ASYLUM-SEEKING, MIGRATION AND CHURCH

At the heart of the gospel is the challenge to see the face of Christ in the stranger, the migrant and the dispossessed. Susanna Snyder's book begins from the stories of those displaced by the currents of globalization, and draws hope from their resilience as well as the actions of those called to be their hosts and advocates. Underpinning all this is a profound theological reflection on our shared humanity and the divine invitation to live as people of faith, not fear.

Elaine Graham, University of Chester, UK

As a migrant myself I deeply appreciate what Susanna Snyder has said about 'flight' and 'fright' as experiences shaping the migrants' self-identity and relations to the church. What makes Snyder's biblically-based reflections on migration so moving and transformative is their rootedness in her personal contacts with the migrants themselves, in their precariousness and vulnerability. I most strongly recommend this book not only to theology students but also to pastors, especially in the USA, where the number of migrants, documented and undocumented, is increasing exponentially. The book will help us make the church a welcoming home to migrants of all faiths.

Peter C. Phan, Georgetown University, USA

A comprehensive and compelling exploration of how people of faith are at the heart of forging a new imagination about migration. In naming the movement from an ecology of fear to an ecology of faith, Snyder challenges us to see the migrant not as a threat but a gift to community. She highlights not only how the Church is reaching out to immigrants but how immigrants are transforming the Church.

Daniel Groody, University of Notre Dame, USA

Asylum-Seeking, Migration and Church addresses one of the most pressing issues confronting contemporary society. How are we to engage with migrants? Drawing on studies of church engagement with asylum seekers in the UK and critical immigration and refugee issues in North America, Snyder presents an extended theological reflection on both the issue of asylum-seeking and the fears of established populations surrounding immigration.

This book outlines ways in which churches are currently supporting asylum seekers, encouraging closer engagement with people seen as 'other' and more thoughtful responses to newcomers. Creatively exploring biblical and theological traditions surrounding the 'stranger', Snyder argues that as well as practising a vision of inclusive community churches would do well to engage with established population fears. Trends in global migration and the dynamics of fear and hostility surrounding immigration are critically and creatively explored throughout the book. Inviting more complex, nuanced responses to asylum seekers and immigrants, this book offers invaluable insights to those interested in Christian ethics, practical theology, faith and social action and mission, as well as those working in the field of migration.

Explorations in Practical, Pastoral and Empirical Theology

Series Editors

Leslie J. Francis, University of Warwick, UK
Jeff Astley, North of England Institute for Christian Education, UK
Martyn Percy, Ripon College Cuddesdon and The Oxford
Ministry Course, Oxford, UK

Theological reflection on the church's practice is now recognized as a significant element in theological studies in the academy and seminary. Ashgate's series in practical, pastoral and empirical theology seeks to foster this resurgence of interest and encourage new developments in practical and applied aspects of theology worldwide. This timely series draws together a wide range of disciplinary approaches and empirical studies to embrace contemporary developments including: the expansion of research in empirical theology, psychological theology, ministry studies, public theology, Christian education and faith development; key issues of contemporary society such as health, ethics and the environment; and more traditional areas of concern such as pastoral care and counselling.

Other titles in the series include:

Asylum-Seeking, Migration and Church

SUSANNA SNYDER
Episcopal Divinity School, Cambridge, MA, USA

ASHGATE

Published by
Ashgate Publishing Limited
Wey Court East
Union Road
Farnham
Surrey, GU9 7PT
England

Ashgate Publishing Company
Suite 420
101 Cherry Street
Burlington
VT 05401–4405
USA

www.ashgate.com

British Library Cataloguing in Publication Data
Snyder, Susanna.
Asylum-seeking, migration and church. – (Explorations in practical, pastoral and empirical theology)
1. Church work with refugees. 2. Church work with immigrants. 3. Forced migration.
4. Refugees–Public opinion. 5. Immigrants–Public opinion. 6. Strangers in the Bible.
7. Social problems–Biblical teaching.
I. Title II. Series
261.8'328–dc23

Library of Congress Cataloging-in-Publication Data
Snyder, Susanna, 1978–
Asylum-seeking, migration and church / Susanna Snyder.
p. cm. – (Explorations in practical, pastoral, and empirical theology)
Includes bibliographical references and index.
ISBN 978-1-4094-2299-0 (alk. paper) – ISBN 978-1-4094-2301-0 (ebook) 1. Church work with refugees. 2. Church work with immigrants. 3. Asylum, Right of–Religious aspects–Christianity. 4. Emigration and immigration–Religious aspects–Christianity.
I. Title.
BV4466.S69 2012
261.8'3–dc23

2012009614

ISBN 9781409422990 (hbk)
ISBN 9781409423003 (pbk)
ISBN 9781409423010 (ebk – PDF)
ISBN 9781409484011 (ebk – ePub)

Printed and bound in Great Britain by the
MPG Books Group, UK.

For all seeking sanctuary.

Contents

List of Figures

Abbreviations

ASIRT	Asylum Support and Immigration Resource Team (Birmingham)
BBC	British Broadcasting Corporation
BCC	British Council of Churches
BEACON	Bradford Ecumenical Asylum Concern
BID	Bail for Immigration Detainees
BMA	British Medical Association
BNP	British National Party
BSA	British Sociological Association
CAFOD	Catholic Agency For Overseas Development
CAP	Church Action on Poverty
CARM	Campaigning – Asylum Seekers and Refugees – Media
CCME	Churches' Commission for Migrants in Europe
CCRJ	Churches' Commission on Racial Justice
CLEAR	City Life Education and Action for Refugees (Southampton)
CLG	Department for Communities and Local Government
COF	Citizen Organising Foundation
COMPAS	Centre on Migration, Policy and Society (Oxford)
COS	City of Sanctuary
CRJN	Churches' Racial Justice Network
CRMC	Coventry Refugee and Migrant Centre
CRN	Churches' Refugee Network
CTBI	Churches Together in Britain and Ireland
CTRIC	Churches Together for Refugees in Coventry
CULF	Commission on Urban Life and Faith
DFID	Department for International Development
EA	Evangelical Alliance
ECSR	Enabling Christians in Serving Refugees
ELR	Exceptional Leave to Remain
ESOL	English for Speakers of Other Languages
ESRC	Economic and Social Research Council
EU	European Union
FBO	Faith-based Organization
FGM	Female Genital Mutilation
GP	General Practitioner
HCIDC	House of Commons International Development Committee
HIV	Human Immunodeficiency Virus
HMSO	Her Majesty's Stationery Office
HO	Home Office

IAC	Independent Asylum Commission
ICAR	Information Centre about Asylum Seekers and Refugees in the UK
IDP	Internally Displaced Person
IND	Immigration and Nationality Directorate (now the UKBA)
IOM	International Organization for Migration
IPPR	Institute of Public Policy Research
JCHR	Joint Committee on Human Rights
JRS	Jesuit Refugee Service
JSOT	*Journal for the Study of the Old Testament*
LCRN	London Churches Refugee Network
MDC	Movement for Democratic Change (Zimbabwe)
MP	Member of Parliament
MPA	Mission and Public Affairs Council (of the Church of England)
MRA	Manager of Religious Affairs (in Immigration Removal Centres)
MU	Mothers' Union
NACCOM	'No Accommodation' Group
NASS	National Asylum Support Service (now Asylum Support)
NGO	Non-Governmental Organization
NHS	National Health Service
NRSV	New Revised Standard Version
OXFAM	Oxford Committee for Famine Relief
RCO	Refugee Community Organization
RSC	Refugee Studies Centre (Oxford)
TB	Tuberculosis
TTI	*Transatlantic Trends: Immigration* survey
UK	United Kingdom
UKBA	United Kingdom Border Agency
UN	United Nations
US	United States
UNDP	United Nations Development Programme
UNHCR	United Nations High Commissioner for Refugees
URC	United Reformed Church
WCC	World Council of Churches
WERS	West End Refugee Service (Newcastle-upon-Tyne)
WRASSG	Wrexham Refugee and Asylum Seeker Support Group

Foreword

I only spent three years as Bishop of Birmingham, but the many wonderful people I met there made a lasting impression on me and taught me a great deal. The same has been true for Susanna Snyder, whose encounters with refugees and asylum seekers in that city, and whose experience of the Church's ministry there amongst these most vulnerable people has been the starting point of this important and challenging book.

Given that the number of asylum seekers and refugees that do end up in the European Union is now relatively small, it is particularly important that we respond to individuals who do seek sanctuary in our countries in a principled and compassionate way. Churches and individual church members are often to be found amongst those offering them hospitality, support and advocacy. Underlying this is nothing other than a sense of having been made welcome in Christ and brought near, as St Paul writes in the second chapter of his letter to the Ephesians, when once we ourselves had been far off. The Church's response to refugees and asylum seekers should be an expression of the truth of Jesus words, 'As I have loved you, even so you must love one another' (Jn. 13:34).

However, this does not mean that we are to be naive or refuse to face up to the complexities of migration in our time. We need to be engaged with these issues in real depth, to assess where the real injustices lie, to identify priorities on that basis, and to understand the challenges of discerning and applying best practice.

Internationally, we need to consolidate and improve arrangements assuring the protection of all those fleeing persecution or escaping situation of conflict and widespread human rights violations, and in our own country we should provide adequate support to those in the asylum system so that they can meet their essential living needs.

In times such as these, when the cuts bite, it should not be the most vulnerable of all who suffer. It usually falls to local refugee groups, and often to churches like many I visit in the North of England, to support those who are struggling to live on the meagre levels of support offered to asylum seekers. It would be tragic if, because of misplaced fears over immigration numbers, we shut our doors to those seeking sanctuary from persecution.

Today no country should have to act alone. International arrangements are in place to ensure that victims of violence and torture, and any in need of international protection, are given a better chance both of surviving immediate crises and of finding security for the future. Whilst the persistence of violence and injustice is regrettable, the international agreements which protect refugees are a mark of human progress, and indeed arise from a virtue common to many religions – the virtue of hospitality to the stranger and the alien.

In 1973, I needed sanctuary from the brutal regime of Idi Amin. Many of my contemporaries were not so lucky. I was received in Britain with great compassion and care – it was almost a home from home. Oh, yes, one room in a communal house sufficed for me, my wife and newborn daughter.

I recall the struggles of surviving on the very limited financial support available at the time, but also the generosity of those who went out of their way to make us welcome, and to ensure that I was able to pursue my studies at Selwyn College in Cambridge. I would like to think that those genuinely needing protection today find that Britain is no less committed to help than its partners in the international community.

I welcome the challenge this book presents not only to the immigration authorities but also to the churches as we are pressed to reconsider both the practicalities and the principles of our engagement with migration and with people seeking sanctuary today.

+Sentamu Ebor
The Most Revd and Rt Hon Dr John Sentamu, Archbishop of York.

Acknowledgements

There are so many people to thank. Stephen Burns encouraged me to start the project, and his enthusiasm and support have remained unwavering. This book began as a doctoral dissertation, and I am indebted to my PhD supervisor, Andrew Davey, without whose patience, brain and sense of humour I would probably have given up on writing long ago. My gratitude also goes to those who have read drafts or chapters, and commented and edited – Anthony Reddie, Paula Gooder, Larry Wills, Elena Fiddian-Qasmiyeh, Peter Kevern, Martyn Percy, Helen Cameron, Catherine Owens and Sue Spilecki. Your time, suggestions, generosity and rigour at different stages and in many ways have all been crucial. Any errors are my own. Thanks also go to numerous others who have offered comments and helped to generate ideas – Dan Groody, Nicola Slee, Ken Leech, Phil Marfleet, Nick Sagovsky, Christopher Duraisingh, Shari Brown, R. S. Sugirtharajah, Matthew Gibney, Luke Bretherton, Anna Rowlands, Marie Marquardt, Manuel Vasquez, Ellen Ott Marshall, Clare Amos, Richard Sudworth, Stephen Pattison, Elaine Graham and Gordon Mursell are amongst them. Sarah Lloyd and the production team at Ashgate have been enthusiastic, meticulous and helpful throughout.

The faculty, students and staff at Episcopal Divinity School and Candler School of Theology, Emory University, are the communities within which this book was planned and written. The students in the two classes I have taught on immigration have helped to get me thinking in new ways and refine some ideas – thank you to all of you for being such fun to teach – and my colleagues at both institutions have been unwaveringly encouraging and supportive. The congregations of St Mary Stoke Newington and St John's Brownswood Park and my colleagues there, particularly Martyn Hawkes, Jonathan Clark and Beryl Warren, must also get a mention: I don't know how many sermons on the 'stranger' you had to sit through during my curacy, but it was a time when much chewing on ideas and many useful conversations happened. I am also very grateful to Martyn Percy and Ripon College, Cuddesdon, for their support during the writing up of the dissertation and for allowing me to use the facilities there, as I am to those at the Queen's Foundation. Michael Gale, in particular, tirelessly reshelved far too many books. Thanks also to the librarians at the Refugee Studies Centre in Oxford and the Sherrill Library in Cambridge, MA. To everyone who allowed me to interview them about their experiences – people seeking sanctuary and those who offer support in so many different ways – a huge thanks.

The Josephine Butler Memorial Trust and the Women's Continuing Ministerial Education Trust provided generous financial support from 2005 to 2008 and at a more personal level, I am grateful for the many friends who have kept me going through the journey and during my own experiences of 'exile' and joy – Chris,

Shari, Donald, Elizabeth, Tanya, Stacy, Becca, Rosie, Rach, Jen, Laura, Lucy, Martyn, Jen, Anya and Zachary, Anne, Sara, Ali and Phil, Gordon, Shelley, Mum and Dad, my sister Julia, Steve and nephews Thomas and Samuel, and Michael must get a special mention – but there are many others. You know who you are. You have put up with a lot. You are my home. Thank you. Finally, to those seeking sanctuary who have inspired, challenged and enriched me, made me laugh and cry and offered me glimpses of an ever surprising God – this book is for you. I hope that the pages which follow may be a small offering in return.

PART I
Setting the Scene

Chapter 1
Encountering Migrants

It was a cold spring day. I had been called and asked whether I could accompany Annette to the Home Office Reporting Centre in Solihull.[1] Sure, I said. No problem. We drove from Birmingham city centre, parked in the multi-storey and took the short walk across the road to the centre. Annette seemed nervous but I didn't think any more of it. It was to be expected. She went through security and into the room where asylum seekers queued to be seen by an official. Nearly an hour must have gone by. I was outside and beginning to get twitchy now too. It shouldn't have taken anything like this long and the waiting area was hardly designed to make you feel welcome and relaxed. Annette suddenly appeared behind some glass; she was waving at me and clearly anxious. The case official accompanying her came out and explained that they were holding onto her as there was a problem – they wouldn't tell me what – and that she seemed to be having an asthma attack. She wanted me to fetch her medication from a drawer in her house. Not having a clue where she lived – she had moved into a new place only three days before – I rummaged in the handbag she had left with me and found some keys and an address on a scrap of paper. I rushed to the car and got hopelessly lost trying to find her room, somewhere in a cul-de-sac in Chelmsley Wood. I felt like a criminal trying the key in every door in the house before entering her tiny room and rifling through the drawers to find an inhaler. No luck. All I could find was a huge bag of medications. I just grabbed it and dashed back to the car. Using one hand to reverse out of the drive, I used the other to phone Shari at Restore. I explained what had happened and she promised to get straight onto Annette's solicitor. I eventually arrived back at the centre, handed over the bag of medications and went through security myself. Annette still seemed distressed, sitting opposite her case official in a cubbyhole. My phone vibrated. I got outside just in time to answer and it was Shari saying that Annette would probably be released if her solicitor could fax a document through immediately. Was there a fax number? Nobody seemed to know. The case official appeared and then disappeared again. All I can assume is that the relevant documentation arrived satisfactorily. Annette appeared at the doorway to the waiting area a few minutes later, looking exhausted and relieved.

---

[1] Names of those seeking asylum are pseudonyms to protect anonymity.

Migration: A Variety of Encounters, a Global Controversy

This personal vignette, from February 2005, offers a glimpse into one kind of encounter that can take place between migrants and members of established populations today. There are plenty of less positive encounters, though, as this experience from June 2011 illustrates:

> The taxi driver started talking as we were on the way back from a grocery store in Cambridge, Massachusetts. He said that he had come to the US from Italy when he was four years old and that he had worked hard all his life. He was from Boston and didn't like Cambridge much. He told me that he had fought in the Vietnam War and protested against it – there were 'morons' in power then – and that the country was going downhill fast now. We should get rid of all the immigrants, he said. He couldn't believe that you could take your driving test in so many languages other than English – this was 'moronic' – and pointed out that they were creating big problems and breeding like crazy. Americans should keep their noses out of other people's business, he reckoned, and thought that the military operations in Iraq and Afghanistan were stupid. Conversely, everyone should stay out of the US. If they didn't, capital punishment was the appropriate response. He told me in no uncertain terms that he thought the best thing to do with the Middle East was to 'nuke' it.

These are simply two of the millions of individual, local and national stories that comprise the global controversy surrounding migration. Migration, a hot social and political potato across the world, is rarely out of the headlines or off governmental agendas and thus, even if not in person, almost everyone is encountering migrants at one remove politically or virtually. In 2011, unrest in Libya, Egypt and Tunisia gave rise to talk about a 'new asylum crisis' in Europe likely to result from a 'massive inflow of economic migrants' (Whitehead 2011) and David Cameron, British prime minister, called upon the public to 'shop' illegal immigrants and those 'wishing to take advantage' of the UK to the authorities (Woodcock and Tapsfield 2011). In the US, comprehensive immigration reform remains a key political controversy and stories about the dangers of illegal immigration abound. The headline 'Asylum Ploys Feed on News to Open Door' ran in the *New York Times* in July – in the wake of the revelation that the woman who accused Dominique Strauss-Kahn, Managing Director of the International Monetary Fund, of rape was an asylum seeker (Dolnik 2011) – and in September, furore erupted over the passing of stringent anti-immigrant legislation in Alabama and when an 'illegal' immigrant was found guilty of drunk driving in Massachusetts (Andersen 2011). In Australia, Prime Minister Julia Gillard tried unsuccessfully to swap 800 asylum seekers whose cases had not yet been determined with 4,000 'genuine refugees' already certified by the United Nations in Malaysia. In Libya, black African migrants who had been working there as casual labourers were attacked and captured by rebel forces claiming that they were Colonel Gadaffi mercenaries

(Pannell 2011). On a trip to Tanzania in 2009, I remember a taxi driver talking about how Burundian and Rwandan refugees were causing problems, taking jobs and causing crime, and how he wanted them to go home. Many other Tanzanians share his views (Hennig 2011).

People tend to have strong feelings about immigration, often negative, and see migrants as a threat to national identity, culture, jobs, resources and security. Migrants are also bringing about significant changes in religious landscapes through the diverse beliefs and practices they carry with them, and some see this as a danger to the traditions and values they have grown up with. Many want immigration – in-migration to their country – to stop. Their hostility is exacerbated by the perception that immigration is on the increase. In August 2011, net migration into the UK was announced to be 21 per cent higher in 2010 than 2009, with 239,000 more people arriving than leaving (BBC 2011). In the US, even though immigration from Mexico has almost halted due to increasingly stringent border controls and changing economic contexts, people still *believe* that many are entering the country without papers. This anti-immigrant climate is having detrimental effects on migrants and would-be migrants, in that it is becoming increasingly difficult for anyone – particularly those who are poor – to gain entry to certain countries and to access basic rights within them. Visas can be virtually impossible to obtain, and detention and deportation of immigrants without them are on the increase, leading to considerable fear, separation from families and places that have become 'home' and, in the worst cases, even death. In the face of this, however, some are stepping forward to support newcomers and calling for more generous immigration and asylum policies. They affirm the need to welcome migrants and value the contributions they make.

Beginnings

This book explores the encounters of churches with migrants and particularly their engagement with asylum seekers in the UK. In 2004, while I was training for Anglican ordination in Birmingham, I decided to start helping at a drop-in for refugees and asylum seekers at Ladywood Methodist Church, where I fumblingly taught some English and assisted in the crèche. We had parties and danced and ate far too much cake. I listened to stories and was angered to hear of the injustices many had experienced in their countries and in the UK and was moved by their courage and resilience. I was also amazed at the energy and commitment of those involved in running the drop-in. Wishing to become more involved, I trained as a befriender with Restore, an ecumenical organization supporting refugees and asylum seekers in the city, and began meeting regularly with Fatima. Having left three older children behind in Cameroon, Fatima lived with her two young children in Nechells. When heavily pregnant, she and her daughter had been placed in detention for 10 days and taken to Heathrow for deportation. They were returned to Birmingham on compassionate grounds, but Fatima still had to report to the

Home Office in Solihull every month and lived in daily fear of a dawn removal raid. Her flat, at the top of a grim concrete tower block in which the lifts smelt of urine, was virtually bare and she had little money for food or toys. However, she soon discovered local playgroup facilities, joined a class to improve her English and became pregnant again. I remember with delight holding her new baby when she was just one day old.

Around the same time, I started a year-long placement at Birmingham Cathedral. It was there that I met Annette, Lucille and Hassan. Annette was from Rwanda and had been imprisoned for failing to support a presidential campaign. In prison, she was subjected to physical and sexual assaults. Lucille was from Burundi and had, like Fatima, been forced to leave her children behind. Hassan, an Iranian, spent much time at the Cathedral helping as a volunteer welcomer and was often there when I dropped in – always smiling and wearing a cross. I helped to organize an awareness-raising evening on asylum-seeking and also co-ran, with an artist in the congregation, a short series of art workshops for asylum seekers. I assisted with the Restore Summer Holiday Programme in 2005, accompanying families on days out to Telford, a nature centre and swimming pools.

The idea to undertake research on this theme emerged soon after my first encounters at the Ladywood Methodist Church. Why, I wondered, were asylum seekers' experiences in the UK so awful and why were churches engaging with them so extensively? Did those seeking asylum feel that these projects were helpful? I was also intrigued as to why Christians volunteered and why certain projects were focused in a particular direction. As well as hoping that my research could enhance church-based support, I also had other more personal motivations. Research is always as much about the 'self' of the researcher as it is about the topic or people being studied (Heywood 2004: 73, 86, Etherington 2004: 99, 109). I had long been interested in issues of justice and development and their relationship to Christian faith, and had, for instance, visited Mozambique in 2003 when it was still recovering from a civil war in which four million people had been displaced. I was also feeling in 'exile' myself. I was passing through theological college and at an in-between stage personally, struggling with my faith, aspects of the institutional church and a sense of not belonging in a diverse theological training environment. A personal sense of being out of place, I am sure, drew me to others who were far more literally and profoundly displaced. Pragmatically speaking, I had a final year to complete at college and was being encouraged to undertake postgraduate work. Time, opportunity, encouragement, personal need and a situation crying out for research thus coalesced.

Since then, I have continued to try to stand alongside people seeking sanctuary. During three years in Northeast London, I worked with the Hackney Refugee and Migrant Support Group to help establish the Hackney Migrant Centre at St Mary Stoke Newington, where I was curate, and I supported campaigns and various refugee networks. I helped out at a computer skills class for unaccompanied asylum-seeking minors in Oxford, before moving to the US in 2009 – first to

Atlanta, Georgia, and then to Cambridge, Massachusetts – where I have lived as a 'non-resident alien' myself.

Aims and Argument

This book examines and critiques current church engagement with migrants in order to bring about improved practice. It asks the questions: how are churches interacting with newcomers, and why? Are there ways in which they could improve what they are currently doing? How might Christians help to transform the attitudes of those, like the Boston taxi driver, who are hostile to immigrants, and bring about changes in immigration and asylum policy? How could they facilitate better encounters between members of established populations and migrants? I argue that Christian communities make substantial, valuable contributions to asylum seeker support and that Christians are prominent among those welcoming and calling for the inclusion of immigrants. Church involvement takes place in a variety of ways, through what I categorize as encounters of service, encounters with the powers, encounters in worship and encounters in theology. By bringing these encounters into conversation with Forced Migration Studies, which will be discussed in Chapter 2, insights from other social scientific disciplines and biblical and theological traditions, I aim to analyse the context in which churches are working and the call placed upon them by Christian faith. I offer critical assessment of their involvement and make suggestions for renewed practice, which I hope will lead towards more faithful and liberatory encounters, not only for migrants, but also for the churches supporting them and for established populations more generally. The book is written for scholars of migration and religion, theologians and ethicists, seminary students, faith communities and faith leaders who are standing alongside immigrants, refugees and asylum seekers – many of whom are themselves migrants. I also aim to speak to Christians who may feel ambivalent about newcomers. While I focus on asylum seekers and the UK, I hope that this book will also prove useful for those studying other types of migration and those living in different countries. Similar threads in terms of experience, attitude, policy, practice and response weave their way across migrant categories, nation-state borders and faith traditions.

The Role of Faith-based Organizations in Society

In order to evaluate the contribution being made by churches to migrant support, it is important to understand the context in which religious communities and faith-based organizations (FBOs) find themselves operating today.[2] Churches continue

---

[2] The term 'faith-based organization' is complex and problematic. As Ferris points out, it 'locks together multiple faith denominations and organizations which may in fact

to engage substantially on social issues despite patterns of declining attendance and the loss of their more-or-less exclusive role as providers of welfare and charity (Prochaska 2006). This contribution is often referred to as spiritual or faithful capital, and takes place against the backdrop of evolving and complex relationships between FBOs and states in Europe and North America. Two contradictory governmental impulses are operative. On one hand, there is a growing enthusiasm about the potential role of FBOs in service delivery, community regeneration and the provision and development of social capital (Baker 2007, 2009, Beaumont 2008, CULF 2006, Davis et al. 2008, Furbey et al. 2006, Graham and Lowe 2009: 155, Sager 2010). Religion, in this sense, is seen by governments as 'cuddlesome' and a valuable partner (Furbey 2010, Bretherton 2010: 34). Cloke puts it this way: 'as state-run welfare services have been hollowed out' in line with dominant neoliberal thinking, so faith-based organizations along with other non-statutory bodies – the 'Third Sector' – 'have often been the principal gap-filler' (2010: 224). The UK Department for Communities and Local Government White Paper, *Communities in Control: Real People, Real Power*, signifies this movement towards more substantial involvement of religious organizations (2008), as does the Coalition government's talk of the 'Big Society'. Sager, reflecting on developments in the US, dates a 'growing devolution of government social services to the nonprofit and private sectors' and 'the increasingly prominent role of religion in politics and policy' to the 1996 Welfare Reform Bill (2010: 17). Interfaith initiatives are particularly welcome, presenting opportunities to build 'bridging social capital' as well as provide services (Weller 2009).

On the other hand, statutory bodies are sceptical about the motivation, impact and efficacy of faith communities perceived to pursue their own agendas of proselytism, promote intercommunal tensions and prevent integration (Farnell 2009). There has been a 'securitization of religion' and fear of links between some strands in Islam and terrorism is ever-present (Bretherton 2010: 35). Reflecting a broader tension between the discourses of secularism and post-secularism, this produces a complex landscape for faith communities to navigate.[3] While 'religious capital' or practical contributions are often welcomed, 'spiritual capital' is resisted (see Baker 2009, Baker and Skinner 2006). Thus, according to Cloke, although the system of contract funding has enabled faith groups to re-enter the policy-making sphere, churches face a dilemma. They can find themselves in

---

bear little resemblance to one another' (2011: 2). I choose to use it here, mirroring its popularity in policy and academic discourse.

[3]   Discussion of the contested term 'post-secular' lies beyond the scope of this book. Post-secularism indicates 'the continuing realization of radically plural societies in terms of religions, faiths and beliefs' and 'the public role and function of religion and religious organizations in our contemporary world' (Molendijk et al. 2010: x); see Habermas (2008), Molendijk et al. (2010), Dalferth (2010) and Ager and Ager (2011) for recent debate.

partnerships of governance that may dilute, or at least press into the background, the very faith-motivations that originally formed the basis of their existence. The more that FBOs have entered into compact contracts, the more they have found themselves locked into centrally-controlled ways of operating … their ethos, and their character can change. (2010: 229)

Bretherton describes this as 'institutional isomorphism' (2010: 43). Some faith-based groups choose to resist co-option and critically challenge governmental approaches and policies: when doing so, to use a phrase coined by Furbey, they are perceived as 'admirably troublesome' (2010, Farnell 2009). In the wake of the global economic downturn, access to funding sources is also increasingly difficult and many FBOs are forced to spend considerable time and energy filling out grant applications in order to secure the future of their work. This is certainly true for many of the Christian organizations working with people seeking asylum in the UK.

Definitions and Parameters

What, though, do I mean by migrant or asylum seeker or church or Christian organization or established communities? Categories, labels and definitions abound in the discourse surrounding both faith communities and migrants and, as Mulvey points out, 'the public generally fail to distinguish between types of migrants and terms are consistently conflated' (2010: 450). It is important to delineate what I mean by these terms for two reasons. First, it will clarify the parameters of this study. Second, it is vital to use all terms and labels carefully, particularly when talking about migration. Labels are socio-politically constructed and convey 'an extremely complex set of values, and judgements' (Zetter 1991: 40, see also Zetter 2007). They have significant consequences and can be used to legitimize oppression. I will introduce them here, and a fuller exploration and critique of some of these categories will follow in Chapter 4.

Migrants, Refugees and Asylum Seekers

Migrant, at a basic level, refers simply to anyone who is 'on the move'. 'International migrants' are defined differently by different countries for statistical purposes, but can broadly be outlined as those 'who cross international borders in order to settle in another country, even temporarily'. The category usually excludes tourists and visitors. Short-term migrants do so for a period of between three and 12 months and long-term migrants for a year or more (IOM 2011b). People journey in diverse ways, and for different reasons, and migrants cannot all be lumped into one box. The term 'voluntary migrants' usually describes those who have made a largely positive choice to move for economic or social reasons. It includes lifestyle migration and low-skilled and high-skilled labour migration.[4] The term 'forced migrants', by contrast, refers to those who have fled their homes involuntarily, whether within their own country or to another state. It includes refugees, internally displaced persons (IDPs), post-conflict returnees and environmental and development displacees (Castles 2002: 1152). 'Illegal migrants' is the term commonly used to describe voluntary or forced migrants who evade official controls and includes those who have been smuggled or trafficked. Following Marfleet, I prefer the terms 'irregular', 'informal' or 'undocumented' to 'illegal' (2006: 165).

The word 'refugee' was probably first associated with the Huguenots in the sixteenth century who described themselves individually as '*réfugiés*' and communally as '*le refuge*'.[5] In 1951, the United Nations ratified a Convention legally defining a 'refugee' as someone who, 'owing to well-founded fear of being persecuted for reasons of race, religion, nationality, membership of a particular group or political opinion, is outside the country of his nationality and is unable or, owing to such fear, is unwilling to avail himself of the protection of that country' (UNHCR 2010: 14). States were obliged to offer refuge to those fleeing persecution which had taken place in another European state before 1951. In 1967, a Protocol lifted the space and time limitations of the Convention and this amended legal definition remains in use today (UNHCR 2010, Loescher and Milner 2011: 191). It includes *activists* (political activity) and *targets* (misfortune of belonging to a particular social or cultural group), and also usually *victims* of societal or international violence through the UN doctrine of 'good offices' (Zolberg et al. 1989: 30). *Individual persecution* is the overriding criterion for granting refugee status.[6] A more common and general definition of a refugee also exists however. Matthew Gibney, for example, describes refugees as 'those people in need of a new state of residence, either temporarily or permanently, because if forced to return home or remain where they are they would – as a result of either the brutality or inadequacy of their state – be persecuted *or* seriously jeopardize their physical security or vital subsistence needs' (2004: 7; see also Sales 2007: 76). Reflecting such slippery usage, I will employ the word 'refugee' as both a precise legal definition and in its more general sense.

The term 'asylum seeker' refers to a person arriving at an international border claiming to be a refugee, but who has not yet been given official legal recognition as such (Gibney 2004: 9–10).[7] An asylum seeker is someone who is formally seeking refugee status in a particular state but who has not (yet) been granted

---

[4]   Betts distinguishes between migrants according to the policy categories they fall into and how they are regulated at an international level (2011b: 1–2).

[5]   For more on the origin of the term 'refugee', see Sassen (1999: 35) and Zolberg et al. (1989: 5–29).

[6]   For more on how understandings of the category of 'refugee' and UNHCR have developed over time, see Loescher et al. (2008), Loescher and Milner (2011) and UNHCR (2010).

[7]   On the roots of asylum, see Schuster (2003: 63–96) and Price (2009: 24–68).

the right to remain there. Legally speaking, it includes anyone who has made an asylum application, whatever his motivation.[8] Given the pejorative connotations of the term, I have chosen to refer to asylum seekers as 'those seeking asylum' or 'those seeking sanctuary' where possible.[9] In the UK, asylum seekers are expected to make an asylum application at the first available opportunity on arriving. While applicants are usually entitled to accommodation, subsistence financial support, free healthcare and legal counsel through the UK Border Agency (UKBA), they are not normally allowed to work until a positive decision on their case has been made. Provision for those appealing a negative decision is more limited. Asylum seekers are also expected to report at immigration centres or police stations and comply with the law. While the government aims to process all cases within six months, many have been waiting for a decision for years and others refused asylum choose to remain in the country, destitute, rather than return to their country of origin. For the purposes of this study and reflecting common usage, a person whose asylum claim has been refused and yet continues to live in the country of destination without documents will also be termed an 'asylum seeker'. People seeking sanctuary – whatever stage their case is at – experience a range of challenges, from lack of shelter, food or English language proficiency through to emotional distress and spiritual dislocation.[10]

While important to understand the legal definitions of these categories from the outset, given their determining impact upon the lives of those labelled by them, I sometimes choose to use the terms asylum seeker, immigrant and migrant interchangeably in the course of this book. This reflects the fact that, in some ways, in the lived experience of migrants, these categories are ambiguous and overlapping (as I will discuss in Chapter 4) and that much of what I say can be applied to underprivileged migrants or those regarded as 'undesirable' in general, not simply to those seeking asylum.

Established Communities and Churches

I use the phrases 'established communities' and 'established population(s)' to refer to the population of the country in which a person is seeking asylum or refuge. This, following Van Hear, is in preference to the more problematic terms 'host' community or 'native' people. As he has pointed out, 'host' community implies a welcome or hospitality which is not always present and 'native' or 'indigenous' people implies aboriginal people and excludes former migrants (1998: 55). The 'established population' in the UK thus includes British citizens, whether born

---

[8]   I use 'he' and 'she' (and 'his' and 'her') randomly and interchangeably throughout the book, to avoid preferencing one gender above the other.

[9]   Referring to asylum seekers as people seeking sanctuary was recommended by the Independent Asylum Commission (IAC 2008b). This suggestion has since been debated, as asylum remains the official legal category (Rabben 2011: 196–197).

[10]   For more on the current asylum process in the UK, see UKBA (2012).

there or naturalized, those with a legal right to residence – including international students and those with work permits – and also people who have been living irregularly in the country for many years.

The term 'Church' is used to indicate the theological idea of the Church or a specific denomination. 'Christian communities', 'churches', 'church-based groups' and Christian FBOs are umbrella terms referring to a variety of Christian congregations, projects and ecumenical groupings. The focus of this study is on the historic mainstream denominations, particularly the Church of England and the Roman Catholic, Methodist and Baptist Churches, though certain mainstream evangelical churches working in this area are also included. Many migrants are members of these churches. While focused on churches, some of the ideas I discuss may have relevance to other faith communities and FBOs. Churches have long been involved with those seeking sanctuary in the UK and their impact upon immigrants' reception and experience has been significant. From encounters with the Huguenots in the sixteenth and seventeenth centuries through to responses to Jews during the 1930s and 1940s and their role in sanctuary movement in the 1980s, Christians can look back at a history of both welcome and hostility towards newcomers.[11] Today, globalization and migration are presenting both considerable challenges and exciting opportunities for churches. The Christian engagement with migrants discussed here takes place against this backdrop.

While not wishing to homogenize groups of people, I, as a British citizen, sometimes refer to established communities in the UK using the pronoun 'we', and newly-arrived migrants as 'they'. I refer to Christian groups and churches variously as 'they' and 'we' in recognition of the fact that I was an outsider to most of the organizations, but also an insider through being a Christian involved in volunteer support.

Outline

This book has four parts. Part I, *Setting the Scene*, provides the methodological and practical context for the study. Chapter 2 discusses the method I used to undertake this research. Situated within the field of Practical Theology and using an action–reflection cycle, I started by gathering a range of experiences of church engagement with people seeking asylum and shaped this using a typological framework. I then brought these experiences into critical interdisciplinary conversation with Forced Migration Studies and Biblical Studies. The goal of my research is transformative and liberatory action. Chapter 3 presents the practical context and starting point for the study. It outlines a range of church activities and

---

[11]   While there has been little systematic written about the history of church engagement with migrants in the UK, some commentary can be found in Panayi (1994), Gwynn (2001), Holmes (1988), Cohen (1994) and Weller (1987, 1989). On the history of sanctuary more broadly, see Marfleet (2011) and Rabben (2011).

projects involved in asylum seeker support in the UK and groups them according to the following categories: encounters of grassroots service, encounters with the powers, encounters in worship and encounters in theology. I also consider the role played by networks and individuals, and draw attention to international action and anti-immigrant Christian responses.

Part II, *Flight and Fright: Experiences of Seeking Sanctuary*, explores and analyses the context within which established society Christians and asylum seekers are encountering one another. Chapter 4, through introducing the major concerns of Forced Migration Studies, offers insight into the global dynamics of migration. What brings migrants to the Global North? What do people face in their countries of origin and after they arrive in a new place? I discuss causes of migration, definitions of migrants, international governance and policy relating to forced migration and the factors affecting the reception and settlement of refugees. I also consider the significance of gender, and the role and impact of faith and faith communities on the experience of forced migrants. Chapter 5 narrows in focus to concentrate on asylum in the UK. I argue that fear among established populations is arguably the most significant underlying cause of the challenges and struggles faced by asylum seekers. These fears take different shapes, from the politico-cultural (seeing migrants as a threat to the nation-state and national identity) to those surrounding economic and welfare resources (seeing migrants as competition for healthcare, jobs, housing, etc.) and those relating to security (seeing migrants as terrorists). I discuss the sectors of the population and locations in which these fears are most prominent and explore the consequences of these fears. These include stereotyping and scapegoating, media hostility, violence towards asylum seekers and increasingly harsh policies and practices of control and deterrence. I introduce the idea of an 'ecology of fear' to encapsulate the vicious circle in which geopolitical insecurity, fears of the established population, negative media discourse and governmental policies and practices serve to intensify each other, which in turn induces fear in migrants. The chapter ends with suggestions from some academics as to how this ecology of fear might be transformed.

Part III, *Encountering 'Strangers' in the Bible*, brings this context into conversation with the Christian tradition. Chapter 6 introduces the wealth of material relating to the stranger in the Bible, from the journeys of Abraham through to the exile, the life of Jesus and the experiences of early Christians. While it is apparent that being strangers is a central theme in the Bible and Judaeo-Christian self-understanding and practice, it is less clear how these strangers are to treat other strangers. I identify two broad strands of responses towards outsiders in the tradition – those made from within an 'ecology of fear' and others made from within what I term an 'ecology of faith' – and explore these in Chapters 7 and 8 respectively. In Chapter 7, I look at the text of Ezra–Nehemiah and the call made within it for the expulsion of foreign wives. While not condoning the message of this text, I suggest that it is important to acknowledge the complicity of the Christian tradition in the exclusion of foreigners. I also argue that it is important to understand why Ezra–Nehemiah is so hostile to outsiders, and discuss the ways in which this hostility is a response to the crisis of exile and to social and economic power struggles taking place. I suggest connections between the ecology of fear then and that which exists now surrounding migration. Understanding and engaging with hostility today is an important first step on the road to transforming it. Chapter 8 moves on to explore a strand of biblical material more positive towards the outsider. Following a discussion of a number of passages which indicate a duty to care for the stranger, I focus on the stories of Ruth and the Syro-Phoenician Woman (Mk 7:24–30) to point out that strangers are often understood to be life-bringers and God-bearers. Both women are liminal outsiders, yet through one-to-one encounters, risk-taking and boundary-crossing on the part of all of the characters, they become sources of new life and transformation for the whole community. I introduce some theological material echoing this idea, particularly from theologies of hospitality, and make connections with the immigration and asylum situation today. Migrants are revitalizing communities, including churches.

Part IV, *Conclusion*, draws together the threads of the book and makes suggestions for enhancing the practice of churches in relation to migrants in each of the four types of encounter outlined in Chapter 3.

Chapter 2

'On the Way' to a Performative and Liberatory Theology

This kind of theology is rooted in the real world and its issues and its suffering. It is intended to arouse conviction and lead to action. It cares for people more than for intellectual coherence, or literary elegance, or academic respectability.

(Forrester 2001: 72)

[T]here is really no other way forward than modestly presenting or offering 'fragments' which may be seen as relevant, true, illuminating and helpful for just practice.

(Forrester 2005a: 16)

This study is situated within the field of Practical Theology, a field which seeks to bring the current experiences, practices, beliefs and concerns – of church communities and society more widely – into critical conversation with Christian scriptural and theological traditions.[1] Practical Theology, like Christian Ethics, is 'concerned with questions of truth in relation to action' (Forrester 2010: 146) and aims to enhance and transform existing practices and understanding. Swinton and Mowat offer a definition: Practical Theology is 'an intricate and complex enterprise' which aims to 'ensure faithful practice and authentic human living in the light of scripture and tradition' (2006: v–vi). In other words, it is 'critical, theological reflection on the practices of the Church as they interact with the practices of the world, with a view to ensuring and enabling faithful participation in God's redemptive practices in, to and for the world' (2006: 6). Practical theologians grapple with specific contemporary situations and take histories and contexts, both individual and shared, seriously. The conversation between *present* experiences and the *past* – 'the wisdom of a religious heritage' – is key (O'Connell Killen and de Beer 1994: viii, Bevans 2002: 7, Pattison 2000b: 139), as this creates the nexus within which new understanding and more 'faithful practice' and 'authentic human living' can emerge. While *all* theology is, in one sense,

---

[1] 'Practical Theology' and 'Pastoral Theology' are often used interchangeably, though the former is often associated with Protestant traditions and the latter with Roman Catholicism; see Pattison and Woodward (2000), Cameron et al. (2010: 21–22) and Cahalan (2010). The terms 'theological reflection' (O'Connell Killen and de Beer 1994, Thompson et al. 2008) and 'contextual theology' (Bevans 2002) are also used to indicate this methodological approach.

practical (Browning 1991: 7), what distinguishes Practical Theology from other theological subdisciplines is that the practices are explicitly reflected upon and the goal of improving practice is consciously articulated. There is no one method for undertaking 'critical reflection on faithful practice' (Graham et al. 2005: 2, Graham 2008). Graham et al. (2005) have grouped a plethora of approaches, priorities and terminology into seven broad and overlapping categories. This study draws largely on that known variously as 'Theology-in-Action', 'Performative Theology' or 'Praxis Theology'.

'Theology-in-Action' or 'Performative Theology'

'Theology-in-Action' is closely related to theologies of liberation (Graham et al. 2005: 170) and has two central characteristics: experience and practice are prioritized over tradition as a starting point and transforming, liberating action is its goal. Liberation Theology emerged within the context of suffering and oppression in Latin America in the 1960s. In his foundational work, *A Theology of Liberation*, Gutiérrez emphasized first that theology should be 'God-walk' instead of 'God-talk'. Theology is properly 'critical reflection on praxis in the light of the Word' – praxis indicating shared value-imbued and justice-constituting practice – and 'doing the truth' or 'orthopraxy' should always precede theologizing (1974: 13, 10). He claimed that the first act of theology involves practice, commitment and contemplation, and the second is theologizing or critical reflection on this praxis in the light of the word of God. Thus, quoting Hegel, theology 'rises only at sundown' (1974: 11). His second related emphasis was that theology should prioritize and start with the experience of the poor. Gutiérrez spoke of doing theology from 'the underside of history' and of God's revelation assigning a privileged place to the parlous and despised (Gutiérrez 1983, Nickoloff 1996: 42, 50–52). The suffering of Jesus could be glimpsed in the great suffering of the poor millions and, if theological reflection was to be valid, solidarity and sharing in the experience of the oppressed were therefore vital. As other liberationists also articulated, theologians could not be 'armchair intellectuals', but rather had to be '"organic intellectuals" (in organic communion with the people) and "militant theologians"' (Boff and Boff 1987: 19). Theology, consequently, had a prophetic function and was committed to bringing about the future liberation of the oppressed (Boff and Boff 1987: 3, Gutiérrez 1974: 14). This mode of doing theology was enacted through the establishment of base ecclesial communities, in which ordinary people were encouraged to use a methodological 'See-Judge-Act' device to reflect communally on their experience in the light of their faith (Dawson 1999, Holland 2005, Segundo 1976: 7–9). Theologies of liberation have proliferated since these early beginnings and now include Black, Feminist,

Womanist, Mujerista, Asian, Minjung, Dalit, Gay and Queer theologies.[2] Each is a 'prophetic theology of a crucified community in a crucified world' (Copeland 2004: 187. Italics omitted).

The notion of 'critical reflection on praxis' has been absorbed and developed in a Northern context as 'Performative' or 'Praxis' Theology.[3] Elaine Graham claims that '[t]heology is properly conceived as a performative discipline, in which the criterion of authenticity is deemed to be *orthopraxis*, or authentic transformatory action, rather than *orthodoxy* (right belief)' (1996: 7). In more recent collaborative work with Walton and Ward, this statement is elaborated: '"*[P]erformative* knowledge*", that is, a way of knowing that is inseparable from doing' affirms that 'practice is both the origin and the end of theological reflection, and "talk about God" cannot take place independent of a commitment to a struggle for human emancipation' (Graham et al. 2005: 170). Christian praxis or faithful action is thus both the starting and end point of theology (see also Swinton and Mowat 2006: 3–27). Praxis generates theological and ethical questions and understanding, and theological grappling with these should result in new, transformative praxis. Authentic theology is developed in and through everyday faithful 'performances', which are also termed 'bodily praxis' or 'pastoral practices'. These embodied practices are 'disclosive', according to Graham, because the normative values of the faith community are constructed in value-informed and directed practice. They 'reveal, and construct, the dominant frameworks of meaning and truth' (1996: 193, 139) and act as 'the agent and vehicle of the divine reality' (1999: 79; see also CULF 2006: 14). Drawing on the work of Bourdieu, she argues that theology is therefore best understood as an embodied, inner wisdom or 'habitus' rather than as an abstract, cerebral discipline. 'Pastoral practice constitutes the *habitus* of faith; it is both inherited and indwelt but infinitely creative: a performative practical wisdom (*phronêsis*) which we inhabit and re-enact' (2000: 110).

A significant caveat must be inserted, namely that there is a difference between performative and liberation theologies. While early liberation theologies clearly focused on the 'preferential option for the poor', some critics argued that the theologians and their works (for example Cone 1990, Gutiérrez 1974) were heavily influenced by systematic theological training. They were liberatory in substance, but not praxis-based methodologically. Conversely, contemporary liberationists will point out that not all performative methodologies aim at emancipatory systemic change.[4] Northern theologians need to be wary of 'expropriating' the rhetoric of liberation theologies 'without engaging their methods' (Myers cited

---

[2] For recent examples, see Kwok (2010), Floyd-Thomas and Pinn (2010), Cheng (2011), Rajkumar (2010) and Reddie (2006a, 2006b).

[3] Examples include Cameron et al. (2010), CULF (2006), Forrester (2001), Graham (1995), Pattison (2000a) and Slee (2004).

[4] I am grateful to Anthony Reddie for pointing out the distinction between substance and method in Liberation and Performative Theologies; see Reddie (2008) for an emerging critique along these lines, particularly in relation to Cone.

in Davey 1995: 62) and of adopting a simply 'cosmetic vocabulary' of 'social concern' or 'liberation' (Gutiérrez 1983: 64; see also Pattison 1997: 11). Lartey has stated the underlying problem as follows: a 'process' approach to Practical Theology risks over-valuing method at the expense of content and a 'way of being and doing' approach risks stressing context and content to the extent that it becomes anti-intellectual and uncritical (2000: 131). While not claiming to be liberation theology, this research has sought to be both performative in method and liberatory in substance.[5]

The Action–Reflection Cycle

The 'performative' or 'praxis' model of doing theology is enacted by means of a cycle – known variously as the 'pastoral circle', 'action–reflection cycle' or 'practical–theological spiral' (Wijsen 2005). This is envisaged and drawn in a range of ways with three, four or five stages.[6] Figure 2.1 synthesizes the models of Ballard and Pritchard (1996: 77–78) and Swinton and Mowat (2006: 95). The cycle begins with 'Current Praxis' [Experience], which involves identifying the situation and outlining what appears to be going on in a prereflective way. This leads onto the second step, namely 'Cultural/Contextual analysis' [Exploration] or the 'excavation of the complex matrix of meanings' within the situation. Insights from social scientific and other nontheological disciplines are used. The third step is critical 'Theological' reflection [Reflection], which is the attempt to understand

Figure 2.1   The action–reflection cycle or practical–theological spiral

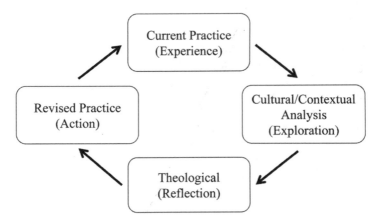

---

[5]   The word 'liberatory' denotes a 'persistent tendency to value freedom' (Lewis Taylor 2003: 27) and is used to distinguish between the emancipatory aim of this study and an authentic 'liberation theology'.

[6]   For examples, see Bevans (2002), Holland and Henriot (1983: 7–8), Lartey (2000), O'Connell Killen and de Beer (1994: 20) and Osmer (2008).

the situation and church practices from the perspective of critical faithfulness, in the light of scripture and tradition. The fourth and final stage is to formulate and enact 'Revised Practice' [Action] (Swinton and Mowat 2006: 95). This four-part cycle is repeated endlessly, forming on ongoing spiral: the revised practice becomes current praxis and so on (Hug 2005: 196, Osmer 2008: 11).

Stage One: Rooted in Current Praxis

Personal Experience and the Importance of Reflexivity

Performative Theology begins with 'participant observation' (Wijsen 2005: 115) or the 'descriptive task' (Osmer 2008).[7] This stage involved exploring the following questions: what is the asylum situation in the UK at present and how are Christian communities responding? I began by reflecting upon what I had learned through my personal involvement in praxis supporting asylum seekers. While a useful starting point, this had limitations. I have only encountered a relatively small number of asylum seekers and church projects and these experiences have been inescapably subjective, partial and constructed. As Swinton and Mowat indicate, '[a]ll reality is interpreted and formulated via an interpretive process within which the researcher is inevitably enmeshed' (2006: 37; see also Hug 2005). Practising 'critical self-reflection' (Swinton and Mowat 2006: 59) – also known as reflexivity – and articulating, as far as possible, my own situatedness and preconceptions are therefore vital. Said draws on the work of Gramsci to make this point:

> In the *Prison Notebooks* Gramsci says: 'The starting point of critical elaboration is the consciousness of what one really is, and is "knowing thyself" as a product of historical processes to date, which has deposited in you an infinity of traces, without leaving an inventory ... therefore it is imperative at the outset to compile such an inventory'. (1991: 25)

What have been my formative experiences and influences and how have my current social, economic and political contexts shaped me? What views and values condition the way in which I see other people and the world? In addition to the motivations, contexts and past experiences already discussed, it is important

---

7   'Praxis' is a slippery word and has its origins in Marxism. Clodovis Boff describes it as the 'sense of the *complexus of practices* oriented to the transformation of society, the making of history' (1987: 6), Min as a 'struggle for liberation in a specific society and history' (2004: 158), Graham et al. as 'denoting the centrality of value-committed action' (2005: 170) and Groody as referring 'to human activity and ministry in the light of God's Reign in history and in the end of time' (2007: 190). I use two terms, 'praxis' and 'experience', to distinguish between shared value-committed actions geared towards liberation and my own personal involvement in this shared praxis.

to note that I am a white, 33-year-old, British, middle-class, ordained Anglican woman – identity facets that have affected the way in which I have engaged with people seeking asylum and understood these encounters. Personal situatedness also affects the very *process* of theological research and reflection. My 'self' has influenced the questions explored, stories gathered and material drawn upon, the way in which analysis has been undertaken and the shape of this book. This is why Bevans claims that '[t]here is no such thing as "theology"; there is only *contextual* theology' (2002: 3). While theological reflection as an 'embodied and passionate process' (Clark-King 2004: 24) is to be embraced, critical self-reflection '*throughout* the research process' is essential as it enables the researcher 'to monitor and respond to her contribution to the proceedings' (Swinton and Mowat 2006: 59. My italics). Moreover, 'critical and analytically accountable forms of reflexivity' are required rather than mere introspection (Finlay 2001: 71). Stating perspectives on oneself is not enough. These perspectives, along with the research methodology and findings, should be critiqued by others and the researcher needs to be willing to change her mind and presuppositions as a result. As Etherington stresses, reflexivity is more dynamic than basic self-awareness: it should open up an active space for exploration (2004: 36–37). I have sought to enter such a space throughout the research process.

Expanding the Horizon: Gathering Experiences in a Shared, Multi-Vocal Context

These limitations and the fact that personal experience is embedded within a wider collective praxis have made drawing on the experience of others essential. So has the shared, multi-vocal context of the study. Evaluating the work of churches acting in solidarity with those seeking asylum – the 'core' praxis explored – requires an understanding of the broader ecclesial and societal *habitus* or 'ecology' within which this praxis takes place.[8] I explore the points at which church praxis and the lives of people seeking asylum and established communities intersect. Gathering examples of as many church practices as possible *and* listening to an assortment of asylum-seeking and established population voices have therefore been vital.

The complex, globalizing world in which we live necessitates engagement with diverse perspectives. One of the criticisms levelled at liberation theology is that it has denied the validity of the experience of the privileged. Min argues that globalization calls for a theology of solidarity – 'solidarity of the different, the solidarity of strangers, the solidarity of those who are other to one another'. He employs the term 'solidarity *of* others' to indicate that 'there is no privileged perspective, that all are others to one another, that we as others to one another are equally responsible' (2004: 82). In recognition of the 'constitutive interdependence

---

[8]   The notion of 'core praxis' is intended to indicate the praxis upon which this study focuses, namely churches' work with asylum seekers. This praxis however takes place within the context of other praxes and experiences, particularly those of people seeking sanctuary and the established population. The term 'ecology' will be explored in Chapter 5.

of all reality', all theologies should reach out beyond their own particularity to others (2004: 138–140). Lartey similarly advocates an intercultural practical theology today which is 'polylingual, polyphonic and polyperspectival. Many voices need to be spoken, listened to and respected in our quest for meaningful and effective living' (2006: 124; see also Isasi-Díaz 1998a: 37, Schreiter 1997: 127–132). As Kwok points out, it is this 'multiplicity of theological voices' that enables 'mutual critique and enrichment' as 'identity is always constructed in relation to others. We cannot understand ourselves without listening to others' (2005: 60). Most importantly, the experiences of people seeking asylum challenge a narrowly monovocal or monocontextual theological approach. All migrants inhabit a variety of spaces, often concurrently, and are constantly required to shift between different cultural, political, social and economic modes, assumptions and statuses. Bedford recognizes, '[t]he experience of migrants is precisely that of a series of epistemological ruptures; time and time again migrants are exposed to "others" in new ways ... When theologians think as migrants and migrants as theologians, epistemological rupture and renewal are almost unavoidable' (2005: 111). She advocates 'learning to speak of God from more than one place' (2005: 112–113). Noting how immigrant identity involves being 'betwixt-and-between', meaning 'to-be-*neither*-this-*nor*-that, to-be-*both*-this-*and*-that, and to-be-*beyond*-this-and-that', Phan likewise suggests a 'multi-perspectival' '*inter-multi-cultural*' theology (2003: 150–151, 154). Any theological work aiming to engage with the polyphonic experience of those who cross borders should make awareness of multiple perspectives a priority. Georgi's reminder 'that biblical proclamation and religion did not originate in niches but at the thoroughfares and junctions of a large world' is also a timely one (2005: 366).[9]

Adopting a 'bricolage' approach

How then have examples of church praxis and experiences of asylum seekers and the established population been gathered? Given the paucity of data on church engagement with asylum seekers in the UK and the complex, fragmentary and ever-changing nature of this engagement, I decided that an overview would be the best starting point for reflection. Not only could this generate a wide range of praxis, voices, experiences and new questions, but it was also the approach most likely to counteract the temptation identified by Pattison to value facts above wisdom, intuition, creativity, illumination, risky speculation and the search for meaning and value (2007: 280–281). Drawing on his notion that 'producing worthwhile and "tasty" theology should be more like organic rather than industrial farming' (2007: 278), the activities of '[c]ontemplation, rumination, reverie, hovering attention – and ... even hovering inattention' (2007: 285. Italics omitted)

---

9   Premnath argues for a 'border pedagogy' which involves boundary-crossing and engagement with diversity (2007a: 5–9). Those researching poverty also 'stress the importance of an *inclusive* approach ... which recognises the validity of *all* voices seeking to challenge poverty' (Beresford et al. cited in Bennett and Roberts 2004: 50).

have been central in this research. 'Bricolage' is the best metaphor to describe my approach. A 'bricoleur' creatively and pragmatically uses an assortment of materials and approaches, odds and ends from a variety of sources, to piece together a jigsaw which can then be interpreted (Neuman 2006: 158).[10]

Between 2004 and 2008, I visited a number of projects and churches engaging with people seeking asylum and spoke with project coordinators and ministers in person and on the telephone. I tried to make my exploration national and cross-denominational in scope, though most of the praxis I investigated lay denominationally within the historic mainstream churches and geographically within England. I drew on personal contacts and met people at conferences who put me in touch with other projects and individuals. I adopted an open, flexible conversational approach, hoping that this would enable the gathering of opinion and allow those with whom I was speaking to lead as well as respond (Swinton and Mowat 2006: 61–65, Bennett and Roberts 2004, Jacobsen and Landau 2003: 191, Osmer 2008: 61–63). I asked questions including: what does this church or project offer in terms of asylum seeker support? Why are you involved in this work, personally and as an organization? What are the strengths of your work and what challenges do you face? I had numerous informal, spontaneous chats with asylum seekers, Christians standing alongside them, friends, neighbours and church-goers, which increased my awareness of the work being done and provided a range of views. Questions about motivations, joys and difficulties were included on an Enabling Christians in Serving Refugees (ECSR) evaluation form in September 2005 and websites, promotional material, journalistic articles and reports provided further context for study. Since 2008, I have kept abreast of changes within some of the projects.

'Hanging out' with asylum seekers
The desire to explore a wide range of church praxis and listen to multiple voices and the adoption of an 'ad hoc' approach runs a significant risk. This is that the voices of people seeking asylum will be lost. As Rieger has warned, 'The postmodern appetite for otherness and difference is so convenient because it does not promote a real alternative ... people on the margins go under in a sea of pluralism. Everything and everybody is thought to be other ... No specific

---

10   Graham refers to 'bricolage' as characteristic of the post-modern age (2000: 106) and McFague advocates an approach like a 'hike' rather than a 'map' (cited in Cameron et al. 2005: 244). Similarities with a multimethod or triangulation approach in the social sciences can be noted. Brewer and Hunter advocate attacking 'a research problem with an arsenal of methods that have nonoverlapping weaknesses in addition to their complementary strengths' (2006: 4. Italics omitted). This is the approach favoured by Swinton and Mowat (2006: 50–51). Incidentally, it can help to avoid the danger of engaging in 'advocacy research' (Jacobsen and Landau 2003: 187, Denscombe 2007: 118–120), which involves researchers finding evidence to corroborate what they have already decided to state. Drawbacks to this approach include its inability to provide a consistent empirical evidence base across the projects.

place is left for the repressed' (2003a: 14). Asylum seekers can be vulnerable to manipulation and exploitation and afraid to participate in research (Kelly 2005). Endlessly confronted with questions by authority figures and often living in flux and fear, daily preoccupations may understandably take precedence over a research project unlikely to bring immediate benefit. A group producing ethical guidelines noted that 'research approaches are in our view very often inappropriate and unethical for a highly vulnerable and ever-changing population' (ESRC Seminar 2006: 203).[11] 'Humanity', 'humaneness' and integrity are vital principles in research (ESRC Seminar 2006, Kelly 2005) and require 'balancing the value of advancing knowledge against the value of noninterference in the lives of others' (Neuman 2006: 131; see also RSC 2007: 164). I wished to avoid engaging in a voyeuristic 'theological tourism' (Thistlethwaite and Cairns 1994) which prioritized my needs as a researcher above those seeking asylum. At the same time, an actualized commitment to the 'preferential option for the poor' (Gutiérrez 2003, Rieger 2003b) was necessary to avoid producing a thoughtless 'theology of good intentions'. Reddie has defined a 'theology of good intentions' as 'a way of responding to situations of injustice, in which the perpetrator fails to take full responsibility for their actions. It is a way of responding to the oppressed and powerless, by refusing to take the experiences or perspectives of these people seriously' (2003: 154). Rieger stresses that only 'an ever closer connection with the margins' can 'keep our resistance honest' and lead to 'new ways of living' (2003b: 188) and Isasi-Díaz that 'it is the word uttered by the oppressed that starts, and sustains the dialogic process of mutuality which stands at the heart of solidarity' (1998a: 37; see also Min 2004: 142, 227). Phan elaborates further:

> A theology out of the context of migration must begin with personal solidarity with the victims of this abject condition of human, often innocent, suffering. Theologians speaking out of the migration experience must 'see' for themselves this 'underside of history' (Gustavo Gutiérrez), 'listen' to the 'stories' of these victims (Choan-Seng Song), preserve their 'dangerous memory' (Johann Baptist Metz), and to the extent possible, 'accompany' them in their struggle for liberation and human dignity (Roberto Goizueta). (2003: 149; see also Castillo Guerra 2008: 250, Gutiérrez 2008)

The experiences, agency and practices of people seeking sanctuary have been central throughout this research (Essed et al. 2004, Loughry 2008: 172). Indeed, the extent to which Christian organizations allow and facilitate the agency of people seeking sanctuary is a key consideration in the analysis which follows.

How, though, can an outsider begin to understand experiences so very different from her own? Rieger's insight that '[t]aking seriously the experience of others

---

[11]   On ethical issues surrounding research on migrants, especially refugees and asylum seekers, see ESRC Seminar (2006), Lammers (2007), Leaning (2001), Schmidt (2007), Temple and Moran (2006) and Van Liempt and Bilger (2009).

begins by listening' is key (2001: 108). Listening helps the outsider to enter into
the stories of others – to experience their experiences to some degree – and so
helps to prevent talk about people behind their backs. Phan pictures listening
as 'dig[ging] deep into the humus of the immigrants' lives' and for him, such
'digging' is important because it 'contributes to building up a kind of concrete
universality, out of particular stories and histories, from below as it were, rather
than the kind of abstract universality and normativity that the dominant theology
attempts to impose on others from above' (2003: 161–162). Listening can, as a
result, create a space for asylum seekers whose voice is not usually heard to have a
voice in knowledge production (see Potts and Brown 2005: 263). In order for this
to happen, the researcher needs to be willing to be challenged by what she hears.
West suggests that scholars need to move beyond 'listening to' *and* 'speaking
for' the oppressed towards a 'speaking with' them. 'Speaking with' avoids the
twin dangers of romanticizing and idealizing the contribution of the 'poor' or
minimizing and rationalizing it (1999b: 136–137). Hearing others on their own
terms is, however, difficult. We are always at risk of silencing the voices of those
on whose behalf we speak. Lewis Taylor identifies the double bind: 'how is it
possible to hear and acknowledge the voice and speech of the subaltern without
engaging in controlling exercises that reinforce their speechlessness?' (2003: 33).
bell hooks puts it more forcefully, suggesting that often intellectual talk

> about the 'Other' annihilates, erases: 'No need to hear your voice when I can talk
> about you better than you can speak about yourself. No need to hear your voice.
> Only tell me about your pain. I want to know your story. And then I will tell it
> back to you in a new way … '. (1991: 54, 151–152)

Migrants need to be given the space to respond or 'witness' as subjects (Oliver
2001). What is more, as migrant experiences are always hybrid, complex and
nuanced, asylum-seeking voices cannot be homogenized. Kwok points to 'the
tensions, contradictions, and fragments that characterize the border subject' (2007:
113) and Bedford notes that a migrant 'from a subaltern culture' who is rooted
in more than one place '*cannot* communicate what he or she wants in' the terms
expected by the dominant culture. Migrants are often not 'understood because
the persons to whom they are speaking do not know their origin or have the
patience to hear their stories' (2005: 108–109). Paralysis is not a solution. While
preventing possible 'charges of misrepresentation and colonial consumption
of the other's experience and insights' (Clark-King 2004: 12), retreating from
research concerning migrants would achieve nothing. Lewis Taylor's four modes
of 'authentic advocacy' offer a possible way through the impasse. If the researcher
acknowledges the problem, involves herself in local resistance, recognizes that her
own freedom is connected with that of those studied and embraces a mysterious
'delirium' which involves recognizing the 'other is also *in* us' (2003: 33–40),

she can be a useful outside partner.[12] Practising reflexivity helps to maintain an awareness of power differentials between the story-teller and listener (BSA 2002: 2, Potts and Brown 2005: 262–263) and vulnerability, self-disclosure and openness on the part of the researcher can build mutuality and trust (Etherington 2004: 22, 25).

In the light of the sensitivities and difficulties mentioned above, however, I chose to 'consult' (ESRC Seminar 2006: 204) those seeking asylum rather than seek their full participation and gathered stories informally through 'hanging out'. 'Hanging out' is a term coined by Rodgers to suggest the kind of 'informal, interpersonal and "everyday" types of encounters' that allow the space for forced migrant voices to be heard (2004: 48). An 'ethical imperative,' it fosters respect, dignity and humanism in research (2004). People seeking sanctuary told me their stories during conversations at English language classes and the post-church coffee counter and while eating ice cream in a nature park. I sometimes asked the questions: where do you find support? What has your experience of churches been? I also undertook one more formal group interview. I tried to be sensitive, made it clear that I was undertaking research and those whose comments are drawn upon consented to their use. Names of people seeking sanctuary are pseudonyms to ensure anonymity (BSA 2002, ESRC Seminar 2006, RSC 2007). I have also supplemented these stories with stories gathered by others, including those found in books and articles.[13] Limitations of this approach should be noted. People seeking sanctuary may have felt more comfortable expressing positive rather than negative opinions of Christian groups to a white, British citizen professionally associated with churches. Need for support from churches and desire to be in good standing with organizations perceived to have formal authority may, in some cases, also have affected responses.

Shaping the Praxis: Constructing a Typological Framework

Gathering a spectrum of varied praxis does not make for easy presentation, and I chose a typological framework to shape the core praxis on which this study is reflecting. Typologies or models can help define a multilayered situation and shape a complex, amorphous plethora of experience into a form which can be explored and discussed. Dulles, twice adopting a 'model-based' approach (1983,

---

12   On the role of 'outsiders' in the theological enterprise, see Bevans (2002: 18–21), Cameron et al. (2010: 73–74), Isasi-Díaz (1998a), Pattison (1997: 227–228) and Sedmak (2002: 14–15).

13   Sources presenting stories of refugees and asylum seekers abound. Published books containing accounts include Bradstock and Trotman (2003), Eggers (2006), Coventry Peace House (2006), Langer (1997), Marfleet (2006), Moorhead (2005) and Rabben (2011). The IAC Hearings (2007–2008) provided a wealth of narrative; see also the films, *In This World* (2003), *Rain in a Dry Land* (2007), *God Grew Tired of Us* (2006), and various reports on destitution, including Malfait and Scott-Flynn (2005) and Jackson and Dube (2006).

1987), notes that '[t]ypological thinking is characteristic of periods when cultural and ideological pluralism abounds. It tends to go with a somewhat skeptical and critical mentality – one that sees the limitations of every theory and commitment' (1983: 35). A model is designed to be a rough and approximate 'ideal case' or, to borrow a term from Barbour, a simplified and schematic 'organizing image' (cited in Dulles 1983: 30–31). As such, models can be helpful tools in research critiquing heterogeneous experience. Dulles divides models used in theology into 'explanatory' and 'exploratory' types, the former synthesizing what is already believed and the latter having the capacity to lead to new theological insights (1987: 24–25). Typologies are inevitably limited and partial and a variety of complementary models should be used. Atherton recognizes that typologies are arbitrary and can 'only provide working frameworks, essentially provisional, never claiming the title of a grand or meta-narrative … typologies are never tidy' (2000: 67–68). In summary, a model is 'a "case" that is useful in simplifying a complex reality, and although such simplification does not fully capture that reality, it does yield true knowledge of it' (Bevans 2002: 31).[14]

I present four exploratory models of church engagement with asylum seekers – 'Encounters of Grassroots Service', 'Encounters with the Powers', 'Encounters in Worship' and 'Encounters in Theology'. They are inevitably artificial, inadequate and overlapping. Not only does the work resist systematization as many individuals, projects and churches are involved in more than one kind of engagement, and sometimes, one activity may fall into two or more categories; but the work is also in constant flux, as the asylum system in the UK changes. The models are designed simply to provide parameters within which the work being done can be meaningfully explored. I resisted any more detailed typological analysis of the examples in order to demonstrate their multistranded and interwoven nature.

Stages Two and Three: Creating Critical Interdisciplinary Conversations

The practical–theological spiral is a conversational process (Graham 1996, Pattison 2000b) and stages two and three of the practical–theological spiral – cultural/contextual analysis and theological reflection – create particular kinds of academic conversation. They seek to bring the praxis outlined in a precritical way in stage one into critical dialogue with various social scientific and theological disciplines. Such interdisciplinary exchange is a distinctive characteristic of all Practical Theology (Ballard and Pritchard 1996: 104, Cameron et al. 2010: 29–32, Swinton and Mowat 2006: 77–80) and the cross-fertilization and mutual criticism it fosters should lead to discovery and deeper understanding. This is because, as

---

[14] Theological works employing typologies include Graham et al. (2005), McFague (1987) and Niebuhr (1951).

Tracy articulates, truth emerges through hard conversation (1988: 18–20).[15] As Lartey has pointed out, however, these conversations are perhaps better described as 'multi-perspectival rather than inter-disciplinary' as a practical theologian cannot deal in their research with the complexity of all the disciplines required (2000: 132). A theologian is not an expert in every area. What is more, establishing a healthy relationship between social scientific analysis and theological reflection requires a delicate balancing act. While some prioritize theological reflection, because theological presuppositions affect the way 'secular' analysis is undertaken (Hug 2005: 201, Swinton and Mowat 2006: 92–94) or because the task of theologians is to offer prophetic comment on society (Wijsen 2005: 120), others suggest that theological reflection should itself be subjected to rigorous criticism by the social scientific insights gained (Lartey 2000: 132–133). This study seeks to engage with the social scientific disciplines on their own terms and is prepared for theological assumptions to be challenged by a critical understanding of the contemporary context.

Stage Two: Exploration and Analysis

The aim of stage two, exploration or cultural/contextual analysis, is to gain a better understanding of the context, *habitus* or ecology within which the praxis is taking place. Exploration can be described as 'the effort to obtain a more complete picture of a social situation by exploring its *historical and structural relationships*. [It] serves as a tool that permits us to grasp the reality with which we are dealing' (Holland and Henriot 1983: 14). Sometimes termed 'socio-analytical mediation' (Boff and Boff 1987: 24), this stage involves the researcher gaining 'insight into the observed practice' (Wijsen 2005: 116). Developing a critical understanding of the ecology within which people seeking asylum and churches are encountering one another in the UK requires analysis drawing on a variety of disciplines (Castillo Guerra 2008: 260). These include history, geography, anthropology, political, economic and urban theories, philosophy and social psychology. Most of these disciplines also need to be considered at multiple levels – global, national and local – in order for a 'deep and rich understanding' of the situation of asylum seekers and the churches' role to be established (Swinton and Mowat 2006: 13–16, 96). A risk must again be highlighted. Pattison rails against mediocrity and woolliness in theological engagement with other disciplines and warns of the dangers of 'trawl[ing] through the human sciences and assembl[ing] a series of insights … which may then implicitly or explicitly be claimed to be of great significance and worth' (2007: 256). He urges an exploration of 'at least one discipline in depth', being clear about its limitations and up to date

---

[15]   For a discussion of revised critical correlation, a method Tracy developed in which theology and other disciplines enter into truth-seeking and mutually critical conversation, see Tracy (1981). While the 'conversation' he refers to is between theology and experience, his insights also apply to interdisciplinary dialogue.

with its findings (2007: 255–259). Lartey similarly challenges a 'pick-and-mix' approach to adopting social science methods (2006: 81).

Introducing Forced Migration Studies

I draw largely on Forced Migration Studies for analysis, a field still emerging and in the process of defining its remit. While almost coterminous with Refugee Studies, which began to emerge as a distinct discipline in the 1980s, it is different in that it is also concerned with involuntary migrants who are not refugees.[16] The term 'Forced Migration Studies' recognizes that many people seeking asylum are not formally acknowledged as refugees and that their situation is enmeshed in complex global patterns of involuntary migration. Forced Migration Studies is itself a multidisciplinary subject. It is a field rather than a single discipline because research into migration and refugee issues necessitates cross-disciplinary endeavour and the use of a range of social scientific standpoints (Brettell and Hollifield 2002, Castles 2000: 19–21, 2003: 22, Marfleet 2006: 7–8). Engaging with and mirroring this field, I draw on insights from a range of disciplines. The burgeoning publication of material in the field, which can be found 'scattered across multiple information repositories', and the ever-changing migration context mean that keeping 'up with new research is always a challenge' (Mason 2007: 149).

Stage Three: Theological Reflection

Stage three of the practical–theological spiral is theological reflection or 'hermeneutical mediation' (Boff and Boff 1987: 24) or 'prophetic discernment' (Osmer 2008). This stage involves evaluating the praxis which has been observed and analysed (Wijsen 2005: 118) by bringing it into conversation with theological and biblical traditions. I decided to focus on biblical narrative as biblical reflection has been neglected to date within practical and urban theologies (Ballard and Holmes 2005: xiv, Latvus 2007, Ballard 2011).[17] Biblical narratives also provide a way of engaging with contemporary stories. As many recount embodied encounters between strangers, connections can be made with encounters between asylum seekers, established communities and churches today. Forrester notes, 'the Bible does not engage with an abstract problem like poverty or pauperism, but with poor *people*, and their lot and standing in God's eyes' (1997: 104). The intention in this stage is to foster 'a transforming narrative' by 'weaving together divine and human stories' (Anderson 2005: 203, 205).

---

[16]   On the background, history and origins of Refugee Studies, see Black (2001) and Chimni (1998, 2009).

[17]   Exceptions include Richardson (2003) and Vincent (2006).

Biblical Studies: foregrounding hermeneutical assumptions

How, though, has such a 'hermeneutical mediation' been accomplished? Postcolonial hermeneutics has provided the primary springboard for reading scripture through a forced migration lens.[18] Its appropriateness stems from two characteristics: the majority of postcolonial scholars define themselves as migrants or exiles – as 'border' subjects living in diasporic communities in the North (Kwok 2005: 44–51) – and its underlying aim, shared with liberation theology, is to bring about the emancipation of the oppressed.[19]

The power and politics infused in biblical texts *and* in the hermeneutical process are foregrounded. According to Segovia, a 'postcolonial optic' recognizes a significant 'shadow of the empire' in the production of ancient texts, in the production of modern readings of ancient texts and in the lives of modern and contemporary readers (1998, 2000: 125–132, Yee 2010: 205–209). The Bible 'is no innocent text' (West 1999a: 77). Those who wrote, translated and selected the texts included in the Bible were affected by the presuppositions of their time – often sexist, racist, imperialist and classist – and by their social, geographical and political location (Kwok 1995: 84, 2005: 7–20, Dube 2000). All who read the Bible are also positioned, interested and conditioned: we are inescapably 'flesh-and-blood readers' (Segovia 1995b). As a result, texts and readings must always be regarded with suspicion and their assumptions exposed. Naive literal parallels between biblical and contemporary situations should also be avoided. Scripture never offers direct correlative answers, but only, according to Clodovis Boff,

> orientations, models, types, directives, principles, inspirations – elements permitting us to acquire, on our own initiative, a 'hermeneutic competency', and thus the capacity to judge – on our own initiative, in our own right – 'according to

---

[18]   The notion of hermeneutics specific to the issue of forced migration is new, but all that can be offered here is a tentative outline of the approach adopted in this study. 'Forced migration lens' is preferred to 'asylum-seeking lens' to indicate that this approach has not been formulated by those seeking asylum. For an introduction to postcolonialism, see Runesson (2011), Yee (2010) and Sugirtharajah (2003: 13–36, 2006a, 2006b). On the development of biblical criticism since the early nineteenth century and the emergence of postcolonial and liberation hermeneutics in the late twentieth century, see Segovia (1995a, 2000).

[19]   Rieger (2003b) indicates that both liberation and postcolonial theologies are concerned with the subaltern subject. Sugirtharajah discusses the similarities and differences between these 'kindred spirits'. One of the ways in which postcolonial theology differs from traditional liberation theology is that '[i]nstead of perceiving the West as demonic, it tries to establish a critical conversation which places the accent on mutual exchange and transformation' and challenges polarised constructions of 'the colonizer as bad, the colonized as innocent' (2006b: 77–81). It emphasizes the hybridized and complex nature of all identities. A postcolonial hermeneutical approach was selected over a liberationist one partly for pragmatic reasons, as it permits a re-reading of biblical texts in the privileged 'metropolitan study' (Sugirtharajah 1999).

the mind of Christ,' or 'according to the Spirit,' the new unpredictable situations
with which we are continually confronted. (1987: 149)[20]

Or in the words of Phan, the aim should simply be to 'discover the possible
relationship between the relationship obtaining between one set of terms (*e.g.*, the
Hebrew exiles and their context) and the relationship obtaining between another
set of terms (*e.g.*, the U.S. immigrants and their context)' (2003: 163).

The Bible is to be read as a source of life for the contemporary world. The text
is critically excavated in order to bring about positive transformation and justice in
the world today, and in this case, the liberation of those seeking sanctuary (see Kwok
1998: 277, Dube 2000: 49). Sugirtharajah argues that '[p]ostcolonial hermeneutics
has to be a pragmatic engagement' (1998b: 113). Recognizing that much biblical
interpretation can be 'boring and petty' Gramscian 'elaboration upon elaboration',
of interest only to small esoteric communities, he stresses that interpretation
should spend more 'energy on religious fundamentalism, suicide bombings, and
asylum seeking, all of which have a great impact on our lives' (Premnath 2007b:
163, 159; see also Sugirtharajah 2006a: 27). Biblical interpretation should help to
'change people's perceptions and [make] them aware of the need for revolution'
(Sugirtharajah 2003: 95).

The whole ambiguous text is to be engaged with, but not every part of the
Bible can be equally affirmed as life-giving for forced migrants. The Christian
scriptures contain a wealth of conflicting material: 'some texts show the indelible
marks of imperialist ideology, while others challenge the dominant power and
have liberating possibilities' (Kwok 2005: 8). McKinlay describes it as a collage
'of voices recorded in print' (2004: 115). Instead of focusing only on texts that
seem appealing, it is important to juxtapose a range of strands and to bring many
different biblical perspectives into intertextual conversation. Kwok suggests a
'dialogical' model for interpretation, 'shifting the emphasis from one scripture
(the Bible) to many scriptures' and 'from a single-axis framework of analysis to
multiaxial interpretation' (1995: 36). The texts explored in this book are drawn
from diverse and conflicting strands within the biblical tradition and explored
from a variety of angles. All texts cannot be regarded, however, as equally valid.
I prioritize texts which promote life, love and justice above those which lead to
death. While inherently oppressive texts cannot always be 'saved' or 'co-opted'
for the oppressed (Mofokeng cited in West 1999a: 87), they can still be mined for
helpful insights and provide illumination into the dynamics of power and exclusion
surrounding asylum-seeking today.[21] Indeed, 'we [can] embrace and transpose the

---

[20]　Colwell similarly criticizes simplistic utilitarian approaches to scripture, arguing
instead that it should be understood as 'transformative narrative'. Scripture contains stories
'through which we are shaped and formed as a people who can live trustfully, faithfully,
lovingly, hopefully, thankfully and worshipfully' (2005: 216).

[21]　This is where Sugirtharajah believes a significant difference between postcolonial
and liberation interpretation lies. Whereas liberationists suggest that all biblical texts can be

ancient texts, and propel them to yield new meanings unenvisaged by the authors of the narratives, in order to meet our contemporary needs' (Sugirtharajah 2003: 2).

A plurality of voices is essential in biblical readings relating to forced migration. Sugirtharajah, borrowing a term from Said, argues that reading 'contrapuntally' helps to 'demystify the received and established framework and read against the grain'. Said believed that it was important to study experiences of the exploiter and exploited together and to avoid binary polarities in reading strategies (Sugirtharajah 2003: 47, 16; see also Kwok 1995: 36, 19). It is in the 'contact zone' (Dube 2000: 58) between oppressed and oppressor that creative and hopeful possibilities for the future can emerge. As we all also 'assume more-or-less fractured, hyphenated, double, or in some cases multiple, identities' in terms of gender, class, ethnicity, nationality and so on, it is vital that our biblical interpretation is also 'hybridized' (Sugirtharajah 2003: 124–125, Kwok 1995: 38, Runesson 2011: 44). A range of hermeneutical frameworks is also required in interpretation (Segovia 2000: 11). Postcolonialism 'is an optic, not the optic, in full engagement and dialogue with a host of other models and other optics' (Segovia 1998: 64). I have drawn on an assortment of commentaries, varied both in terms of the hermeneutical framework they employ and the contexts within which readings have been undertaken.

Finally, the voices of those 'on the move' and excluded are prioritized. At a textual level, submerged and silenced voices of strangers need to be uncovered. Speaking of the oppressed more generally, Weems points out that their voices appear 'as random aberrant outbursts in a world otherwise rigidly held together by its patriarchal attitudes and androcentric perspective' (1991: 76). We need to scrutinize texts for what and who is missing in order to recover stories that have been suppressed or misrepresented (Sugirtharajah 1998a: 18). This requires imagination (Runesson 2011: 119, Kwok 2005: 30). At an interpretive level, readings offered by those who know what it feels to be 'on the move', 'in-between' and excluded are also given priority. According to Sugirtharajah, readings which take place in a betwixt and between 'interstitial cultural space' will help 'the post-nationals in their metropolis and the subnationals in their refugee settlement [to] work out a relevant hermeneutics' (1996: 427–428). The biblical analysis in this study seeks to draw, as much as possible, on commentaries provided by those who inhabit such an 'interstitial' space.

---

rescued and life-giving if interpreted correctly, postcolonial scholars recognize that there is often a problem with the text itself (2006b: 78; see also 2001: 239–241, 2002: 103). While he perhaps overdraws the contrast – Mofokeng and Isasi-Díaz, who suggests that 'only those parts of the Bible which allow and enable a true liberative understanding of Hispanic women are accepted as revealed truth' (1998b: 274), would regard themselves as liberationists – the point that the authority of the Bible is open to question is well made.

Stage Four: Towards Transformative and Liberatory Action

The final stage of the practical–theological spiral is action or renewed practice or 'practical mediation' (Boff and Boff 1987: 24). According to Wijsen, its objective is 'to demonstrate conditions for the possibility of innovating the practice under investigation' and it is achieved through 'pastoral planning' (2005: 120). This study aims to result in liberatory action. Research into the suffering of others can only be justified if alleviating that suffering is an explicit objective (Turton 1996: 96), and Forrester relentlessly advocates for an approach which starts where the 'shoe pinches' and leads to some vision of and power for change (Morton 2004: 35–36). He stresses that theology should address the oppressed first and, only then, policy-makers, citizenry and the Church with a disturbing message. It needs 'to "rekindle utopian energies", to nurture a vision of God's future, to call on people to seek equality with eagerness and commitment' (Forrester 2001: 72, 251). Sung similarly recognizes the need to develop a liberating 'horizon of utopian desire' by dreaming 'of a free world, a world liberated from all kinds of oppression and objectification of human beings'. He suggests that, in time, this horizon can be 'further developed and appears to us as a *project* for a new society (sometimes, in Christian circles, as *God's project*)' (2005: 5–6; see also Min 2004: 227–228). This study seeks to support those seeking sanctuary in their quest for new life in a new place, and justice and liberation are its underlying goals. It does this through sketching a renewed *habitus* or ecology in which Christian solidarity with migrants could take place and suggesting a number of ways in which encounters between churches and people seeking sanctuary might be enhanced. Echoing Castillo Guerra's aims for theologies of migration, I hope to point towards the generation of 'a society of *convivencia*' and to 'empower [asylum seekers'] economic, social, cultural, political, and religious rootedness. Such commitment has to be accompanied by the task of humanization of the societies of destination, so that they are hospitable societies' (2008: 262). I hope to point towards 'new ways of living together and new ways of building community' (Rieger 2003b: 187).

While easy to talk about such transformation, it is much harder to bring about in practice. Petrella has criticized liberation theology for becoming 'stagnant' since the decline of socialism through lacking a 'historical project' to deliver on its promises. It seems 'incapable of moving from critique to the construction of alternatives that could give concepts such as "liberation" and "the preferential option for the poor" renewed vigor' (2006: vii, 17). Talking about oppression, marginality and having visions for liberation can actually be counterproductive if there is no concrete attempt to move beyond them (Premnath 2007b: 155). This book cannot, however, enact renewed practice and presents no detailed action plan. It rather offers a vision of a more faithful ecology within which renewed praxis could take place and a few general but realistic suggestions for practice within this ecology. The focus is on moving forward positively together and on creative reconstruction rather than simply on denunciation (Schreiter 1997: 127–132).

Suggesting 'gradual steps' is, I believe, often more productive than attempting to induce 'millenarian revolutionary fervor' (Petrella 2006: ix).

An Endlessly Repeating Spiral: 'Fragmentary' Provisional Findings

A key assumption of performative theology is that this four-part cycle is repeated endlessly. It is best drawn as an ongoing spiral. Performative theology is a modest and fragmentary approach which makes no claims to completeness or final answers. Forrester refers to theology as generating 'puzzling reflections in a mirror' (1 Cor. 13) (2000: 18), quoting Rilke who recognized that '[t]he story of a shattered life can only be told in bits and pieces' (cited in Forrester 1999: 129). For Forrester, it is essential that practical theologians 'quarry' to

> obtain the fragments that serve as road metal, the living stones that make our homes and churches, the grit that provokes the oyster to produce pearls, the crystals that concentrate light into visions, the fragments that generate utopias, that build up jigsaws of meaning and that nourish the activity of truthfulness, love and justice which is the practice of God's Reign (2004b: 437).

We should inject any theological fragments we uncover into public debate (2000: 155). Such fragments only ever offer partial truth and limited understanding and we must therefore continue with the hard, tiring, dangerous, often unnoticed task of theological 'quarrying' (2004b: 437). The action–reflection cycle must be repeated again and again in order to ensure that our understanding is always growing and deepening. Theological discoveries are transitory, providing 'shafts of light into situations and issues rather than final answers or durable solutions. It is, in a way, "throwaway" theology that always has to reinvent its tasks and methods. As such, it must always be flexible and provisional' (Pattison and Woodward 2000: 14). Good theology must always be 'tentative' and humble (Lartey 2006: 19, 103–105, Pattison 2000b: 137, Sedmak 2002: 159). It is perhaps migrants who speak of God from multiple locations who 'remind us with particular poignancy that all theology is "on its way"; the *via theologica* requires a *theologia viae*' (Bedford 2005: 113). Kwok, describing border passage as 'a continuous journey and not a fait accompli', calls for a 'theology of "not quite" to articulate the grief, loss, and tensions of the border subject' (2007: 104, 113). People seeking sanctuary point us towards a realization that 'God is that which cannot be fully grasped by our language and bound by our experiences and fantasies. God always exists outside any totalitarian effort and resists any attempt of full narration' (2007: 114). There is a growing body of literature emerging around migration and theology, and in this book, I simply hope to make a contribution to an important conversation and to stimulate further research.

Summary

This chapter has discussed how a performative and liberatory theology has been attempted in this study and, in the process, identified some of its key assumptions. The practical–theological spiral forms the structure of this book. The following chapters will explore current praxis, Forced Migration Studies, Biblical Studies and suggestions for renewed practice in turn.

Chapter 3
Supporting Asylum Seekers:
Church Activities and Projects

How are churches responding to the needs and desires of asylum seekers? What kinds of Christian projects, services or events are being created and resourced? Do these take place at congregational, local, regional, national or international levels? Are Christian groups working alone or partnering with other organizations? This chapter explores these and other questions and presents a broad-brush picture of church engagement with people seeking sanctuary in the UK.

The work of churches and Christian FBOs can be divided into a range of encounters, following the typological framework laid out in Chapter 2.[1] In everyday speech, the word 'encounter' denotes coming across someone or something unknown and usually for the first time. More literally, to encounter means to 'unexpectedly experience or be faced with (something difficult or hostile)' or 'an unexpected or casual meeting'. It has its roots in the Latin 'in contra' meaning 'against' (Pearsall 1998: 607). 'Encounter' implies a coming into contact of entities hitherto unassociated that contains the possibility of mutual opposition and antagonism. Contacts between those unfamiliar to each other can and often do result in considerable fear, resentment and suspicion. While an 'encounter' can remain simply that – a point of connection at two entities' edges – it can also develop into deeper relationship. 'Encounter' can indicate a range of connections of different intensities which change over time.

Encounters of Grassroots Service

[F]or I was hungry and you gave me food. I was thirsty and you gave me something to drink, I was a stranger and you welcomed me. (Mt. 25:35)[2]

---

[1] While the following examples specifically concern asylum-seeking in the UK, the four categories also have relevance to work being undertaken with immigrants and refugees in other national contexts; see Appendix 1 for a list of projects in the UK, US and elsewhere. For more on faith-based support and activism in the US, see Daniel (2010), Hondagneu-Sotelo (2008), Groody and Campese (2008) and Slessarev-Jamir (2011: 131–165). For other typologies of FBOs, see Unruh and Sider (2005), Clarke (2008), Ferris (2011) and Orji (2011).

[2] All biblical quotations are taken from the New Revised Standard Version (NRSV).

'Encounters of Grassroots Service' are to do with the pastoral care of individuals and represent the 'cuddlesome' face of religion valued by governments.[3] They are person-centred and rooted in the activities of befriending, listening, visiting and service provision. Much activity lies within this model and is undertaken through organized, multistaffed and multi-agency funded projects as well as through the small-scale ad hoc responses of particular congregations and individuals. Most of these encounters involve volunteers and are responses to the perceived practical and pastoral needs of those seeking asylum. They are often a first reaction to someone seeking sanctuary stepping over the threshold of a church. The following examples give a flavour of the work being done.

Restore is a project of Birmingham Churches Together which 'seeks to help, welcome, and support refugees and asylum seekers' (Restore 2011a). Established in 1999 on the initiative of local churches, it has had one part-time and three full-time members of staff. It has focused on befriending, and volunteers have been trained and linked with individuals seeking asylum to offer support, guidance and practical help. In 2007, 51 families or individuals were offered a new befriending match (Restore 2008: 6) and in 2010, Restore received 112 new client referrals (Restore 2011b: 4). Restore has organized a summer holiday programme for children and social activities for men and women, such as visits to art galleries, botanical gardens and swimming. It also operates as a resource for satellite church groups in the area that provide varied English language classes, drop-in sessions where people can come in for conversation or various services if they wish, and befriending activities. For example, Solihull Welcome has offered tea and chat to those waiting to sign on at the Home Office Midlands Enforcement Unit, and a drop-in session and English class have been run at a Methodist church in Ladywood. Restore points those seeking sanctuary in the direction of legal support and has helped to found the Hope Projects, including a fund and housing to support destitute asylum seekers, a fund for children and mothers without access to public funds, and counselling (Hope Projects 2011). Restore has worked with a range of organizations from the Birmingham Law Centre through to ASIRT (Asylum Support and Immigration Resource Team), doctors' surgeries and the Refugee Council. Church members have accompanied individuals to court hearings and welcomed newcomers into their homes.

In Newcastle-upon-Tyne, asylum seekers have come to the West End Refugee Service (WERS) for advice, clothing and drop-in sessions with workers from Northumbria Police (community links), Your Homes Newcastle Move-on team, Victim Support and other non-statutory organizations. Based in a former vicarage, the project has also operated an emergency hardship fund and offered

---

3   This model has similarities with Atherton's vignette of partnership and reconciliation labelled 'neighbourly discipleship: transforming localities' (2000: 93) and the activity Schaeffer categorizes under 'Church as Protective Community' (1990: 44). It includes activities categorized under a 'project' or 'service' model and 'community work' model by Logan (2000: 144).

a professional counselling service and English language classes. While WERS is not explicitly Christian, many volunteers have been and church-linked sources including the Church Urban Fund have provided significant funding (Cross 2005, WERS 2011). In 2008, WERS had five part-time employees, whose work included providing advice drop-ins in the community, home visits and training for volunteer befrienders. WERS has networked with other local voluntary groups and has a large 'client' body: in 2007–2008, '5189 contact episodes were recorded at the drop-in advice sessions and visiting surgeries' and '6300 visits were made to the clothing store' (WERS 2008). It has been the place to which most local organizations, from the Cathedral to the police, refer those seeking sanctuary. The Boaz Trust in Manchester, established in 2004, has focused on supporting destitute asylum seekers. In 2011, they provided accommodation for 50 asylum seekers and five refugees in eight houses and through a network of local host families. Working with the Red Cross, the Boaz Trust has also helped to establish five destitution projects in the Northwest region, which have provided food parcels and cash support. The organization has been open most days to provide clothes, food, advice and 'Meaningful Lives' activities and classes (Boaz Trust 2008, 2011).

Diverse agencies throughout the UK offer similar services. The Coventry Refugee and Migrant Centre (CRMC) (formerly the Coventry Refugee Centre), set up in 2000 by a Methodist minister and which later became an independent organization, has had statutory funding and run a variety of activities. One team has focused on asylum seekers and another on supporting refugees for six weeks after they get leave to remain. Hillfields Christian Fellowship Church has contributed food parcels and money, and the Mothers Union (MU) has helped with nappies and baby milk. CRMC, with Churches Together for Refugees in Coventry (CTRIC), has made subsistence grants to those seeking sanctuary. The Jesus Centre, an initiative of the Jesus Army, has been open on weekends to provide laundry, meals and medical services. The Coventry Peace House, established in 2004, has acted as a night shelter for destitute asylum seekers. A Sikh Gurdwara has provided an evening meal, Roman Catholics have provided financial allowances for individuals, and students from Warwick University have made up food parcels. Many volunteers at CRMC and the Peace House have been Christian (Hall et al. 2005). Asylum Welcome in Oxford, established in 1996 by a group of friends connected with the Black and White Christian Fellowship, has also broadened out from its largely Christian roots. The project has facilitated volunteer visits to detainees in Campsfield Removal Centre as well as provided drop-ins, an education advice team, photography and football projects, practical information, holiday activities, help finding lawyers and accommodation, four youth clubs for different ages, IT courses and training for local refugee community organizations (Asylum Welcome 2008).

The services also vary widely. Bradford Ecumenical Asylum Concern (BEACON) has offered asylum seekers temporary accommodation with volunteer hosts, welcome and refreshments for those waiting for appeals to start at the Asylum Hearings Centre in Thornbury, and the 'McKenzie Friend' befriending project (BEACON 2008). In Southampton, City Life Education and Action for Refugees (CLEAR) has organized English language sessions, a cinema club, football, social events, casework, business advice and mentoring and a bicycle recycling workshop. Part of the Pioneer Churches Network, it has had links with Tearfund and worked with the City Council and Refugee Action (CLEAR 2008). In Bristol in 2004, St Nicholas of Tolentino Church in Easton offered sanctuary to a Rwandan woman and a Colombian man threatened with deportation (BBC 2004). Wrexham Refugee and Asylum Seeker Support Group (WRASSG) was established in 2001 as a response of local churches and others to the dispersal of asylum seekers to the town. With the backing of Wrexham Borough Council, WRASSG has supported two weekly drop-ins, at local Methodist and Salvation Army churches, that offer friendship and practical help, including distribution of fresh fruit and vegetables provided by the local health board as well as advice and referrals. The Diocese of St Asaph has contributed to the project financially (Church in Wales 2008). Congregations in Northern Ireland have offered activities from English language classes to cooking sessions, mother and toddler groups and befriending (Kerr 2008).

In London, a plethora of organizations serve asylum seekers. Aiming to 'accompany' and 'serve' all those seeking sanctuary, the Jesuit Refugee Service (JRS) has prioritized work with those who are detained and destitute. Volunteers and staff have visited and corresponded with detainees in removal centres, producing news sheets to keep people in touch with developments in their countries of origin (JRS 2007: 48).[4] The London office has been open three days a week for a drop-in, offering lunch and an opportunity for those who are destitute to obtain travel assistance grants. Asylum seekers have been able to access computers, seek referrals to medical and legal services and also work as volunteers. In 2007, individuals from 31 countries made 3,110 visits to JRS. JRS has also operated a voucher exchange scheme and in 2007, £7,700 of vouchers were exchanged for cash each month (JRS 2007: 48–49).[5] The Memorial Baptist Church in Plaistow has accompanied people to doctors' surgeries and housing departments, helped to furnish houses and stood bail when needed (Baptist Union n.d.). The Notre Dame Refugee Centre, based at the French Church in Leicester Square, has catered for French-speaking Africans and hosted a twice-weekly

---

[4]   Removal centres are not part of the formal prison chaplaincy system. Managers of Religious Affairs (MRAs) are appointed to oversee the provision of religious services for detainees. Some MRAs act as traditional chaplains, while others are dependent on local clergy and lay people who act as chaplains in a paid or voluntary capacity. Often chaplaincies are part of local support groups offering pastoral care, prayer and worship and some hand out Bibles or put people in touch with legal services when requested to.

[5]   As will be explained in more detail in Chapter 4, those seeking asylum are sometimes given vouchers for specific shops as subsistence payments. Voucher exchange schemes give asylum seekers cash for these, enabling them to purchase food and other essential goods from cheaper or more appropriate stores.

drop-in offering general, health and legal advice, counselling, English lessons, food parcels, clothes and lunch. A chaplain has made links between the church and the centre (Notre Dame 2008, Bloqueau 2005). Praxis, a 'place for displaced people', was started as a Christian initiative in 1983 (though is now independent) and its Chief Executive Vaughan Jones is a United Reformed Church minister. Praxis is based in East London and has supported migrants through befriending, football, advice, community empowerment and by providing a clothes store and healthcare in conjunction with the Red Cross and Médicins du Monde. They have also offered voucher exchange, a community café and an interpreting service (Praxis 2008). St Mary Stoke Newington has provided a building within which the Hackney Migrant Centre could base a weekly drop-in and the London Churches Refugee Network (LCRN) launched a fund in 2007 to collect money and distribute resources among destitute asylum seekers. Its patrons have included bishops from the Church of God of Prophecy, the Roman Catholic Church and Church of England, and representatives of the Methodist and United Reformed Churches. The Bail Circle, based in London under the auspices of the Churches' Racial Justice Network (CRJN), draws on a network of people to provide sureties for those seeking bail for removal centres. The coordinator has offered case support to individuals including through finding legal advice, challenging inappropriate removals and organizing emergency medical intervention (de Raadt 2006).

Some organizations with a broader social justice agenda have also funded and supported local grassroots service projects. In 2001, a six-person international Church Mission Society team worked alongside a partner Christian charity, Folkestone Migrant Support Group, for six months to support families and assist integration (Morgan 2004, 2006). The Bradford Mothers' Union has supported a baby clinic for those seeking asylum in a city centre health centre, offering conversation and friendship and collecting clothing for young children (Haigh 2008).

Encounters with the Powers

> Speak out for those who cannot speak, for the rights of all the destitute. Speak out, judge righteously, defend the rights of the poor and needy. (Prov. 31:8–9)

'Encounters with the Powers' designates activities of lobbying, campaigning, advocacy and transforming attitudes in relation to asylum aimed at the established population – and particularly people or structures with power. Wink defines the 'Powers That Be' as 'more than just the people who run things. They are the systems themselves, the institutions and structures that weave society into an intricate fabric of power and relationships. These Powers surround us on every side. They are necessary. They are useful ... But the Powers are also the source of unmitigated evils' (1999: 1). 'Powers' indicates both people with authority on asylum matters in the UK and the systems, institutions and structures which influence the experiences of those seeking sanctuary. These include governmental departments, politicians, the civil service, the media, local authorities, key public and corporate figures and think tanks. Activities that encounter the powers represent 'admirably troublesome' religion (Furbey 2010) or what Smith names as the 'disruptive potential' of religion to 'turn the world upside-down' (1996: 1). Some encounters are individually focused and involve witnessing on behalf of those seeking asylum in court hearings or representing them to their MPs. The clergy at Newcastle Cathedral, for example, have acted as witnesses in the cases of Iranian members of the congregation claiming asylum on grounds of religious persecution. Other work is locally oriented, aiming to raise awareness and tackle myths held by members of a congregation or community. Encounters which take place at a national level usually challenge asylum policies and systems.[6]

Advocacy has been a strong emphasis of JRS. The UK director has had numerous public speaking engagements to raise awareness about the legislation faced by those seeking sanctuary and JRS has published responses to government legislation, in conjunction with other bodies such as the Methodist Church and Quakers. They have collaborated with campaigning organizations including Asylum Rights Campaign and Church Action on Poverty (CAP) and written to MPs concerning parliamentary bills. The monthly *JRS–UK News* contains policy and legislation updates and JRS has had a voice on the Greater London Authority Refugee and Community Forum (Zanre 2005). The director of the Boaz Trust has established NACCOM – the 'No Accommodation' Group – an informal partnership of organizations committed to supporting destitute asylum seekers and ending destitution, and is a prominent advocate for asylum seekers at local, regional and national levels – working with other charities on projects such as City of Sanctuary (Boaz Trust 2011). The Boaz Trust has also had a multimedia presentation on asylum, destitution and the work of the Boaz Trust called the 'BOAZ Roadshow' (Boaz Trust 2008). The coordinator of Restore in Birmingham has chaired the Refugee Strategy Network (which coordinates the voluntary sector on asylum in the West Midlands) and Hope Housing, spoken at local churches and also had a wider national role, being invited to offer input at national events on asylum. She has attended the Board Meeting of the West Midlands Strategic Migration Partnership, involving members of the regional UKBA. Restore, moreover, generated a study into destitution in Birmingham in order to produce an evidence base to challenge policies of destitution and to improve services offered (Malfait and Scott-Flynn 2005). CTRIC has held open meetings for church members and organized 'Celebration of Cultures' evenings. In 2004, it distributed 5,000 copies of *Facts, Myths, Truths and Stories: Asylum Seekers and Refugees in Coventry* and, in 2005, a part-time outreach worker to churches and church schools was appointed (Hall et al. 2005). EmbraceNI works 'to promote a positive response to

---

[6]   This model has similarities with Atherton's 'vignette' of partnership and reconciliation labelled 'national discipleship: reformulating policies' (2000: 110) and the activity Schaeffer categorizes under 'Church as Prophetic Witness' (1990: 45).

people seeking asylum, refugees, migrant workers and minority ethnic people in Northern Ireland'. Its approach has included producing a CD-ROM and leaflets designed to tell the stories of new arrivals and to provide information on asylum, refugees and migration. It has encouraged more churches to support migrants and works with agencies, MPs and Members of the Local Assembly to try and ensure that newcomers are treated fairly (Kerr 2008, EmbraceNI 2008).

Denominations and ecumenical groupings have also made a contribution in terms of national advocacy. The sets of principles published by CCRJ (Deeks 2006, Weller 2007) were designed to present united Christian policy recommendations and to encourage more churches to become involved in support. The United Reformed Church passed a resolution in 2003 to tackle hostility towards asylum seekers and produced a leaflet encouraging churches to get involved (URC n.d.).[7] The Evangelical Alliance (EA), in conjunction with others, has tried to influence the decision-making process on asylum claims in relation to those who have converted to Christianity. Representatives met with the Immigration and Nationality Directorate (now the UKBA) in February 2004. In February 2005, the 'Churches Main Committee' (representing a range of Christian and Jewish groups, including the EA) presented a submission to the Home Office outlining problems within the asylum system. Further meetings and correspondence followed and in 2007, guidelines for caseworkers were amended. Nicholas Coulton, Sub-Dean of Christ Church Cathedral in Oxford, reinforced this campaign by writing to the immigration minister Liam Byrne in April 2007 to challenge poor understanding about conversion on the part of adjudicators and the unreasonable questions used to verify someone's Christian faith. This letter was also published in *The Times* (Coulton 2007). In June 2007, the EA hosted a Symposium on the Persecution of Christian Asylum Seekers in the House of Lords (Coton 2007: 7–8, Coulton 2008).

Another significant ecumenical Christian engagement with the powers seeking to have a direct political impact has been coordinated by CAP. In 2005, it launched a campaign – Living Ghosts – to highlight and challenge policies inducing destitution among those seeking sanctuary (CAP 2008). In 2005, over 45 Church leaders signed a statement in support of the campaign and Nicholas Sagovsky, then Canon Theologian at Westminster Abbey, took CAP's endurance challenge to live for a week on the food and income of a refused asylum seeker in July 2008. CAP is part of the Still Human, Still Here campaign, a coalition aspiring to end the destitution of refused asylum seekers, which has also been independently backed by the Archbishops' Council of the Church of England and the Catholic Bishops' Conference of England and Wales. CAP has supported the Let Them Work campaign of the Trades Union Congress and Refugee Council, calling for those seeking or refused asylum who have been in the UK six months to be allowed the right to work. In 2006, the Commission on Urban Life and Faith

---

[7] Other denominational responses include Methodist Church (2011a, 2011b), MPA (2005) and Office for Refugee Policy (2004).

called the government to take a responsible lead on asylum policy and condemned policies which denied asylum seekers the right to work (CULF 2006: 90). The Children's Society has produced a report revealing and condemning destitution among asylum-seeking and refugee children, based on research in Birmingham (Clarke and Nandy 2008).

Church leaders have been outspoken in challenging the powers. In addition to the involvement already mentioned, Church of England bishops have engaged with all parts of the legislative process as immigration and asylum legislation has passed through the House of Lords. For example, the bishops of Winchester and Ripon and Leeds spoke on 13 June 2007 during the second reading of the UK Borders Bill challenging measures relating to detention and deportation policies and restrictions on appeals (Hansard 2007). Leading up to the 2005 general election, the Bishop of Ripon and Leeds and the West Yorkshire Ecumenical Council called for a revision of asylum policy and an end to the fuelling of hatred (Ekklesia 2005). A letter to *The Times* on 4 May 2005, signed by the Anglican Bishop of Oxford, URC Moderator, Roman Catholic Bishop of Portsmouth, Methodist President of Conference and the Free Church Moderator similarly called upon citizens to 'challenge candidates to give priority to ensuring just and compassionate treatment for those who have come to this country seeking asylum' and criticized poor handling of asylum claims. In November 2008, the Archbishop of York publicly condemned as 'unmerciful' the immigration minister's suggestion that asylum seekers, lawyers and supporters were 'playing the system' (Sentamu 2008). The Dean of Birmingham Cathedral chaired the 'Celebrating Sanctuary' Refugee Week Committee between 2001 and 2005, which aims to raise awareness of the lives of those seeking asylum in the city and brings together refugee community groups and secular and faith-based advocacy organizations in public support of newcomers. Islamic Relief has participated by setting up a refugee camp as an exhibit. The Bishop of Coventry has hosted multifaith meetings and met with MPs regarding asylum legislation, and the 'West Midlands Regional Church Leaders Forum' organized a conference for a Voluntary Sector Regional Strategy Group for Refugees and Asylum Seekers in 2004 (Hall et al. 2005).

Seeking to influence both attitudes and policy, the Independent Asylum Commission (IAC) was established in 2007. Called for by Canon Nicholas Sagovsky in 2005 at the annual Gore Lecture at Westminster Abbey (Sagovsky 2005), it was founded in conjunction with the Citizen Organising Foundation (COF) and various faith communities.[8] Chaired by a former High Court Judge and the president of the Association of Muslim Lawyers, the IAC examined the national asylum system and made recommendations for improvements (IAC 2008a, 2008b, 2008c, 2008d). It conversed with those seeking sanctuary, their

---

[8]　It followed an enquiry into Lunar House by the South London Citizens in 2005, of which Sagovsky was a part, which was initiated after some church members in South London were appalled by hearing the experiences of those seeking asylum at the Home Office processing centre.

supporters and the UKBA. Christian engagement in and consequent influence on its findings were crucial, particularly in terms of input into the commission's regional hearings. The grassroots knowledge which church-based groups had gleaned of the experiences of those seeking sanctuary, as well as asylum seekers themselves connected with these groups, provided much of the evidence on which its recommendations were based. Citizens for Sanctuary – a COF campaign with substantial church involvement – has been working towards making the recommendations of the IAC a reality. Successes to date include public actions to prevent asylum seekers in Middlesbrough having to walk 12 miles and back to a police station in Stockton to report to the Home Office, and garnering a commitment by the Coalition government to end the detention of children by May 2011. This campaign involved Nicholas Sagovsky dressing up as Father Christmas and attempting to deliver gifts to around 35 children detained at Yarl's Wood Immigration Removal Centre in December 2009 (Citizens for Sanctuary 2011, Cox 2011).[9] The Archbishop of Canterbury publicly supported this call for the end of child detention and has expressed concern about the lack of asylum seekers' right to work and their protection if returned to countries of origin. He has also affirmed the significant contributions made by refugees to British life (Williams 2008, 2010a, 2010b).

Churches have been strong opponents of the British National Party (BNP) and its anti-immigration agenda. Speaking before a BNP rally held in Stoke on Trent in September 2008, for instance, the Bishop of Stafford called on Christians to oppose the party and churches gathered at a city centre church on the day of the rally for a prayer vigil for peace and reconciliation (Gold 2008).

Encounters in Worship

> All the ends of the earth shall remember and turn to the Lord; and all the families of the nations shall worship before him. (Ps. 22:27)

'Encounters in Worship' refers to engagement with people seeking sanctuary in the context of Christian liturgy and prayer. Such encounters take different forms. They occur in and through the regular worship services of congregations (often on Sundays), special services focusing specifically on those seeking asylum and related issues, and the nurture of those wishing to convert to Christianity. Many people seeking asylum turn up at church services. At Birmingham Cathedral

---

[9]   This governmental commitment has come under question, however, as later in 2011, UKBA opened a 'pre-departure accommodation centre', Cedars, which contains families in attractive buildings and grounds through boundary fences and the security firm, G4S (Gentleman 2011). For more on the origins and activities of Citizens for Sanctuary, as well as a COF campaign supporting undocumented migrant workers, Strangers into Citizens, see Ivereigh (2010: 129–158).

for example, Annette, Lucille and Hassan were regular members of the Sunday morning congregation and Celine turned up at one service hoping to find peace, pray and chat. The Nazarene Church in Longsight, Manchester, has taken steps to ensure a warm welcome is offered to those seeking sanctuary who attend their Sunday morning worship. Newcomers have been invited to serve Holy Communion and to read lessons, and the congregation aims to sing in Spanish, English and French every week so as to include as many present from different countries of origin as possible (Brower 2008).

Opportunities for worship and spiritual exploration specifically deigned for people seeking asylum and those who support them are sometimes also offered. Conferences, such as those held by the Churches Refugee Network (CRN) or Enabling Christians in Serving Refugees (ECSR), have opened and closed with a time of worship. Prayers, readings and songs that focus explicitly on themes of welcoming the stranger and justice are often chosen. The worship at the CRN Conference in May 2008 was entitled 'Walking with Strangers' and included prayers based on Matthew 25 such as 'Forgive us Lord when we do not recognize you as a stranger walking with us ... Open our eyes so that we may remember you in the brokenness and emptiness of the stranger'. At a service held in Westminster Abbey for the launch of the London Churches Refugee Fund in June 2007, a confession explored the suffering of those who were destitute and included the hymn, 'When I needed a neighbour, were you there'. There have also been services held on the World Day of Migrants and Refugees and a retreat entitled 'you know how a stranger feels ... ' took place at Worth Abbey in 2006 for supporters of those seeking sanctuary. I led a biblical reflection for a weekend organized by Restore for asylum seekers and volunteers of varied faiths in Birmingham in 2006, focusing on the stories of Abraham and Hagar and including candle-lighting as a symbol of prayer. Restore has also invited people seeking sanctuary to participate in group retreats to Iona. When I visited the St Mary Magdalene Centre for Refugees and Asylum Seekers in London, I participated in a time for prayer during which a candle was passed around in silence as meditative music was played.

While prayers, readings, songs and reflections are often chosen or written for the particular occasion, resources are also sometimes drawn from anthologies and websites. *Entertaining Angels* contains a wealth of material on the theme of refugees and asylum-seeking drawn from all over the world, including confessions, ideas for Refugee Sunday, a children's liturgy and intercessions (Duncan 2005; see also Duncan 2002). The Iona Community has published a 'Refugee Evensong' and Jagessar has composed a 'Service of Word and Table' around the theme of seeking asylum (Jagessar 2008). JRS has provided confessions, readings, reflections and intercessions written by refugees from all over the world and those who support them, and resources for Bible study and worship can be downloaded from an ECSR/Lifewords website (JRS 2005, 2008, ECSR 2008). Various denominations also provide worship resources for their member churches on asylum-seeking and migration. For example, a webpage for Methodist Refugee Sunday on 22 June 2008 offered information, a Bible study, hymn, prayers and readings suggestions

(Methodist Church 2008). The Catholic Agency for Overseas Development (CAFOD) provides liturgical resources on the theme of refugees (CAFOD 2008) and CAP compiled material on asylum-seeking to be used at services on Poverty Sunday in 2006 (CAP 2006).

The nurture of those wishing to convert to Christianity also takes place in some churches. Newcastle Cathedral began welcoming Iranians seeking sanctuary into the congregation after a sign outside saying 'welcome' in a variety of languages attracted one man who soon brought friends with him. Some of these 11 or so Iranians were Catholic and others Muslim, by birth if not by practice. When two children were born, some asked for their baptism and for their own confirmation and reception into the Church of England. Preparation classes followed, Bishop Hassan Dequhan-Tafti, a former Anglican bishop in Iran, joined the diocesan bishop for the service and churchwardens became godparents to the babies. A discussion group was continued at the request of the group (G. Miller 2004, 2005, Coulton 2008).

Encounters in Theology

> They said to each other, 'Were not our hearts burning within us while he was talking to us on the road, while he was opening the scriptures to us?'. (Lk. 24:32)

As these encounters will be discussed in greater detail in the course of the chapters which follow – this book is itself an example of these encounters – I will only offer a brief outline of this model here. 'Encounters in Theology' indicates engagement with people seeking sanctuary through theological reflection. These encounters are manifest in the choice of biblical verses for project tag lines, the worship resources mentioned above and a growing body of academic work. Many theological encounters have, to date, focused on the theme of welcoming the stranger, drawing on passages such as Matthew 25 and Hebrews 13:2, or on the experience of the Holy Family which forms part of many Christmas and New Year reflections (see for example Jones 2000).

Expanding the Picture

While these models indicate much of the work being done to support people seeking sanctuary, there are in addition a number of other layers of engagement – feeding into all of these encounters – worth noting. A number of national networks draw together and resource church-based groups engaging with people seeking sanctuary. The CRN organizes an annual conference to facilitate networking and information sharing and emails have also been sent to CRN members containing information about changing legislation, countries of origin and cases. CRN seminars have been convened at Westminster Abbey to discuss asylum-related issues. ECSR was established in 2001 as an initiative of Tearfund, the Baptist Union and the Salvation Army, with a mostly evangelical membership and, before folding in 2011, it operated a website providing a range of information and organized conferences. The National Catholic Refugee Forum, founded in 2000, has similarly organized training workshops and conferences. Tearfund has produced resources for Christians wishing to respond to the needs of asylum seekers by setting up a befriending project (Powell and Leather 2002), as have the Baptist Union (Baptist Union n.d.) and the Church of England (MPA 2005). The Methodist Church has a webpage aiming to provide resources to churches on all aspects of immigration and asylum (2011c). Individual Christians are also involved with people seeking sanctuary through their day-to-day work, whether as social workers, judges, civil servants, doctors, lawyers or teachers. In 2006, the 22 Senior Immigration Judges based at Field House in London included a Methodist Lay Preacher, Anglican Lay Reader and Anglican self-Supporting Minister as well as practising Jews and Muslims.

Finally, work on asylum-seeking and refugee issues at an international level involving Christians from the UK – directly or indirectly – should be mentioned.[10] JRS works on international campaigns to address some of the root causes of forced migration, including the use of child soldiers and landmines. The Churches' Commission for Migrants in Europe (CCME), based in Brussels and drawing on the experiences of churches across Europe, works to influence EU policy concerning migrants in an inclusive direction and designated 2010 as a year of European Churches Responding to Migration (CCME 2011). The World Council of Churches (WCC) has long been concerned with migration, and in 2007, launched a 'Global Platform for Reflection and Analysis' focused on the theme of 'Finding Sanctuary: Migration, Community and the Churches'. A variety of reflections were submitted and a summary posted online (WCC 2008). In 2012, the WCC convened an international working group to produce a new theological statement on migration.

Summary and Postscript: Hostility

This chapter has introduced some of the encounters between people seeking sanctuary and church communities in the UK through outlining key features and examples of four different models of engagement. A postscript must be inserted. While many Christians support those seeking asylum, some do not. Jean-Paul, seeking sanctuary from a life in the Congo, recounted how one church in Birmingham he had attended for a while 'did not know' about asylum seekers and refugees or was simply not interested in helping: 'it was not so friendly'

---

[10] This is akin to what Atherton calls 'international discipleship' (2000: 134). Schaeffer also talks about international work, including that of the World Council of Churches (1990: 39–42).

(Group Interview 2007). One minister mentioned that some in her congregation had reservations about welcoming those seeking sanctuary on the grounds that they could be doing something illegal, and I have given talks in Christian contexts where people have been hostile or misinformed about the issues. Migration Watch, an independent think tank that calls for greater limits on immigration, has been chaired by a practising Anglican and has included the president of Christian Solidarity Worldwide among its advisory board (Migration Watch 2011). Lord Carey, the former Archbishop of Canterbury, supporting the Cross-Party Group on Balanced Migration (authored by Migration Watch), said that we 'have to question whether the unprecedented levels of immigration that we are now seeing can truly contribute to the "common good"' (2008). More extremely, a number of BNP members self-identify as Christian, including five ministers on a 2008 published membership list (BNP 2008). Christian support for those seeking asylum cannot be assumed.

PART II
Flight and Fright:
Experiences of Seeking Sanctuary

Chapter 4

Flight: The Global Dynamics of Migration

> While movements of people across borders have shaped states and societies since
> time immemorial, what is distinctive in recent years is their global scope, their
> centrality to domestic and international politics and their enormous economic
> and social consequences. (Castles and Miller 2009: 3)

What brings migrants, including asylum seekers, to the Global North? What do
people face in their countries of origin, en route and after they arrive? This chapter
provides an overview of the international dynamics of migration, placing the
activities outlined in Chapter 3 – and the UK asylum context with which they
engage – into a wider context. Castles, an eminent forced migration scholar, has
stressed the importance of engaging with a broad, global picture. Warning against
overemphasizing the 'subjective and cultural aspects of forced migration' and the
'tunnel vision' which can result from national, short-term policy driven research, he
asserts the need for analysis at micro and macro levels, and believes that 'specific
studies of specific groups or situations [should be] informed by broader studies
of global social, political and economic structures and relationships – and vice
versa' (2003: 21–26; see also Marfleet 2006: 7–8). In order respond effectively
to migrants in our own contexts, we first need to understand more about migrant
experiences across the globe.

Contemporary Migration Flows: 'Something New Afoot'

In an influential book first published in 1993, Castles and Miller announced the
'age of migration' (2009). While there has always been international movement –
humans are inherently migratory, having moved about in search of food, shelter,
work and opportunities since time began – they suggest that it 'has never been as
pervasive, or as socio-economically and politically significant, as it is today' (2009:
299). Something 'new is afoot' (Castles 2004). The number of people moving in
all directions across the globe has increased significantly in the last 60 years,
with an estimated 214 million migrants worldwide at present. This equates to 3.1
per cent of the world's population and represents a significant increase from 150
million in 2000. The figure could rise to 405 million by 2050 (IOM 2010, 2011).
By the end of 2010, there were approximately 43.7 million forcibly displaced
people, including 15.4 million refugees and 27.5 million internally displaced
persons (IDPs), as well as an estimated 12 million stateless persons worldwide

(UNHCR 2011a).[1] At any one time, there are thought to be 2.5 million people in forced labour, including sexual and domestic exploitation, as a result of trafficking (UN Initiative to Fight Human Trafficking 2011). In 2005, it was estimated that around 800,000 people were transported over borders each year by smugglers at a turnover of 10 billion US dollars (Moorhead 2005: 37). Migration has become a big business.

Wide-ranging and interrelated transformations in international politics and economics have led to this new era of migration, including the end of Cold War, the development of the European Union and the multifaceted phenomenon known as globalization (Koser and Lutz 1998). Fresh types of civil war are also constantly emerging and human rights abuses are endemic (Castles 2004). Defined by its 'increasing numbers, shifting geographies, changing migrant profiles, feminization, new policy responses and changing migration strategies' (Koser and Lutz 1998: 4), this era of new migration has is seeing increasing numbers of immigrants arriving in the Global North (Sales 2007: 30). It is this which helps to explain why immigration and asylum have become such significant items on the agenda of many Western governments.[2]

Causes of Migration

So, why do people move? Arango outlines a 'colourful, variegated mosaic' of theories to explain contemporary patterns and trends in migration (2004: 22).[3] A first group of theories concentrate on *micro-level* factors: that is, they suggest that migration occurs as a result of positive decisions made by specific individuals or groups to seek a better life or income elsewhere (Arango 2004: 22–23). *Macro-level* explanations, by contrast, recognize the significance of global structural factors in encouraging people to move (Arango 2004: 24–27). Sassen argues that 'migrations do not simply happen' but are rather produced, patterned and embedded in specific historical phases and 'shaped by existing politico-economic

---

[1]   'Stateless persons' refers to individuals 'not considered as nationals by any State under the operation of its law' as well as 'persons with undetermined nationality' (UNHCR 2011a: 37).

[2]   I use the terms 'Global North' and 'Global South' to designate countries often described respectively as belonging to the 'first' or 'developed' and 'third' or 'developing' worlds. While still problematic in terms of geographical inaccuracy and the homogenization of diverse countries, the former terms at least have fewer hierarchical connotations than the latter. I use the term 'Western' to indicate a style of government historically associated with North America, Europe and Australasia; see also Castles and Miller (2009: 7–12) and Sales (2007: 21–43) on new migration. Some dispute this view, arguing that we 'are *not* living in an unprecedented "age of migration"' (Zolberg 2001: 12).

[3]   For a range of migration theories, see Brettell and Hollifield (2002), Castles (2007), Cohen (1996), Hammar et al. (1997), Massey et al. (1998), Sassen (1988b) and Solimano (2010).

systems' (1999: 155). A 'geopolitics of migration' exists in which sending and receiving countries are agents. Structural factors affecting migration include the globalization of economic activity – particularly the operation of markets and the North–South economic divide – the increasing ease of communication and transport, the formation of transnational and regional institutions and agreements, and the public-political struggle around human rights which helps to shape immigration policy (Sassen 1999: 150–155, Spencer 2011: 9–11, Castles 2007: 39–40). The role of large institutions such as states and corporations should not be underestimated, nor should demographic disparities between areas with weak economies but high fertility rates and areas with fast-growing economies but declining fertility (Castles 2002; see also Massey et al. 1998: 277).

Meso-level factors comprise the 'intermediate, relational level that stands between the micro level of individual decision-making and the macro level of structural determinants' (Arango 2004: 29). Faist (1997, 2000) is among those who highlight the importance of 'sets of interpersonal relations that link migrants or returned migrants with relatives, friends or fellow countrymen at home' (Arango 2004: 27–28). These transnational kin networks provide vital financial, social and cultural capital for the migration process: that is, they often offer money, information about the migration process, understanding of the new society, employment, accommodation and support (Castles 2007: 35–36, Solimano 2010: 30). As a result, they can be instrumental in a person's initial decision to move, affect the choice of route and destination and provide 'the basis for processes of adaptation and community formation' in the new country (Castles 2007: 36). The migration industry including traffickers, 'travel agents, lawyers, bankers, labor recruiters, brokers, interpreters, and housing agents' (Castles 2007: 36) constitutes an additional meso factor. Both types of network – kin and migration industry – have a 'multiplier effect', being cumulative and self-perpetuating: the more those from a particular family and community migrate and use them, the more likely others will do so in the future (Arango 2004: 28, Castles 2007: 37). This 'crucial' intermediary level helps to explain why there are still so few migrants out of most places and why there are so many out of very few places (Faist 1997, 2000).

Arango points out that 'migration is too diverse and multifaceted to be explained by a single theory' (2004: 15, 30–33). Macro, meso and micro factors all help to explain why certain individuals migrate to certain places and at certain points. While macro structural dynamics should not be underemphasized, it must be remembered that migrants are also 'social beings who seek to achieve better outcomes for themselves, their families and their communities by actively shaping the migratory process' (Castles 2007: 37). They are proactive agents and micro factors are significant. These three sets of factors are moreover economic, social *and* political in nature. Arango in fact emphasizes that, while most theories focus on economics, '[t]he relevance of the political dimension nowadays can hardly be overstated' (2004: 31). Not only can political conflicts lead to emigration, but conflicts of interest in receiving countries and the ability of governments to control migration – particularly through admissions policies – have a significant impact on whether, where and how people choose and are able to move (Castles 2007: 42–45, Arango 2004: 31). These theories focus predominantly on South-to-North migration, but it is important to recognize that movements of people are multi-directional, criss-crossing the globe in infinite ways.

Refugee Migration: A Complex of Push, Pull and Intervening Factors

In-country political push factors
In thinking about why people become forced migrants, and in particular refugees and asylum seekers, *political push* factors are critical.[4] Persecution 'for reasons of race, religion, nationality, membership of a particular social group or political opinion' is the defining characteristic of a refugee according to the 1951 United Nations (UN) Convention (UNHCR 2010: 14). The Convention came into being following the Second World War and the persecution of the 1930 and 1940s, particularly the Holocaust. It was also designed for those fleeing the Soviet bloc to the West – in other words, it was created for explicitly political reasons – and so as Marfleet points out, welcoming refugees was often more a means of 'ideological self-assertion' for Western governments than a humanitarian gesture (2006: 151; see also Loescher 1993). While the Convention focuses primarily on individual persecution, certain regional agreements – notably a Convention adopted by the Organization of African Unity in 1969 and the Cartagena Declaration of 1984 relating to Central American refugees – as well as international human rights norms, have since allowed for responses to group displacement caused by civil strife, general violence and violation of human rights (Loescher and Milner 2011: 191).[5]

The overriding immediate push factors for refugees have remained persecution, violence and conflict (Zolberg et al. 1989). Mass, collective displacement is often related to violence and conflict, while individually-based persecution may be related to a broader range of factors. Violence and conflict frequently have their origins in ethnic tensions. According to Harff and Gurr, '[i]n 2002 about two-thirds of the world's 15 million international refugees were fleeing from ethnopolitical conflict and repression' (2004: 1). Religious difference and hostility can also play a role. Infamous refugee-generating civil wars include those which took place in the Balkans and former Yugoslavia in the 1990s, Ethiopia and Eritrea from the 1960s to the present day and Rwanda in 1994 (Harff and Gurr 2004:

---

[4] 'Push' factors are those which negatively encourage people to move *away* from a particular location. 'Pull' factors are those which positively encourage people to move *to* somewhere else; see Kunz (1973).

[5] There had also been group-based approaches to refugees prior to the creation of UNHCR in 1950 and the 1951 UN Convention, including responses to the Spanish Civil War and the creation of the League of Nations (1919), United Nations Relief and Rehabilitation Administration (1943) and the International Refugee Organization (1946); see Zolberg et al. (1989: 18–27).

11–14). In 2010, the highest number of asylum claims were filed by people from Zimbabwe, followed by Somalia, Democratic Republic of the Congo, Afghanistan and Colombia (UNHCR 2011a: 26), countries all experiencing internal unrest and conflict.[6] This evidence suggests, as Mark Gibney points out, that 'the most violent countries in the world produce nearly all of the world's refugees' and that 'refugees almost always flee to countries where human rights practices are better than they are in their respective countries of origin' (2002: 16). In an analysis of the top 10 countries of origin of asylum seekers to the EU in 1990–2000, repression of minorities and ethnic conflict were present in all of these and civil war in seven (Castles and Loughna 2005: 60).[7]

The deeper context: underlying and exacerbating push factors
These immediate in-country political push factors are, however, usually caused or exacerbated by features of the broader domestic and international contexts in which they take place. Conflict and violence do not occur in a vacuum. As Collinson points out, 'we need to be asking why [a particular] group is vulnerable or persecuted or lacking basic protection' by analysing the 'dynamic and varied social, economic, political, and environmental *institutions* and *processes*' at work and paying close attention to changes in social relations and the political economy (2011: 309, 311).

Looking through an historical lens, refugee flows are frequently a symptom of pre-existing political fault lines. The end of the Cold War is partly responsible for generating a number of so-called 'new wars'. According to Harff and Gurr, when the bipolar world order dissolved into an insecure 'ethnically fragmented multipolar system', there was an '"explosion" of ethnopolitical conflicts' (2004: 10, 17). This has manifested itself in 'the enduring tension between states that want to consolidate and expand their power and ethnic groups that want to defend and promote their collective identity and interests'. Internecine wrangling over power and resources helps to explain why it was that in the early 1990s, 31 countries had major ethnic wars (2004: 1, 17; see also Schmeidl 2001). These wars are also new in that they take place on a larger scale and over a shorter period of time than before, and result in more violence against non-combatants through the use of weapons such as landmines (Loescher 2000: 194, Marfleet 2006: 152).[8] Political fault lines go further back still. Arbitrary state boundaries were

---

[6]   Origins of asylum claims differ from origins of refugees. In 2010, Afghanistan, Iraq, Somalia, the Democratic Republic of Congo, Myanmar, Colombia, Sudan, Vietnam, Eritrea and China were the top refugee producing countries (in that order) (UNHCR 2011a: 15).

[7]   The top 10 countries were the former Yugoslavia, Romania, Turkey, Iraq, Afghanistan, Bosnia and Herzegovina, Sri Lanka, Iran, Somalia and the Democratic Republic of Congo (Castles and Loughna 2005).

[8]   See Kaldor (2001) and Duffield (2001) for more on 'new wars', and Newman (2003: 12–15) for an argument that patterns of conflict have not changed since the end of the Cold War.

imposed during the colonial era and, when the colonial powers hastily withdrew in the 1950s–1970s, they usually left behind weak states in the grip of fragile ruling cliques. The nation-forming processes which followed often involved the expulsion of minorities (Castles 2000: 176, Loescher 1993: 12–13) and anyone deemed to threaten elite power and wealth. Large numbers of refugees today can therefore be regarded as ongoing symptoms of 'unfinished nation-building and state formation processes' resulting from the transformation of large empires and small communities into a world of nation-states. When a 'people' and a 'land' do not match, destructive attempts to 'alter people' to make them fit can take place (Westin 1999: 41–42. Italics omitted). Nations with an imperial past share in the underlying blame for refugee flows today. The nation-state system itself cannot be exonerated. As Sassen recognizes, not only do '[s]tate-building processes contribute to mass flight and mass expulsions' but old concepts of state belonging do not fit with present realities (1999: 83–84). Haddad goes as far as to suggest that refugees are 'an inevitable if unintended consequence of the international states system' (2008b: 1).

The causes of forced displacement are also related to current geopolitical, economic and environmental systems and dynamics. Collinson points out that changes in the 'distribution of power and wealth' between individuals and groups at sub-national, national, regional and international levels tend to generate competition and conflict. If money and power are unequally shared or shifting and 'up for grabs' – whether within or between countries – people are likely to fight. The institutions and interactions mediating these shifts can also provoke unrest (2011: 312–316). She suggests that the capitalist economic system is fundamentally culpable: global capitalism 'by its very (exploitative) nature, generates mass poverty and destitution and creates profound social, political and economic transformations that are likely to be associated with processes of exclusion, dispossession, violence, and/or persecution' (2011: 317). Relationships between states, the power and actions of multinational corporations and shifting environmental patterns can all play a background role (Betts 2009: 11). External military intervention provides an example. Intrastate conflicts involving foreign military intervention are the second strongest predictor of refugee migration (Schmeidl 2001: 84–85) and it is no coincidence that UK asylum applications from Afghanistan and Iraq rose during the 'wars on terror' initiated by the US and UK in these countries. In 2007, Afghanis were the largest single group of refugees in the world (3.1 million, 27 per cent) and Iraqis the second (2.3 million). Together they accounted for almost half of the people of concern to the United Nations High Commissioner for Refugees (UNHCR 2008a: 8).[9] These external military interventions were, in large part, a consequence of Western foreign policy

---

[9]   These statistics exclude Palestinians, who were in fact the largest group of refugees at this time. UNHCR has only recently begun to include all refugees, including those outside its official mandate, in statistical analysis.

priorities, security agendas, alliances and economic power – what some have called contemporary imperialism (Chimni 1998).[10]

In situations on the ground, the immediate causes of flight are in fact similarly multifaceted. The term 'complex emergencies' signifies the frequent coincidence of violent internal political or ethnic conflicts with natural disasters, deterioration of state authority and public services, food insecurity, disease, environmental devastation and economic collapse (Loescher 2000: 194, Keen 2008: 1–3). Environmental degradation has usually been overlooked as a cause of forced migration, as have underdevelopment and poverty. Each factor can, on its own, encourage people to flee. It has been estimated that the 'accumulated impact' of environmental and natural disasters affects an 'average of 211 million people' every year (UNHCR 2006: 27) and development-induced displacement and resettlement, that is people being uprooted to make way for infrastructure construction such as dams, irrigation, roads, mines, industries and urban conurbations, affects on average 10 million people per year (UNHCR 2006: 28).[11] Poverty can tip the balance in favour of a person's decision to flee. In their analysis of the top 10 countries of origin of asylum seekers to the EU in 1990–2000, Castles and Loughna discovered low income in half and low life expectancy in three (2005: 60). Therefore, as Sales puts it:

> The causes of conflict and violence that propel refugee flight are linked to those that cause poverty and economic dislocation and that propel people to move in search of better material opportunities. As conflicts are increasingly related to the breakdown of state structures, the economic and political causes of movement are difficult to disentangle. (2007: 75)

The personal decision to flee: pull and meso factors

Why do certain individuals flee when others do not and why do refugees end up in one place rather than another? Pull and meso factors again come into play. According to Castles and Loughna, decisions to seek asylum in the West are always shaped by a combination of push, pull and 'intermediate factors and migration mechanisms' (2005: 54). However bad the situation pushing people away, hope of a better future is often a secondary motivator. Pull factors include the possibility of protection and security, strong economies and health and welfare provision. Choice of destination is likely to be affected by the country's geographical proximity and whether or not there are past colonial links, a common language, similarities in culture and diaspora communities there (Castles and Loughna 2005: 61). Meso,

---

[10]   External military intervention includes the supply of arms. Zolberg et al. emphasize the impact of using refugees as a foreign policy instrument: refugees are political tools, having a propaganda function in 'cold wars' and a direct armed use in 'hot wars' (1989: 273).

[11]   For more on the relationship of the environment to refugee flows, see McAdam (2011), Lambert (2002), Wood (2001), Black (1998). For more on development-induced displacement and resettlement, see de Wet (2006), Mehta (2009) and Padovani (2006).

intermediate or intervening factors are even more significant. Communication with earlier migrants and the 'migration industry' will affect the destination of a refugee (Castles and Loughna 2005: 62). Asylum seekers can have little choice in the matter, simply ending up wherever they have been taken by smugglers or agents. The impact of an individual's personal and social circumstances should also not be underestimated. It is usually those with some education, political influence and financial resources – that is, greater agency – who are able to seek asylum in the West. Passage to a country hundreds or sometimes thousands of miles away is only affordable for those who have been well-paid. The extremely poor far more often find themselves displaced within their own country as IDPs or in a refugee camp in a neighbouring one.[12] Only an estimated 17 per cent of refugees live outside their region of origin (UNHCR 2011a: 11). As Van Hear puts it, in the context of a stringent international migration regime, 'there is a hierarchy of destinations that can be reached by migrants and asylum seekers, according to the resources – financial and network-based – that they can call upon' (2006b: 127). International migration usually requires the financial resources of the whole household and, for the poorest, migration outside their own country is rarely an option (2006b: 134).[13] The admissions policies of different states, as for all forms of migration, also determine refugee patterns and flows.

Defining Migrants, Refugees and Asylum Seekers

The complexity of factors affecting who, why and where someone becomes a refugee or an asylum seeker problematizes the simplistic definitions usually employed, including those I sketched in Chapter 1. As already outlined, the 1951 Convention makes individual persecution the criterion of refugee status and assumes that the persecutor is internal to the state (Zolberg et al. 1989: 25). A refugee is, legally speaking, someone who has been forced to move *against their will*, motivated by *political* push factors. Asylum seekers are in a similar category, as they have 'sought international protection [but their] claims for refugee status have not yet been determined' (UNHCR 2011a: 37).[14] An economic migrant, by

---

[12]   For more on IDPs, see www.internal-displacement.org [accessed: 16 August 2011], Koser (2011a) and Weiss and Korn (2006).

[13]   Castles and Loughna note that high population density and a high adult literacy rate are features of the countries which produce most asylum seekers to the West. These features indicate the presence of human capital enabling such journeys (2005: 54).

[14]   UNHCR points out that 'a person is a refugee from the moment he or she fulfils the criteria set out in the refugee definition. The formal recognition, for instance through individual refugee status determination, does not establish refugee status, but confirms it' (2008a: 13).

contrast, is commonly understood as someone who *voluntarily* travels to another country in hope of better *economic* prospects, motivated largely by pull factors.[15]

These current categorizations are inadequate as almost no movement is entirely voluntary and motivated solely by pull factors or wholly forced and affected only by push factors. A rigid forced-voluntary dichotomy cannot be maintained (Loescher 1993: 163–164, Collinson 2011: 319–320, Van Hear et al. 2009). Moreover, economic, political and social factors intertwine and mutually reinforce one another. The notion of a 'migration–asylum nexus' (UNHCR 2006: 56) encapsulates this complexity. People moving often have 'mixed motivations', fleeing violence and persecution *and* 'seeking to build new lives and to send remittances to dependents back home' (Castles and Van Hear 2011: 292), and so-called economic migrants and refugees have also increasingly used 'the same routes and intermediaries, including smugglers' (Sales 2007: 75, Van Hear et al. 2009: 13). They are often brought to the same destinations and refugees may perform a 'secondary migration', moving on to seek better economic opportunities after arriving in safety. '[A]ge-selective asylum migration' also involves a younger member of the family being positively chosen to apply for refugee status so that s/he can help support the family back home (Sales 2007: 75). With the decline in economic immigration in the West after the oil crisis in 1973, many looking for work submitted asylum applications as all other legal means of entering Western countries were cumulatively closed off and the restrictions on asylum since the 1990s have meant that asylum seekers have been forced increasingly to move as undocumented migrants (Castles and Loughna 2005: 41).

Faced with this tangled asylum-migration web, scholars have produced a plethora of possible migration and forced migration typologies (Castles 2004, Suvin 2005: 112, Bookman 2006: 32–39, Vervotec 2006). Given the 'diversification, proliferation and intermingling' of categories (Castles 2002: 1151, Suvin 2005: 114), they are all inevitably limited. A simple model based on two key variables is most helpful. Drawing on Van Hear's notion of a continuum of migration, which recognizes that force, choice and agency operate in different combinations in all types of human movement (1998: 43–44), and Betts' recognition that most migration exists on a 'spectrum' between 'volition and coercion' and is 'motivated by a mixture of economic and political factors' (2009: 4), it can be drawn as shown in Figure 4.1.

Social and cultural factors interplay with both variables, affecting levels of agency and the reasons for movement, and Collinson also suggests that the slowness or suddenness of migration may be a key factor in determining how forced or voluntary it is (2011: 319). Every migrant, refugee and asylum seeker is unique and could find themselves anywhere along either axis. Each has her own

---

[15]   Temporary and seasonal labourers, people contracted to work for industries or companies and female domestic workers, as well as those travelling from Eastern Europe to the UK or Central America to the US, are among those usually lumped together in this category.

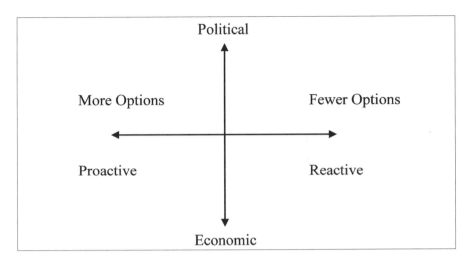

Figure 4.1   Model of migration

mixture of motivations and pressures and, as Turton claims, 'there is therefore no such thing as "the refugee voice": there are only the experiences, and the voices, of refugees' (2003: 6).[16] He agrees with Malkki that 'refugee' is not 'a label for a special, generalisable "kind" or "type" of person or situation' but 'a descriptive rubric that includes within it a world of socio-economic statuses, personal histories, and psychological or spiritual situations' (cited in Turton 2003: 14).

Given this, church-based groups need to be wary of all narrow definitions. They fail to encapsulate the complexity of the motivations and backgrounds of those who claim asylum. Asylum seekers should also be *allowed* to desire a better life with enhanced economic and social opportunities. In the effort to support asylum seekers and gain public goodwill, many Christians understandably edit out these possible secondary motivations: they want to distinguish between those who are vulnerable and the so-called economic 'scroungers' the majority of the public dislike. In the process, they risk devaluing the claims of newcomers whose reasons, while legitimate, are not solely political. It is also important to remember that definitions have largely been constructed for political ends. Zetter points out that 'who is a refugee is as much a matter of pragmatic political interpretation as one based on international law or supranational humanitarian imperatives' (1999: 50) and Schuster argues more specifically that the distinction between a voluntary 'economic migrant' and an involuntary 'political refugee' enables governments to privilege the violation of political rights over socio-economic rights in granting asylum (2003: 57). All labels inherently involve a political and ethical choice and definition 'has a bearing on matters of life and death' (Zolberg et al. 1989: 3–4). Even the term 'migration–asylum nexus' needs to be used with

---

16   Agier (2008) has attempted to delineate 'the refugee experience'.

care as it has become too closely associated with South-to-North migration and migration management agendas in the Global North (Castles and Van Hear 2011: 296, Crisp 2008). Governments may claim that asylum seekers are really irregular immigrants as an excuse to limit the numbers they admit.

The Forced Migration Regime: Searching for Durable Solutions to a Growing 'Problem'

Forced migrants are widely regarded as a 'problem' requiring a 'solution'. International agencies, national governments and local communities all wish to control their flows. For some, this is in order to relieve the suffering of those forced to flee. For most however, it is for the benefit of countries being asked to host them. Joly describes a 'new asylum regime' which has emerged in the context of the era of 'new migration' (2002: 2; see also Crisp 2003). Signifying a 'paradigm shift', it

> is characterized by the search for solution rather than protection, by the diversified categories of persons of concern to refugee agencies such as UNHCR, by its humanitarian rather than human rights bias, by the trans-sovereign character of initiatives and many other features ... [and] the significant role of refugees as deliberate or unwitting movers of international policy and intervention. (Joly 2002: 2)

The institutional players or 'actors' in this regime are predominantly industrialized governments working through intergovernmental bodies and supra-national agreements such as the UNHCR, the EU and NGOs. The twin desires to manage migration and find durable solutions to forced migration – that is, solutions which enable the forcibly displaced to 'attain integration and citizenship' (Martin et al. 2005: 227) – lie at the regime's heart.[17]

Regional Containment: Refugee Camps, Repatriation and Local Integration

The most common means of addressing forced migrant flows is to offer temporary protection and humanitarian aid to people within their country of origin (as IDPs) or in refugee camps in neighbouring countries. Known as regional containment, this approach aims to prevent the uprooted from travelling too far and its ultimate goal is repatriation. Van Hear argues that the 'new forced migration paradigm' 'seeks to contain both conflicts and forced migrants in their regions of origin. This

---

[17] UNHCR, wishing to avoid the negative associations of the term 'asylum', has adopted the phrase 'refugee protection and durable solutions in the context of international migration' in order to maintain the integrity of its mandate (Crisp 2008: 2). Global migration management will be discussed in more detail in Chapter 5.

new configuration can be seen as part of a wider "migration management" push whose purpose is to reduce the numbers of unwanted migrants who reach western countries' (2006a: 214, Agier 2011: 30–31).

Refugee camps, designed to provide temporary safety, shelter and sustenance for forced migrants, are established under the auspices of the UNHCR and/or governments and run by statutory bodies and NGOs. Alongside this in certain countries, UN peacekeepers and Western military personnel are sent into war zones to defuse the conflict. That voluntary repatriation is the solution favoured by the international community (UNHCR 2011a: 17, Crisp 2004: 4) helps to explain why most refugees only ever reach a neighbouring country. Pakistan, Iran and Syria were the top three refugee-hosting countries in the world in 2010 when Afghanistan and Iraq were the top refugee-producing countries (UNHCR 2011a: 14). Two and a half million refugees are estimated to have returned home in the last five years, compared to only 444,000 resettled through programmes in third countries (UNHCR 2011a: 17).[18]

While repatriation 'in safety and dignity' (Martin et al. 2005: 227) may be the ideal long-term solution, some researchers argue that the interim 'encampment is bad for everyone' (Verdirame and Harrell-Bond 2005: 272). According to Verdirame and Harrell-Bond, epidemics and environmental degradation are rife, ethnic identity can be radicalized, community disintegrates and the fundamental right to freedom of movement is violated. It also creates a setting in which the 'arbitrary exercise of power' is easy (2005: 271). Refugee camps can become militarized and create 'refugee warriors' – men committed to violent conflict on behalf of their ethnopolitical group – who plunder the camps for recruits and money (Loescher 2000: 198). Humanitarian aid can thereby indirectly bolster the resources of warring parties (Terry 2002: 27, 219). Control and confinement, 'forced passivity' and poor education can negatively impact on refugees, leading to emotional, psychological and interpersonal struggles as well as frustration and desperation (Wigley 2006: 168, Feyissa and Horn 2008), and as most humanitarian funds are channelled into emergency subsistence relief, little is done to address underlying societal problems (Loescher 2000: 195). Agier describes the refugee camp as an 'authentic desert' and a form of being 'imprisoned outdoors', where those whom the world considers undesirable 'remnants' are kept waiting in 'a kind of social quarantine' or non-existence *'on the margins of the world'* (2008: 39, 61–62, 2011: 1, 52). Humanitarian intervention is complicit in migration management, he argues, and 'borders on policing' (2011: 4). Smillie and Minear note the existence of a bewildering 'plethora of international groups' whose humanitarianism is undermined by foreign policy imperatives, domestic considerations and a 'Me First' attitude in the 'scramble … for attention and funds' (2004: 163, 183). Thus, while there are some winners as well as losers in camps and camps can have the advantage of keeping refugees on the international

---

[18]   They are labelled third countries, as the country of origin is the first and the country to which a person initially flees is the second.

radar (see for example Fiddian-Qasmiyeh 2010, 2011), emergency camp-based responses cannot be considered sufficient 'to help people restart their disrupted lives' (Martin et al. 2005: 234).

One of the other durable solutions for refugees also usually emerges within their region of origin. This is 'local integration that occurs when the first refugee haven permits the new arrivals to remain as legal residents and potential citizens' (Martin et al. 2005: 227). Many Rwandan refugees from the 1994 genocide, for example, assimilated into Congolese, Tanzanian and Burundian societies. Local integration takes place on an ad hoc basis and legal residency is offered by governments who sense that they have little choice to do otherwise.[19]

Solutions in the West: Resettlement, Asylum, Policing the Borders and Internal Controls

When policies of regional containment fail to stem refugee flows, because individuals have resources to travel further afield or the ongoing situation forces them to, Western governments fall back on other methods to inhibit the arrival and impact of those seeking asylum at their borders. In the process, they work against the other two possible durable solutions currently favoured by the forced migration regime, namely resettlement in a third country and political asylum (Martin et al. 2005: 227). Most countries are unwilling to take more than a handful of refugees on resettlement programmes, which act as 'an international responsibility sharing mechanism'. Only 98,800 refugees were resettled in new countries by UNHCR in 2010, the vast majority in the US (71,400) (UNHCR 2011a: 18–19; see also Joly 2002: 7). The Gateway Protection Programme, launched in the UK in April 2003, has resettled just over 3,000 refugees in areas such as Sheffield, Norwich and North Lanarkshire in the seven intervening years (HO 2011: 23).[20] As already indicated, seeking asylum in the West is also relatively rare. In 2010, while there were 15.4 million refugees, only 845,800 asylum claims were made and a mere 22,090 of these were received in the UK (UNHCR 2011a, 2011b).[21] Asylum applications

---

[19]   For a discussion of the varied experiences of camp and locally integrated refugees, see Malkki (1995).

[20]   The Gateway Protection Programme receives people directly from refugee camps in Africa and Asia and offers to resettle up to 750 individuals per year. Refugee Action is the main voluntary sector provider for this programme; see www.refugee-action.org.uk/ourwork/projects/Gateway.aspx [accessed: 15 August 2011]. A few refugees with close ties to the UK are also resettled on the Mandate resettlement scheme. Resettlement was the founding intention of the UNHCR. The United Nations Relief and Rehabilitation Administration, formed in November 1943, became the International Refugee Organisation in 1946 and resettled 1,039,150 people who had been displaced by the war between mid-1947 and the end of 1951. In 1949, the office of the UNHCR was launched and continued the work of resettling political refugees at an international level (Marrus 2002: 340–345).

[21]   This compares with 180,600 asylum applications in South Africa, 54,300 in the US and 48,100 in France (UNHCR 2011a).

did, however, increase in the UK in the late 1990s and, as I will discuss in the next chapter, the admission of asylum seekers is believed to have a variety of social, economic and political drawbacks. Western governments have therefore severely clamped down on asylum (Joly 2002: 5–6, Crisp 2003). Not only are very few asylum seekers given legal permission to settle in the UK – only about one-quarter of the asylum applications received in 2010 are estimated to have resulted in initial grants of asylum, humanitarian protection or discretionary leave (HO 2011: 19) – but mechanisms have also been introduced to prevent potential claimants from reaching the border and to ensure that their situation while waiting for a decision is as uncomfortable as possible. The borders are carefully policed and internal controls are stringent.

Proactive Global Solutions: Addressing Root Causes

These approaches all tend to be reactive and benefit national governments and established populations more than they do refugees. Only a few of those forcibly displaced are resettled or granted asylum in a third country and refugee camps as a means to eventual repatriation clearly have drawbacks. For Smillie and Minear, there is overall a 'relative underfunding of prevention in relation to remedial action. The humanitarian enterprise is better at staunching wounds than at anticipating and preventing injury' (2004: 19). An approach recommended by many forced migration scholars, therefore, is to address proactively the root causes of refugee movements and thereby stem them at their source.[22] Loescher has been a prominent advocate. He asserts that taking large-scale preventative action to avert the crises which cause refugee flows is essential and calls for a 'new, comprehensive, and humane approach' (1993: 205). Sustained economic and political support in fragile contexts is required, involving human rights monitoring, development assistance and the construction of democratic institutions. As he puts it, the 'real refugee problem is that political, economic, and security conditions in the home country are so bad that citizens feel compelled to leave' (1993: 181). International rapid reaction capability and safe haven policies should be established, and early warning mechanisms clearly need to be improved (Martin et al. 2006: 62). Monitoring situations where human rights are abused and assisting unstable countries before wars erupt could defuse refugee-producing situations before they have begun. Given that political violence is predictable, Mark Gibney argues that 'every serious human rights abuse in the world constitutes a failure of refugee protection' (2002: 27). The arms trade must also be scrutinized and challenged as small arms play a significant role in fuelling conflicts within states (Martin et al. 2005: 252).

A concerted development effort could help to lessen refugee flows. The notion of a 'migration-development nexus' points to the ways in which migration can

---

[22]   Castles and Van Hear note a recent return to discourse about tackling root causes, its popularity having dipped after the 1980s and 1990s (2011).

facilitate development which can, in turn, reduce the numbers of people leaving their countries of origin. Transnational ties formed through migration result in financial and social remittances (including ideas concerning human rights or democracy) as well as 'brain circulation' or knowledge transfer: migrants can therefore, in effect, act as 'productive development agents' (Faist 2010: 81, Solimano 2010: 63–70).[23] At an economic level, financial remittances combined with efforts to build infrastructure and industry and raise living standards could reduce forced migration caused or exacerbated by poverty. This ironically indicates the necessity of allowing some migration in order to reduce mass migration. Governments and other international bodies are increasingly recognizing that through what they term 'well-managed' migration, developing country poverty could be substantially reduced (DFID 2007, World Bank 2006, HCIDC 2004: 3). In 2007, developing countries received official remittances of $251 billion, which was double that received through official aid and two-thirds of foreign direct investment. In addition, unrecorded remittances may have equated to half of the recorded amount (Lindley 2011: 251). This said, it is debatable whether remittances do aid development overall. Sometimes, for example, they may only succeed in improving the well-being of particular families or be spent on fuelling conflict (Castles and Miller 2009: 60–61). Ongoing development and aid spending is vital and the effects of adjusting current trade policies could be considerable.

At the level of civil society, the transfer of ideas and processes facilitated by migrant–homeland ties could help to improve the material, legal and governance infrastructures in certain countries, especially in contexts recovering from war (Martin et al. 2005: 249–252). At the same time, the risk of 'brain-drain' needs to be recognized. A report exploring the links between poverty and migration stated that it is 'inefficient and incoherent for developed countries to provide aid to help developing countries to make progress towards the Millennium Development Goals on health and education, whilst helping themselves to the nurses, doctors, and teachers, who have been trained in, and at the expense of, developing countries' (HCIDC 2004: 28). Returning refugees need to be reintegrated and war-torn societies require assistance in their efforts to rebuild (Loescher 2000: 212–213). Peace-building is key (Milner 2011). As Van Hear argues, the best solution is to improve 'living conditions or human security in places that are now sources of forced migration and displacement, so that migration becomes a matter of choice rather than necessity' (2006a: 221).

Addressing root causes is not, however, as obvious a solution as it may seem at first. Not only do root causes ultimately 'lie in the imbalances of power and resources in the global political economy, and addressing them would require a major transformation in the distribution of power and resources worldwide' (Castles and Van Hear 2011: 287), but tackling them is based on the problematic

---

[23]   For more on the links between migration and development, see the Global Forum on Migration and Development at www.gfmd.org [accessed: 9 February 2012], Castles and Miller (2009: 50–78) and Skeldon (2010).

notion of 'transforming societies' – an approach which resonates with the colonial 'civilizing mission' and 1960s Western modernization theories (Castles and Van Hear 2011: 298). Most governments in the Global North assume that migration from poor countries should be stopped entirely and therefore prefer to focus on present, short-term control rather than engage with longer-term, underlying solutions, which might threaten vested interests (Castles and Van Hear 2011: 297, 302).

Reforming the Regime: Working Together and Renewing UNHCR

Essentially, what is required is the 'development of more comprehensive and cohesive strategies to address forced migration in its complexity' (Martin et al. 2005: 3). A forced migration regime needs to tackle root causes while also strengthening protection and pursuing all of the durable solutions mentioned above – repatriation, local integration, resettlement and political asylum (Crisp 2004: 7). Global governance of refugees is 'more robust' than that of other types of migration, comprising 'a set of norms, rules, principles, and decision-making procedures that help define states' responses to refugee flows' (Loescher and Milner 2011: 189; see also Betts 2011b). However, as this regime struggles to cope with the volume and complexity of forced migration today, significant reshaping is necessary. First, collaboration between states, government departments, civil society, UNHCR, NGOs and other regional and international bodies is essential and could be improved (Betts 2009, 2011a, Loescher et al. 2008: 125–126, Chimni 2001). Martin and colleagues advocate democratization (allowing diasporan communities to participate) as well as dialogue and cooperation between receiving and source states (2006: 4–5, 227). Loescher argues that an 'internationally harmonized migration policy' also 'needs to be broadened and backed by a visionary approach to interrelated global issues such as security, trade and development, human rights, and migration' (2000: 215). Due to global power imbalances, cooperation has so far necessitated participants making explicit connections between 'refugee protection and issue-areas in which Northern states have had an interest' such as security, immigration and trade (Betts 2011a: 55).

Second, and related to this, UNHCR requires reform. UNHCR, as the actor given responsibility by the international community to protect refugees, needs to increase its transparency, secure and manage financial resources more effectively and play an enhanced 'facilitative and catalytic role in mobilizing other actors to fulfill their responsibilities'. Susan Martin and colleagues suggest 'the creation of a UN High Commissioner for Forced Migrants' (2005: 3–4) and Loescher and colleagues suggest a new UN Migration Organization and UN Peacebuilding Commission to work in conjunction with UNHCR (2008: 125–126). Loescher and Milner agree that UNHCR needs to concentrate on coordination and advocacy (2011: 205). Given 'the highly politicized environment within which it works', UNHCR also needs to become more politically astute and engaged. While needing to work with states' interests in order to have leverage, it needs to avoid *serving* them (especially in their reluctance to admit people and the ways in which governments earmark UNHCR donations for particular countries, regions or activities) and thereby jeopardizing the integrity of its own mandate to protect refugees (Loescher and Milner 2011: 201–206). The definition of a 'refugee' according to the 1951 Convention is also no longer adequate (Kneebone 2003, Loescher 1993: 163–165). A new regime which acknowledges the complex and overlapping categories of forced (and voluntary) migrant is essential and the international legal system should be reformed 'to include protection for the full range of forced migrants needing international attention' (Martin et al. 2005: 3). Given that in 2005, only 146 out of 191 UN member states were signed up to the Convention, the gathering of more signatories is crucial (Sales 2007: 70, Martin et al. 2006: 63).

Models of Adaptation: Factors Affecting the Reception and Settlement of Refugees

What happens to forced migrants at the other end of flight, if and when people are admitted into a country in the Global North? Churches supporting those who are resettled or seeking asylum need to have an understanding of the factors that affect their adaptation, often termed integration, into a new society. Integration, widely stated as the goal of immigrant policies and projects, is a multidimensional process and a debated and variously defined term (Ager and Strang 2008: 167). Valtonen defines it as the 'process by which immigrants and refugees engage with, and become part of their resettlement society' (1998: 41). Berry uses the term *acculturation* to indicate the process of migrant adjustment to being in contact with another culture and society. He models different strategies for acculturation (1992: 82) (see Figure 4.2).

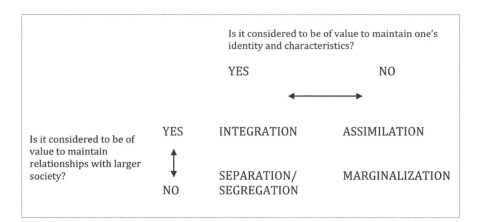

Figure 4.2   Berry's different strategies for acculturation

He suggests four possible outcomes of the encounter between minority groups and larger society. *Assimilation* indicates submersion within the dominant society and *Separation* (chosen)/*Segregation* (imposed) means the maintenance of identity and minimal relations with larger society. *Marginalization* involves the loss of group identity and exclusion from larger society and *Integration* signifies participation in the dominant society while maintaining self-identity. Integration leads to lower stress levels than separation and is in fact the commonly preferred migrant strategy (1992).[24]

Ryan and colleagues (2008) challenge this interpretative model as well as medical, psychosocial stress models that understand the clinical disorders, coping strategies and personal relationships an individual may have as critical factors explaining integration outcomes. The former is too focused on cultural contact and the latter too focused on individuals. Instead, they prefer the term '*migrant adaptation* to describe the process through which individuals seek to satisfy their needs, pursue their goals and manage demands encountered after relocating to a new society' and argue that *resources* are the 'means by which individuals satisfy needs, pursue goals and manage demands'.[25] These resources are personal, material, social and cultural and migrants' adaptation 'depends largely on their ability to regain lost resources (e.g. social support) and gain new ones relevant to the host environment (e.g. proficiency in the host language)' (2008: 7, 13). Ager and Strang suggest considering the 'foundations', 'facilitators' and 'social connections' which enable refugees to attain integration through and in the key domains of employment, housing, education and health (2008). All three models are valuable. While resources are certainly significant and the models of Ryan and colleagues and Ager and Strang are more comprehensive, reflection on how asylum seekers relate to a new culture and society is particularly relevant to the discussion in Chapter 5. I use the term 'adaptation' in recognition of the fact that integration – often used in everyday speech to mean full participation in the established society – is not necessarily the outcome of immigration into the UK. I use the four categories suggested by Berry to distinguish between possible adaptation outcomes. So then, what factors or resources affect the adaptation outcome? What leads a certain refugee or asylum seeker to integrate, assimilate, separate/segregate or be marginalized? While making generalizations and adopting a blanket approach are unhelpful (Bloch 2002: 201), I will outline a number of interrelated ones.

Circumstances of Migration and Relationship to Country of Origin

The first two closely related factors affecting the nature of adaptation are the circumstances of migration and a refugee's relationship to his country of origin

---

[24]   Joly suggests three main options – assimilation, separation and integration (2004: 145).

[25]   These needs are basic physiological and psychological ones, such as food, accommodation, a stable and safe environment, a sense of belonging, meaningful activities and feelings of control (Ryan et al. 2008: 8–9).

and position within it. Experiences prior to migration such as traumatization and whether refugees are 'anticipatory' (left slowly, after preparation) or 'acute' (left suddenly) will affect acculturation processes (Doná and Berry 1999: 176).[26] The circumstances of migration affect a refugee's settlement (Bloch 2002) and Ryan and colleagues argue that 'migrant groups at risk of poor adaptation are those who enter the resettlement process with a low level of resources ... once an initial loss has occurred, this will beget future loss. For example, when a person enters the asylum process, they are at risk of entering what Hobfall (2001) terms a *resource loss spiral*' (2008: 14).

Joly has moreover demonstrated that if someone has been part of a collective project of a society, such as opposition to a dictator, they will see exile as a continuation of that project, maintaining a close relationship with their homeland and aiming to return home. Some members of the Movement for Democratic Change (MDC) are a contemporary example, having an active political organization in the UK geared at bringing about transformation in Zimbabwe.[27] This may lead to a lack of desire to assimilate to the new society. Conversely, if refugees have had no part in a collective project, being for example genocide victims, they are unlikely to envisage return.[28] Joly labels the former Odyssean refugees and the latter Rubicon refugees (2004: 143, 1996). Odyssean refugees are oriented to the past and their homeland and their '*us*' includes all those engaged in the same political struggle. Often involved in transnational political associations, interaction with the reception country only goes as far as it is relevant to engagement with their homeland society. Rubicon refugees, by contrast, see assimilation into the new society as an option and the boundary between *us* and *them* is decided in relation to the reception country. The organizations they are involved with usually assist with settlement and ensure support and opportunities for the group (2004: 164–174).

Van Hear discusses the effects of transnationalism, that is, people having 'multiple allegiances to place' (1998: 4), and notes that the greater the ambivalence towards home and/or a new country, the weaker a migrant's roots will be in a single territory and the stronger the claim to a diaspora condition. If such a claim is made, adaptation is most likely to take the form of integration or separation as understood in the Berry model.[29] In the light of these findings, it is notable that in a

---

[26]   Kunz (1981) makes this distinction between 'acute' and 'anticipatory' refugees.

[27]   See their website – www.mdcukandireland.org – for more information [accessed: 22 August 2011].

[28]   Kunz (1981) similarly defines three different types of relationship with a home country which affect settlement – majority-identified (views shared by population not government), events-alienated (alienated from population due to events or past discrimination) and self-alienated.

[29]   Portes disagrees, arguing that 'transnational activities can act as an effective antidote to the tendency towards downward assimilation' and actually 'facilitate successful adaptation by providing opportunities for economic mobility and for a vital and purposeful group life' (1999: 471–472). Transnationalism will be discussed in more depth in Chapter 5.

survey undertaken by Bloch of Somali, Tamil and Congolese refugees in Newham, East London, only 43 per cent of respondents saw Britain as home. Moreover, while 10 per cent said that they definitely did not want to return home, 71 per cent said that they did want to if the circumstances were right (2002: 142, 145).

Country of Origin and Characteristics of Individual Migrants

Two other interrelated factors affecting adaptation are a person's country of origin itself and his personal characteristics. According to Vervotec, 'country of origin' comprises 'a variety of possible subset traits such as ethnicity, language[s], religious tradition, regional and local identities, cultural values and practices' (2006: 31). Those who come from former colonies of the new nation, for example, are likely to have more of a cultural, religious and/or linguistic connection with the established society. Thirty-nine per cent of those interviewed by Bloch in Newham claimed that language had significantly affected their adaptation. Tamils and Somalis arrived with better English and a longer history of migration than the Congolese (2002: 184–185). Cultural knowledge – another factor necessary for successful communication and navigating social norms – is also important (Ager and Strang 2008). Country of origin can affect employment, with people from high income countries often working in finance and business, while those from low income countries are more likely to find themselves in the retail, wholesale, health and social work sectors (Vervotec 2006: 18–19). Finally, those coming from warmer climates can find the winters of northern countries hard to cope with: 4 per cent of those interviewed by Bloch claimed that the weather had affected their adaptation (2002: 188). For Bloch, language skills, educational background and employment experience are simply part of a migrant's *individual* characteristics (2002).[30] These characteristics, along with a person's health, physical attractiveness, financial resources and other skills, can assist or 'constrain' certain behaviour in the new society (Ryan et al. 2008: 7–8, 13).

Social Networks and Refugee Community Organizations

A third pair of factors to consider is the role of social networks and refugee community organizations (RCOs).[31] Social connections can help people to overcome isolation, alleviate personal and material problems and provide a space for sharing a collective sense of loss and patterns of meaning (Joly 1996, Ager and Strang 2008, Strang and Ager 2010). Ryan and colleagues label personal relationships which provide emotional, informational and tangible support as 'social' resources (2008: 7).

---

[30]   Vervotec describes these characteristics as 'migrants' human capital' (2006: 31. Italics omitted).

[31]   For examples of RCO projects, see Community Links (2005). There are also broader immigrant community organizations and Migrant Hometown Associations.

Bloch regards the voluntary sector as a crucial component in the settlement of refugees, and particularly RCOs, which can assist and sustain those who arrive 'without kinship ties and support networks'. Volunteering opportunities created by RCOs and NGOs can help people to experience 'self-esteem and feel they are contributing' (2002: 161, 172) and refugees sometimes also see volunteering as a route into paid employment, a means of self-improvement and a way of demonstrating to established communities that they are 'good citizens' (Yin Yap et al. 2011). RCOs are involved in an array of activities, notably information-provision, advice, advocacy, education, interpretation, cultural outings, social clubs, political engagement and 'the chance to meet and exchange news from home' (Bloch 2002: 162). The value of RCOs has, however, been questioned recently. Zetter and colleagues suggest that dispersal of asylum seekers since 1999 has led to RCOs being less involved in integration and more in defending the basic rights of asylum seekers, filling gaps in government provision and adopting a defensive role at the 'edges'. They mostly lack resources to offer education, training and employment programmes which could aid long-term integration into the labour market and are generally unwilling to be part of formalizing networks. Being labelled as RCOs may also perpetuate a group's marginality (Zetter et al. 2005, Griffiths et al. 2005). Vervotec suggests that in light of their proliferation, community organizations are no longer effective in terms of representation because governments and local authorities find this array hard to relate to. It can take a long time 'to develop effective community organizations which can deliver services and impact on local decision-making' and many prefer to have a low-profile in the current anti-immigration climate (2006: 28). Aside from formal RCOs, informal friendship and contacts with others from the same home country or region in the same immigration situation – for example, being an asylum seeker waiting for a decision on a case or appeal – can create 'social bonds' and offer valuable support (Ager and Strang 2008: 178, Strang and Ager 2010: 596–598). This, in turn, can affect a person's desire to integrate, assimilate or separate and the emotional and psychological resources they require to do so.

Responses of the Established Communities: Attitudes and Policies

The final pair of factors is the most critical. Regardless of how successful RCOs and social networks are or how strong adaptation wishes and pre-existing skills, a refugee's ability to adapt to the new society and the form that this takes is largely dependent on the attitudes and policies of the established community. Adaptation is a two-way process (Strang and Ager 2010: 600–603, Hollands 2001: 295) and as Vervotec puts it, the 'usually chequered responses by local authorities, services providers and local residents' are key (2006: 31. Italics omitted). Ryan and colleagues describe established community attitudes and policies as an 'environmental constraint', one of 'a range of barriers' which a migrant can encounter 'in his or her attempt to gain resources in the host environment' (2008: 13), and Joly argues that for Rubicon refugees, the 'outcome of their group formation will be largely determined by host-related factors' (2004: 174). The nature and effect of established community attitudes and policies are the focus of a detailed discussion in Chapter 5, but I will introduce them briefly at this point.

Established community attitudes play a considerable role. Thirteen per cent of those interviewed by Bloch in Newham said that they believed racism and discrimination had affected their settlement (2002: 188) and Valtonen notes that, while positive social interaction with the established community can encourage integration, negative interaction is likely to encourage separation, segregation or marginalization. Stereotypes hinder 'successful social interaction with the receiving society' and established society pressures to assimilate can be counterproductive (1998: 51). The friendliness or hostility of established communities and the resulting ability (or not) to make 'social bridges' – that is contacts outside one's own ethnic, religious or country group – can significantly aid or hinder adaptation (Ager and Strang 2008: 179–180). Intimately related to these attitudes, government policy has a considerable effect on the nature of adaptation. The top factor named by 41 per cent of those interviewed by Bloch as affecting their adaptation was immigration status (2002: 188). A person's legal status determines their entitlement to a range of rights, from healthcare, housing, social security benefits and education (including English language classes) to freedom, as well as what employment they are allowed or likely to obtain. The level of access accorded to different categories of immigrant is directly determined by national and local government policies (da Lomba 2010, Vervotec 2006: 31, Bloch and Levy 1999, Phillimore 2009: 53). Nine per cent of those surveyed by Bloch explicitly claimed that unemployment had affected their ability to adapt. This is because without participation in the labour market, it is very difficult for newcomers to maintain self-esteem, develop a new position or 'role' in society, gain contact with people outside their immediate community and meet their cultural obligations such as supporting an extended family (Bloch 2002: 188, 91, Hynes 2011, Valtonen 1998). The type of housing in which asylum seekers and refugees are placed can also affect adaptation (Vervotec 2006: 22) as can dispersal and detention policies which, as indicated above, often disrupt social networks (Hynes 2011, Bloch 2002: 195–197, Griffiths et al. 2005: 210, Robinson et al. 2003). Refugees in Glasgow, for example, expressed that they felt more 'at home' if their communities were safe and peaceful and if they had a sense of stability (Ager and Strang 2008: 183–184). The ability to access to state structures, including government services – 'social links' – also matter to newcomers (Strang and Ager 2010).

All of these policies and practices are rooted in a country's understanding of nation, citizenship, rights and multiculturalism. Ager and Strang therefore see these as the foundational factor affecting adaptation outcomes: a nation's sense of identity 'incorporates certain values; and these are values that significantly shape the way that a concept such as integration is approached' (2008: 173–174, Strang and Ager 2010, Bloch 2002: 84–88). A particular nation's integration policies are also influenced by 'interaction with other national political economies and migration regimes' (Papadopoulos 2011: 37–38). It is policies and attitudes, above all else, that have the power to and often do push new arrivals into marginalization, assimilation or segregation.

The Significance of Gender: Experiencing Forced Migration as a Woman

A thread long neglected by scholars, policy-makers and practitioners in the forced migration field was the significance of gender (Hajdukowski-Ahmed et al. 2008: 2, Busher 2010, Lykes 2010, Martin and Tirman 2009, Forbes Martin 2004).[32] This is surprising given that about 50 per cent of all migrants are women. Women have different experiences of the pre-migration, migration and post-migration stages from men as well as particular needs. Given that 'every stage of displacement ... is gendered', Mertus argues that it is vital to filter refugee movements and uprooted populations through a 'gender lens' (2003: 252). This section aims to create such a lens while recognizing that women's experience cannot be homogenized. Each uprooted woman, as each man and child, has her own unique combination of motivations, experiences and difficulties.[33]

Reasons for Flight

The reasons for women fleeing are often different from those for men. Gender-related persecution and violence are prevalent. As Freedman notes, in times of both war and peace, '[w]omen's bodies become sites of symbolic struggle between opposing sides, and also sites of repression' because 'women are seen as bearers of national identity, producers and reproducers of national boundaries, identities and cultures' (2007: 49–50). Control of women's bodies and sexuality is practised in a variety of ways, the most common being female genital mutilation (FGM), forced pregnancy or abortion, persecutory laws, domestic violence, wartime sexual violence, rape and sexual exploitation by the so-called 'protectors' including UN forces (2007: 50–68, Leaning et al. 2009). If fleeing due to political persecution, Crawley points out, it has more likely been because of a male family member's activity or being in 'low level' supportive roles. Women's political activism thereby often takes place within, or is framed by, the 'private sphere' (1999: 321, Cenada 2003).

---

[32] On refugee children and unaccompanied minor asylum seekers in the UK, see Watters (2008: 63–94), Ahearn et al. (1999), Kohli and Mitchell (2007) and Rutter (2006). On the experiences, needs and challenges faced by those claiming asylum because of sexuality, see for example McGhee (2001a, 2001b), Berg and Millbank (2009) and Bohmer and Shuman (2008: 236–241). On refugees and asylum seekers with disabilities, see Ward et al. (2008).

[33] Freedman points out that '[w]omen's migratory experiences are influenced not only by their position as women, but also by their class, race or ethnicity, their age and their sexual orientation'. She suggests the importance of gender as a 'relational concept', considering the differences between men and women (2007: 16–18); see Meertens (2004) and Turner (2004) on factors relating to men.

Deciding to Migrate

Being a woman can also affect the decision about whether to migrate: is it desirable or possible? Freedman points to a variety of 'social, economic and political obstacles' faced by women. There may be 'gendered social roles and norms' within a country which forbid a woman travelling alone. It may be hard to find financial resources for travel as women are often financially dependent, and there is a risk of violence or sexual abuse on the journey. Being primary caregivers of children, women are also usually understandably reluctant to leave them behind (2007: 25–26, Cenada 2003). The factors holding a woman in her community of origin are, on the whole, likely to be greater than those holding a man.

Exclusion from Rights

If they do seek resettlement or asylum, the nature of their persecution has a considerable effect on whether women are likely to be granted refugee status. Violence against women in the 'private sphere' is largely ignored in the 1951 Convention which concentrates on political persecution in the public arena, and acts such as forced marriage, FGM, honour killing or forced sterilization are often just attributed to 'cultural differences' (Freedman 2007: 69, Pickering 2011, Sadoway 2008: 245).[34] Women face major obstacles in proving that rape or sexual abuse constitutes serious harm and 'persecution', even if performed by government or peacekeeping forces, and claims for asylum made in UK on this basis are often refused (Crawley 1999: 322). If a woman's experiences can be compared to those of some women in the receiving country, 'her plight is more likely to be minimized' (Sadoway 2008: 245). Crawley argues that 'a wide variety of assumptions … effectively serve to exclude the experiences of many women seeking protection':

> Women's experiences are conceptualized as 'private' – *private to personal relationships, private to cultures, and private to states* – and therefore beyond the scope of international protection efforts. In addition, women's *resistance* is depoliticized, in part because it frequently occurs within the geographically and conceptually 'private' sphere of the home, family or the community (1999: 329).

---

[34] Chantler notes that even though gender-based persecution is increasingly recognized as fitting with the Convention – through including women as members of a particular social group – this is not unproblematic. Not only do countries where the domestic violence or FGM took place 'need to be portrayed as "backward"', but it continues to relegate women to the private sphere (2010: 109–111). Freedman points out that the very distinction between 'private' and 'public' is false, as 'violence against women occurs everywhere in the world, and all of this violence can be considered … not as the expression of an aberrant individual act, but rather as part of a larger system of social relations' (2007: 68). For more on the inadequacy of the Convention for women, particularly on the public–private dichotomy, see Crawley (2001).

Research undertaken by the Refugee Women's Resources Project notes how the Home Office has often dismissed women's claims of torture. Kenyan women have been told in refusal letters that they could not have been tortured, raped or sexually assaulted on the basis that 'there was a vociferous human rights debate' going on there. Where it has been acknowledged, it has been put down to the 'misbehaviour' of individual police officers or prison wardens. Activities, such as distributing leaflets for a political party or defending women's rights, have also not been regarded as significant enough to have provoked persecution (Cenada 2003: 126). Refugees are 'essentialized' – ungendered and desexualized (Callamard 1999: 197) – but at the same time, assumed to be male. According to Treacher and colleagues, such 'homogenization renders women's experience invisible and silent, simultaneously wiping out differences between women' (2003: 1).

The asylum process itself exacerbates the likelihood that persecution for female gender-based reasons will be dismissed. Proving sexual violence requires a medical certificate that most women lack, and Freedman notes that some decision-makers assume all women are simply copying other stories of rape (2007: 89). Many are moreover understandably reluctant to relive their horrific experiences, especially in front of a male immigration officer (Hayter 2003: 12), and shame, guilt and fear of rejection from their own community can be powerful inhibitors (Cenada 2003: 126). Stories can change over time, as women try to tell them more accurately, and this can cause their credibility to be challenged (Pickering 2011: 87; see also Rabben 2011: 179). Despite UNHCR Guidelines regarding the protection of women and girls (1991, 2008b) and Home Office guidelines on gender-specific considerations and interview practice, insensitivity and ignorance of gender issues remain widespread among caseworkers (Freedman 2007: 102, Pickering 2011: 82).[35] As women's cases are often complex, few male lawyers know how to deal with them effectively (Cenada 2003: 127). Even where the significance of female gender is acknowledged, women are frequently portrayed as 'using their perceived "vulnerability" to "take advantage" of Western states ... using their reproductive capacities to make themselves even more vulnerable or to gain extra benefits from an overly generous welfare state' (Freedman 2007: 133, Pickering 2011: 87). Conversely, if they demonstrate ingenuity, strength or intelligence, some assume that they have overstated their vulnerability and exaggerated their stories (Sadoway 2008: 248; see also Burman 2010). '[E]rratic and capricious' decision-making on female asylum cases is not unique to the UK (Pickering 2011: 82, 57–92). This may help to explain why so few women relative to their presence in migration flows become asylum seekers. Few detailed statistics on asylum-seeking according to sex or age exist, but in 2007, only 30 per cent of principal asylum applicants in the UK were female (HO 2008: 9; see also Freedman 2007: 24–27).[36]

---

[35] There are also guidelines concerning sexual violence against refugees (Lykes 2010: 74).

[36] The proportion of women varies according to country or origin. For example in research carried out in 2001, only 14 per cent of claimants from Iran and Sudan were women compared to over 56 per cent from Eritrea (Freedman 2007: 28). This contrasts

Gender-specific Adaptation

If waiting for asylum decisions or given leave to remain, women have different adaptation experiences from men. While some needs are common, such as gaining language skills, adequate housing and refugee status, they are less likely to have been educated (Reed 2003) and may have responsibility for children, needing childcare support and/or maternity care (Kennedy and Murphy-Lawless 2003). They may also be recovering from rape or FGM traumas: tailored psychological support and counselling is then essential (see Decker et al. 2009). Women often find themselves without a usual family support network or role and can feel physically vulnerable and isolated. It is, for example, more difficult for women to attend language or vocational classes due to cultural constraints and the need for childcare and transportation (Forbes Martin 2004: 136) and women can be treated as if they are of little importance (Zabaleta 2003). Feelings of isolation are intensified if they are forced to wait indefinitely for men held in detention centres (Reed 2003: 116). These challenges are not unique to women in the UK. Loss, living 'in limbo', economic hardship and difficulties raising children were identified by Sudanese refugee women in Canada as four significant experiences undermining their identity and mental well-being (Hayward et al. 2008).[37] Freedman notes the particular difficulties for women who are themselves detained or dispersed. In detention, women are often denied adequate healthcare and psychological support, 'kept in unsuitable conditions, with poor food and insufficient provisions for hygiene' and sometimes experience 'sexualised and racialised abuse by guards'. Mixed gender accommodation is particularly problematic for those used to gender segregation in their own cultures (2007: 154–160).[38] Regarding dispersal, being moved near to birth can inhibit access to expert healthcare and translators, and a minimal weekly allowance means that HIV-positive women struggle to buy milk formula (2007: 162–166).

Understanding the differing experiences of asylum-seeking men and women could enhance church-based support. As Freedman notes, NGOs can exacerbate women's disempowerment if they are not careful – either through ignoring 'gender as an issue altogether or else refer[ring] to the supposed "vulnerability" of women seeking asylum without seeking to understand the real needs of female asylum seekers' (2007: 124).

---

with a large number of migrant women who work and send remittances home (Ehrenreich and Hochschild 2002). It is surprising to note that in 2007, only 14 per cent of principal male applicants were granted asylum at an initial stage compared to 22 per cent of women (HO 2008: 9).

[37]   Vervotec notes that among 'migrants in London generally, women migrants have a far lower employment rate (56%) than men (75%)' (2006: 20), while Kofman and colleagues suggest that female refugees can actually find it easier to adapt and access income and social rights (2000: 73).

[38]   See also report by Legal Action for Women on Yarl's Wood (2006).

The Role and Impact of Faith Communities

The significance of faith in the lives of forced migrants and the role played by FBOs in supporting refugees have similarly been neglected. Hendrickson and Seegmiller point out that 'the majority of refugee studies do not touch on religion at all, despite the centrality of religion in the experience of many displaced people' (2007: 5; see also Goździak and Shandy 2002: 129). Refugees and asylum seekers manage experiences of fear, marginalization and hope through a range of strategies, including negotiations of religious identity and practice (see for example, Fiddian-Qasmiyeh and Qasmiyeh 2010, Fiddian-Qasmiyeh 2011, Balci 2007). Research addressing this deficit has begun to emerge, and I will draw on a range of case studies – given the overlapping nature of voluntary and forced movement – to demonstrate how significant faith and religious organizations can be at all stages of the migration process (Mayer 2007).

Leaving and Travelling

Religion can, as already noted, play a role in creating or exacerbating the situations which encourage people to flee (Shandy 2002, Chaillot 2007). More positively, migrants often draw on religion in the process of deciding whether to leave as well as during the journey. Hagan and Ebaugh have revealed that many Guatemalan Mayan migrants seek spiritual and practical support and advice before leaving for the US, and churches may contact kin or potential sources of legal help at their destination on their behalf (2003: 1150). Among 202 departing undocumented Central American and Mexican migrants Hagan surveyed, 78 per cent turned to God to assist them in deciding whether to migrate and four out of five 'prayed to God, a saint, a religious icon, or sought counsel from trusted local clergy within several days prior to embarking on their journey'. While some of this was for help with practical concerns, including money, securing coyote[39] and care for those left behind, their most important concern was protection: 68 per cent requested protection on the journey in prayer, especially in terms of personal safety and security (2008: 7–9). Clergy provide information about dangers, safe routes and prayer books including a directory of shelters and legal services. In addition, they offer 'religious sanction for the migration, a kind of spiritual travel-permit that has huge symbolic value' (2008: 13–14; see also Jansen 2008: 69–70). In journeys often full of danger and despair, religion can provide – as Dorais suggests following interviews with Vietnamese refugees in Montreal – a 'source of hope and comfort' (2007: 60).

---

[39]   A coyote is someone immigrants pay to accompany them in their journey across the desert from Mexico into the US.

Adapting

What role does religion play for those who reach their destination and begin to build a new life? Many migrants arrive in a new country with strong religious affiliations and continue to practise their faith. In a 'snapshot' of religious affiliation at Oakington Immigration Reception Centre in Cambridge, only 9 per cent of detainees stated that they had no religion or were atheists or failed to fill in the question about religious adherence. Nearly 75 per cent were Christian or Muslim. A chaplain claimed that there was 'at any point a *minimum* of between 30–40% of the population who actively subscribe to some form of religious observance' (Pirouet 2006: 169).

Psychological, emotional and spiritual support

Faith can, at one level, provide a valuable psychological and spiritual resource. The Oakington chaplain quoted above claimed that many draw strength from spiritual care and/or recommit to faith while in detention and McMichael has demonstrated how Islam provides an important source of stability for Somali refugee women trying to reconstruct their lives in Melbourne, Australia. Islam acts as a source of home and community, provides a framework for understanding new experiences and offers calming routine practices. One woman, Haweye, explained: 'Our religion is very important. It is good, we love it, and it has a very important role. It protects us from a lot of things. If we have a problem we turn to Allah and ask for help' (2002: 183). Research has frequently demonstrated the positive value of religious belief for health (Pepitone cited in Goździak 2002: 143). Not only can faith offer solidarity through giving common identity, but music, prayer, scripture, worship and community can also reduce emotional pain and stress related to fear, anxiety and uncertainty. Religion can offer a sense of control and order (Goździak 2002, Jansen 2008: 76, Parsitau 2011). For Nuer refugees from Southern Sudan in the US, Christian identity has served as a vehicle for social reconstruction (Shandy 2002) and in his study of Vietnamese in Canada, Dorais found that religion played a role in defining identity and meaning-making in the new context (2007). One Catholic man stated, 'Those who participate in the activities of the Vietnamese Catholic community are happy because it gives a meaning to their life' and a Buddhist woman said, 'A religious life is the only way to remain mentally balanced ... so many people visit pagodas in order to find inner peace' (Dorais 2007: 65). Religion helps many migrants to find a new sense of identity and 'delineate an alternative cartography of belonging' (Levitt 2003: 861). Some seek out a worshipping community familiar from their past, while others choose to form or join new churches, mosques, temples and gurdwaras. These are sometimes connected with a country, region or language of origin (Chaillot 2007). Some become more devout in exile or change religious affiliation (Dorais 2007: 61, Carulla 2007). Church attendance is very important to many Filipina workers in the Netherlands and migration can actually lead to a new or renewed 'religious quest', including 'new questions about faith, church, and God' (Jansen

2008: 69). Some migrants arriving in the Global North express criticism of the liberal, dwindling churches they find and look for opportunities to evangelize members of established populations.

Practical, social and political role

Religious networks and FBOs, such as those described in Chapter 3, also play a practical and social role. Migrants choose which projects and bodies – faith-based or otherwise – they seek assistance from and make use of them to become involved in the new society. According to Hirschman, being part of a religious community can provide 'respectability or opportunities for status recognition and social mobility that is denied in the broader society'. From 'potluck dinners to job referrals', religion offers avenues for social advancement, leadership, community service and respect, social, cultural and socio-economic roles (2007: 414; see also Hagan and Ebaugh 2003: 1150, Stepick et al. 2009, Eby et al. 2011, Goździak 2008, Ley 2008). Given that the workplace is often not open as an avenue for settling for many asylum seekers (at least for a period of time), participation in religious communities presents a viable alternative strategy. It is also possible that individuals from countries with majority Muslim populations, such as Iran, may strategically convert to Christianity in the UK in order to claim asylum on the basis of religious persecution. Levitt has suggested that religion can be 'a potential catalyst for humanitarian activism or a cosmopolitan embrace' on the part of transnational migrants. Exploring four immigrant communities in Boston, she argues that '[b]elonging to religious institutions socialized members into receiving-country politics' while also enabling continued participation in homeland affairs (2008: 767–769).[40] They gained political skills and received a 'crash course in civics', facilitating their participation in both arenas. Faith communities

> bring people into contact with fellow believers who do not all come from the same country. Sometimes, migrants even find themselves sharing a pew with someone who is native-born. They hear sermons and participate in activities that influence how they think about changing the world and shift how they put these into practice. (2008: 778)

Jayaweera and Choudhury similarly note the role played by Islam in the UK in community building through its 'values of compassion, generosity and kindness, and its emphasis on civic responsibility', as well as outreach to the community and service provision with partners. Mosques also provide an avenue for statutory access to new migrant communities (2008: 120).

Refugee resettlement in the US is largely undertaken by faith-based organizations (Eby et al. 2011, Goździak 2008: 183), and McSpadden has shown how Ethiopian and Eritrean refugees resettled between 1979 and 1992 by religious

---

[40] The four communities were Muslims from Pakistan, Hindus from Gujarat, Protestants from Brazil and Irish Catholics from Donegal; see also Levitt (2007).

congregations or volunteers experienced greater 'psychological well-being' and higher employment and schooling rates compared to those resettled by agency caseworkers (1998: 159–160). Volunteers had time, were less affected by state expectations, developed strong personal links with the refugees and could provide wide contacts in the 'normal' job arena. They fostered personal 'kin type' relationships, congruent with Ethiopian and Eritrean family support for single men, and seemed to facilitate socio-economic upward mobility (1998: 163). As Eby and colleagues put it, 'faith-based actors' support of resettlement increases refugees' local integration prospects, especially by enhancing social connections in the community that have a positive impact on other aspects of integration' (2011: 2; see also Scott 2003).

Churches are, in short, places where refugees can make friends (D'Onofrio and Munk 2004: 43, Marfleet 2006: 230). Ahmad, a Muslim asylum seeker from Afghanistan, spoke of arriving in Nottingham and meeting 'so many friends in church. They were interested in me. I thought to myself: they're nice, lovely people. They always chat to me and ask about things'. Hassan described being 'over the moon' when a woman in the congregation he was worshipping with introduced him to Restore in Birmingham: 'Even when I feel very sad, I feel like there is a place I can go and ring the bell, where they listen to people.' Compared with more formal organizations which operate on an interview, time-allocated basis, churches can provide – as Hassan put it – 'a door which is open to people' and a safe space in which 'open conversation' is possible. Ali spoke of Restore being a 'friend' and Jean-Paul of it providing a context in which he can relax. Church volunteers and staff come along and listen to people's experiences without a particular political or institutional agenda.[41]

Hirschman concludes that '[r]eligious beliefs and practices can serve as ballast for immigrants as they struggle to adapt to their new homeland' and summarizes the importance of religion to migrants as 'the search for refuge, respectability, and resources' (2007: 396, 413). Part of the ability of religious institutions to play this role lies in their access to valuable resources – such as alternative vision, principles, personnel, finances, buildings, broad geographical networks, grassroots information and moral credibility – which can be mustered for a good cause (Snyder 2011, Eby et al. 2011, Smith 1996, Cloke 2010, Orji 2011, Graham and Lowe 2009: 155). These can also be used to influence public opinion and political debate. Local, national and international FBOs can, through advocacy, bring about changes in policies affecting migrants (Wilson 2011, Eby et al. 2011). Ferris has

---

[41]   These comments were all made during Group Interview (2007). While most FBOs with which I have had contact work with people from a range of faith backgrounds and explicitly guard against evangelism, certain groups may wish to convert non-Christian asylum seekers. This said, it is important to recognize that some working with Christian groups as volunteers or paid workers do not self-define as Christian, and as noted, some asylum seekers look for opportunities to evangelize the established population. The possibility of conversion is therefore two-way.

suggested that non-governmental organizations and particularly churches listen to the grassroots voices of those seeking asylum in a way that statutory organizations rarely do. They

> possess certain strengths which challenge the hegemony of governments. They control funds and human resources which governments may need. They have access to information which may contradict government sources. They may have constituencies capable of mobilizing public opinion ... the Churches stand out from NGOs since they possess not only large numbers of adherents but also a certain moral authority which may be used to sway public opinion (1990: 175).

She also notes that faith communities usually have some unrestricted funding and are not tied to the legal definition of a refugee, which allows a certain freedom of activity, and recognizes the benefit of being 'part of a vast global network of communities that are linked to each other' (2011: 12).

A caveat
Religion is not, however, always a positive factor in the lives of migrants at the adaptation stage. It can be a source of tension or conflict in a new country as different groups negotiate identity, beliefs and power. In Europe, Muslims are faced with the challenge of inhabiting a society which tends to associate Islam with fundamentalism and extremism (Behloul 2007). Goździak also notes that for women, religion can play an ambivalent role, 'serving as a source of resiliency as it both facilitates and impedes integration processes'. While refugee women can find comfort in their faith, they can also experience oppression at the hands of male religious leaders and be excluded from practising certain rituals that could be valuable (2008: 189–190). Religion can foster female subservience. Patel tells the story of a Kenyan asylum seeker, dependent on a Pentecostal church in London for accommodation and food, who felt 'exploited because she [was] made to do all the cleaning and cooking and other domestic chores for the people that she [was] staying with' (2010: 10–11).[42]

The Dangers of Becoming 'Monsters of Concern'

There are also dangers churches need to be aware of when offering support, some of which are shared by humanitarian organizations. Humanitarianism is 'deeply ambiguous' (Agier 2011: 5) and Terry points out that '[g]ood intentions are not enough' (2002: 216). At one level, secular and faith-based humanitarian efforts can often be reactive, disjointed and piecemeal. Greater coordination, professionalism and self-monitoring would improve the support offered. Weiss quotes Smillie: 'one of the greatest problems facing NGOs today is the fragmentation of effort,

---

[42]   For more on the nexus between migration, gender and religion, see Bonifacio and Angeles (2010).

the hundreds of look-alike organizations spawned more by charity than clarity of purpose. Fragmentation is the amateur's friend, a haven for wheel inventors' (2001: 226). While referring primarily to humanitarian intervention in contexts of conflict and poverty, Smillie and Minear's call for a 'more disciplined NGO community' (2004: 236) is equally necessary among the plethora of migrant and asylum-supporting NGO groups in the Global North. Professional expertise, including a rooting in sound academic research, experienced financial, personnel and operational management, excellent training and frequent evaluation would be beneficial, and FBOs are increasingly working towards this (Martin 2001, Ferris 2011). By increasing collaboration between humanitarian and other organizations, a vital grassroots perspective could be introduced into the level of global governance (Kjaerum 2002: 204).

It is also possible to exacerbate the disempowerment and dependency sometimes experienced by those seeking sanctuary. Humanitarianism, according to Barnett, 'contains elements of both emancipation and domination' – or, in other words, paternalism – which equates to 'interference with a person's liberty on the grounds that it is in his or her best interests' (2011: 107). While he argues that it is sometimes necessary to use privilege to assist others and bring about change, refugee agency and participation are crucial. Harrell-Bond, questioning Western notions of compassion which are often 'inherently ethnocentric, paternalistic and non-professional', claims that humanitarians need to facilitate rather than impose aid and be accountable to those whom they wish to help. Quoting O'Neill, she warns of the dangers of becoming 'monsters of concern' (1986: 26, 363). Refugees can be placed in a helpless role and then expected to be grateful or blamed for developing a 'dependency syndrome' (Harrell-Bond 1999). They are 'talked about' and there is rarely care without control (Agier 2011: 4, Barnett 2011: 107). Agency, by contrast, 'centralises people, conceptualised as social actors who process their own experiences and those of others while acting upon these experiences … [It] claims space for moral responsibility and accountability' (Essed et al. 2004: 2). Acknowledging and prioritizing the agency of migrants – affirming and facilitating people's potential for resourceful and creative adaptation – is essential (Kibreab 2004: 23–24). Sima Wali, an Afghani exile in the US, was helped by a businessman to dial her sister's friends in Washington and paid for the call when she first arrived. She writes, 'I was embarrassed that my first act in the US involved receiving help I couldn't repay'. Given that she had been a member of a ruling family, she found such extreme loss of status difficult to bear (1994: 132–133). Hayward and colleagues note that Sudanese women in Canada struggled with the mental health support offered to them by the medical profession, preferring to draw on their own 'culturally grounded coping strategies or healing practices'. As they summarized, 'We want to talk, they give us pills' (2008: 204–205). Churches need to ascertain from migrants what services and approaches would be helpful rather than assuming they know what these are.

Another difficulty is that refugees are constantly portrayed as vulnerable victims, often for well-meant reasons. NGOs and churches do so because such a portrayal is likely to elicit charitable support and funding. Enemies and friends can thereby ironically both create dehumanizing stereotypes of forced migrants. As Summerfield notes, governments and the conservative social sectors 'paint asylum seekers as resilient and wily' while their supporters, 'the liberal and radical social sectors', tend to 'pitch asylum seekers as people who had no choice but to run from their countries, innocent of any thought other than to escape further persecution, torture and the risk of death. They do not conjure up resilience, but vulnerability, weakness and damage' (2005: 111; see also Winder 2005: 466, Malkki 1997: 224). Whether portrayed positively or negatively, asylum seekers 'are rarely regarded as ordinary human beings who have or are going through extraordinary circumstances' (Hynes 2011: 42). Zetter in fact suggests that the refugee regime itself perpetuates the notion that refugees are 'a problematic category of people constituting a burden of dependency on the international community' (1999: 73).

Recognizing personal motivations for working alongside asylum seekers helps to guard against the pitfalls mentioned above. As Harrell-Bond notes, 'Refugees attract "volunteers", often people with no specialized training who behave as though they "need refugees more than refugees need them"' (1999: 150). Guilt can influence our responses as can being undervalued. Kristeva warns against engaging with the 'other' out of guilt and suggests that the 'foreigner's friends, aside from bleeding hearts who feel obliged to do good, could only be those who feel foreign to themselves' (1991: 23). Vaux argues that we must be constantly introspective as 'the weakness of others is a terrible temptation ... We enjoy our power, and by implication the other person's weakness. This is not altruism at all, only a hidden and profound selfishness' (2001: 8, 114). While no action for another is entirely selfless and everyone has mixed motivations, naming and owning these motivations is important so that supporters do not end up using asylum seekers subconsciously for their own ends.[43] Churches would do well to remember the warning posed by Ignatieff, that fulfilling strangers' *needs*, defined by rights or basic necessities, is very different from helping them to *flourish*, something which also involves the intangible qualities of love and belonging, dignity and respect and ultimate meaning (2001: 10–16).

Summary

This chapter has introduced the concerns and findings of Forced Migration Studies. The ways in which awareness of these may enhance the work being done by churches to support migrants will be drawn out in more detail in the conclusion. Having concentrated primarily on the global context and explored dynamics

---

[43]   See Keen (2008: 116–140), Smillie and Minear (2004: 11) and Verdirame and Harrell-Bond (2005) on vested interests and duplicity in humanitarian work. On ethical challenges faced by humanitarian NGOs and FBOs and ways of establishing accountability, see Orobator (2008).

Chapter 5

Fright: The Dynamics of Fear within Established Populations

Foreigner: a choked up rage deep down in my throat, a black angel clouding transparency, opaque, unfathomable spur.

(Kristeva 1991: 1)

Fear is at the root of the big challenges in our sector. Fear in refugee-producing countries, and fear in rich countries, and of course in the boats, container trucks and airports in between. In all three places, there are merchants of fear looking to manipulate and increase it for their own unholy ends.

(Board 2008)

Having explored some of the global dynamics surrounding forced migration, I now turn in this chapter to focus on the experience of people seeking asylum in the UK. Responses of established populations, as I have argued, are arguably the most significant factor affecting the reception and adaptation of migrants. Often rooted in fear, the reaction of many to newcomers is a 'choked up rage' (Kristeva 1991: 1). This chapter seeks to explore some of the reasons lying behind this fear and the effects of this fear on the lives of those seeking sanctuary.

The Pervasive Reality of Fear

Fear – 'the belief that someone or something is dangerous, likely to cause pain, or a threat' (Pearsall 1998: 670) – has become an underlying feature of most Western societies. People are afraid of an array of possible occurrences and this is, in large part, due to the profound changes brought about by globalization. Globalization is a slippery term and its precise definition varies according to context (Groody 2007: 13). Broadly speaking however, it can be understood as the system of 'networks' and 'flows' of financial capital, information, technology, people, organizations, political governance, images, brands and ideas burgeoning across the contemporary world (Castells 2000a, Appadurai 1996). While such networks and flows are not new, their current volume, speed and intensity are unprecedented (Held et al. 1999: 431, Rosenau 2004: 27, Short 2004: 22), leading, at one level, to a greater connectivity and similarity between nations and peoples, in economic, cultural, political, spiritual and criminal domains (Held et al. 1999: 2). At another level, there has been a fragmenting and entrenching of local cultures and identities and an increased competition between these – a phenomenon expressed in the phrases 'glocalization' (Robertson 1995) and the 'clash of civilizations' (Huntington 1996). There is thus a 'precarious balance' and continual tension between '"flow" *and* "closure"' and '"flux" *and* "fix"' (Meyer and Geschiere 1999: 2). Short prefers the active term 'globalizing' as it 'capture[s] that sense of becoming and longing' (2004: 2) and for Rosenau, the contradictory localizing/globalizing, centralizing/decentralizing and integrating/fragmenting tendencies at micro- and macro-levels are best labelled 'fragmegration' (2004: 24). Globalization can be summarized as the complex, dynamic and interweaving set of economic, cultural, social and political processes which are simultaneously homogenizing and fragmenting – or 'fragmegrating' – communities across the world.

Migration is a key strand in these globalization processes. Movements of peoples are a cause and consequence of other global flows. Short has described migration flows as 'the human face of globalization' (2004: 18) and Bauman characterizes the contemporary age as 'liquid life' in which fluidity and mobility is displacing human fixity (2005; see also Sassen 2006a: 74, Urry 2003: 61). Even those who do not travel physically 'can dash or scurry or flit through the Web, netting and mixing on the computer screen messages born in opposite corners of the globe' and television allows a jumping 'in and out of foreign spaces with a speed much beyond the capacity of supersonic jets and cosmic rockets' (Bauman 1998: 77).[1] In the words of Appadurai, 'the warp of [stable communities] is everywhere shot through with the woof of human motion' (1996: 33–34). This pervasive movement is 'part of a transnational revolution that is reshaping societies and politics around the globe' (Castles and Miller 2009: 7).

This profound reshaping is not universally welcomed. While many enjoy the significant benefits that it brings, fluidity, interconnectedness and fragmentation can also be deeply unsettling. There is a widespread perception that the world is in crisis and Furedi has argued that Western societies are 'increasingly dominated by a culture of fear'. In a search of the Reuters database, he found that the usage of the term 'at risk' increased from 2,037 mentions in 1994 to 18,003 mentions in 2000 (2005: vii, xii). Economic and social fragmentation has contributed to isolation, vulnerability, insecurity and sense of lost control. Fear and panic are self-fulfilling, and even simple problems or threats can spiral into 'questions of human survival' (2005: 67, xiii). Beck refers to a 'world risk society' (1999) and argues that the risk society's 'normative counter-project, which is its basis and motive force, is *safety*' and that 'one is no longer concerned with attaining something "good", but rather with *preventing* the worst'. Solidarity can ironically arise from this sense of shared anxiety (Beck 1992: 49). These risks do not even have to have a sound evidence-base in reality for them to shake societal foundations: '*it is cultural perception and definition that constitute risk*' (Beck 1999: 135; see also 2006: 7). Fear has

---

[1]   For a biography of Bauman, and an introduction to and critique of his thought, see Tidball (2004). Coleman and Eade critique Bauman's model for 'slippery fluidity' (2004: 6).

become a defining feature of our times (Pain and Smith 2008, Linke and Taana Smith 2009).

Globalized life is full of uncertainty and anxiety (Bauman 2005: 1–2, 1998: 117, 2001) and as Urry points out, 'one effect of global markets is to generate "wild zones" of the increasingly dispossessed', that is, areas perceived in the West to be characterized by politically, economically and civically weak states. These are believed to impinge dangerously on the West: 'The flows from the wild zones of people, risks, substances, images and so on increasingly slip under, over and through the safe gates, suddenly and chaotically eliminating the invisibilities that had kept the zones apart … the spaces of the wild and the safe are chaotically juxtaposed' (2003: 130–131). He suggests that the 'enemy' can be defined as 'global risks that have few borders or boundaries and that can be as much within the society as without'. Migrants, terrorists, diseases and viruses, environmental and health risks and the current global economic downturn can all be included in this category (2003: 133). There is a sense that these all, along with the crisis of global warming, represent Armageddon for the human race.

Immigrants, particularly asylum seekers and those without documents, provide one focus for this pervasive fear: they are seen as a prime threat. While fear and the perception of newcomers as threat are not inevitable, talk of a migration crisis is widespread and in 'virtually every world capital, the flow of people is regarded with alarm' (Weiner 1995: 1). According to Marrujo, 'immigration has become a metaphor for risk' (2003: 19), or in international relations and political science discourse, migration has become 'securitized'.[2] In the 2008–09 *Citizenship Survey* in the UK, 77 per cent of respondents thought that immigrant numbers should be reduced (CLG 2010: 68) and in 2010, the *Transatlantic Trends: Immigration* (TTI) survey found that 65 per cent of the British public viewed immigration as more of a problem than an opportunity (2010: 19). In a survey in Coventry undertaken by Ward in 2005–2006, only 14 per cent of refugees and asylum seekers interviewed felt that the established population had a positive or welcoming attitude towards them (2008: 30). Asylum seekers are perversely seen as a *group* threat, despite having to prove their *individual* persecution: they are invariably referred to as 'hordes' or 'floods' (Marfleet 2006: 154). Their very definition, moreover, connects them with fear. As Nyers points out, the 1951 Convention 'discursively produces the refugee as a human being identified by a close relationship with the human emotion of fear'. While this may elicit sympathy, 'human beings who are defined by their fear have a long history of being simultaneously defined as social outcasts, lacking full reasoning capacity, and incapable of presenting an autonomous, self-governing form of personal subjectivity' (2006: xvii). But what is it about asylum seekers that turns them into a particular target for fear? What makes them appear

---

[2]   For examples of the view of migration as 'crisis', see Mote (2003) and Moxon (2004). While the extent of the sense of crisis and fear is novel, threads of fear as well as welcome can be found in every past century (Holmes 1988, 1991, Panayi 1994, Winder 2005). Securitization will be discussed in more depth later in this chapter.

so dangerous? I will explore three threads of anxiety – politico-cultural, security-existential and economic-welfare concerns – in turn.[3]

Politico-cultural Fears: Seeing Migrants as 'Transrupting' the Nation-state and National Identity

A first set of fears is rooted in the threat which migrants are believed to pose to the British nation-state culturally and politically. In a report by the Information Centre about Asylum and Refugees in the UK (ICAR) that explored public attitudes to asylum seekers and refugees, a major established population concern was a dread of losing a sense of national and local identity through being 'overwhelmed' (D'Onofrio and Munk 2004: 27). The concept of the nation-state fuses three separate elements – a 'people (culture, language, religion, history)', a 'territory (land, resources, economy, geography)' and a state '(legislation, rule, administration, political control, power)' – into one unit (Westin 1999: 41). Or as Vervotec puts it,

> some sense of identity is presumed to characterize a people; this identity/people is believed to be contiguous with a territory, demarcated by a border; within the border, laws underpin a specific social and political order or system; this social order – which is conceived to be different from orders outside the border – both draws upon and reinforces the sense of collective identity. (2007: 158)

The 'people' are traditionally understood to be of one ethnicity and even one class (Balibar and Wallerstein 1991: 84) and thus, according to Castles, a nexus exists between the nation-state ideal and racism (2000: 169).[4] Religion, specifically belonging to the established church, was also a traditional pillar of British identity and a key determinant of the rights and status of inhabitants until the nineteenth century (Sales 2007: 177, Cohen 2003: 64). Such an understanding of nation and nationality is, famously, a myth: nations are simply 'imagined communities' (Anderson 1991), a mere 'mirage' (Winder 2005: 464). Britain was only formed by the Act of Union in 1707 and has always had 'fuzzy' frontiers (Cohen 1994: 7) and a strong Nonconformist tradition. It also has a long history of division and dissent around gender, class, region (Hall 2000: 229) and, indeed, religion. The national myth nevertheless remains a powerful one (Pickering 2001: 83–84, Soysal 1994: 166–167) and it is being fundamentally 'transrupted', to coin a word used by Hesse, by contemporary migration. The movement of people across borders is acting as a 'discrepant that opens up the nation to different challenges, interrogations and

---

[3]   Similar fears are present in the US (Fennelly 2008, Deaux 2006: 40–58).

[4]   Gellner claimed, 'homogeneity of culture is *the* political bond' (1997: 29).

representations' (2000a: 16).[5] Appadurai goes as far as predicting that the nation-state is 'on its last legs' (1996: 19).

Transnationalism

The growth of transnationalism can be held partly responsible. Transnationalism describes the reality that 'many migrants today intensively conduct activities and maintain substantial commitments that link them with significant others (such as kin, co-villagers, political comrades, fellow members of religious groups)' living in different nation-states (Vervotec 2007: 149). These activities are intense and continuously recurring, and involve 'a regular and significant commitment of time by participants' (Portes 1999: 464, Faist 2010: 83). Vervotec notes their effects in three broad domains. Socio-culturally, transnationalism involves migrants developing an orientational 'bifocality' 'to here and there'. Politically, it results in dual citizenships, multiple allegiances and governance at a global level. In the economic domain, it can assist development in countries of origin (largely through remittances) and facilitate cross-border capital flows and investment (2007, Faist 2010: 90–91). While at a 'small-scale and everyday' level, transnationalism affects groups and individuals, over time it can bring about sweeping changes for 'families and communities in places of origin, wider populations surrounding transnational networks, and entire societies' (Vervotec 2007: 171). Transnationalism can be practised by powerful institutional actors such as states and multinational corporations or at a lower-key, personal and grassroots level (Portes et al. 1999: 221, Faist 2010: 88–89).[6]

Connected with these transnational practices has been the development of 'diaspora' communities. Diasporan existence is a collective form of permanent living in a country other than that of origin and involves a migrant group connecting with the new society *and* maintaining links and a sense of identity connected with their homeland. As they respond to 'dwelling-in-displacement', members of diasporan communities accommodate to and resist their new society as they hold in tension 'the experiences of separation and entanglement, of living here and remembering/desiring another place' (Clifford 1999: 223–224).[7]

---

[5]   Hesse describes a transruption as 'any series of contestatory cultural and theoretical interventions which, in their impact as cultural differences, unsettle social norms and threaten to dismantle hegemonic concepts and practices. Transruptions transcend or overcome any initiative to dismiss their relevance, and continually slice through, cut across and disarticulate the logic of discourses that seek to repress, trivialize or silence them' (2000a: 17. Italics omitted).

[6]   Transnational activities are not new, but 'the high intensity of exchanges, the new modes of transacting, and the multiplication of activities that require cross-border travel and contacts on a sustained basis' are novel (Portes et al. 1999: 219).

[7]   For more on transnationalism and diaspora, see Brubaker (2005), Cohen (2008), Faist (2010, 2000), Pries (1999), Van Hear (1998), Vervotec (1999, 2007) and the journals, *Global Networks: A Journal of Transnational Affairs* (Oxford: Wiley-Blackwell) and *Diaspora: A Journal of Transnational Studies* (Toronto: University of Toronto Press).

'Super-diversity' and multiculturalism

Alongside and partly as a result of these developments, contemporary migration has exponentially increased the variety of people present in localities.[8] A plethora of nationalities, ethnicities, cultures, religious affiliations, ages, genders and sexual orientations rub alongside one another. Reflecting on London, Vervotec notes that recent years of immigration to the UK have 'brought with it a transformative "diversification of diversity" not just in terms of ethnicities and countries of origin, but also with respect to a variety of significant variables that affect where, how and with whom people live'. He labels this interplay of factors as 'super-diversity' (2006: 1). Given that diversification is 'not a matter of increased numbers but relative change in a given locality' (2006: 21), even a small and insulated rural community with only a handful of newcomers, commuters or tourists, is likely to have been affected.[9]

For Beck, this reality is best conceptualized as 'cosmopolitanization'. A 'cosmopolitan outlook' means having a '[g]lobal sense, a sense of boundarylessness' (2006: 3), but whereas this outlook in the past was positively chosen by an elite – they opted to be cosmopolitans – 'cosmopolitanization' refers to forced or

> latent cosmopolitanism, *unconscious* cosmopolitanism, *passive* cosmopolitanism which shapes reality as side effects of global trade or global threats such as climate change, terrorism of financial crises. My life, my body, my 'individual existence' become part of another world, of foreign cultures, religions, histories and global interdependencies, without my realizing or expressly wishing it. (2006: 19)

Successive British governments have adopted what Koopmans and Statham term a 'multicultural pluralist' strategy to deal with this reality – more commonly known as multiculturalism. An approach which attempts to facilitate the co-existence of super-diverse communities in a given territory, it contrasts with largely 'ethnocultural exclusionist' (ethnic descent continues to be the predominant criteria for citizenship) and 'civic assimilationist' (citizenship is open, but requires conformity to the dominant established community culture) approaches, adopted in Germany and France respectively. In the UK, the state has offered immigrants and minority ethnic communities political, social and economic rights, while at the same time allowing them the freedom to retain cultural distinctiveness and protecting them against discrimination through race relations legislation (2000b: 196).[10]

---

8   Not all migrants – for example tourists or those working on very short-term visas – would consider themselves transnational actors or part of a diaspora.

9   Difference can also be encountered virtually through the Internet, TV etc.

10   For more on multiculturalism and other citizenship strategies, see Brubaker (1992), Castles (2000, 2002), Favell (2001), Freeman (2007), Gutmann (1994), Hansen (2000), Hansen and Weil (2001), Hesse (2000b), Kymlicka (1995, 2001) and Parekh (2000).

'Transrupting' citizenship and sovereignty: multicultural and postnational challenges
These practices and realities are banging nails into the coffin of the nation-state by
breaking apart 'the conceptual nexus identities–borders–orders' (Vervotec 2007:
163). This is happening in two significant ways. First, traditional understandings
of *citizenship* which assume a people and a land are intimately linked have been
transrupted. Multiculturalism decisively cuts the traditional link between being
a democratic citizen and belonging to a particular ethno-cultural group (Castles
2000: 187; see also Castles and Davidson 2000: 6–7) and 'imagined communities
– be they ethnic, religious, or in other forms' have become 'transterritorial and
centripetal' (Jacobson 1996: 133). Joppke puts it this way: '[m]ulticulturalism
challenges a fundamental principle of the nation-state: the congruence of political
and cultural boundaries' (1998a: 31).[11] Increases in postnational membership
categories – people having global horizons, commitments and affiliations – are also
contributing to this crisis in citizenship (1998a: 23). Transnational and diasporic
groups profoundly challenge 'traditional ideas of nation-state belonging' as their
'identity is not primarily based on attachment to a specific territory' (Castles 2002:
1157) and many people now relate to more than one nation-state (Faist 2000: 313;
see also Clifford 1999: 220, Sayyid 2000).[12]

Second, the link of the state or power-base with a particular land or country is
no longer certain. This transrupts established notions of *sovereignty* and is largely
due to postnational challenges. Castles has emphasized how power (state) is slowly
being divorced from territory (country) (2000: 187). The 'flows of investment,
trade, and intellectual property are inextricably linked with movements of people'
and this means that governments are finding it increasingly difficult to control their
borders (2004). As sovereignty is essentially rooted in the ability of states to control
their borders, the unauthorized crossing of these national borders fundamentally
violates it (Hollifield 2007: 64). Add to this the institutions of global governance
(UN, World Bank, EU, NGOs etc.) and the superseding of nationally-based rights
by international human rights based on the notion of universal personhood, and the
authority of the nation-state seems most definitely under question (Soysal 1994:
157).[13] Faist points out that transnational communities can also 'serve as platforms

---

[11]   Koopmans and Statham term this the 'multicultural challenge' (2000b); see also
Hollifield (2007: 64) and Beck (2006: 66).

[12]   Koopmans and Statham describe these as 'postnational challenges' to citizenship
(2000b); see also Hollifield (2007: 78).

[13]   See Castells (2004: 356–364), Benhabib (2004), Jacobson (1996) and Sassen
(1998a: 69–71) for more on the challenge posed by international human rights to the
nation-state. The end of empire is also significant in that it brought about a melancholia
implicated in contemporary racisms directed against immigrants, asylum seekers and other
groups (Gilroy 2004: 133); see also Hall (2000: 212), Rutherford (2005: 79) and Rosenau
(2004: 31).

to challenge the authority of governments in emigration states by launching opposition groups outside their reach' (2000: 313).

The extent of transnationalism and the degree to which the nation-state system is transrupted should not, however, be exaggerated. To quote Short, the 'nation-state has not wilted in the sun of globalization' (2004: 26). There are still relatively few migrants – approximately 3.1 per cent of the world's population – and most focus considerable attention on their new localities. As Faist puts it, most immigrants 'are rather parochial transnationals ... immigrants and their descendants retain and develop new local attachments and ties while being engaged in border-traversing activities' (2000: 290) and 'global flows have to be anchored locally in specific places' (2010: 87). Friedman recognizes that 'the transnational requires a national' (2004a: xiv) and multiculturalism is still 'a way of controlling difference within the nation-state framework' (Castles 2002: 1157). While the nation as a culturally homogeneous unit may be in decline, the state is still strong. Not only does the nation-state system continue to be the prime source of migrants (Joppke 1998a: 5), but nation-states still have the ability to control entry through their borders and are the key regulators of migration (Hollifield 2007: 78). Assimilation and citizenship are still the major emphases in nation-states (Joppke and Morawska 2003) and human rights are granted through and in a nation-state (Soysal 1994: 157, Joppke 1998a, 1998b). What is more, the future of multiculturalism is by no means guaranteed. In February 2011, British prime minister David Cameron criticized the 'doctrine of state multiculturalism' on the basis that it encouraged different cultures to inhabit segregated worlds, a factor which he implied had fostered the development of Islamic fundamentalism. 'Community cohesion' has, since the unrest in cities in northern England in 2001, become the overriding state goal (McGhee 2005, Jayaweera and Choudhury 2008, Thomas 2009, CLG 2010, Spencer 2011: 220–223).

Ordinary fears: 'things aren't how they used to be'
Whatever the reality, and although people may not articulate the sense of threat as a challenge to citizenship and sovereignty, there is a widespread feeling that national identity and British culture are under threat.[14] This feeling – ordinary or everyday fear – is focused around the perception that the Britain people know and love is shrinking before their very eyes. Those from many different backgrounds in the established population regard immigrants, people with 'alien' values, religions, cultural codes and political ideologies, as the major source of this threat.[15] As an

---

[14]   This feeling is also present among some church members. In a survey in 2008–2009, Christians were more likely to think that immigration should be substantially reduced than other religious groups or those with no religious affiliation (CLG 2010: 70; see also Scott 2003). Isin and Wood argue that such fragmentation of identity is only true for the consumerist 'rising classes in advanced capitalism' (1999: 151).

[15]   Cuisine and arts (theatre, music, visual) brought by immigrants are often exceptions to this rule, being welcomed by many. Curry, for example, is now the national 'British' dish.

Institute of Public Policy Research (IPPR) report investigating public attitudes to asylum in Birmingham, Camden, Cardiff, Norwich and Weymouth recognized, 'Cultural and social problems are frequently blamed on asylum seekers ... These include a decrease in community cohesion, an apparent undermining of British identity, and population growth' (Lewis 2005: 36). One woman's comment summed up this fear: 'I know this sounds awful but why can't they conform to our ways? They stick together and bring down an area' (Lewis 2005: 37. Italics omitted). In 2010, 48 per cent of British people in the *Transatlantic Trends* survey felt that immigration was having a negative impact on British culture (TTI 2010: 19).

According to Castles, the fear becomes especially 'acute when the Other comes from former colonies, where their otherness (expressed both through phenotypical and cultural difference) has been constructed both as inferiority and as a danger to "Judeo-Christian civilization"' (2000: 191). These fears are a form of 'new racism' (Toğral 2011, Ibrahim 2005: 164, Kundnani 2001). The term 'new racism', while acknowledging the ongoing nature of traditional racism, points to the reality that 'current racist discourses are being dominated by the so-called "insurmountability" of cultural differences' (Toğral 2011: 222). Lewis quotes a survey in 2004 which found that while 85 per cent of respondents would not mind Australians moving into their area, the corresponding figures for black Africans and Iraqis were 39 and 16 per cent respectively (2005: 42). The 2008–09 *Citizenship Survey* found that more white people thought that immigration should be substantially reduced than any individual ethnic minority group (CLG 2010: 70).[16] The association of Middle Eastern countries with Islam may explain the fact that Iraqis were the most feared: fears of an Islamic politico-cultural-religious takeover and 'anti-Muslim racism' (Kundnani 2007) are rife. In 2010, 53 per cent of the British public in the *Transatlantic Trends* survey worried that Muslims were integrating poorly (TTI 2010: 27).

Asylum seekers as 'bare humanity': the particular threat of being in-between
Why are certain immigrants such as asylum seekers or irregular migrants, rather than migrants in general, the focus for this fear? One possible explanation is that asylum seekers represent the archetypal stranger. While overstating the extent to which ethnicity is no longer significant, Sivanandan is right to point out that asylum seekers are bearing the brunt of a 'xeno-racism' – 'xeno' meaning stranger – 'a racism that is meted out to impoverished strangers even if they are white' (2001: 2; see also Kundnani 2001, Malloch and Stanley 2006: 58). There is something about *strangers* that evokes a profound sense of fear.

---

[16]   See also Castles and Davidson (2000), Hall (2000: 238), Kundnani (2007), Marfleet (2006: 278), Schuster and Solomos (2004) and Solomos (2003: 237). In one survey, 'race' proved to be the most significant concern especially among lower socio-economic groups, above concerns regarding welfare and economic competition (Dustman and Preston 2003).

Strangers are those who represent transience, ambiguity and hybridity and disrupt fixed categories and stable identities: they are in-between people.[17] Simmel defined a stranger as someone 'who comes today and stays tomorrow. He [*sic*] is, so to speak, the *potential* wanderer: although he has not moved on, he has not quite overcome the freedom of coming and going'. The stranger is thus an ambivalent figure, who embodies a tension between 'nearness' and 'farness', 'indifference and involvement' (1950: 402–404). Drawing on Simmel, Pickering argues that strangers are 'neither Other nor not-Other. That is why they upset the normative structures of assessment and censure'. They exist in a 'continual contact zone between belonging and unbelonging'. Strangers are transgressive, bringing 'the periphery into the centre, difference into the same, unfamiliarity into familiarity, in ways which unravel the certitude and resolution in the idealisation of home' (2001: 204, 218).

Strangers – unknowable but proximate people – are thus deeply unsettling.[18] As Jonathan Smith puts it, 'While the "other" may be perceived as being either LIKE-US or NOT-LIKE-US, he [*sic*] is, in fact, most problematic when he is TOO-MUCH-LIKE-US, or when he claims to BE-US' (1985: 47). It is people who inhabit the edges of the familiar, but are at the same time different, who tend to seem most threatening: they expose our own hybridity and ambivalence. Consequently the unknown stranger, according to Sennett, 'can dominate ... the perceptions of people who are unclear about their own identities, losing traditional images of themselves' (2002: 48; see also Bauman 2001: 115). Kristeva, drawing on Freud, suggests that the stranger is the repressed elements within the self (1991). Given this, 'Confronting the foreigner whom I reject and with whom at the same time I identify, I lose my boundaries ... I lose my composure. I feel "lost," "indistinct," "hazy"' (1991: 187).

While all transnationals and migrants are to an extent 'Betwixt-and-Between' (Phan 2003: 150), someone seeking sanctuary epitomizes this figure of the 'stranger'. As I have noted, a paradox exists that the nation-state system continues to wield considerable power while national identity is under threat. One result of this is that people are ever more desperately holding onto national identity and attaching greater symbolic value to place as a fixed point amid global fluidities (Bauman 2001: 110–111, 2004: 112). We are stuck in the 'imaginary of the nation-state' (Appadurai 1996: 166) and identity remains firmly rooted in specific geographically- and historically-defined places (Kibreab 1999). Hastrup and Olwig argue that this 'place-fixation' leads us to see mobility as a pathology (1997: 6).[19] Asylum seekers are, unlike most other immigrants, doubly strange and

---

[17]   For an introduction to the stranger in social thought, see Papastergiadis (2000: 62–75).

[18]   Lofland defines a stranger as 'anyone personally unknown to the actor of reference, but visually available to him [*sic*]' (1973: 18. Italics omitted).

[19]   Weil claimed that nationhood is the central form of modern collectivity (1987: 95) and Heidegger emphasized the importance of dwelling and being placed (1971). Warner,

estranged. While all migrants move, those seeking sanctuary often continue to shift from temporary accommodation to temporary accommodation after arriving in the UK. They never have a fixed abode. Moreover, within the nation-state system, asylum seekers are quite clearly 'matter out of place' (Douglas 1984: 41). They have left their country of origin and not yet been legally accepted in another. They have renounced one citizenship but not received a new one. Quoting Beck, 'if a "monogamy of place" is characteristic of the modernity of the nation-state, then internal biographical globalization represents a kind of *polygamy of place*' (2006: 43).[20]

Malkki suggests that refugees' 'loss of specificity' in terms of culture, place and history is held as threatening in a world where nations, culture, peoples and societies are assumed to be territorially bounded. She argues that refugees are liminal in this order and 'confront [it] as a symptom of its own fragility and endangerment'. They are usually depicted as 'bare humanity', meaning 'human in the most basic, elementary sense' (1995: 11–12). In a world in which full humanness is linked to nationness, 'denying the nationness of an "other" is denying its subjectivity' (1995: 257). Agamben has similarly argued that refugees are reduced to 'bare life' (*zoē*) – meaning natural or animal life without the political freedom and identity understood to constitute a full human being (*bios*) – and are included only through being excluded and when their 'state of exception is declared and materialized' (1998, 2005 in Owens 2011: 139). Refugees break 'the identity between the human and the citizen and that between nativity and nationality', thereby bringing 'the originary fiction of sovereignty to crisis' (Agamben in Owens 2011: 137).[21] Nyers puts it more simply: 'refugees are allocated characteristics – speechlessness, invisibility, passivity – that are the obverse of the sovereign identity of citizenship' (2006: xiv). As a result they are depoliticized and 'are represented as a mishap, an accident that scars the moral and political landscapes of the international order' (2006: 9). A refugee's existence 'is not a full humanity (full in the sense that he or she is cultured, capable of reasonable speech) but a thin humanity' (2006: 95). Thus while refugees represent the failure of the nation-state system, they also perpetuate or reinforce it as a social construction: they are, in fact, its 'inevitable if unintended consequence' (Haddad 2008b: 1; see also Betts 2009: 54–56). Watson

---

however, suggests that identity is no longer rooted in fixed places (1999). For a discussion of different perspectives, see Lovell (1998).

[20]   Irregular migrants similarly move about within the country and are in a comparable situation, but unlike those seeking asylum, many wish to or do retain official citizenship in their country of origin.

[21]   Agamben's discussion of the refugee in relation to sovereign bio-power has been very influential in recent scholarly work and provokes considerable commentary and critique. For an introduction to his thought and a critique, see Owens (2011). Agier argues that refugee camps act as spaces of extraterritoriality – 'kinds of place that are outside of all place' – which serve to exclude and bring into question the real existence and social identity of refugees (2011: 180–181, 2008: 49).

writes, 'the concept of the refugee reinforces the modern understanding of the political: that each individual belongs to a bounded territorial community of citizens ... the refugee is the exception to the citizen norm' (2009: 35).

While like 'us' in their basic humanity, asylum seekers' lack of rootedness and state challenges our deep-seated need to be culturally and politically placed in a national context. Moreover, they are often rendered speechless and passive. Ironically, those seeking asylum embody our own unsettledness, as Rutherford articulates:

> Asylum seekers symbolise the paradox of modernity – the historic opportunity to make a life for one's self, but at the same time the experience, in the promise of a better future, of a fearful loss of security, familiarity, home ... The asylum seeker is the modern day stranger, a portent of the destructive, liberating, frightening, cruel, exhilarating powers of modernity. The loss of a previous way of life personified in the asylum seeker echoes our own experience of loss. (2005: 72–73)

This feeling is only exacerbated when the 'stranger' is not alone, but comes in considerable numbers, a reality manifest in the language of liquids used to describe those seeking sanctuary. Our longing to be rooted in a soil, revealed in 'territorializing metaphors of identity', is threatened by the 'human floodtides, waves, flows, streams, and rivers' of the 'uprooted' (Malkki 1995: 15–16; see also Sandercock 2003: 111, 123). For Malloch and Stanley, at a time when travel and identities are monitored so carefully, 'asylum seekers represent a "self-selected", paperless, rootless and shifting force' (2006: 54).

Locating politico-cultural fear

Evidence gathered on regional differences in attitudes to asylum 'is inconclusive and in some cases contradictory' (Crawley 2005: 9) and opinion differs as to where fear, of all three kinds outlined here, originates and is most pronounced.[22] With regards to politico-cultural fears, there is some evidence to suggest that it is those who have had little contact with difference who are most anxious. The ICAR report noted that in Oakington and Bicester, people were 'worried about changes or potential changes in their communities that they perceive as drastic and beyond their control'. Such anxieties were less common in areas where asylum seekers and minority communities had already been present (D'Onofrio and Munk 2004: 31). Those who have had little contact with foreigners or minority ethnic communities can be extremely anxious about the possibility of what they consider an 'urban problem' encroaching on their environments. Attitudes towards

---

[22]   For detailed discussion of the ways in which different factors – geographic, socio-economic, gender, age, education, religious affiliation, ethnic background – affect attitudes to asylum, see Crawley (2005) and CLG (2010: 68–75).

immigration in areas with higher ethnic diversity tend to be more tolerant (CLG 2010: 72, Saggar 2003: 185).

Those reflecting on urban contexts, however, point out that cities are 'worlds of strangers' (Lofland 1973) already characterized by fault lines between class, ethnic, cultural and religious groups (Ellin 1997, Graham 2004a, 2004b, Virilio 2005) and fear of those who are different (Sennett 1993, 2002). It is here where dispersed asylum seekers are usually placed. Just as with other migrants, even where their 'share in the total population is more modest, their uneven distribution over districts and wards may still make them clearly visible' (Penninx et al. 2004: 4). It is therefore also in these 'embodied sites' (Short 2004: 128–130) where fears about the arrival of more strangers are likely to be palpable. Sandercock claims national identity is most profoundly unsettled in 'mongrel cities' as the imaginary of 'national space'

> involves a sure knowledge (if one is British) that down the street there is, for example, an English butcher's shop, a Protestant or Catholic church, an English pub, and not a Halal butcher, Buddhist temple, or gay bar ... the national issue of migration becomes a struggle which is played out at the level of the locality in terms of an experience of threat and loss, and the desire to reassert control over one's territory, one's spatial *habitus* (2003: 112–113).[23]

The comment that they 'bring down an area' came from a woman in Birmingham, and such fears are often held by Londoners who have long experienced diversity as the norm. In the 2008–09 *Citizenship Survey*, the proportion of people who believed immigration should decrease was roughly the same in rural (53 per cent) and urban (51 per cent) areas (CLG 2010: 71).

Economic-Welfare Resource Fears: Seeing Migrants as Competition for Resources

A second set of interrelated fears appears more banal. Many in the established population are anti-asylum as they believe that asylum seekers increase competition for already scarce jobs, housing, benefits and healthcare. People think that those seeking sanctuary are emptying the pot of available tax-generated income, a suspicion given credence by the report that the total bill for supporting asylum seekers in 2000–2001 came to £835 million, equating to £34 for every household (BBC 2001). Economic impacts are as much of a concern as cultural change (Lewis 2005: 7). The ICAR report outlined major concerns related to health (notably fear of longer waiting lists and catching diseases from asylum seekers), housing and local services (anxiety that house prices will decline or asylum seekers will jump the queue for tenancies) and resentment towards supposed preferential treatment (being given mobile phones and fully furnished houses) (D'Onofrio and Munk

---

[23] Sandercock defines a mongrel city as one 'in which difference, otherness, fragmentation, splintering, multiplicity, heterogeneity, diversity, plurality prevail' (2003: 1).

2004: 27–28; see also Lewis 2005: 27–31, TTI 2010, Ward 2008).[24] These fears are captured in the well-rehearsed claims that those seeking asylum are 'scroungers' or 'spongers'. It is significant that in Ward's survey in Coventry in 2005–2006, 73 per cent of established society respondents saw asylum as '*only* a form of economic migration to the UK' (2008: 22; see also Watson 2009: 41–42). Sivanandan argues that while the 'rhetoric of demonisation' may be xeno-racist with regards to asylum seekers and refugees, 'the politics of exclusion is economic' and 'poverty is the new Black' (2001: 2). It is, in other words, the new strangers' lack of wealth and the perceived association of this with disease and limited education that is leading to their exclusion. Even some from minority ethnic communities, who could relate to the experience of immigration and may have themselves been a focus for the politico-cultural fears outlined above, express considerable concern about asylum seekers 'in terms of economic threats' (Lewis 2005: 10, Ward 2008: 28).

Zones of social exclusion
Social deprivation and exclusion are widespread in the UK. A survey revealed that by the end of 1999, about 14 million people in Britain – 25 per cent of the population – were 'objectively living in poverty'. Nine million could not afford adequate housing, 10.5 million adults could not afford one or more essential household goods such as carpets and telephones and around three million adults and 400,000 children were not properly fed (Pantazis et al. 2006: 1–2). Debt, unemployment, fuel poverty, a high incidence of mental health issues and the struggles of lone mothers are features of every urban context. Extreme deprivation is often focused in particular urban localities. Lister adopts the term 'place poverty' to talk of a concentration of individual poverty in a particular neighbourhood and notes that there is a 'spatial polarization' between these and the better-off (2004: 70). While recognizing the divergences between and within areas, she notes a number of interrelated factors in disadvantaged neighbourhoods which can be physically and mentally damaging, engender powerlessness and erode morale. These include 'poor housing, a run-down physical environment; neglected public space; inadequate services and facilities; lack of job opportunities; and high levels of crime and anti-social behaviour' (2004: 70). People inhabiting such areas are stigmatized with labels such as 'underclass' and associated with delinquency, undeserving 'welfare dependency', crime, violence and anti-social behaviour. They have little genuine voice of influence and are given little power (2004: 72, 107–112, 170–175).

Short describes places characterized by poverty, collapse, risk aversion, exclusion and resistance as 'black holes' (2004: 50), a term he borrows from Castells. Castells argued that regions where the already socially excluded were being further disadvantaged by globalization – whether the whole continent of Africa or poor urban ghettos in the West – could be understood as 'black holes

---

[24]   For more on asylum seekers as a threat to health and welfare, see Geddes (2005) and Poore (2005).

of informational capitalism' defined by '"lock in" trajectories of marginality' (2000b: 165–167). While many urban areas are regenerating and gentrifying as a result of global capitalism, there are 'sharp increases in socioeconomic and spatial inequalities within major cities of the developed world' and 'new forms of peripheralization' (Sassen 2006a: 152, 195). Mendieta describes these peripheral zones as 'invisible cities' within cities and of the experiences of immigrants and refugees as 'indigent other[s] … who build their enclaves in the shadows of the glamorous city of transnational capital' (2001: 23, 17). Those pushed to the peripheries – deprived long-established communities as well as newer 'indigent others' – cannot access the benefits of the emerging local and global networks (Davey 1999: 383) and are effectively 'confined to invisibility' (Massey 2007: 216).

Locating economic-welfare fears
Ironically, it is precisely those already struggling with deprivation who are expected to host those seeking sanctuary. To quote D'Onofrio and Monk: 'Dispersed asylum seekers, as well as refugees, are often housed in places of high levels of social and economic deprivation, characterised by violence and anti-social behaviour, and where the local attitude towards asylum seekers is likely to be unreceptive' (2004: 17–18; see also Vervotec 2006: 22, Kundnani 2001: 47). Given that asylum seekers are among the most impoverished people in British society for reasons which will be discussed later in this chapter, fears of competition for already scarce resources in terms of healthcare, housing, employment and even charity handouts are not surprising.

The roots of fear can thus lie in reasonable assessments of concrete realities. As Kramer points out, 'distrust is not always irrational' (2004: 157). The IPPR survey discovered that the more vulnerable someone feels to economic competition, the more likely they are to be concerned about asylum seekers. Attitudes are strongly influenced by an individual's immediate environment and social class. While economic competition did allow 'some people to justify racial prejudice in apparently rational terms … many others were genuinely fearful of losing hard-won resources' (Lewis 2005: 12, 15, 27). The ICAR report similarly recognized that social deprivation was a key factor determining attitudes to 'strangers'. It quotes a resident of a Newcastle council estate: '[Y]es, they have had a bad life […] but who hasn't?!' (D'Onofrio and Munk 2004: 31. Italics omitted). There is a concern that the UK has insufficient room for everyone wanting work and better standards of living (van Selm 2005: 1) and that material resources, already thinly-spread among those in areas of deprivation will be spread even more thinly when shared with those who have never contributed to the tax system or communal life in other ways. Asylum seekers – who are not permitted to work unless they have been waiting over 12 months for a decision on their case – are considered to contribute neither social nor economic capital. Pain and Smith note a 'strong relationship between marginality and fear' (2008: 4) and as Castles puts it, 'at a time of economic decline, sharing a shrinking social cake with new groups appears as a threat to the conditions of the local working class' (2000: 191).

While these concerns may be more pronounced in dispersal areas of deprivation, they are by no means their exclusive preserve. They have also 'permeated swathes of the population where no tangible threat exists' (Rutherford 2005: 83). The ICAR survey discovered that in areas where immigration centres existed or were proposed – that is, where there had been little if any contact with asylum seekers in the community – people feared asylum seekers as a *potential* burden on services (D'Onofrio and Munk 2004). Economic-welfare fears also vary according to the state of the economy. Economic boom leads to greater generosity towards migrants, while recession fosters fear of competition over jobs (Joly 1996: 21). During the current global economic downturn, restrictive attitudes towards immigrants, including those seeking sanctuary, are likely to have increased (TTI 2010: 11, Koser 2011b).

Security-Existential Fears: Seeing Migrants as Death-Dealing Terrorists

A final set of concerns revolves around the threat that people seeking asylum are believed to pose to national and personal security.[25] While security is an inherent concern in a globalizing world, since the attacks which took place on 11 September 2001 in the US and on 7 July 2005 in London, it has become an overriding concern of governments and publics in virtually every corner of the globe. A key facet of this obsession has been the emergence of a 'migration/asylum-security nexus' (Huysmans 2006: 1, Zanchettin 2005: 163) in which migration and asylum-seeking are linked with terrorist threats.[26] Applying for asylum is believed to be an easy route of entry for terrorists and anyone doing so is therefore treated with immense suspicion. Malloch and Stanley have collected evidence showing how asylum seekers have been linked in the press with the making of ricin, planning terrorist attacks, terrorist hijackings and membership in the Taliban. Indeed, '[a]ccording to the *News of the World* (2003): "Britain is now a Trojan Horse for Terrorism"' (2006: 57).

While there was always a 'general unease' about immigration and asylum, in recent years they have been perceived as a more serious 'existential threat' (Huysmans 2006: 47). Revisiting Hobbes' observations of life in the seventeenth century, Huysmans explores why it is that migrants are so easily seen to threaten our national security and, by extension, our very existence. Hobbes believed that human life is shaped by primal fear of violent death and the unknown (Blits

---

[25]   All three sets of fears outlined in this chapter could be understood as fears for security (Huysmans 2006: 67–84, van Selm 2005: 3, Watson 2009, Tirman 2004, Hampshire 2009: 109). I use the term 'security' to refer to this set of fears only, as this is how security is commonly understood in public discourse.

[26]   For more on the securitization of migration, see Guild and van Selm (2005), Hampshire and Saggar (2006), Lazaridis (2011), Rudolph (2006) and van Munster (2009).

1989: 418) and this basic, abstract fear of death is transformed into something tangible by locating it in agents who are different from us and have the power to kill us. Thus 'the fear of the other is an objectified fear of death' (Huysmans 1995: 58). When migrants or asylum seekers become linked with terrorism, they become identified as carriers of death who are negatively and stereotypically defined as undifferentiated 'non-I's. Reasoning as the threatened host, Huysmans concludes, 'Migration causes violence, and violence kills ... the migrant carries death and who wants to host death?' (1995: 60; see also 2006: 52).

Asylum seekers are also often regarded as dangerous because they are held responsible for other criminal activity, from street muggings through to rape and murder. Fear of crime was a significant factor identified in various surveys (Lewis 2005, D'Onofrio and Munk 2004, CLG 2010, TTI 2010, Ward 2008). One man interviewed stated, 'Most of them have got a knife or a blade. They're brought up different to us' (Lewis 2005: 39. Italics omitted). In a documentary shown in May 2004, fears of both terrorism and crime were apparent. Campaigners against plans to turn an old naval site in Lee-on-the-Solent into an accommodation centre for asylum seekers equated them with terrorists, fearing that they would blow up the Swanwick air traffic control centre or the local oil plant. Others were terrified of being raped or of contracting HIV. They feared the breakdown of community cohesion, an increase in crime and a consequent drop in property prices (*Dispatches* 2004). Malloch and Stanley point out an 'extensive association between asylum and criminality' and drawing on an article in the *Observer* in 2003, note how asylum seekers have been associated with '"gang warfare", drug trafficking, kidnapping, corruption, as well as the trafficking of people for the sex industry' (2006: 57). These security-existential fears flourish in outer-urban, suburban and rural areas as well as in urban contexts where terrorist attacks are deemed most likely (Swanstrom 2002, Graham 2004a).

People seeking sanctuary present particular targets for this kind of fear because they are perceived to embody indiscriminate violence and chaos. Members of the established population subconsciously fear that the breakdown of society, civil anarchy and death refugees have witnessed is somehow contagious, that refugees are portents of doom. According to Matthew Gibney, refugees are 'human examples of how states can sink into violence, torture and oppression. As representatives of these undesirable features of social life, it is not surprising that refugees are often construed as carriers of the instability and insecurity that led to their initial departure' (2002: 41). Rutherford describes them as 'harbingers of a troubled world' (2005: 72). Asylum seekers are moreover associated with illegality because, for reasons that will be discussed later in this chapter, many arrive through illicit channels, using smugglers and without legal documentation. They are believed to slip deviously through borders, changing their identities and adopting aliases to manipulate and con others for their own no-good ends (Malloch and Stanley 2006: 57). Squire describes the equation of asylum and 'illegal immigration' in the phrase 'asylum-seeker-cum-illegal-immigrant' (2009: 12). Asylum seekers epitomize those described by Bauman as vagabonds: 'The tourists travel because *they want to*; the vagabonds because *they have no other bearable choice* ... The immigrant, travelling illegally and experiencing immigration controls, is the "other" of the elite capitalist' (1998: 93).

The ethnic and religious backgrounds of those seeking asylum intensify this negative association. Usually presented by the media as young black or Asian men, they personify what Alexander terms as the 'triple pathology' of race, gender and generation associated with violence and disorder (2000: 124–125). The fact that many asylum seekers are Muslim or come from Muslim-majority countries and have, by definition, been pushed to the edges of their own societies establishes an immediate connection in many minds with the disenfranchised members of Al-Qaida responsible for the 9/11 attacks and London bombings on 7 July 2005.[27]

The Corollaries of Fear

Fears surrounding national identity, socio-economic competition and security exacerbate one another. As Sandercock recognizes, the 'threats are multiple: psychological, economic, religious, cultural. It is a complicated experiencing of fear of the "Other" alongside fear of losing one's job, fear of a whole way of life being eroded, fear of change itself' (2003: 4). People believe that 'uncontrolled migration leads to social breakdown' (Watson 2009: 6) and asylum seekers are seen as both 'culpable' and 'threatening' (Squire 2009: 56–57). How though does this nexus of fear play out in practice? What are its consequences for those seeking asylum and for established communities?

Stereotyping and Scapegoating: Using Migrant 'Strangers' as Convenient 'Others'

Fears relating to asylum seekers actually have certain positive uses for the established population. This is because they can act as a fertile seed-bed for the stereotyping and scapegoating of those who are feared, activities which Beck argues are a key strategy for coping in our fear-ridden world. People convince themselves that '[w]hat is happening here need not be overcome here, but can be deflected in one direction or another and can seek and find symbolic places, persons, and objects for overcoming its fear'. As a result, '*displaced* thought and action, or *displaced* social conflicts are especially possible and in demand'. Thus,

> the risk society contains an inherent tendency to become a *scapegoat society*
> ... The very intangibility of the threat and people's helplessness as it grows
> promote *radical and fanatical reactions and political tendencies* that make

---

[27]   Afghanistan and Iraq, unstable countries with predominantly Muslim populations, were two of the top five sources of asylum claims in the EU between 1990 and 2000 (Castles and Loughna 2005: 51). On the effects of 9/11 on Muslims in the US, see Iftikhar (2008).

social stereotypes and the groups afflicted by them into 'lightning rods' for the invisible threats which are inaccessible to direct action (1992: 75).

Stereotyping, or 'othering', involves assigning a group of individuals certain characteristics that homogenize 'them' and differentiate them as a group from 'us'. According to Pickering, it takes place through constructing binarisms or 'large blocks of unchanging sameness grouped under different category headings. These homogenized blocks are hierarchically arranged and differentially assigned as "essence" and "difference"' (2001: 210). Scapegoating involves the ejection or exclusion of those who have been 'othered'. Having reduced, essentialized, naturalized and fixed difference, the process of stereotyping 'symbolically fixes boundaries, and excludes everything which does not belong' thereby pathologizing it/them (Hall 1997: 258, 265. Italics omitted). It silences the 'others' and can summarized as

> that strange process through which two or more people are reconciled at the expense of a third party who appears guilty or responsible for whatever ails, disturbs or frightens the scapegoaters. They feel relieved of their tensions and they coalesce into a more harmonious group. They now have a single purpose, which is to prevent the scapegoat from harming them, by expelling and destroying him [*sic*]. (Girard 1996: 12)[28]

These two related processes are useful in helping established communities to cope with all three sets of fears relating to asylum-seeking. In politico-cultural terms, they allow members of the established community to blame those seeking sanctuary for the loosening of national identity moorings. Bauman points out that the 'truth' of nations depends on defending them against outsiders and that nations seem to 'focus their self-defence on locating, segregating, disarming and banishing the *strangers* rather than *enemies*: those aliens in their midst who are crystallizations of their zealously, but ineffectively, suppressed ambivalence' (1992: 687).[29] Those seeking asylum provide ideal raw material for stereotyping and a ready group against whom the so-called nation can be defended.

Yet at the same time, when this bolstering of national identity fails, asylum seekers also provide 'others' over and against whom a new identity can be delineated. All identity depends on a stereotyped 'other': we define who 'we' are

---

[28] See Girard (1986, 1996, 2001) for more on his theories. These processes are complex and multifaceted and have been discussed extensively in a range of disciplines from psychoanalytic, social identity and boundary-formation theories to postcolonial, feminist and racism studies and anthropology. Examples include Barth (1969), Bhabha (1994), Brown (2000), Douglas (1984), Hall (1997), Kristeva (1982), Tajfel (1981) and Walton and Hass (2000); see Cohen (2006: 89–109) on theories of xenophobia.

[29] See also Beck (2006: 73–74), Castles (2000) and Papastergiadis (2000: 59).

by not being 'them' (Sampson 1999: 116, Pickering 2001: 83).[30] The search for new identities is a defining feature of a world in which fixed points seem to have collapsed (Bauman 2005: 6) and 'the distinction between Self and Other – one important aspect of any identity – has become especially salient as people acquire more and more Selves and relate to more and more Others' (Rosenau 2004: 48). Bauman argues that new identities are likely to be rooted in contrived 'cultures' or 'neotribes' (1992: 696–697) and those seeking asylum provide a convenient 'other' over and against which such 'neotribes' can be formed.[31] First generation African-Caribbean immigrants can, for example, distinguish themselves from those seeking asylum just as easily as can white suburban citizens born in the UK. Asylum seekers can also provide an outlet for racism no longer 'acceptable' against minority ethnic communities.

In economic-welfare terms, people seeking asylum provide a scapegoat for the strains on welfare resources and competition over housing and jobs (see Castles 2000: 191, Sales 2007: 221) and in security-existential terms, they provide a convenient face for terrorists and criminals onto which fears can be projected. With the end of the Cold War, moreover, Western nation-states had lost their prime enemy and were looking for new ones (Isin and Wood 1999: 158, Matthew Gibney 2002: 40). While Arabs had long been feared and rising anti-Muslim sentiment was in fact an extension of pre-existing Orientalist frameworks, the growth of Islamic terrorism represented by 9/11 provided a convenient substitute enemy and happened to coincide with a rise in asylum applications in the West. Migrants and asylum seekers thus provide convenient stereotypes and scapegoats in a range of ways. They are among those Hall describes as being 'symbolic bearers of a complex pattern of change, diversification and "loss" for which they are only the most convenient scapegoats' (2000: 230; see also Cohen 2006: 12, Marrujo 2003: 21). Exemplifying Bauman's notion that people 'seek pegs on which they can together hang their individually experienced fears and anxieties', asylum seekers can be understood as a perfect and available 'peg community' (2001: 16). Incidentally, scapegoating also enables people seeking sanctuary to be blamed for their own problems, thereby exempting the established population from any guilt that might spur them to help. Rutherford points to the 'singular brutal narrative: Their plight is of their own making. We owe them NOTHING' (2005: 79). As a result, asylum seekers end up being useful to established communities despite protestations to the contrary.

---

30   On identity formation, see Braidotti (1994), Corbey and Leerssen (1991), Gutmann (1994), Hall (1996), Kristeva (1982, 1991), Lévinas (1993) and Theunissen (1984).

31   Rosenau outlines 12 worlds of response to the age of fragmegration. Of these, resistant and traditional locals and globals, exclusionary locals and all four private worlds are likely to reject outsiders (2004; see also Friedman 2004b: 73–74).

Attacks on Asylum Seekers: Media Hostility and Public Violence

Stereotyping and scapegoating have almost entirely negative consequences for those seeking sanctuary. The most overt way in which these fears manifest themselves is through extreme verbal and physical hostility. Colville argues that four out of five national daily tabloid newspapers with an estimated combined readership of over 17 million people have been full of anti-asylum spin. Between 1 January 2000 and 1 January 2006, he found that seven tabloid newspapers produced 8,163 articles mentioning asylum seekers. The term 'bogus asylum seekers' appeared 713 times, 'criminal' and 'asylum seekers' on 538 occasions together and 'crime' and 'asylum' appeared together 945 times. They were also associated with rape 50 times and madness 271 times (2006b: 16–17).[32] Asylum seekers have been accused of roasting the royal swans on a spit (Sullivan 2003) and of eating donkeys (*Daily Star* 2003), bringing in TB and HIV, being scrounging benefit shoppers and terrorist bombers.[33] Littlejohn, writing in the *Sun* on 1 September 1998, announced that 'Britain is now open house to the scum of the Earth. We have become the world's dustbin'. While many of these headlines emerged a while ago – 2003 was when the *Sun* ran an 'Asylum Madness' campaign – on 6 October 2008, the *Daily Mail* contained an article praising fierce control of migration (Slack 2008). The headlines with which this book started reveal that media hostility continues to present a problem.[34]

Violent physical attacks have also been numerous. Fifty-seven per cent of refugees and asylum seekers interviewed in Coventry in 2005–2006 reported that either they or someone they knew had experienced racial harassment or violence (Ward 2008: 32). Colville relates how one 45-year-old Turkmenistani refugee was walking in a park with his wife and 10-year-old son in August 2005, when a local man unleashed dogs on them and all three members of the family were left bleeding on the ground. On the east coast of England, two men mowed down an Iraqi asylum seeker with a car and on the south coast, three men charged into a house and battered with iron bars an Iraqi man who they thought was an asylum seeker and a rapist (Colville 2006a: 7). Kundnani similarly relates a series of incidents that took place in Glasgow after dispersal, including a six-year-old girl having toxic liquid poured over her head, thugs with baseball bats attacking a five-year-old African boy in a playground and a 22-year-old Kurd being stabbed to death on an estate. Commentators explained that this murder had been provoked by delivery of new furniture to asylum seekers' homes (2007: 84).

---

[32]   The newspapers were the *Sun*, *Daily Mail*, *Daily Express*, *Daily Star* and Sunday's *News of the World*, *Mail on Sunday* and *Express on Sunday*.

[33]   See ICAR (2004, 2007), Kundnani (2001) and Malloch and Stanley (2006) for more on media presentations.

[34]   Not all media presentation has been hostile. For example, the *Independent* gave substantial positive coverage to the Independent Asylum Commission in 2007–8 and the BBC followed the story of a man from Sudan sympathetically (*The Asylum Seeker* 2004).

Policies and Practices of Control

Fear also has significant effects on the nature of asylum policies and practices in the UK. The state is expected to manage and defuse 'risks' to its population (Malloch and Stanley 2006: 55; see also Nyers 2006: 53) and governmental policy interventions on asylum have therefore been numerous. Far from being a 'soft touch' as some commentators claim (Mote 2003, Moxon 2004), the watchwords in the UK on asylum, as elsewhere in the Global North, are control, restriction and prevention. As Sales puts it, 'The trajectory of asylum policy has been to treat asylum seekers with suspicion, as a risk to society rather than as people themselves at risk' (2007: 152). Migration, including asylum, forms a key element in the contemporary British policy agenda. New Labour prioritized migration in its legislative agenda (Somerville 2007: 1) and the Coalition government is following their lead. The predominant goal of the government is to 'control', or in more recent policy discourse, 'manage' migration (Flynn 2005, Layton-Henry 2004) for the benefit of the established population.[35]

There is a desire to gain from the benefits which labour migration can bring, while not weakening national identity, security, cohesion or the legitimacy of the nation-state. In order to continue facilitating economic growth through transnational trade, investment, markets and services, immigration is central (Castles 2004). However, countering the fears outlined above depends on limiting migration. Hollifield labels this the 'liberal paradox: the economic logic of liberalism is one of openness, but the political and legal logic is one of closure' (2007: 64, Geddes 2008: 188). Therefore, rather than aiming at a zero-immigration 'Fortress Britain' that allows no one entry, governments – starting with New Labour – have sought to *manage* migration (Flynn 2005). This involves adopting a two-pronged approach, based on making 'a sharp distinction between immigrants with valuable skills, recruited legally through the work permit system or through other schemes, and asylum seekers, who have been attacked as illegals seeking to evade immigration controls' (Layton-Henry 2004: 331). The logic is one of 'selective exclusion' based on distinctions between 'productive' (desirable) and 'unproductive' (undesirable) migrants (Squire 2009: 24, Flynn et al. 2010: 103). According to Flynn, a system designed to allow in beneficial migration co-exists with 'draconian measures' against the 'spontaneous component of global migration' which 'emerged during the 1990s as an element in a survival strategy pursued by growing numbers of impoverished workers' using the 1951 Convention (2005: 484, 478). Managed migration is 'structured around business interests' and 'the migrant's duty is to be useful, first and foremost, to established business, and only after that to him/ herself' (Flynn 2005: 480–481). The White Paper, *Secure Borders, Safe Haven* (HO 2002b) signified the beginning of this approach (Sales 2007: 149, Somerville 2007: 22) and was followed by a five-year strategy, *Controlling our Borders:*

---

[35]   Global governance of migration (excepting refugee migration) has not been strong to date and remains in emerging stages (Ghosh 2000, Kunz et al. 2011, Martin et al. 2006).

Making Migration Work for Britain (HO 2005) and *A Points-based System: Making Migration Work for Britain* (HO 2006b). While still wishing to attract the 'brightest and best', as the Coalition's Home Secretary put it (Spencer 2011: 252), the Coalition government has taken a harder line. It seeks to reduce net migration by tens of thousands, including through stricter controls on foreign students and the number of family visas obtainable. They have also introduced a temporary cap on the number of non-EU highly skilled immigrants (Flynn et al. 2010, TTI 2010: 19). Asylum seekers and refugees, in such a system, are seen as an extreme threat to 'the orderly form of managed migration flows' (Flynn 2005: 463). The result has been a motley assortment of policies, as Somerville points out:

> The direction of policy has been paradoxical: on the one hand, a commitment to economic migration, and on the other, the development of a tough security framework that allows no unauthorized or 'illegal' migration and fast end-to-end processing of asylum seekers. In addition, anti-discrimination measures have been reinforced and at least partly amalgamated under an agenda of 'integration'. (2007: 4; see also Layton-Henry 2004: 332, Sales 2007: 180–181)

Sales notes that this period has been marked by 'constant organisational change' (2007: 168), exemplified by the frequent alteration of the name of the government department responsible for migration and asylum, currently the UK Border Agency. It is also clear that even while policies are opposed to 'illegal' migration, the contribution made by irregular migrants, including asylum seekers, to the British economy is considerable and covertly welcomed, be they working in restaurants, cleaning jobs, fruit-picking, nannying, the sex industry or factories (Kundnani 2007: 55–62). Marfleet notes how often irregular migration has been 'praised' and acted as 'capitalism's "lubricant"' (2006: 165–168, 172) and Kundnani claims, 'Britain's hypocrisy is to want only the work and not the worker, creating an underclass that can service society without being a part of it' (2007: 62). This paradoxical '*mélange*' approach to migration is shared by other countries in Europe (Geddes 2000: 1, 2003, Gibney and Hansen 2005: 84). While they differ in detail and there is no unified system on all aspects of admission policy (van Selm 2007: 91, Schuster 2000: 129), EU member states do co-operate at an intergovernmental level on restricting asylum (Geddes 2008, Joly 1996: 44–85, Lavenex 2001). Boswell and Geddes in fact suggest that since 2009, 'a common EU migration and asylum policy' can be said to be emerging (2011: 7).[36]

---

[36]   In 2009, the Lisbon Treaty was ratified and the Stockholm Programme for 2010–2015 established. For details of these and other EU policy, legislation and co-operation on asylum, including a discussion of its benefits and disadvantages, see Boswell and Geddes (2011: 150–175) and O'Sullivan (2009). EU policy on asylum and immigration tends to focus on border restrictions rather than tackling root causes of refugee flows (Haddad 2008a: 196, Lavenex 2001: 202, van Selm 2007), although Boswell and Geddes point

Asylum policy has resembled a 'patchwork' (O'Sullivan 2009: 238) and restrictionist policies and practices in the UK operate in two broad areas.[37] One set of measures is designed to hamper entry to the nation-state territory and thereby prevent individuals making an asylum claim. This '(b)ordering' – as van Houtum and Pijpers call it – functions to make 'a divisive order in an assumed chaos' (2008: 160–162). A second set of measures aims to exclude those who manage to get past these border controls. People seeking asylum face a plethora of policies and practices designed to prevent their permanent residency in the country. As van Houtum and Pijpers suggest, '(b)ordering and (b)othering go hand in hand' (2008: 162). This, in turn, is intended to deter others from making asylum claims (Gibney and Hansen 2005). Despite its commitment to providing sanctuary for those genuinely fleeing persecution and its claims of efficiency – 'fair, effective, transparent and trusted' were the key words linked to a Home Office Report in 2006 (HO 2006a) – the UK asylum system often proves to be complex, ineffective in making good decisions and unfair to asylum claimants.[38] Or in the words of the Independent Asylum Commission, it is not 'fit for purpose' (IAC 2008a).

Close the borders!
Instruments and processes introduced to hamper entry have included new visa requirements, carrier sanctions on airline and shipping companies, pre-inspection regimes (immigration officials known as 'airport liaison officers' operating at selected foreign airports to deter travel), interdiction, international safe havens and safe third country agreements (Gibney and Hansen 2005, Watson 2009: 47–48).[39] From 1999, immigration officials were allowed to employ force and increasing use is being made of new electronic surveillance technologies, including fingerprinting and checking the biometric data of would-be arrivals (Sales 2007: 103).[40] Somerville notes how successful the Labour government was at this 'key policy goal' of reducing initial claims: the total of 84,130 applications in 2002 was reduced to 25,710 in 2005 (2007: 65). This fell further to 17,790 in 2010 (HO

---

out that it has also 'exerted some more benign influences' including outlining minimum standards for reception and procedures (2011: 165).

[37]   Hammar has distinguished between policy at the border (regulation of flows of immigration and control of aliens) and policy in society (immigrant policy) (1985: 7–10; see also Geddes 2008, 2003: 40–43, Sales 2007: 102); see Kneebone (2009) and Gibney (2004) for discussions of asylum policy in the US, Canada and Australia, and Price (2009: 200–244) for restrictions on asylum in the US.

[38]   Multiple reports have criticized the asylum system. For overall critiques, see IAC reports (2008b, 2008c, 2008d) and JCHR (2007). Refugee Council and Amnesty International have also produced numerous reports.

[39]   Mountz explores the use of islands to detain and process asylum seekers, arguing that Australia, Canada and the US exercise considerable border enforcement strategies at the 'front end' (2011).

[40]   For more on these border measures, see Gibney (2006), Guild (2006) and HO (2005).

2011). Such border controls tend to drive those seeking asylum into the hands of professional smugglers as the only way to circumvent them (Väyrynen 2005: 146). Far from reducing fear therefore, these measures to prevent entry only exacerbate the association of asylum seekers with dangerous criminality.[41]

The asylum process: fast-tracking, detention and deportation
The asylum process is shaped to facilitate the refusal of the vast majority of claims and to do so as rapidly as possible (Somerville 2007: 65–66, Gibney and Hansen 2005: 79–82).[42] At a European level, the UK opted into the Dublin Convention, formulated in 1990 and enforced in 1997, which prevented asylum seekers from making applications in more than one country, allowed them to be returned to 'safe' countries and ensured that 'manifestly unfounded' applications would be fast-tracked and usually rejected (Geddes 2008: 78–79). Dublin II, which replaced this in 2003, allowed adults to be returned to another country if they had passed through it whether or not it was the 'first safe country' (Sales 2007: 122, Boswell and Geddes 2011: 151).

Fast-track procedures have been introduced and extended in every UK immigration and asylum act from 1999 to 2009, involving ever-increasing restrictions on the right of asylum seekers to appeal against a negative decision as well as the use of detention.[43] In 2002, specific removal targets were set, detention of claimants for up to six months was permitted and centres were pointedly renamed 'removal centres'. The Act of 2004 supported increased removals to 'safe third' countries and enlarged removal centre capacity.[44] One of the aims of the New Asylum Model, introduced in *Controlling our Borders* (HO, 2005) and brought into force in March 2007, was to process 90 per cent of asylum claims within six months by 2011.[45] Each asylum applicant was allocated a single 'case-handler', expansion of detention facilities was planned and removal targets set. The Home Office reported that 46 per cent of new applications made in June 2007 were completed within six months (HO 2008: 4). Overall in 2010, only 25 per cent of initial asylum claims were approved (17 per cent through grants of asylum

---

[41]   See also Koser (1998), Kundnani (2007: 69) and Sales (2007: 105).

[42]   For an introduction to asylum processes in the UK and US, see Bohmer and Shuman (2008), O'Sullivan (2009), Spencer (2011: 45–81) and Price (2009). On asylum seekers' experiences of processes in both countries, see Rabben (2011).

[43]   Key legislation includes the Asylum and Immigration Appeals Act (1993), the Asylum and Immigration Act (1996), the Asylum and Immigration Act (1999), the Nationality, Immigration and Asylum Act (2002), the Asylum and Immigration (Treatment of Claimants, etc.) Act (2004), Immigration, Asylum and Nationality Act (2006), the UK Borders Act (2007) and the Borders, Citizenship and Immigration Act (2009). Speeding up of the adjudication process has also taken place in the US (Price 2009: 231).

[44]   See Bloch and Schuster (2005) for more on the developing use of detention and deportation.

[45]   For more on the New Asylum Model, see O'Sullivan (2009: 256–257).

and 8 per cent through grants of leave to remain on other grounds) while 19,695 asylum applicants left 'voluntarily' or were forcibly removed (HO 2011: 26).

The IAC undertook a formal review of the asylum system in 2007 and, in line with the findings of other agencies, identified considerable flaws. People were required to apply for asylum 'as soon reasonably practicable' (HO 2002a) when entering the country, which could be difficult as understanding of the system or a grasp of the English language may be lacking at that point. There were moreover only a limited number of Asylum Screening Units with restricted opening hours (IAC 2008b: 22).[46] Legal aid provision for asylum seekers was dramatically reduced in 2004–2005, driving down the quality of legal advice and making the mounting of a solid case very difficult (BID and Asylum Aid 2005). Difficulties accessing legal representation if detained are especially pronounced (IAC 2008d: 17).[47] There have also been problems with interviews, including poor translation, which results in key facts being incorrectly translated and later undermining a case, poorly qualified interviewers and inappropriate or insensitive questioning.[48] Country of origin information has also not always been up-to-date or relevant (IAC 2008b: 26). The speed with which decisions are sometimes now made provides inadequate time either for a proper case to be mounted or for the Home Office case owner to form a comprehensive picture. A single forum for appeal, the Asylum and Immigration Tribunal, was established in 2004 and the amount of time allowed for lodging an appeal reduced. The 'culture of disbelief' and preoccupation with timescales and targets often cloud judgement (Refugee Council 2007), and case backlogs and delays remain considerable (Spencer 2011: 69–70).[49]

---

[46] Since the IAC review, the number of units has been reduced to one, namely Lunar House in Croydon. The majority of asylum claims have to be submitted here, though exceptions allowing people to submit claims elsewhere are occasionally allowed on health or mobility grounds.

[47] At the time of writing, an Early Legal Advice Pilot (ELAP) which aims to address lack of access to legal advice is being tested by the government in various localities. It is still to be decided whether this pilot will turn into a national programme.

[48] Fatima experienced difficulties on both legal and translation fronts, having a succession of legal representatives who requested considerable fees but who failed to produce professional services and make headway on her case and a translator at her initial interview who inaccurately translated her claim that her husband was a member of the 'opposition' party into his being a member of the governing party. For further examples of the effects of practices and policies, see Rabben (2011), Coventry Peace House (2006) and IAC (2007–2008).

[49] Similar problems can be found within the US asylum system, resulting in arbitrary asylum decisions and a wide disparity between immigration judges in terms of the percentages of applications they approve (Price 2009: 228–231). In 2007, there were 450,000 unresolved or legacy asylum cases in the UK. While 63,000 of these individuals were granted approval by 2009 under a Case Resolution Programme and the government claimed to have resolved 403,500 of these cases by March 2011 (Home Affairs Committee 2011), backlogs continue.

The Act of 2004 challenged the credibility of asylum seekers if they could not produce a passport, had a false document, had destroyed a travel document without good reasons or refused to answer questions (HO 2004, Bohmer and Shuman 2008: 84–108). Yet given the strictness of border controls and the situations which most are fleeing, the likelihood of being able to travel on and/or produce official, coherent identification is slim.[50] The result of all these practices is that a considerable number of poor initial decisions are made and a high rate of cases go to and are won on appeal. The figure was 27 per cent in 2010 (HO 2011: 20). While UNHCR Guidelines on the Detention of Asylum Seekers state that it should only be used if people are a danger to the public, a 'flight risk' or have not established their identity, the use of detention is on the increase across the globe and often arbitrarily (Watson 2009: 49, Welch and Schuster 2008). In the UK, 12,575 asylum seekers entered detention in 2010, including 300 children (HO 2011: 27), and some people have been held for years (Welch and Schuster 2008: 145).[51] Detention not only denies people their basic human right to freedom, but conditions are often inadequate, as was indicated in relation to women in Chapter 4 (IAC 2008d, Bloch and Schuster 2005, JRS 2004). Being incarcerated alongside criminals also succeeds in increasing asylum seekers' perceived association with illegality.[52]

Deportations have increased considerably in recent years, to the extent that scholars are writing of the global 'deportation regime' (De Genova and Peutz 2010) and suggesting that the US is a 'deportation nation' (Kanstroom 2007). In the UK, 29,040 refused asylum seekers were deported in 2006 (Gibney 2008: 146) and removals of principal asylum claimants increased by 91 per cent between 1997 and 2005 (HO 2006a: 6). Deportations often take place through dawn raids and excessive use of force is commonplace, sometimes involving children and occasionally even resulting in death (Fekete 2005, IAC 2008c). The Labour government even opposed some judiciary rulings against certain deportations (Squire 2009: 73). There are also anomalies, in that, for example, Zimbabweans and certain stateless people have been refused asylum but not deported as their home country is not deemed safe.[53] Even when refugee status is granted, there is

---

[50]   The UNCHR recognized in 1948 that refugees might need to use illegal means to escape and Article 31.1 of the 1951 Convention explicitly stated that receiving states should not 'impose penalties' on those who arrive in 'their territory without authorization' (UNHCR 2010: 29).

[51]   As noted in Chapter 3, while the Coalition government promised to end child detention by May 2011, it is unclear as to whether this promise has been kept. Government figures show that in December 2011, 17 children were being held in detention, including 10 at a new family unit at Cedars (HO 2012).

[52]   In the US, people who make an asylum claim at a border are transported immediately to jail and while some are released following an interview, many remain in detention (Welch and Schuster 2008: 142).

[53]   The UK remains signed up to the European Convention on Human Rights, which prohibits the return of asylum seekers to countries where they could face torture and death.

no guarantee that this will lead to permanent residency and citizenship in the UK. *Controlling our Borders* (HO 2005), the relevant parts of which were incorporated into law in 2006, led to a pilot project returning unaccompanied asylum-seeking children and established that the granting of refugee status could be reviewed after five years (Sales 2007: 151). This again may only feed fears however, as 'those with a temporary or precarious status may actually have greater difficulties entering into positive relations with established residents than those with (or heading for) permanent residence' (Rudiger 2006: 4).

Being treated as terrorists
Asylum seekers are also increasingly being excluded through legislation aimed at combating terrorism. As a result of the 2001 Anti-Terrorism, Crime and Security Act, suspected terrorists who happened to be immigrants could be interned 'regardless of the decision on deportation' and a further Act in 2006 explicitly stated that asylum was to be denied to terrorists (Somerville 2007: 41, Hampshire 2009: 120). More specifically, the 2001 Act has allowed the British Secretary of State to increase the number of people denied refugee status. It has done so by expanding the understanding of what constitutes an act negating the obligation to offer protection, beyond those already identified in Article 1(f) of the 1951 Refugee Convention – crimes against humanity, serious non-political crimes or acts contrary to the purposes and principles of the UN (UNHCR 2010: 16; see Zanchettin 2005: 154). The 2006 Act gave the government explicit power to deny refugee protection on national security grounds and increased immigration officers' powers to check individuals' identity. The 2007 Act allows immigration officers to search and arrest anyone suspected of an offence relating to obtaining asylum support on 'reasonable suspicion'. In fact, association of asylum with national security risks has allowed 'a rejection of the normal operating rules' of political procedure, allowing the 'threatened state' to introduce otherwise unacceptably 'illiberal' and 'pernicious' policies (Watson 2009: 1, 26–27, Hampshire 2009: 119, Boswell and Geddes 2011: 42). These policies, and accompanying political statements, again only serve to exacerbate the association of asylum seekers with terrorism, fuelling public anxieties (Rudiger 2007). That discrete portions of anti-terror legislation deal with asylum and immigration and vice versa has according to Somerville entrenched 'the connection between the two in law' as have comments such as those made by Beverly Hughes, then Minister for Immigration and Citizenship, that the measures of the 2001 Bill were 'designed to enhance intelligence and information gathering, to restrict people suspected of involvement in terrorism, *to prevent abuse of asylum*' (Somerville 2007: 39–41).

Known as the principle of *non-refoulement* (1951 Convention, Article 33) (Kneebone 2009: 11–14), Tony Blair, as prime minister, suggested that this commitment might have to be re-examined (Statham 2003: 166–167). This prohibition is in fact also a non-derogable international legal principle. On statelessness in the UK, see UNHCR/Asylum Aid (2011).

Deterrence by humiliation: welfare, dispersal and destitution

Other measures focus on the treatment of asylum seekers while they are waiting for a decision and after they have received a negative decision. These aim to 'demagnetise' the UK by '*lowering* support or *excluding* asylum seekers from services' (Somerville 2007: 67). Schuster describes these measures as a 'second line of defence' (2000: 123). The adoption of a European Commission directive in 2003 concerning minimum standards for the reception of asylum seekers has, as Ghanea points out, allowed the UK authorities to claim that they are protecting human rights while deterrence remains the keynote (2007: 124, 128). From 1993, asylum seekers were offered inferior social and housing support, with benefit levels set at 70 per cent of income support – insufficient to ensure a living standard above the poverty line (Hynes 2011: 8). In 1996, cash benefits were replaced with vouchers for those claiming asylum in-country rather than at the border and for those appealing a decision, and in 1999, vouchers were introduced for all asylum seekers and the National Asylum Support Service (NASS) was established to act as the conduit for all asylum seeker assistance.[54] Asylum seekers were no longer allowed to receive benefits and the voucher scheme was widely denounced, as 70 per cent of organizations working with asylum seekers claimed that asylum seekers experienced hunger and 96 per cent said that asylum seekers could not buy essential items as a direct result (Mynott 2002: 113). It excluded people in a cash economy (Sales 2002: 465). Voucher exchange schemes, including those offered by FBOs mentioned in Chapter 3, became a lifeline.

The Act of 1999 also introduced compulsory dispersal. According to Vervotec, by 'its peak in 2003 the dispersal system had spread 54,000 asylum seekers to 77 local authorities across Britain' (2006: 22). Aiming to take pressure off the Southeast, reduce costs, aid integration and fill unwanted housing as well as primarily to deter asylum applications (Savage 2005: 226, Somerville 2007: 69), the policy of dispersal has had a range of negative consequences 'premised on a "no-choice" basis' (Hynes 2011: 85). It has separated those seeking sanctuary from sources of support, in the form of friends, family, community and faith-based networks, particularly as people can be moved without choice at any time (Griffiths et al. 2005: 46–47, Hynes 2011: 160–162). Dispersal has made access to good legal, translation, health and education services difficult (Hynes 2011: 130–144) and English language provision is rarely adequate (Phillimore 2009: 58). In 2007, free English lessons for asylum seekers were abolished in England (Mulvey 2010: 254). Many have to relocate several times, increasing a sense of 'limbo' (Hynes 2011: 105, Hynes and Sales 2010: 51) and they have often been placed in inappropriate locations, where people have little experience of receiving immigrants or where they are already struggling with issues of deprivation (Hynes 2011: 72–88, Vervotec 2006: 22, Kundnani 2001, Robinson et al. 2003: 132). Mynott has illustrated the 'appalling' nature of most accommodation. Research

---

[54] NASS funded refugee service providers, notably Refugee Council and Refugee Action, to provide 'one-stop' services. NASS has been renamed Asylum Support.

undertaken by Shelter in 2000 discovered that nearly one-fifth of asylum seeker accommodation was unfit for human habitation, 19 per cent was infested, 28 per cent overcrowded and 83 per cent exposed to unacceptable risks of fire (2002: 118; see also Hynes 2011: 123, Hynes and Sales 2010: 51). Hynes points out that the main impact of dispersal and NASS (now Asylum Support) has been asylum seekers' 'feeling of loss of control over their lives and a sense of liminality, or limbo' (2011: 114).

While phasing out the voucher system for most, the Act of 2002 (Section 55) denied any support if a claim had not been made soon after arrival and withdrew the concession allowing asylum seekers to apply to work after six months.[55] People seeking asylum were left with no means to support themselves. A Refugee Council survey of organizations working with asylum seekers found that 74 per cent had witnessed clients being refused support after having applied for asylum within a few days of arrival, 74 per cent reported clients being forced to sleep rough and 74 per cent reported that clients lacked essential items including clothes and toiletries (2004b: 7). In 2004, electronic monitoring of those appearing adult was introduced to restrict movement and to prevent illegal work and refused asylum seekers were denied free access to primary healthcare and hospital services (Sales 2007: 146, 150). In November 2005, the Law Lords overturned Section 55 arguing that it breached human rights, but those whose claims and appeals are refused and reach 'end of process' can still find themselves destitute. Section 4 (Hard Case) support – in the form of accommodation and vouchers – is only provided for those who agree to voluntary return. This equated to £35.39 per week in 2010 (Spencer 2011: 63). Those unwilling or unable to return to their country of origin have no choice but to slip into the urban underworld, sleeping rough, working in the irregular economy or taking handouts from friends. While exact numbers are impossible to ascertain, it was estimated that there were between 1,000 and 2,000 destitute asylum seekers in Birmingham alone in 2005 (Malfait and Scott-Flynn 2005) and research conducted on behalf of refugee-supporting agencies found that over 40 per cent of people using refugee agencies were destitute (Smart and Fullegar 2008). The IAC claimed that while only 9,365 are on Section 4 support, there are approximately 283,500 refused asylum seekers remaining in the UK (2008c: 31). Destitute asylum seekers include 'heavily pregnant women, torture survivors, the mentally and phsycially ill, and older people' and they are at risk of increased vulnerability to ill health, sexual exploitation, stigmatization, illegal working, criminal activity and becoming victims of crime (IAC 2008c: 20, 22).[56]

---

[55]   One ruling suggested that refused asylum seekers would soon again be allowed to work, providing that their country of origin was deemed too dangerous to return to; see www.bailii.org.ew/cases/EWHC/Admin/2008/3064.html [accessed: 23 December 2008]. In July 2010, the Supreme Court ruled, in line with an EU directive, that asylum seekers whose appeals have not been dealt with within 12 months must be given the right to work.

[56]   Other reports on destitution include those initiated by Amnesty International (2006), Centre for Social Justice (2008), Open Door (Prior 2006) and Refugee Action (2006).

The aim of these humiliating measures has been to create 'an insulated immigration path for asylum seekers where they are separated from mainstream society (and often from their communities, through relocation) until a decision on their status has been made' (Somerville 2007: 74; see also Hynes 2011: 20, 190, Phillimore 2009: 58). Those who are in the asylum system can thus be described as 'denizens', people partially excluded from social, economic and political belonging in the nation-state. The measures have also succeeded in turning many of those who reach end of process into 'helots', people 'without access to democratic rights, property or protection' (Cohen 2006: 149, 1994: 186–190). Given that welfare benefits are not a significant 'pull factor' for aspiring refugees, these measures have done nothing to deter asylum applications (Bloch and Schuster 2002: 401, Geddes 2005: 168–169). What they have done is construct asylum seekers as 'culpable subjects' (Squire 2009: 117) and establish a system of 'new apartheid' (Mynott 2002). This new apartheid inhibits asylum seekers' ability to start adapting to the new context (Sales 2002: 474, Bloch 2002: 87–88) which ironically works against the government emphasis on 'community cohesion' and integration. Their poverty coupled with the denial of the right to work also forces some asylum seekers to enter the irregular economy thereby fulfilling the twin prophecies that they are an 'undeserving burden' on the welfare system and involved in illegal activities (Sales 2002: 457–458, Suvin 2005: 117).[57]

Breaking Spirits and Generating Anxiety: The Perspective of those Seeking Sanctuary

Fears of the established population, embodied as they are in such hostility, policies and practices, can do considerable harm to migrants. They provoke high levels of reflected fear. Wilson has suggested the 'broken spirit' as a metaphor for the 'fracturing of the soul, self, and identity' that can take place (2004: 110). The asylum process, with its culture of disbelief, bureaucracy and physical force, can be a considerable source of distress for those within it. Silove points to growing evidence that asylum seekers 'constitute the most traumatized of the wider refugee population', noting how many have experienced torture, human rights violations, family deaths and other traumas before arriving in the Global North. The adversarial processing of claims and its other faults are only likely to exacerbate this (2004: 17–19). The length of time involved in waiting for a decision on appeals, despite government fast-track targets, leads to uncertainty, anxiety and a sense of life being 'on hold' and makes planning for the future difficult (Sales 2007: 190–193). At Birmingham Cathedral, Annette and Lucille

---

[57]   Boswell and Geddes point out that these 'practices of exclusion' have been hard to enforce, as they can face judicial challenge and delivery organizations tend to have an 'inclusive logic'. Governments also realize that such exclusion tends to create more rather than fewer problems (2011: 172).

routinely responded to my weekly enquiry as to whether they had had any news on their cases: 'Still waiting'. Dispersal can result in 'social and psychological exclusion' (Bloch and Schuster 2005: 503, Kundnani 2001: 47, Hynes 2011: 190) and the denial of the right to work forces most into passivity and dependency. Asylum-seeking children can find it hard to gain access to schooling as schools worry that they will drain valuable resources (Sales 2007: 204). Many adults live in fear of being uprooted to a new city where they know no one, or of being sent to a removal centre or deported after a dawn raid.

As a result, many asylum seekers experience health difficulties, from depression and anxiety to miscarriage (Bradstock and Trotman 2003, BMA 2008). Given the restrictions on access to healthcare, it can be difficult to find treatment even if the need is acute (Kelley and Stevenson 2006). Summerfield personally assessed over 800 asylum seekers and refugee survivors of organized violence and persecution during the 1990s and 'saw plenty of unhappiness, frustration, anger and humiliation' and high levels of posttraumatic stress disorder and depression (2005: 103). While previous exposure to trauma, whether before departure or en route, increases the risk of these, Silove recognizes the 'substantial contribution of postmigration stresses in perpetuating trauma-related symptoms ... Most of these stresses are the direct consequence of restrictive policies applied to asylum seekers' (2004: 23).[58] Asylum seekers' experiences of humiliation and 'mis-recognition' (O'Neill 2010: 247) make it even harder to adapt to a new situation, and the effects of knowing oneself part of a stigmatized group should not be underestimated. The ICAR report found that one concern of asylum seekers was the negative perceptions of local people (D'Onofrio and Munk 2004: 31). A Kosovan woman at the Ladywood drop-in in Birmingham spoke of her depression and isolation in 2005, saying that she often did not want to leave her flat. She was anxious about letting her children play outside as she had heard stories of children being kidnapped and believed that the police would do nothing to help a Kosovan family. Such stigma can easily be internalized and lead to shame. As Pattison recognizes,

> Groups and individuals who fall into a state of long-term toxic unwantedness, abomination and abjection find themselves the objects of inarticulate stigma and rejection to others and often to themselves ... To be excluded, unwanted, treated as defiled, and shamed by self and/or others is to risk death – social, psychological, personal, or even physical. (2000a: 183; see also Lister 2004: 117–120, Sales 2002: 474)

Feelings of despair and fear can be especially intense for those who experience detention or destitution. One man described how he felt being interned:

---

[58]   Reflecting on the risks taken and suffering experienced by those crossing the US–Mexico border, Groody refers to the journey of migrants as a way of the cross (2009b).

Detention is an awful experience ... When I arrived, I was placed on 24 hour suicide-watch. As time went on I became more and more depressed. I had no motivation and nothing to look forward to. I attempted to end my life three times. When I had failed in my suicide attempts, I decided to starve myself to death. (Cited in Harding 2006: 7–8)

Another 25-year-old Sudanese man who was refused support under Section 55 and had no choice but to live rough, claimed: 'I feel depressed and hopeless. I feel less than human – like an animal. I hate myself ... I wouldn't have to answer any more questions if I was dead' (cited in Harding 2006: 14). A Burundian woman who fled in 2003 was refused asylum, and found herself pregnant and destitute. She described her situation to an interviewer:

I've lived with friends some of the time. You stay, maybe one month, and they ask you to leave, you go to another friend, you stay may be six months and they ask you to leave. You stay two days here and two days there. Sometimes you go in the streets – walking. Sometimes you go to the pub – to pass the time ... The most difficult is that when I walk outside I get cold ... Sometimes I'm hungry and have nowhere to eat. You get tired from too much walking in the street. When I'm on the streets at night I feel bad. I don't like this life because I have nothing to do and I'm not feeling well. (Cited in Coventry Peace House 2006: 8)

Fear of deportation led Ramazan Kumlaca to hang himself in Campsfield while awaiting deportation to Turkey in 2005 and Zekria Ghulam Mohammed, a 27-year-old Afghan, hanged himself in his flat in Glasgow in 2004 after his claim had been refused and NASS support withdrawn. His friends explicitly commented that his life in the UK had left him 'ashamed' and 'broken' (Fekete 2005: 59). In March 2010, the bodies of an asylum-seeking family who had just received a negative decision from UKBA were found at the bottom of a tower block in Glasgow (Hynes 2011: 183). If voluntary repatriation or deportation to the country of origin occurs, those who have sought sanctuary may find themselves again the victims of persecution or even dead (Fekete 2005: 27).[59]

A note of caution must be added. It is important to avoid assigning asylum seekers 'a sick role' (Summerfield 2005: 111) and pathologizing them as vulnerable, ill and depressed. Suffering is often used as yet another stick to beat migrants with, reinforcing perceptions that they are a burden on healthcare and welfare systems (Silove 2004: 19). Many people seeking sanctuary exhibit courage, joy and hope and the experience of a complex bundle of different emotions is a universal human one. Refugees are simply 'normal people who are forced to deal with abnormal

---

[59] Hassan – mentioned in Chapter 1 – on returning to Iran in 2008, was forbidden from leaving the country for 30 years. This destroyed his hopes of moving to the US to marry and start a new life there; see Vijayakumar and Jotheeswaran (2010) on suicide and posttraumatic stress disorder among asylum seekers.

and traumatic situations' (Hayward et al. 2008: 196). Some resist marginalization and fear through creating and maintaining social networks, 'speaking out' and protesting (Hynes 2011: 156, 176). At the same time, many enjoy opportunities for training, leaning English and volunteering and those who gain refugee status can begin a new life. Annette, for instance, undertook courses in hairdressing and administration and is now a British citizen. She recently moved to Tennessee to marry. Fatima was granted leave to remain and has brought her children from the Cameroon to live with her. Hassan claimed that he felt safe when he arrived in the UK. Some also speak of the hospitality and welcome they have received from members of the established population. Arun spoke of meeting 'so many friends in church … nice people', and there is often much fun shared at organized events (Group Interview 2007).

An Ecology of Fear

Despite these glimpses of hope, it is clear that fear has deep, broad roots and far-reaching consequences. There is what I term an ecology of fear engulfing the nexus between established communities and people seeking asylum. The term 'ecology' stems from the Greek words *oikos* (household) and *logos* (knowledge), and literally means 'knowledge of the household'.[60] It is most commonly used to mean 'a branch of biology that deals with the relations of organisms to one another and to their physical surroundings' (Pearsall 1998: 586). It can also be used metaphorically to indicate a range of interconnected characteristics or ideas (for example, Pattison 2000: 69). I use 'ecology' in both metaphorical-conceptual and literal ways. Metaphorically, I use it to indicate an interconnected set of emotional reactions, attitudes, behaviour patterns and language which evolve in contexts dominated by fear or faith. It is literal in that it also refers to the real, changing relationships between organisms (asylum seekers, established population, politicians, the media and so on) in specific physical environments (the UK, cities, churches, communities and so on). In short, 'ecology' refers to *a material and ideological environment in which mutually reinforcing patterns of thinking, feeling and acting define relationships between individuals and groups.* 'Ecology' indicates a space within which different kinds of encounter can happen.

The ecology of fear surrounding migrants can be depicted as a vicious circle in which fears of the established population feed negative media discourse, public acts of hostility and restrictive policies and practices. Such discourse, hostility, policies and practices, coupled with international geopolitical insecurity, only serve to intensify the anxieties and hostility of the established population and induce fear in migrants. As Kundnani puts it, the logics of suspicion and deterrence

---

60   Crosby states that 'the root word of ecology, as ecumenics, is also *oikía/oikos*. Ecology is merely the study of the world as a basic organism, as a basic global household' (1988: 266).

feed one another in dangerous and mutually-reinforcing ways (2001: 45; see also Squire 2009: 145, Hynes 2011: 196). The result is a dystopian context dominated by a sense of crisis and anxiety (see Figure 5.1).

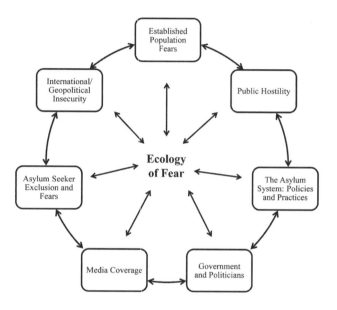

Figure 5.1   The ecology of fear

Such an ecology of fear is pernicious as it escalates a number of disparate and sometimes unrelated worries into a generalized, widespread paranoia. People start to suffer the delusion that migrants are 'out to get them'. While there may be short-term benefits of having a ready-meal scapegoat, the ecology of fear does nothing to help established communities in the long-run and has devastating effects on those seeking sanctuary. It leads to a paralysis in which everyone becomes stuck in the present moment – an asylum 'Groundhog Day' – which substitutes easy short-term scapegoating for the hard slog of seeking effective long-term solutions that might address the underlying roots of fear. As Furedi puts it, fear 'breeds an atmosphere of suspicion that distracts people from facing up to the challenges confronting society' (2005: xvi).

This ecology of fear is neither accidental nor spontaneous, however. It cannot simply be attributed to abstract forces of globalization or to 'an intense emotional reaction to a real or perceived danger' (Nyers 2006: 51) on the part of members of established populations. Fear is also actively produced by specific groups who may benefit from it. Fear 'has to be lived and made' (Smith and Pain 2008: 2). Politicians and governments are the predominant generators of fear.

They formulate the policies that help to create and sustain anxiety and, as Sales recognizes, 'Government policy is not simply a response to the real or imagined fears of the public ... Through constructing immigration controls it has created and sustained divisions and legitimised the racist attitudes that demand ever-further controls' (2007: 237). Restrictionist policies, coupled with the rhetoric of 'securitization' and clamping down, encourage people to believe that there is a crisis. When the government then fails to meet its own strict targets, the crisis-mentality intensifies and people clamour for more control (Bloch and Schuster 2005: 509, Kundnani 2007: 180, Hampshire 2009: 119, Mulvey 2010). As Squire puts it, 'policy-initiatives often produce and reproduce the "problems" that serve as justification for such practices' (2009: 16). The apparent confusion within the policy agenda, in that it serves to exclude migrants while at the same time prohibits discrimination, also feeds anxiety and uncertainty. The agendas of community cohesion and immigration restriction and deterrence seem incompatible (Zetter et al. 2006: 7, Hynes 2011: 3, Layton-Henry 2004: 331, Schuster and Solomos 2004: 283). That governments 'dominate and shape the public discourse on asylum' (Statham 2003: 174) becomes obvious when comparing the situation in the UK with that in the US. As Welch and Schuster point out, 'the perceived threat of asylum seekers in the US is quietly contained within government agencies and not a publicly shared construction' (2008: 146).[61]

This comes about largely because migration is a valuable token in party political games and is exploited to win votes (Dummet 2001, Moorhead 2005: 35). Migrants, especially poor or so-called 'illegal' ones, provide a useful scapegoat, as I have discussed, for any problems surrounding welfare provision, and they offer an enemy at a time when political polarization in the UK has diminished and the evils of the other party can no longer provide a rallying cry.[62] Larson points out how politicians often use suspicions of out-groups as a means of distraction, justification and aggrandizement (2004: 43) and according to Robin, fear is useful for politicians wishing to generate a sense of unity: '[Fear] is a political tool ... created and sustained by political leaders or activists who stand to gain something from it, either because fear helps them pursue a specific political goal, or because it reflects or lends support to their moral and political beliefs – or both' (2004: 16). As politicians also think (or at least claim to think) that their election success is dependent on strict immigration and asylum policies, the result is a political consensus between the major political parties that firm control of migration will be

---

[61]   Welch and Schuster suggest that in the UK, politicians and the media have driven 'noisy panic', whereas in the US, there has been more of a 'quiet panic'. Both panics have facilitated detention, the former through justifying it and the latter through keeping it out of the public eye (2008).

[62]   See also Huysmans (2006) on the political nature of the securitization discourse. Asylum has usually only been granted for the self-interest of the state, whether for reasons of foreign diplomacy, in order to shore up the image of being a liberal democracy or to meet a need for labour (Loescher and Scanlan 1986, Schuster 2003: 55).

the shared watchword (Sales 2007: 153, Gibney 2003: 29). The asylum card was played blatantly in the 2005 general election with Michael Howard, then leader of the Conservative Party, advocating withdrawing from the 1951 Convention and imposing an annual quota on refugees (Somerville 2007: 128), and in the 2010 British Election Study, while public concerns surrounding the economy dominated, immigration was in second place (Flynn et al. 2010: 107). This said, Flynn and colleagues note that immigration featured little in the 2010 election campaign itself, as mainstream politicians have begun to recognize that 'there is more pain than gain in talking up or talking down on immigration' and 'discretion [is] the better part of valour' (2010: 103). Asylum and immigration have proved more fertile soil for far right politicians, however. The BNP won 4.3 per cent of the vote across the seats it contested in the 2005 general election and made 'asylum clampdown' one of its 2006 council election manifesto commitments (BNP 2006, Kundnani 2007: 135). The BNP and UK Independence Party promised 'radical change' during the 2010 general election campaign (Flynn et al. 2010: 104).

The media are also culpable. The agenda may be set by government and political elites (Kaye 1997: 180), but the media interprets and presents this agenda to the public. Bralo and Morrison point out that the media 'command the lines of communication between those who are "in the know" and the structured ignorance of the general public' (2005: 188). As evident in the headlines already outlined, their coverage is often biased and lacking in nuance (Mares 2003; see also ICAR 2004). While the tabloid press is the greatest culprit, even the BBC used tabloid language such as 'swamped' on an Asylum Day in July 2003.[63] Fifty-three per cent of the established population Ward interviewed in Coventry claimed that the media was their main source of information on asylum (2008: 42). Kundnani accuses the press of positively using the issue of asylum 'to effect a mood of populist outrage against an imagined "liberal elite" who, it is claimed, have sold out the British people'. They combine 'mock populism and state-sponsored racism' to promote 'a new commonsensical popular racism directed at asylum seekers' (2001: 48). It is likely that the media has a significant impact on public opinion through 'attitude formation by repeated patterns of representation' (Hargreaves 2001: 27; see also O'Neill 2010: 125–133, Watson 2009: 21).

Numerous other influences on the ecology of fear include the EU, employers, lawyers, lobbyists, the judiciary and the NGO sector (Watson 2009: 21). As Somerville points out, 'the "engine room" of policy development is made up of professions, agencies, departments, think tanks and interest groups of the modern polity' (2007: 117). Conflicting interests from all sorts of public and private bodies and mass opinion play a part in shaping the ecology of fear. The general public cannot be entirely exonerated and understood as passive victims of forces beyond their control either, regardless of the IPPR report finding that respondents saw themselves as 'powerless bystanders' (Lewis 2005: 21). Politicians and the media

---

[63]   See news.bbc.co.uk/1/hi/programmes/asylum_day/default.stm [accessed: 10 December 2008].

claim to be responding to public opinion and indeed, in a survey conducted in February 2005, 49 per cent of respondents said that immigration and asylum was one of the three most important political issues. Seventy-eight per cent argued that government policies on asylum and immigration were not tough enough and 60 per cent supported withdrawing from the 1951 Convention (YouGov/*Mail on Sunday* 2005). Seventy per cent of British respondents in the *Transatlantic Trends* survey in 2010 believed the government to be doing a poor job on immigration (TTI 2010: 19). The public also drives the ecology of fear.

It is almost impossible to unravel the precise dynamics of the 'relationship between politicians, public and media' (Colville 2006a: 9; see also Bloch and Schuster 2002: 405). Fear, according to Pain and Smith, is 'simultaneously everyday and geopolitical': everyday fears and national or global fear-inducing discourses and practices sustained by those in power are 'inter-reliant and complementary' (2008: 7). An ICAR report on media impacts describes the existence of 'a signification spiral' or 'deviancy amplification spiral', meaning

> different communicators – large and powerful newspapers, officials, local audiences, political groups – who respond to one another interactively. While each is aware of the others, each has a distinctive agenda. The model suggests that communications can share common elements that through contact with others are reinforced, or amplified. (2004: 11)

What is clear, as Sandercock points out, is that discourses of fear produced are potent: 'portraying certain groups as fear-inducing surely serves to some extent to produce the very behaviours that are dreaded, while also increasing the likelihood that such groups will be victimized (through hate crimes and/or official brutality) with relative impunity' (2003: 124). Two opposite dangers thus exist. The first is conceiving the ecology of fear as intrinsically woven into the fabric of society. This falls into the trap of making nobody responsible for the consequences of fear. The second danger is to scapegoat one group – the public, politicians or the media – for all the ills which befall migrants.

Transrupting the Ecology of Fear

How might this ecology of fear be transrupted and an alternative ecology brought about? Where might we begin to look for hope? As Squire points out, the 'exclusionary politics of asylum are not inevitable' (2009: 32). Engaging with and addressing the fears of established populations is regarded as essential by a number of scholars. Given that adaptation is a two-way process involving migrants and established communities (Spencer 2003: 6), the anxieties and needs of both must be taken into consideration for an effective way out of the ecology of fear to be found. Dismissing or condemning all established community fears outright is only likely to play into the hands of the far right (Hansen 2003: 32).

As Sandercock suggests, fears 'need to be communicated and negotiated ... It is a long-term process of building new communities, during which such fears and anxieties cannot be dismissed but need to be worked through' (2003: 125, 138. Italics omitted). Ward similarly suggests that 'open debate and genuine mediated exchange' could help to address established population frustrations and grievances (2008: 46–47).

Facilitating contact between members of established communities and migrants has the potential to break down barriers and debunk false stereotypes. As the ICAR report states, 'understanding is most effectively encouraged by setting up contacts and establishing links between local people and asylum seekers' (D'Onofrio and Munk 2004: 43).[64] Bauman suggests that while problems may be 'gestated in the "space of flows," ... they need to be confronted and tackled in the "space of places"' (2004: 113). 'Everyday' or 'small acts and practices' are important in bringing about change (Pain and Smith 2008: 14). Some urban geographers advocate embodied connection between different groups of people. They call for the planning and nurturing of diverse, creative cities in which these connections can be fostered, as this could enable urban super-diversity to become a source of celebration rather than anxiety. Rogers suggests that the city needs to be a place 'of easy contact' (1997: 167) and Sennett recognizes the city as a place where people can grow through contact with diversity (1993, 2002). He claims that the 'modern city can turn people outward, not inward; rather than wholeness, the city can give them experiences of otherness' (1993: 123). Amin advocates 'the daily negotiation of difference' and 'prosaic interaction' in urban contexts (2002: 9–12) and Sassen suggests the global city as a place in which new citizenships could be worked out and the disadvantaged can find a voice in local, everyday ways (2006b).[65] As Castles and Miller claim, 'The global city with its multicultural population is a powerful laboratory for change' (2009: 258). Vervotec suggests that policy-makers should therefore ask themselves: 'what kind of forums, spaces and networks should be created and supported to stimulate inter-relationships of newcomers and settled communities?' (2006: 30).

Contact, by and of itself, does not however ensure positive encounters (Amin 2002: 11). It also needs to be accompanied by the provision of accurate information about asylum seekers and a commitment to avoid inflammatory discourse. The public is currently substantially misinformed and misled. Winder noted that in one poll, respondents thought that immigrants made up 20 per cent of the UK population whereas it was only 4 per cent, that Britain took 25 per cent of the world's refugees whereas it was only 2 per cent and that an asylum seeker received £113 per week whereas it was only £36.54 (2005: 440). The ICAR report noted that 'attitudes

---

[64]   See also TTI (2010: 7), Hollands (2001), Sales (2007: 238), Sampson (1999: 237–239), Temple et al. (2005: 45) and Valtonen (1998).

[65]   Gilroy similarly suggests that 'hetercultural metropolitan life' and 'convivial metropolitan cultures' act as a 'bulwark against the machinations of racial politics' (2004: 131–132); see also Cohen (2006: 189–194) on 'everyday cosmopolitanism'.

and experiences established prior to initial contact will influence whether people seek or avoid inter-group contact and what the effects of such a meeting will be'. Providing people with facts is one way of encouraging more positive attitudes and ensuring that when members of the established population do come into contact with those seeking asylum, the encounter is likely to be congenial (D'Onofrio and Munk 2004: 15, 55–56; see also TTI 2010: 6). Hollands similarly discovered that even supporters require better understanding: '[I]f humanitarian commitment is not combined with political awareness of refugee issues and ethnic relations, in other words of the structural context in which contact with refugees takes place, then disappointment may well result in the withdrawal of commitment and even new prejudices' (2001: 312). Providing people with a better understanding of the realities of asylum-seeking could improve their immediate reactions towards those seeking sanctuary when they come across them and also help to shift underlying negative attitudes (Robinson 1998: 158, Papademetriou 2003: 53, Ward 2008: 31). Informing people, for example, that the UK received only 5 per cent of the total asylum applications in the world in 2007 (UNHCR 2008a: 14) and that many of these applicants have professional qualifications would challenge two widely held myths.[66] The highest current source of in-migration to the UK is students. The IAC has also suggested the need to alter the primary discourse from 'asylum' to 'sanctuary', as the latter word has more positive connotations for the general public (2008b).

Another set of proposals for slicing through the vicious spiral focuses on reforming the asylum system and establishing fairer asylum, immigration and citizenship policies. If the system and policies are just, effective and efficient, fears will gradually be allayed. As well as calling for root causes of refugee movements to be tackled, various bodies have made a range of specific recommendations concerning decision-making processes and the treatment of those seeking sanctuary.[67] Some scholars have also suggested more radically that legal routes for refugee immigration should be expanded, notably through resettlement programmes and ushering in a world of open borders (see Gibney and Hansen 2005: 88–89). Sales, for example, advocates 'freedom of entry and residence' for asylum seekers and Hayter and Schuster are among those who call for an end to border controls (Sales 2007: 233, Hayter 2004, Schuster 2003: 276). Others disagree, arguing that the best solution is to close the borders more tightly. This would, they argue, take the heat out of established community fears by making it clear that the UK was not a 'soft touch'. A third set of voices seeks a midway point between the two poles in the models of multiculturalism and cosmopolitanism

---

[66] Myth-busting can, however, have the opposite effect and encourage people to focus on the myth (Ward 2008: 46).

[67] Castles suggests addressing disparities between North and South is vital (2007). For recommendations regarding processes and treatment, see Amnesty International (2006), Centre for Social Justice (2008), IAC (2008b, 2008c, 2008d), Kelley and Stevenson (2006), Lewis (2005) and Refugee Council (2004a, 2004b).

(Beck 2006, Benhabib 2004, Cohen 2006, Parekh 2008). These point towards some form of managed immigration and asylum system coupled with legislation promoting equal opportunities and rights for all.[68] Hall, for instance, argues for an 'agonistic' democracy and a more inclusive Britishness, which holds together the particular and universal (2000: 235–237) and Young suggests that '[t]he freedom to cluster should also be paired with an openness to unassimilated otherness' (2000: 224). Squire calls for a 're-enactment of citizenship and asylum' that moves away from the logic of exclusion and deterrence and towards 'a specifically mobile "post-territorial" conception of citizenship' embedded in both discourse and institutions of governance (2009: 183–185).

Related to the suggestions for the development of everyday cosmopolitanisms and multicultural forms of citizenship, a more personal, existential and psychological angle to tackle fear could be through constructing and nurturing a different understanding of ourselves as human beings. We need, it is argued, to adopt a cosmopolitan and hybrid mindset. Kristeva suggests that embracing our own 'stranger within' could enable us to encounter those who are different more positively and openly (1991), and various scholars suggest that recognizing and affirming human hybridity – that is, that each person contains a mixture of identities, motivations, feelings and perspectives – is an effective means of de-essentializing identities and transrupting stereotypes. Bhabha, writing from a postcolonial perspective for example, suggests that a hybrid strategy 'makes possible the emergence of an "interstitial" agency that refuses the binary representation of social antagonism' (1996: 58; see also Papastergiadis 2000). Others propose the value of embracing transitory and shifting 'nomadic' identities (Bauman 1992: 693–694, Huysmans 1995: 68). For Beck, a 'realistic cosmopolitanism' is rooted in identities that understand the self as both similar to and different from the 'other' (2006: 48, 58). The 'self' and the 'other' can therefore no longer be seen as diametrically opposed, and this could encourage members of established communities to discover more of an affinity with those seeking asylum. Such a cosmopolitan or hybrid mindset is partly brought about subconsciously through the everyday, ordinary encounters in urban contexts mentioned above.

Alongside a new cosmopolitan, 'other'-oriented self-understanding, some point out the need for a new vision. Sandercock suggests the importance of resacralizing and re-enchanting our cities. Her utopia is '*cosmopolis* … a city/region in which there is genuine acceptance of, connection with, and respect and space for the cultural Other, and the possibility of working together on matters of common destiny, the possibility of togetherness in difference' (2003: 2). Robin argues that moving beyond a defining logic of fear requires a 'vision of positive justice, some ideologically grounded hope for radical change' (2004: 165) and O'Neill calls for a 'radical democratic imaginary' to 'transgress the current regressive discourses

---

[68] Matthew Gibney provides a discussion of these views, rooted in the divergent ethical positions of communitarianism and humanitarianism (2004). For a discussion of different possible modes of incorporation, see Koopmans and Statham (2000a, 2000b).

and practices by states' (2010: 257). This new vision often emerges through acts of political resistance and 'turbulence' on the part of migrants, which 'critically interrupt the exclusionary operations of state governance and national belonging', combined with 'solidaristic engagements' of members of established communities standing alongside them (Squire 2009: 147, 165–166). O'Neill notes the role that can be played by alternative media and diasporic voices in transforming the imaginative landscape (2010: 133–141).

While these suggested solutions all have merits, none will transrupt the ecology of fear alone. Fear is rooted in a range of factors and varies infinitely according to an individual's personality and pre-existing views on race relations, social justice and Britain's place in the world (Lewis 2005: 13), as well as age, ethnicity, gender, geographical and cultural location, educational background and class. Time is also required for attitudes to change and fears to dispel (D'Onofrio and Munk 2004: 57). An ecology of fear cannot be transformed overnight.

Summary

This chapter has explored the dynamics of fear surrounding asylum-seeking in the UK today, dynamics that churches may benefit from understanding in more depth. The causes and consequences of fear have been explored and a pervasive ecology of fear identified. A number of proposed methods for transrupting this ecology and thereby improving the situation both for those seeking sanctuary and members of the established population have also been outlined. No easy solution or quick fix is apparent. In the face of these challenges and proposed solutions, I now wish to turn to the question: does Christianity have anything to contribute to discussions concerning how the ecology of fear may be transrupted? Do the scriptural and theological traditions have any useful insights into fear and how it can be dealt with? Are Christian communities any good at acknowledging and grappling with fear of strangers and, if so, how do they recommend breaking through it? It is to exploring these questions that the next three chapters turn.

PART III
Encountering 'Strangers' in the Bible

Chapter 6
Approaching 'Strangers'

We shall not cease from exploration
And the end of all our exploring
Will be to arrive where we started
And know the place for the first time.

(Eliot 1959: 48)

A Montage of Texts and Themes

'Strangers' and 'strangeness' are motifs embedded at the heart of the Judaeo-Christian tradition. They weave their way through it as a recurring thread. In almost every book of the Bible, explicitly or implicitly, the interconnected themes of journeying, alienation and encountering outsiders are explored. The peoples of God frequently found themselves wandering or experiencing exile in foreign lands and it is this which explains the pervasiveness of the thread. Fascination with strangeness is also a response to universal and perennial human preoccupations. Mursell suggests that it reflects the 'urge to migrate [that] has characterized human civilization since earliest times' (2005: 4) and Brueggemann claims that the Bible is addressed to 'the central human problem of homelessness (*anomie*)' (2002: 200). Life as strangers is double-edged in the Judaeo-Christian tradition in that, while affirmed as a God-given and fruitful calling, it is also peppered with a painful longing for home and roots. The following fragmentary montage provides an overview of the range of material and writing on the theme.[1]

Nomadic Forefathers: Setting Out and Being 'On the Move' in Genesis

The Bible begins with numerous stories about people 'on the move'. Genesis grapples extensively with what it means to live as outsiders and among strangers and the expulsion of Adam and Eve from the Garden of Eden, the banishment of Cain and the scattering of the people at Babel all occur within its first few chapters.

From 11:27, Genesis is dominated by a sense of travel (West 2006: 74) and in 12:1–2, the story of Abram begins with a 'wrenching departure' (Brueggemann 2002: 17). Abram is summoned by God to leave behind all that defines him – his

---

[1]   See also Brueggemann (2002), Carroll R. (2008), Daniel (2010: 13–39) and Mursell (2005).

country, people and father's household – for the sake of only vague promises of a new vision and abundant life (West 2006: 84). He becomes a migrant. While this migration is depicted as necessary to enable a new future for humanity – 'Abram must go *so that* others will be blessed by God' (West 2006: 85) – their continual movement and consequent nomadic existence means that home for the patriarchal family in the present is an elusive reality.[2] They always live as outsiders and strangers. Abram is described as a *ger* or 'sojourner' in the lands of Egypt (12:10) and his status, power and blessings significantly stem from this identity. The covenant is made with Abram precisely when he is an alien (17:8) and the appearance of God as angels in Genesis 18 is framed between references to Abraham as a vulnerable *ger* (17:8, 19:9, 20:1, 21:34). Abraham travels from Ur to Harran to Canaan, travelling its length and breadth (13:17) and passing through Egypt, Mamre, Beersheba and Moriah. Amos concludes, 'Abraham is always and everywhere a *ger*, and this fact dominates his story from beginning to end' (2004: 142).[3] These wanderings continue in the lives of his descendents, Isaac, Jacob and Joseph.[4] As West puts it, '[t]he line that God will choose as the vehicle for the blessing of all humankind will be this line of nomadic wanderers, and not the city dwellers' (2006: 77). Movement also dominates the story of the exodus and the wilderness wanderings.[5] Clines has described the entire Pentateuch as a narrative of journeying, one full of '"travel" stories' where 'everyone seems constantly on the move' (1978: 108) and, according to Feldmeier, 'foreignness is stressed time and time again in the patriarchal narratives … *Being a stranger is life according to the promise*' (1996: 242–243; see also Gooder 2000: 109). Significantly, God was always with his people on their travels: 'God can command the departure; but he remains with them from resting place to resting place' (Westermann 1986: 157).

There are also moments of settlement depicted in the Pentateuch, however, and movement is not considered universally desirable. Amos notes how Cain is described as a wanderer and fugitive and condemned to the 'Land of the Restless Life' as a punishment (2004: 30) and Walls distinguishes between 'Adamic' (punitive) and 'Abrahamic' (redemptive) forms of biblical migration (cited in ter Haar 2008: 38). The central goal of all the movement was moreover to find the Promised Land, a land which the people could eventually inhabit. As Inge

---

2   Ruiz describes Abram and Sarai as 'economic refugees from Canaan' (2007: 26) and Habel suggests the call is part of a 'migration narrative' (1995: 116–117).

3   The historicity of the Abrahamic narratives is widely doubted, but the theological narrative remains significant. For discussions of historicity and nomadism, see De Vaux (1961), Provan et al. (2003: 117–119), Soggin (1999: 98–103), Van Seters (1975: 13–38) and Westermann (1986: 74–79). Finkelstein and Na'aman (1994) offer archaeological perspectives.

4   Fontaine (2010) reads the story of Joseph in conversation with contemporary human trafficking and Wong (2010) explores patriarchal dreams of migration alongside the experience of Chinese immigrant women in Hong Kong.

5   On the exodus and wilderness wanderings tradition, see Childs (1974), Meyers (2005), Gooder (2000: 101–107), Mauser (1963: 20–36) and Noth (1972: 115–130).

suggests, the 'anticipation, the promise, is of landedness, a *place* which is rooted in the word of God ... Israel is a people on a journey because of a promise, and the kernel of all its promises from Yahweh is to be given the land, to be *placed*' (2003: 37).[6] There is flux between movement and rest, migration and settlement.

The Crisis of Exile: Casting a Moving Shadow over the Hebrew Bible

Having eventually established a settled kingdom ruled by a monarchy, the kingdom soon divided and the people of Israel found themselves once again subject to domination, uprooting and deportation (Brueggemann 2002: 68, Inge 2003: 40). Judah fell under Babylonian control in c.605 BCE and following rebellions by the Judahites, the Babylonians imposed deportations on two occasions in c.597 and 586 BCE. Ahn has described this era as 'the forced migrations period' (2011: 46). The second time the people in Jerusalem were placed under a lengthy siege and the city was destroyed. The damage indicated in the Bible is extensive. The temple, royal palace and homes were burned, the city walls were demolished, vessels and treasures were carted away from the temple and senior priests, royal officials and local leaders were rounded up. Some of these were executed and many others forced into exile (2 Kgs 25, Jer. 52). According to Zech. 7:14, the land was in ruins. Their 'experience is of being in and belonging to a land never fully given, never quite secured' (Brueggemann 2002: 13).

The exact number of deportees to Babylon and the conditions in which they found themselves are disputed. Whatever the precise realities, the exile clearly traumatized those deported and those left behind. While the exiles seem to have been given a level of personal, religious and economic freedom (Miller and Hayes 2006: 494), there are indications that they may have been used for forced labour (e.g. Isa. 9:4, 10:27, 14:25) and drafted into the Babylonian army (Smith 1991: 77–79). More significantly, as Farisani puts it:

> For those who were deported, as opposed to those who remained in the land, the downfall of the state of Judah meant a deep social uprooting. They had lost not only their homes but also their land and a social status which was usually influential; often they had been torn from their clans or even families and as a rule were deprived of the solidarity provided by kinsfolk. (2004b: 381)

According to Smith, the exile 'was a punishing experience' (1989: 31, Smith-Christopher 1997, 2002) and their condition 'daily reminded Judeans that they were no longer an independent people' and contributed to the development of a 'minority consciousness' (Smith 1989: 53). Mintz describes it as a symbolic as well as a real catastrophe. Not only was Judah crushed as a state, but communication

---

6   See also Brueggemann (2002: 8–13, 67–83) on the centrality of land and settlement.

with God was also cut off because sacred service and sacrificial offerings could no longer be made in the Temple (1996: 19–20).[7]

The exile formed the predominant material, psychological and spiritual context for the writing and compiling of the Hebrew Bible. Brueggemann demonstrates how exilic dislocation is manifested in the grief of Lamentations, the despair found in Isaiah 40–55 and the danger of self-preoccupation evident in the stories of Joseph, Esther and Daniel. Brueggemann concludes: 'Exile is the decisive event in the Old Testament for faith as for history … Exile, however, is not primarily geographical. It is a cultural, liturgical, spiritual condition; it is an awareness that one is in a hostile, alien environment where the predominant temptation is assimilation' (1997: 4–11, 115).[8] Carroll describes the Bible as 'the great metanarrative of deportation, exile and potential return' (1997: 64) and Neusner argues that while the story of exile and return to Zion encompass what happened to only a few families, their genealogy became *the* history of Israel. The Torah rendered the exile 'normative and mythic, turning an experience into a paradigm of experience' (1997: 226–228).

Jesus in the Gospels: 'Queering' Settled Place

The experience of being strangers in a strange land thus became the defining essence of Jewish identity and it is possible that Jesus partly 'understood his message and ministry as the beginning of the end of Israel's exile' (Evans 1997: 328, Wright 1996: 126–127). What is more, the Gospels indicate that Jesus lived as a wandering 'stranger' among others who inhabited the edges of society. In the Gospels of Matthew and Luke, Jesus is portrayed as being 'born on the road', as his parents travel for the census and then flee to Egypt. He was an itinerant preacher who stood alongside the marginalized and he 'migrated' from heaven to earth and back again (Senior 2008: 23–24). The whole period of the incarnation can be understood as the 'displacement' of God towards his people (Naish 2005: 48, 58–64). Jesus travelled extensively and encouraged his disciples to do the same, taking little with them. He called the disciples to leave their families and homes to follow him (e.g. Mk 1:16–20, 6:6–13, Mt. 8:18–22, 10:34–39) and they journeyed from place to place in Galilee, around Jerusalem and beyond into the surrounding territories. He was, according to Myers, suggesting that the Twelve were 'to take on the status of a sojourner in the land' (Mk 6) (1988: 213).[9]

---

[7]   For debate surrounding numbers and conditions of the deportees and the extent to which the exile signified a crisis, see Ackroyd (1968: 20–38), Carroll (1998) and Mein (2006: 54–73).

[8]   Ahn (2011) interprets various biblical texts as literature written by first to third generation immigrants and makes comparisons with contemporary migrant contexts and experiences.

[9]   Gundry (1993: 307–308) and Witherington (2001: 210–211) suggest that Jesus' call was for a reliance on hospitality rather than a radical ascetic itinerancy.

Moxnes describes Jesus as a 'displaced person' (2003: 67), arguing that his life was a challenge to conventional fixed notions of identity based on place and that he called his disciples to be similarly dislocated from static understandings of identity. Protesting against Roman imperial domination, Jesus 'queered' place, meaning that he questioned 'settled or fixed categories of identity, not accepting the given orders or structures of the places that people inhabit' (2003: 5). Through his lifestyle and sayings suggesting 'no-place' (for example Mk 6:4), 'not-yet places' (for example Mk 1:16–20) and alternative places (for example Mk 3:31–35, 10:28–30), he challenged identities rooted in the three key social institutions of household, kinship, village (2003: 49–71). Jesus thereby questioned the value of household and village activity and 'their power to grant or withhold honor' and entered into a liminal identity 'for those who had left the male space of the household' (2003: 68, 91). Place was transgressed and transformed by a 'vision of a new symbolic order' which challenged the 'area of paternal authority over household and village life, and placed his followers in imagined households with God as their father ... By contrasting the present "kingdom" under Herod Antipas with "the kingdom of God," he defined Galilee differently' and created a 'New Spatial Ordering – an Economy of the Kingdom' (2003: 106, 140, 154, 156).[10]

Early Christian Communities of *Paroikoi*: 1 Peter to the Church Fathers

Given Jesus' example, it is hardly surprising that the early Christian communities also regarded themselves as 'strangers' or 'sojourners'. They saw themselves as dislocated on this earth and being en route to a heavenly home, an attitude that may have stemmed from the extensive travels of their leaders and their own experiences of social marginalization. The early Christians were extremely mobile, travelling to spread the gospel and dependent on local Christian communities to provide hospitality. Malherbe points out that churches were 'established in important cities on the major trade routes ... early Christianity shared in the mobility of its society. The preachers were themselves transient' (1983: 63–64). Such mobility was relatively easy in the first-century Roman Empire and according to Meeks, Paul travelled nearly 1,000 miles in his reported career (2003: 16–19). Senior also recognizes that 'in the highly mobile and interconnected Mediterranean world of the first century AD the early Christians were not strangers to the experience of dislocation caused by violence and persecution' (2008: 26). They were a religious minority and a target for hostility because of their different views and way of life.

---

[10] For more on Jesus as a disrupter of social norms, see Brueggemann (1997: 69), Crossan (1991: 346, 421–422), Hobbs (2002), Koyama (1993: 284–285) and Theissen and Merz (1998). Horsley disputes this, suggesting that in passages such as Mk 3:31–35, Jesus is renewing the covenantal community rather than rejecting the family or disrupting society (2001: 196–197).

The New Testament epistles reveal a preoccupation with strangeness and sojourning. The first letter of Peter, probably written between 73 and 92 CE, is addressed to 'aliens' and 'exiles' in the diaspora of Asia Minor (1:1, 2:11). Elliott notes that one of the Greek words used is *parepidemos*, meaning transient visitors, pilgrims or sojourners. The other is *paroikos*, meaning foreign or 'other', and refers to a 'displaced and dislocated person, the curious or suspicious-looking alien or stranger'. Paradoxically, these 'strangers in a strange land' are simultaneously 'at home with' God (2005: 23–25). In Greek society, *paroikoi* denoted a real historical, political-legal and social condition of someone with higher status than a *xenos*, a complete foreigner with no legal protection, but who still experienced social, commercial and political restrictions (2005: 24–25, 37–38). In times of turmoil and adversity, the *paroikoi* were likely to be scapegoats of social animosity because of their 'in-between' status (2005: 69). While not technically *paroikoi*, the use of the word 'Christian' (4:16) in the letter shows that others perceived them to be a sect within society. They were 'the outsiders, strangers both socially and religiously. As such they constituted a potential danger to the public order and social weal' (2005: 79). In 1 Peter, this dislocation is turned into a virtue: 'The Christians are strangers in this society – and this is precisely their vocation; that is what they are supposed to be ... "Foreignness" and membership of the people of God are thus opposite sides of the same coin' (Feldmeier 1996: 256, 262. Italics omitted). The 'displaced and disenfranchised' are offered a place to belong in the household (*oikos*) of God (2:5, 4:17) and a distinctive communal identity as God's elect (1:1, 2:4–10). Christianity thus provided 'homes for the homeless' (Elliott 2005: 77–78, 181). The Letter to the Hebrews, also written to those experiencing persecution, was similarly premised on the idea of the people of God as wanderers, travelling through this land towards their eternal heavenly home. The people see themselves as 'strangers and foreigners on earth' as Abraham and his descendants were (11:13) and claim, 'here we have no lasting city, but we are looking for the city that is to come' (13:14). Their situation is likened to being in a liminal place in the wilderness (3:7–4:13) (Lincoln 2004: 35).[11]

This emphasis on travel, sojourning and strangeness as a way of life continued well beyond the first century. The *Didache*, a treatise compiled at the beginning of the second century, points to the existence of itinerant prophets who visited settled Christian communities administered by bishops and deacons. One section tells these communities, 'Let everyone who comes in the name of the Lord be received' (12.1) (Niederwimmer 1998: 183). The *Epistle of Diognetus*, a late second or early third century document, demonstrates that Christians were clearly designating themselves as sojourners by this time: 'They live in their own countries, but only as aliens. They have a share in everything as citizens, and endure everything as foreigners ... They busy themselves on earth, but their citizenship is in heaven' (cited in Wogaman and Strong 1996: 17). According to Feldmeier the *Second Letter of Clement* depicts Christians as sheep among wolves in society: 'So παροικία –

---

11   Käsemann (1984: 19) offers relevant commentary on Hebrews.

the sojourn of the non-citizen in a foreign place, the foreign parts per se – also became the self-description of the Christian community' (1996: 263). Augustine similarly saw Christians as strangers in the earthly world in exile from their home in the heavenly 'City of God' (1972) and Feldmeier points out that 'in the third and fourth century the term παροικία then found its way into the terminology of church administration as "parish", "parochial" etc.' (1996: 264).

The Restless Essence of the Christian Life

Wayfaring, movement and restlessness have become intrinsic to Christian self-understanding. Migration continued to define Christianity in its first seven centuries, with believers travelling from Syria to Egypt to India to the Western Mediterranean (Phan 2008). Pilgrimage, the practice of travelling to holy places, exemplifies this sense that Christians are a people 'on the move'. Origen noted trips to the cave in Bethlehem in the third century and Eusebius recognized that people were congregating in Jerusalem in the fourth (Sellner 2004: 72–73). Colambanus (c.543–615) referred to himself as a *peregrinus* and after years at a monastery in Bangor, Wales, decided to become 'an exile for the sake of Christ'. Originally from Ireland, he travelled to establish communities in Burgundy and Italy (Harpur 2002: 42–44). In the Middle Ages, pilgrimage was undertaken by any who could afford to and was used as a metaphor for life (Platten 1996: 12–14) and Christians continue to pilgrimage to places including Taizé, Iona, Lourdes, Jerusalem and Mexico City today.[12]

Mursell suggests that a 'fundamental sense of transience, of never fully being at home where we are, is part of our spiritual make-up, part of the restlessness that is at the heart of our vocation as human beings' (2005: 12–13) and Georgi describes 'the people of God [as] a community of sojourners, constantly on the road, never taking possession, always seeking the city that is to come' (2005: 368). Feldmeier affirms the Christian task as to be 'practising strangers' (1996: 270) and Moltmann has argued that Christians are journeying in hope towards the future (2002). Naish puts it this way: '*every* Christian, and the Church as a *whole*, is displaced in relation to the world by virtue of his or her calling' (2005: 18). Sheldrake also suggests the importance of journeying across boundaries and of being nomads as '[t]he presence of God acting in the within of all things is always strange and elusive, overflowing boundaries into what is "other"' (2001: 67). The poet T. S. Eliot conceived of life as a circular journey moving away from home, searching for meaning and connection, and returning to where we started at the end of life:

---

[12] For more on pilgrimage and journeying in the spiritual life, see Bartholomew and Hughes (2004), L. Byrne (2000), Eade and Sallnow (2000), Harpur (2002), Harris (2010), Hermkens et al. (2009), Hughes (1986), Hume (1984) and Vanier (1997).

Home is where one starts from ...
We must be still and still moving
Into another intensity
For a further union, a deeper communion ...
In my end is my beginning. (1959: 27)[13]

Merton similarly spoke of his life as being on a road: 'My Lord God, I have no idea where I am going. I do not see the road ahead of me. I cannot know for certain where it will end ... you will lead me by the right road though I may know nothing about it' (1958: 70). More controversially, Hauerwas and Willimon have described Christians as 'resident aliens', people who are called to live in the world but as people who are radically 'other' and who live differently from the society around them: the church exists as 'an adventurous colony in a society of unbelief' (1989: 49).[14]

Summary and Emerging Questions

Being strangers is a central theme in the Bible and in the history of Judaeo-Christian self-understanding and practice: the people of God often find themselves being uprooted and on the 'outside'. It is a theme drawn upon by a number of those reflecting theologically on asylum-seeking, refugees and migration (for example Hoffmann 1989, McLoughlin 2005, 2006, Senior 2008). What is less clear though is how these strangers are to treat other strangers. How are they to approach those they do not know and those who are different from them? While there is often talk of *the* biblical attitude towards strangers – one leaflet encouraging support of asylum seekers notes 'the unequivocal call of the Bible to care for the stranger in our midst' (URC n.d.) – a plethora of responses can in fact be found.[15] Smith-Christopher points out that 'in most periods of Israelite history, including the time of monarchical power, exclusionary attitudes coexisted with idealistic laws which sought, for example, to codify the traditions of "hospitality to the stranger"' (1996: 119). For example, while the Abrahamic narratives and Isaiah 55–56 seem to be positive towards outsiders, other post-exilic texts such as Ezra–Nehemiah seem to be far less welcoming. A similar mixture of attitudes can be pointed to in the New Testament. The early Christian communities seemed to suggest that on the one hand, strangers were to be welcomed and included – they were intentionally cosmopolitan communities – but on the other, they were to separate themselves

---

[13] 'Journey of the Magi' (Eliot 1990) explores a similar theme, as do some poems of R. S. Thomas (2000: 308, 364, 456).

[14] See also Hauerwas (1981) and Nazir-Ali (1998). Brueggemann challenges this separatist understanding of the Church (1997: 13).

[15] Keifert similarly claims, 'the biblical vision invites me to give up my self to the point of opening up myself to the perspective of the stranger' (1992: 78).

as God's elect from outsiders. Both 'centripetal and centrifugal thrusts' can be discerned (Elliott 2005: 108).[16] Responses towards strangers can, however, be grouped broadly into two strands – those made from within an 'ecology of fear' and those made from within what I describe as an 'ecology of faith'.[17] I explore these in the next two chapters in turn.

Before turning to the texts, though, a crucial difference between the strangers in biblical narratives and contemporary migrants must be noted. Those seeking sanctuary in the Global North today are a minority and established populations a majority. In biblical times, Judaeo-Christian communities were usually the minority. Those they were viewing as strangers were thus the larger nations and communities – the powerful majority – that surrounded their struggling enclaves. It is important to bear this in mind throughout the textual readings in the next chapters.

---

[16]   Brett (1996: 11), Levenson (1996: 145, 168), McKinlay (2004: 22–36, 132) and Sparks (1998) similarly point to the diverse attitudes to 'others' in the Bible.

[17]   These strands are comparable with what Brueggemann terms 'trajectories' (1993). Jacobs used the terms 'faith' and 'fear' oppositionally with regards to pastoral care and counselling (1987).

Chapter 7
Ecology of Fear: Ezra–Nehemiah

Then, in the midst of this celebration, the student raised his hand and asked simply, 'What about the Canaanites?' Suddenly all the uncomfortable feelings I had been repressing about the Bible for years flooded me. Yes, what about the Canaanites? and the Amorites, Moabites, Hittites? ... I now began to see some complicity, for over and over the Bible tells the story of a people who inherit at someone else's expense. (Schwartz 1997: ix–x)

This chapter explores responses made to strangers in the Bible from within an ecology of fear. These invariably call for their exclusion or destruction. While many Christians choose to dismiss texts condoning hatred or violence, they form a significant strand in both the Hebrew Bible and New Testament and should not be ignored. Focusing on Ezra–Nehemiah as an example, this chapter explores the following questions. What insight can such biblical texts offer into contemporary dynamics of exclusion surrounding migration? What do they suggest about the factors which lead to the emergence of an ecology of fear in which someone deemed a stranger is regarded as a threat to be removed?

Dealing with 'Foreigners': Introducing Ezra–Nehemiah

The books of Ezra and Nehemiah narrate the return to Judah of some of the Israelites sent into exile in Babylon in c.597 and 586 BCE. Having defeated the Babylonians, the Persians took control of the area in 539 BCE and administered Judah as a province of their empire, within the Satrapy of Beyond the River (Williamson 1987: 48–50, Blenkinsopp 1988: 61). Ezra, a scribe and priest, and Nehemiah, an appointed governor, were among those sent home by the Persian authorities to rebuild and re-establish Jerusalem's temple, walls, community and law at different times. Ezra–Nehemiah tells the story of their attempts to do so.

There is considerable debate as to when the books were written and completed in their final form and by whom, as well as disagreement about the dates that Ezra and Nehemiah arrived in Jerusalem.[1] Three points are clear. First, Ezra–Nehemiah was composed and edited during the post-exilic period, a time when the people of Israel were trying to come to terms with the profound crisis that had befallen

---

[1]   For a discussion of authorship, chronology and textual structure, see Blenkinsopp (1988: 41–54, 2009: 86–92), Clines (1984: 16–24), Farisani (2004a), Japhet (1994), Williamson (1987) and Wright (2007).

them and their continued subjection under the Persian Empire. Past events and a sense of ongoing precariousness would almost certainly have come together to establish an ecology of fear and the authors were responding from within this. According to Clines, the books 'should be seen as an attempt at self-understanding on the part of Ezra's community which has experienced a fulfilment of the divine promises of restoration, but is still "in great distress" (Neh. 9:37) because of Persian overlordship' (1984: 26). Second, the text was written by persons with power and authority in the newly reconstituted Jerusalem community. The authors were probably former exiles or those closely related to them and readers enter into the story through the eyes of Ezra and Nehemiah (Farisani 2004a: 223). Third, the text is less important as a historical document than as a theological one and exact dating and authorship need not be a major concern. Indeed, it is probable that 'the gap between texts and the real world remains as unbridgeable as ever' (Carroll 1991: 124) precisely because the text was designed to convey a theological message rather than historical detail. It is with the theological message of Ezra–Nehemiah, rather than with a detailed historical account, that this chapter is primarily concerned. This said, it seems likely that Sheshbazzar (replaced at an undefined point by Zerubbabel) – the first returnee mentioned in Ezra – returned in 538 BCE to rebuild the temple, Ezra in 458 BCE to restore the community and re-establish the law and Nehemiah in 445 BCE to rebuild the walls. Nehemiah returned for a second time in 432 BCE (Japhet 1994: 208, Throntveit 1992: 2–3, Williamson 1987).

The Clear Demands: Get Rid of your Foreign Wives! Separate from the Peoples of the Land!

The most striking aspect of Ezra–Nehemiah is the repeated call made for the dismissal of foreign wives and the extreme animosity expressed towards the 'peoples of the land'.[2] The reaffirmation of the law and covenant, initiated by Ezra and reinforced by Nehemiah, includes a demand that all Israelite men married to foreign women are to divorce them. Ezra denounces marriages of Israelites with the 'peoples of the lands' in unambiguous terms (Ezra 9:1–4, 10–12) and demands that the people of Judah make confession and 'separate [themselves] from the peoples of the land and from the foreign wives' (Ezra 10:11). What is more, when individual cases were heard, no provision was made for the divorced women or for their children (Throntveit 1992: 56). The 'peoples of the land' are also held in 'dread' (Ezra 3:3) and negatively associated with opposition to the rebuilding of the temple (Ezra 4:4). Nehemiah is equally harsh. He forbids *all* foreigners from entering the temple: 'When the people heard the law, they separated from

---

[2]   The difference between 'foreigners' and 'peoples of the land' will be discussed below. Ezra–Nehemiah is not the only post-exilic text to express such an antipathy towards intermarriage; see Gen. 24:3, for example (Amos 2004: 134).

Israel all those of foreign descent' (Neh. 13:3).[3] Those condemned for opposing the rebuilding of the wall are Samaritans, Ammonites, Ashdodites and Arabs (Neh. 4) and he later echoes Ezra's more specific concerns about foreign wives (Neh. 13:23–27). Ezra–Nehemiah thus appears to be a profoundly xenophobic text. Foreigners and in particular, foreign wives, are to be completed excluded from the community. It is a 'cautionary tale' (Anderson 2009: 47) and Clines is right to be 'appalled by the personal misery brought into so many families by the compulsory divorce of foreign wives … [and] outraged at Ezra's insistence on racial purity' (1984: 116). Williamson suggests that the treatment of mixed marriages in Ezra 9–10 and Nehemiah 'is among the least attractive parts of Ezra–Nehemiah, if not of the whole [Old Testament]' (1985: 159) and Schwartz describes Ezra 9:11–12 as 'the most xenophobic utterance' the Bible makes 'about drawing the border of Israel by kinship' (1997: 86).[4]

Grappling with Unpleasant Texts

If a naive literal parallel was to be made between the text and contemporary migration, the demands of Ezra and Nehemiah could be taken as an encouragement to ignore newcomers at best and positively seek their removal from local and national communities at worst. Given, though, that such a hermeneutical approach is flawed for reasons already outlined in Chapter 2, how should such a text be dealt with today? One approach, understandably favoured by Christians standing alongside migrants, is to disregard the books altogether. Those trying to encourage people to be more open to immigrants and asylum seekers are unlikely to turn to a narrative which presents such an unhelpful counter-message. Commentators from a northern evangelical tradition have tended to focus on the 'spiritual' messages which can be gleaned, sidestepping awkward xenophobic elements. Dave Cave, for example, concentrates on the problems caused by compromise and the watering down of the requirements of the religious life. He suggests that 'wife' in Hebrew could mean 'concubine' or 'cohabitor', implying that the issue at stake is probably adultery rather than foreignness (2003: 81–82). For him, Ezra–Nehemiah points to the reality that '[i]t is so easy for things to creep into the life of the church through wrong relationships and unholy alliances. Once things, or people, which are nothing to do with God move into the body of Christ, it does not take long for the rot to set in … Holiness is not negotiable; cleanse the temple!' (2003: 181).[5]

---

[3]   Throntveit describes the three sets of exclusions of foreigners in Neh. 13 as attempts to reform 'holy space', 'holy time' and a 'holy congregation' (1992: 122).

[4]   Other Jewish scholars note exclusionary tendencies in the text. Olyan writes of a 'powerful discourse of purity' promoting the 'idea that aliens defile' (2000: 82) and Japhet describes the view of Ezra–Nehemiah concerning those who remained in the land as being that 'there are no such people at all!' (1983: 113).

[5]   Brueggemann (2008: 91–117) discusses a range of strategies people employ to deal with difficult and unpleasant texts.

Neither the texts themselves nor the issues of xenophobia and exclusivism can be so easily bypassed, and I prefer two alternative ways of dealing with such texts. The first reads the books from the perspective of its submerged voices – the excluded strangers – and involves acknowledging the complicity of the wider Judaeo-Christian tradition in fostering hostile attitudes towards foreigners. Ezra–Nehemiah is exposed as one of many texts which contain inherently oppressive and life-denying elements. The second approach involves mining Ezra–Nehemiah for helpful insights into the contemporary migration situation and the exclusionary mentality which surrounds it.

Exposing the Christian Tradition: The Perspective of the Excluded in an Ecology of Fear

Interpreting Ezra–Nehemiah from the standpoint of those excluded is no easy task. This is because the voices of outsiders are usually silenced in ecologies of fear. The foreign women do not speak in the text and are thus prevented from defending their cause, as are the men who have married them. All who disagree with the viewpoint of the author and the characters of Ezra and Nehemiah are marginalized. It is precisely these voices, though, that from a forced migration hermeneutical standpoint should have priority. It is vital to read between the lines and pay 'close attention to the minor characters in it, so that we may hear the other side of the story' (Fewell 2004: 127). Imagining what it must have been like for the foreign wives and their children in Ezra–Nehemiah, Fewell writes,

> In some ways the biblical world and the (post)modern world are not so very far apart. Children suffer in both as a result of the theology and politics of adults. Should we not find our lives interrupted, disrupted, and unsettled by this? Should we not read between the lines of both the Bible and our culture? Should we not speak out and act on behalf of the children? (2004: 134).[6]

Farisani (2004c) has paid particular attention to the voices of those deemed strange in Ezra–Nehemiah and reveals that not only were foreign wives to be cast off, but the 'peoples of the land' were also prevented from participating in the rebuilding projects initiated by the returnees (Ezra 4:3). Certain characters (Sanballat, a Samaritan, Tobiah, an Ammonite, Geshem, an Arab and a prophetess Noadiah) are portrayed as threatening 'enemies' of Nehemiah (Neh. 6:1–14) and as having consistently opposed his work. But their opposition is far more likely to have been a *reaction* to their unfair treatment than its cause and 'needs to be seen as the only legitimate means left for them to protest against their exclusion' (2004c: 36). For these people, as well as the foreign wives and the men who had married them,

---

[6]   Fewell offers an imaginative reading of the text from the perspective of Jonathan, son of Asahel, who opposed the proposal to remove wives and children (Ezra 10.15) (2004).

the story told in Ezra–Nehemiah is one-sided and oppressive. Farisani points out that no shred of religious law could have legitimated the women's dismissal and it seems unlikely that the Persians would have demanded such an unpopular and unachievable policy (2004c: 41).[7] He concludes that both the exclusion of the 'peoples of the land' from the building projects and the dismissal of foreign wives were the result of 'ethnic "constructions"' and the abuse of ethnicity for Ezra and Nehemiah's own ends (2004c: 42–43; see also Anderson 2009). Honouring the perspective of the submerged 'peoples of the lands' requires exposure of their unjustified exclusion and a denunciation of the text which endorses it. The ecology of fear within which Ezra–Nehemiah was written had profoundly unpleasant consequences.

A Range of Dubious Texts, Themes and Practices

Ezra–Nehemiah is one of a number of biblical texts which could be used to justify the exclusion of outsiders. Ecologies of fear were prevalent in biblical times. Smith-Christopher suggests, 'Even the most casual familiarity with the Hebrew Bible enables one to see that there are many texts that could be used to justify racist and oppressive attitudes and policies towards anyone considered the "foreigner" or the "enemy"' Foreigners, on the whole, 'are to be killed, conquered, or at the very least avoided' (1996: 118, 121).[8] While he perhaps overstates the case, in that it is usually only people who compete with Israel for the land who are regarded as problematic (Wills 2008: 27–39, 45–46), a brief survey substantiates his broad claim. The exodus, often acclaimed as an act of divine liberation, was an oppressive episode for any who were not Israelites. Egypt was depicted as an enemy and God promised to annihilate 'the Amorites, the Hittites, the Perizzites, the Canaanites, the Hivites and the Jebusites' (Exod. 23.23). This was so that his people could take over and inhabit their lands.[9] Associating with these 'foreigners' displaced and destroyed by the Israelites, indigenous peoples in particular have struggled with the exodus narratives (Ateek 2006, Warrior 2006).[10] The Hebrew Bible depicts the Israelites as a 'chosen people' and describes their attempts to establish a separate nation. This required the labelling of the inhabitants of Palestine as 'foreigners' and 'enemies' and the denial of their rights and identity

---

[7] Carroll has suggested that Noadiah's opposition to Nehemiah is 'a mark in her favour' (1992: 96; also cited in Farisani 2004c: 35). Klein (1999: 819) argues that no demand is made to dismiss already existing mixed marriages in Nehemiah. This contrasts with Ezra 10.11.

[8] On violence in the Bible, see Nelson-Pallmeyer (2005) and Schwager (2000).

[9] Deut. 2:34, 3:6, 7:1–6, Josh. 12, Ps. 83 and Isa. 13 offer examples of calls to exterminate 'foreign' peoples and their enactment.

[10] Fernandez has suggested that the experience of Filipino migrants to the US is ironically more like an 'Exodus-toward-Egypt' than one away from it (2006); see also Tulud Cruz (2010: 311).

(Whitelam 1996, Said 1988). As Kwok notes, the 'exclusion of the Other is closely related to the concept of election' (1995: 89). At the end of the book of Esther, we learn that 'the Jews struck down all their enemies with the sword, slaughtering, and destroying them' (Est. 9.5) and various texts, including the so-called 'Curse of Ham' (Gen. 9:18–27), have been used to justify racism.[11] Biblical violence towards 'ethnically different' women, including Jezebel and Hagar, has subtly legitimated the denigration and exclusion of women labelled in similar ways (McKinlay 2004, Williams 1993, Trible 1984).

The Hebrew Bible is not the only source of negative attitudes towards strangers; exclusive elements are also found in the New Testament. Levenson is right to point out that any attempt to make an 'unreflective contrast between a closed, ethnocentric Judaism and an open universal Christianity' is increasingly incredible (1996: 167). Although the Pauline Church is often understood to have been an inclusive and cosmopolitan community, the ecology of fear was not entirely absent. One commentator on Ezra–Nehemiah cites 2 Corinthians 6:14–15 as evidence that Paul also called believers to separate themselves from all outside the community (Holmgren 1987: 75; see also 1 Cor. 5:9–13) and according to Boyarin, Paul's desire for a universal, unified humanity in Christ actually meant that all people were to be merged into a common, dominant culture. The transcendence of the particularities of gender, ethnicity and class through baptism (Gal. 3:27–28) has thus, indirectly and unintentionally, encouraged racism and oppression (1994: 24, 233, Castelli 1991, Kwok 2005: 89–93). The line between inclusion and imperialism is very thin. Anti-Semitism, in particular, can be perceived in a number of New Testament texts. Freyne points out how anti-Jewish rhetoric helped community building in the Matthean and Johannine communities (1985) and Stegemann argues that Titus is xenophobic and 'heterophobic', as it stigmatizes a deviant group by negatively associating it with Jews and Cretans (1996).[12]

Key Christian doctrines can facilitate 'othering'. Monotheism, a central tenet of the Hebrew Bible, and dualism, implicit in the divine/human nature of Christ of the New Testament, have both contributed to an insider–outsider mentality. Brown Douglas argues that the rooting of Christianity in a 'closed' monotheism with a jealous God and the dual divine/human nature of Christ – the Christological paradox – have interacted problematically (2005: 20): 'In effect, Christianity's theological core compels the need to define difference, be it the difference between Christians and non-Christians or divinity and humanity' (2005: 22). It is this emphasis on defining difference, she believes, which has contributed to Christianity's fuelling of 'white racist fury' and its provision of 'a "sacred canopy" for certain inequitable power relationships' (2005: xiii, 9). Heyward has similarly suggested that in 'a dualistic praxis' such as Christianity, '"the other" is always better or worse, more or less, than oneself or one's people. Identity is forged and known by contrast and

---

[11]   See Anderson (2009), Felder (1991), Sadler (2005) and West (2006: 16–17).

[12]   For a discussion of the construction of the 'other' in a range of biblical texts, see Wills (2008).

competition, not by cooperative relation' (1998: 202). Christianity has thus, albeit unintentionally, fostered the desire and need to exclude.

History has often reflected the exclusionary mentality of these founding texts and doctrines.[13] With the conversion of Constantine and resulting intertwining of Christian ideology and imperial power (Carroll 2001: 171), exclusionary biblical texts came to be exploited for political ends and gained the backing of secular force. Schwartz suggests that because of the extensive dissemination and influence of biblical texts in a post-Constantinian world, they became the 'foundation of a prevailing understanding of ethnic, religious, and national identity as defined negatively, over against others. We are "us" because we are not "them." Israel is not-Egypt'. Biblical narratives have, as a result, been 'deployed against whatever "Canaanites" people wanted to loathe, conquer, or exile' (1997: x). The Middle Ages witnessed episodes of hostility towards those perceived to be strange. Not only were Jews scapegoated for many evils in society, frequently experiencing persecution and expulsion (Wistrich 1999), but the Crusades and Inquisition directed against Muslims and heretics epitomized the cruelty of a stranger-fearing Christianity. Even Kristeva, who claims that the Pauline Church began as a broad-based community, suggests that 'Christian cosmopolitanism bore in its womb the ostracism that excluded the other belief and ended up with the Inquisition' and recognizes that medieval monasteries and churches only offered hospitality to Christians (1991: 86–87).

In modern times, the Church had an ambivalent role in the slave trade (Thomas 1997) and colluded with European imperial expansion involving the military conquest of 'foreigners'. It was also slow to challenge the brutal exclusion of all kinds of difference practised by the Nazi regime in the 1930s and 1940s. Racism has been present within the Church since its beginnings and stories of exclusion and rejection are prolific, such as those told by Caribbean immigrants who arrived in the UK after the Second World War.[14] The Bible has been wielded to justify the oppression and killing of those labelled 'outsiders' in conflict situations in South Africa, Israel and Ulster (Akenson 1992) and the JRS peace education coordinator in Burundi suggests that most of theological justification for 'violent armed re-conquest of power' in his context has emerged from reading the Old Testament (cited in Orobator 2005: 152). Wars fought in the name of Christian faith have been numerous and, as I have already indicated, religion can play a significant part in generating refugee flows. According to McTernan, over half of the conflicts in the world as recently as 2003 had a religious component (2003: xiii) and contemporary religious fundamentalism – Christian as well as that found

---

[13]   Pattison suggests that a 'shadow side' exhibited by Jesus during his ministry became incarnated in the Church (2007: 229–242).

[14]   See Aldred (2005), Barton (2005), Beckford (2000), Byron (2002), Gordon-Carter (2003), Haslam (1996), Isiorho (2002), Leech (2005), Milwood (1997) and Schotsmans (1993); see Anderson (2009) on the ways in which Ezra–Nehemiah has intersected with racism and segregation in the US.

in other faiths – should also not be forgotten (Morris 2006, Armstrong 2001). Termed 'furious religion' by Berger (cited in Forrester 2005b: 35), it tends to lead to the 'othering' of those who hold a different view (Blair 2008). Today in the US, some among the Christian Right have been at the forefront of calls for immigration restriction. They cite Romans 13:1–5 to argue that earthly authorities and laws (including immigration laws) are effectively God's laws and must therefore be obeyed, and claim that Christians have a special duty to family, community and nation and that nation-state boundaries are ordained by God (see, for example, Edwards 2007).

Acknowledging Our Complicity

The attitudes and actions described in Ezra–Nehemiah with regard to so-called foreigners are in good company and Christians need to acknowledge the complicity of their faith tradition in fostering ecologies of fear and endorsing the exclusion of strangers, foreigners and those perceived to be different in all sorts of ways. Pretending that xenophobic passages do not exist or putting exclusionary practices down to misinterpretation are not viable options. Some texts are inherently hostile towards the outsider and were written with the explicit intention of justifying or encouraging their removal or destruction. As Nelson-Pallmeyer puts it, 'religiously justified violence is first and foremost a problem of "sacred" texts and not a problem of misinterpretation' (2005: xiv. Italics omitted). Naming the exclusionary strand within the Christian tradition is a matter of honesty, integrity and theological credibility. In a volatile contemporary world, Forrester has argued that we need a 'more realistic theology', one that engages 'far more directly and urgently with the realities of religion in all their diversity and power, and with theologies some of which may seem primitive and savage, but which have a continuing power to touch the heart and elicit courage, brutality and self-sacrifice as well as love and a passion for justice' (2005b: 24, 9). Doing 'realistic theology' in relation to migration requires an acknowledgement that texts such as Ezra–Nehemiah exist and that they have potential to foster exclusion or worse. It also requires recognition that some Christians today inhabit ecologies where the stranger is feared and suspected and that all, in different ways and at different times, marginalize and oppress strangers.

Exploring Ezra–Nehemiah in Relation to Contemporary Migration and Asylum

The second way in which texts such as Ezra–Nehemiah can be dealt with is to mine them for useful insights. As Nelson-Pallmeyer suggests, there is no need to throw away our 'sacred' texts: 'In fact, we can learn as much or more from their distortions of God, God's power, and human power as we can from their positive insights' (2005: 135). While the context in post-exilic Judah was obviously very different from the twenty-first century Global North and naive parallels cannot be drawn, the characteristics of ecologies of fear and the dynamics of exclusion are to some extent perennial. Interrogating these texts can therefore enhance our understanding of the difficulties experienced by migrants today. The overall message of the text is not to be endorsed or excused, but the detail of the text may deepen our understanding of those who are currently hostile towards foreigners. This reflection on approaching the expulsion of foreign women in Ezra–Nehemiah is helpful:

> [T]here is no denying that the breaking up of families was a horrible thing ... Modern readers are caught up in a dilemma between imposing their own moral standards upon an alien age and negating their legitimate impulse to make moral judgments about human behaviour. Perhaps rather than making moral judgements, it would be more rewarding to attempt to sympathise both with Ezra and those whose marriages were broken up. (Clines 1984: 118)

Entering into the lives of Ezra and Nehemiah and the experiences of those around them is likely to yield more insight than dismissing them out of hand. According to Grabbe, it is important to read 'both synchronically and diachronically' because it 'is by listening to the entire chorus of the text that we begin to tap its riches' (1998: 196–197).

The authors of Ezra–Nehemiah were rooted in and aimed to address the challenging situation in which the Israelite community found itself after the exile. The exile had been a traumatic upheaval and the people in Judah continued to face subjugation under the Persian authorities. The post-exilic context was thus understandably undergirded by anxiety and apprehension: it was one which tended to foster an ecology of fear. This ecology of fear was defined by certain characteristics, and it is these which help to explain why foreigners, and foreign women in particular, were the objects of so much concern and hatred.

Coming to Terms with the Crisis: Restoring a Lost Past and Explaining the Exile

The first significant characteristic to note is the desperate need the Israelite community had to understand and come to terms with the exile. The people were mourning a lost past and looking for an explanation for what had happened. Blenkinsopp suggests that Ezra–Nehemiah was in fact written with the very purpose of giving 'the people back their history, a usable past which will enable them to see that their lives have meaning even in an imperfect world, even in the absence of political autonomy' (1988: 37). Establishing recent events as positive, divinely intended steps in the history of salvation, the authors hoped, would renew Israel's sense of legitimacy and authority (Williamson 1987: 79, Throntveit 1992: 10).

Recapturing a Lost Past: A 'Second Exodus' and Three Projects of Restoration

The people of Israel, particularly those who had been in exile, were desperately trying to recapture and restore a lost past. Establishing continuity with the pre-exilic situation was therefore crucial to them and according to Williamson, accomplished in two ways – through the use of typologies and by pointing out institutional continuities (1987: 81–86). Typologically speaking, the authors decided to portray the return to Judah as a 'second exodus'. The notion of a 'second exodus' came from references to restoration and return in Isaiah (42:13–16, 43:14–21, 52:11–12) and the words *'alah* (Ezra 1:3, 7:6–7, 8:1), meaning to go up, and *ma'alah* (Ezra 7:9), meaning going up, were used to describe the first exodus before they were used to describe the waves of return in Ezra–Nehemiah (Throntveit 1992: 44, Klein 1999: 678). Ezra probably chose to 'go up' to Jerusalem on the first day of the first month (Ezra 7:9) because this was when the Passover was commemorated, a festival that specifically recalled the first exodus. A number of other significant connections between the return from exile in Ezra–Nehemiah and the exodus include a concern for proper worship, Moses' delegation of authority (Exod. 18:13–27) being comparable to Ezra appointing judges (Ezra 7:25), the common themes of despoiling Egyptians and slavery (Ezra 9:1, 9) and the failure to keep the covenant (Throntveit 1992: 45–51).

Turning to institutional continuity, three separate projects of restoration were initiated by the returnees in Ezra–Nehemiah: they attempted to rebuild the temple, the community and the walls. Each project aimed to ensure and demonstrate that the present would be exactly like the past. The restoration of temple worship is portrayed in ways that clearly link it with the first exodus *and* the first temple, and comparisons made between the new and old temples are manifold.[15] The altar is put on its original foundations, the first sacrifices reinstituted were regular morning and evening burnt offerings and the first festival the people celebrate on their return is the Feast of Booths (Ezra 3:3–4, Exod. 29:38–42, Lev. 23:42–43, Throntveit 1992: 23, Klein 1999: 691). The first temple had been dedicated in connection with this festival (2 Chron. 5:3) and the celebration of the Passover (Ezra 6:19) provides another link with the exodus (Klein 1999: 714).[16] The community was also restored through the reinstatement of the law and by clarifying who legitimately

---

[15]   People returned with cultic vessels and other gifts (Ezra 1:7–11, 7:14–20, 8:24–34), evoking memories of those carried on the exodus (cf. Exod. 3:21–22, 12:35–36) and restoring what Nebuchadnezzar had taken away from the Temple of Solomon (Throntveit 1992: 16–18). Williamson has pointed out how the very language in Ezra 1:6–11 consciously intends to evoke the exodus (1987: 84–85). Miller and Hayes point to conflicting traditions about the temple restoration and who was responsible (2006: 512–513). The condition of the temple before its restoration is also unclear: it may have been totally destroyed but Jeremiah 41 indicates that the altar may still have been standing (Provan et al. 2003: 292). The temple was finished in c.515 BCE.

[16]   Ezra 3:7–8 reveals that the cedars of Lebanon are paid for and brought through Joppa in the same way (2 Chron. 2:16), masons from Sidon and Tyre are used (1 Chron. 22:4) and work begins in second month (1 Kgs 6:1) (Throntveit 1992: 24, Blenkinsopp

belonged to it.[17] Re-establishing the law was the primary task of Ezra (7.10) and its importance is emphasized by its climactic position in Nehemiah 8 (Williamson 1987: 76). Extended lists of community members were designed to articulate who legitimately belonged to the 'people of Israel' by demonstrating their links to pre-exilic families. As Throntveit notes, in Ezra 2 people were named by their family names, either with reference to a pre-exilic ancestor (2:3–20) or to a pre-exilic town (2:21–33) (1992: 19). These links were more ideological than real, as the authors wished to demonstrate that the post-exilic community and traditions in Jerusalem were descended directly from and almost identical to the pre-exilic 'old Israel' (Blenkinsopp 2009: 83–84).[18] Rebuilding the wall around Jerusalem, the task given to Nehemiah, was the third aspect of restoration. This was as much about restoring the 'essential unity' of the community as it was about defence of the land (Throntveit 1992: 78).[19]

The desire to restore is a feature of most ecologies of fear. As I suggested in Chapter 5, many people today also hanker after a mythical lost national past in relation to immigration and asylum. Such an emphasis on restoration is, however, almost always problematic as the desire to restore is more about nostalgia than renewal. Fear tends to slide people backwards into the familiar rather than propel them forwards into the new. While finding a way to grieve as 'communities of honest sadness' and holding onto the old (Brueggemann 1997: 4–5. Italics omitted) may be important for those experiencing exile of any kind, it can stunt communities if this is all that is done. As Mursell suggests, memory should serve three functions: it gives individuals and communities a story, past and identity; it defines people over against prevailing system of control; and it helps them to imagine and anticipate a new future (2005: 33–35). Too strong a focus on restoration tends to restrict the possibilities of memory to the first two. Ezra–

1988: 100). The 12 male goats (Ezra 6:17) express the completeness and universality of the newly dedicated temple, representing the 12 tribes of Israel.

[17] There is debate concerning what exactly the 'Law' was that Ezra was seeking to restore in Ezra 7. Usually presumed to be the Torah, the law of Moses, Blenkinsopp argues that it is in fact 'Deuteronomic law supplemented by ritual legislation in the Pentateuchal corpora conventionally designated P and H' (1988: 155, 152–157). Soggin suggests other possibilities, including that it may have been law found in the 'Temple scroll' at Qumran (1999: 314).

[18] The almost identical list in Nehemiah 7:5–73a reinforced the connection. Ezra 2:2 and Nehemiah 7:7 list 12 leaders and in Ezra 8, an emphasis on the number 12 and its multiples signifies a 'theology of community', implying 'that the Israel of Ezra's time is the true Israel, the complete Israel' (Klein 1999: 731). The figure of Zerubbabel may also have been mentioned in order to emphasize continuity in leadership, as he is elsewhere depicted as a 'messianic' figure and a member of the Davidic family (for example Zech. 4, Hag. 2:20–23) (Miller and Hayes 2006: 518).

[19] The celebration at the completion of wall (Neh. 12:27–43) lists Levitical musicians and cultic personnel and is in 'keeping with liturgical orthopraxy' (Blenkinsopp 1988: 343–345).

Nehemiah may have gained a new story and identity in the face of Persian control and past oppression, but a new future was neither imagined nor enacted. The only future they seemed able to conceive was a return to a mythical, rose-tinted and pure past – the past as it should have been.

Blaming mingling with foreigners
As well as wishing to recapture a mythical past, the authors of Ezra-Nehemiah were looking for someone or something to blame for its loss and for the exile. The destruction of Jerusalem and deportations that had taken place were believed to be a divine punishment for unfaithfulness. The community had transgressed a law and been defiled as a result, and God had worked his anger out through the actions of the King of Babylon (Ezra 5:12).[20] God had used foreign nations on numerous previous occasions to chastise and rebuke Israel (for example 1 Chron. 5:26, Isa. 10:5, Amos 6:14) and marriages with foreigners had been forbidden a number of times (Exod. 34:15–16, Deut. 7:3–4). While some prominent Israelites had married outside their own people, including Moses (Exod. 2:21; Num. 12:1) and David (2 Sam. 3:3), foreigners and foreign wives in particular were usually seen as a grave threat to faith and purity. For example, 'foreign women' are held responsible for the undoing of Solomon (1 Kgs 11:4, cf. Neh. 13:26). The flouting of these prohibitions was fixed upon by Ezra, Nehemiah and those around them as an explanation for what had happened. The word *ma'al* (faithlessness), used in Hebrew to indicate a serious sin, is mentioned five times specifically in relation to intermarriage in Ezra (9:2, 4, 10:2, 6, 10, Throntveit 1992: 52) and the penitence and confession the people offer is directly connected with the sin of foreign association (Neh. 9:1–2).[21] The authors believed that relating to those outside their community too closely had caused their recent trauma. The overwhelming urge to blame when a disaster strikes or society seems to fall apart is a recurrent one – an urge evident in the scapegoating of migrants today.

The 'Foreigners' … or 'Peoples of the Land' … or 'Strangers'

The second characteristic of post-exilic Judah to note is that those termed 'foreigners' were probably not in fact members of other nations at all. Who, then, were they? While it is never entirely clear 'whether "foreigners" denotes truly alien peoples, like Moabites or Ammonites, or whether it refers to all those, including Jews, who were not directly related to the people who had returned from exile' (Klein 1999: 850), most commentators agree that it was the latter. The authors of Ezra–Nehemiah, sympathizing with those who had been in exile, were using the

---

20   See also 2 Chron. 36:17. Smith cites Ezek. 20 and 22 as evidence that the exile is regarded as a punishment for defilement (1991: 90).

21   Nehemiah 13:1–3 indicates that it could rather have been the law in Deuteronomy 23:3–8 forbidding the admission of any Ammonite or Moabite up to the tenth generation to the assembly of the Lord that had been broken.

terms 'foreigners' and 'peoples of the land' interchangeably to refer to anyone who had not been in exile. The *am ha'arets* (peoples of the land) were clearly distinguished from the *golah* community (returned exiles) (for example Ezra 4:4) and it is these 'peoples of the land', not primarily people of other nations, from whom the former exiles wished to separate. Ezra, Nehemiah and their fellow exiles considered themselves to be 'special' (Smith 1991: 83) and holier than those who remained in Judah. McKinlay explains:

> in the eyes of the returnees ... these surviving inhabitants of the land, referred to now as 'the peoples of the land' to distinguish them from those who had experienced the purifying ordeal of exile, were not a part of the true Israel. But not only were they not a part of the Israelite community, they were now considered pollutants, and regarded as virtual Canaanites. (2004: 27)

The 'true Israel' is portrayed only as those who returned from exile. Everyone else was deemed an outsider (Klein 1999: 668, Blenkinsopp 2009: 83–84). Ezra and Nehemiah were thus dealing with what they perceived as the 'enemy without' (foreigners) *and* the 'enemy within' (Knoppers 2007). The description offered by Douglas is particularly apposite: the 'people of the land' were 'the immigrants, refugees and displaced persons who now inhabited Judah' and the exclusions applied to these and to the residents of former northern kingdom (2001: 36). [22]

When it comes to the foreign women who were to be dismissed, it seems probable that Ezra and Nehemiah were also primarily concerned about Judahite women who came from families which had not experienced exile (Eskenazi and Judd 1994: 269–270, Blenkinsopp 2009: 64). [23] It is significant that those most vociferously labelled 'foreign' and excluded were *women*. Camp suggests that '[w]hile it is possible that "Israelite" men were marrying outsider women more often than vice versa, it seems just as likely that we are dealing here with the gendered rhetoric of strangeness as much as anything else' (2000: 335; see also Anderson 2009: 56). [24] Being 'foreign' in Ezra–Nehemiah is intimately linked with

---

[22] Throntveit claims that the 'peoples of the land' were descendants of people planted in the northern kingdom by the Assyrians under their policy of deportation after fall of Samaria 722 BCE (2 Kgs 17:1–6) (1992: 25).

[23] Camp notes that *zar* and *nokri*, the terms used to describe the women (for example Ezra 10:10–11, Neh. 9:2), have 'a variety of connotations, often overlapping, in the Hebrew Bible. They can refer to persons of foreign nationality, to persons who are outside one's own family household, to persons who are not members of the priestly caste, and to deities and practices that fall outside the covenant relationship with Yhwh' (2000: 40–41).

[24] The focus on foreign *wives* could represent a 'sociological situation in which Judean men were marrying foreign women but not giving their daughters as brides to foreign men, perhaps because the foreign brides brought as dowries actual land holdings titularly claimed by members of the *Golah* community' (Camp 1991: 24). It does seem likely that many men returned from exile without families and so needed to marry women from those who had stayed in Judah. It could also be because wives become part of the husband's family,

being female. Women were on the 'outside' in a patriarchal society and the tensions between the *golah* community and the *am ha'arets*, for reasons which will become clear later in this chapter, had little to do with them. So-called foreign wives acted as convenient pegs on which men could hang their intra-communal tension.

Given that it was a conflict between and about the *am ha'arets* and the *golah* community in post-exilic Jerusalem that resulted in the demands to end contact and intermarriage between these two groups and with other outsiders, the issue seems to have been less to do with outright xenophobia and more about power-play between competing related groups within a fragile and bruised community. The worst problem for Ezra and Nehemiah was not the people completely 'other' to them – foreigners from different nations who spoke different languages and had different gods – but those who were close to them and yet now seemed strange.

Useful light is thrown on the contemporary migration situation. Underlying the repeated talk about keeping immigrants and asylum seekers out because of the damage they are doing to Britain or the US rumble tensions between political parties, socio-economic classes, liberals and communitarians, globalists and localists and people of different religious views. Migrants, like the foreign wives in Ezra–Nehemiah, often find themselves caught in the crossfire of conflicts that have little to do with them. They simply happen to embody elements of the groups or issues deemed problematic. Questioning the subtext of the situation is therefore vital. What is going on beneath the conflict between members of established communities and those seeking sanctuary? The fears identified in Chapter 5 may be a presenting symptom of underlying tensions between different classes or groups within the established population or they could be a secondary consequence of racism felt towards second or third generation Black and Asian immigrants. Is immigration the field on which an ideological battle between liberal humanitarians and conservative nationalists is being played out? Or does the fact that asylum seekers are *strangers* lie at the heart of their problems? It is also interesting to remember that while Middle Eastern asylum-seeking males are often particular targets for hostility today, women still bear the practical brunt of discriminatory policies and systems, as they do in Ezra–Nehemiah.

A Religio-Ethnic Necessity: Purifying and Unifying the Community

Why was it was that many in the *golah* community wished to exclude the so-called 'foreigners' or peoples of the land? Ideologically speaking, the *golah* community believed that it was essential to eject all that polluted their religious life and to establish a clear sense of group identity. They wished to be pure. For those inhabiting a post-exilic ecology of fear, expelling the 'peoples of the land' was a religious *and* ethnic necessity. Turning to Smith-Christopher:

---

meaning a greater danger of foreign practices being imported than if daughters left to marry foreign men (Camp 1991: 24). These reasons are not, however, incompatible with women also being used as scapegoats when it came to the writing of the text.

Ezra defined the terms of the marriage crisis both ethnically (by citing the national/ethnic categories of Canaanite, Hivite, Perizzite, etc.) and religiously (by citing such terms as 'the Holy Seed'). In this case, acceptable marriages would be those within a religious and ethnically defined group ... Ezra was engaged in a serious dispute *with other Priests* on the issue of 'foreigner' and 'insider'. (1996: 124–125)

Smith-Christopher notes an emphasis on priestly terminology and concerns in Ezra. The word used to describe the 'abominations' of the foreign peoples usually refers to ritual or religious sins (for example Ezek. 7:3, 16:22) and the use of the priestly term *bdl*, meaning 'to make a separation' (for example Ezra 10:11), 'reflects the priestly writer's obsessions with "separations" between the pure and impure' (1996: 125).[25] In Ezra, this religious term is used 'to accomplish social ends, namely the avoidance of social "pollution"', a factor unsurprising for a group under extreme stress. The exiles, having experienced intense social and political threats as a minority in Babylon, would have felt the need to create a 'culture of resistance' to preserve their cultural and ethnic identity. A 'minority group consciousness characterized by social borders delimiting the "inside" and "outside" of the group, and also by concerns for purity and group integrity' would have resulted (Smith 1991: 83–86). He explains how this tightly defined identity would have persisted on their return to Jerusalem:

> The exiles formed a community not only self-consciously defined – a 'Hibakusha' community – a community of 'survivors' who returned to Palestine, but who also formulated a theology of innocence and purity against the defilement of those who remained behind complete with social structures to accommodate the communal solidarity requirements. (Smith 1991: 97)[26]

It is significant that the term 'survivors', *hannish'ar* (Ezra 1:4), is used of those who returned, as it has the theological connotation of 'remnant' (cf. 1 Chron. 13:2, Neh. 1:2–3) (Klein 1999: 678). The word indicated their holiness.[27] The exclusion of foreign women in Ezra can thus be understood as an act of identity reaffirmation though practices of 'boundary maintenance' (Smith-Christopher 1994: 257).

Religious concerns also seem to have rattled and motivated Nehemiah. The term *bdl* is found in Nehemiah 9:2 and Nehemiah made a number of explicitly religious reforms. He expelled Tobiah the Ammonite from a special chamber in

---

[25]   See Smith (1989: 145–149) for more on the use of *bdl*.

[26]   'Hibakusha' was a term used by Japanese survivors of the atom bomb.

[27]   Other words and phrases used indicating holiness include 'holy seed' (Ezra 9:2), 'Jews' (e.g. Ezra 1:11, 8.35, Neh. 7:6) and 'the assembly of the Exile' – *qāhāl haggōlā* – which is unique to Ezra–Nehemiah. It suggests a corporate identity 'not definable by a territorial or political referent' (Hoglund 1991: 66) and therefore one more to do with ethnic and cultic purity.

the temple (Neh. 13:4–9), reinstalled Levites (Neh. 13:10–13, 30), re-emphasized the Sabbath and suggested that mixed marriages were an act of evil and treachery against God (Neh. 13:27). The conflict between the *golah* community and the *am ha'arets* was probably a conflict between strict Yahwists who 'sought to bring the priesthood and religious establishment into conformity with a conservative position, a position based primarily on the laws of the book of Deuteronomy' and priestly Yahwists who were far less rigid. According to Miller and Hayes, that Eliashib the High Priest had installed Tobiah 'demonstrates that the high priest and priesthood were far more open to religious relationships with foreigners' than was Nehemiah who expelled him (2006: 534, Douglas 2004: 5).

This said, it is important to reiterate how intimately interwoven concerns regarding ethnic, cultural and religious identity were.[28] Blenkinsopp notes that the returnees performed 'a religious colonization with a definite religious agenda, namely, the creation of a self-segregated, ritually pure society', but, given that many of those who were excluded were YHWH-worshippers, 'what is at issue is a theory of *ritual ethnicity* rather than simply what we would call religious affiliation' (2009: 229, 67. My italics). He argues that the marriage programme was designed to confront the problem of 'how to maintain the characteristic way of life, the religious traditions, even the language (cf. Neh. 13:23) of a community, against the threat of assimilation' (1988: 201, cf. 363). That half of the offspring of mixed marriages were believed not to be able to speak the language of Judah would have made a significant dent in sense of cultural collective self (Neh. 13:24, Ruiz 2009). The loss of Israelite geopolitical autonomy also meant that the people were more likely to use religious beliefs and practices to ground their self-identity (McNutt 1999: 209). Wills notes the occurrence of the terms 'Judah' and 'Judean' (*yehudim*) over 30 times in Nehemiah 1–7, arguing that this 'heightened sense of the term … *affirms* group identity': 'The We of ideal Israel is constituted in response to the Other' (2008: 80).[29]

This preoccupation with religio-ethnic identity led, incidentally, to conscious and dangerous manipulation of the existing scriptural tradition. Olyan has shown how earlier texts such as Leviticus 18:24–30 and Deuteronomy 23:3–9 were elaborated and 'interpreted in Ezra–Nehemiah in an expansive manner that allows them to provide support for the exclusivist program of the leaders of the returnees'. Whereas before, anyone with an Israelite father was considered an Israelite (for example Gen. 46:20), now an alien had become a person 'with any foreign blood' (2000: 88–89; see also Blenkinsopp 1988: 175, Fishbane 1985: 115–119, 143).

---

[28] Scholars debate whether religious and/or ethnic-cultural identity was the primary concern; see Blenkinsopp (1988: 176, 185), C. Hayes (2002: 7–8, 10, 30–34), Throntveit (1992: 57) and Eskenazi and Judd (1994: 275) on the ways in which these concerns intersect. Clines (1984: 116–118) and Sparks (1998: 318–319) argue that it was more exclusively a religious matter.

[29] *Yehudim* in Ezra–Nehemiah is variously translated as Judean or Jew, depending on when a scholar believes a clear sense of Jewish identity emerged.

The framing of intermarriage in terms of cultic pollution was innovative and 'consolidate[d] the rhetoric against exogamy with the rhetoric of uncleanness in a new and powerful way' (Camp 2000: 56).[30]

At a time when British national identity and other socio-economic and political identities seem increasingly fragile, the longing to define who 'we' are has become more pronounced, just as it seems to have become for the *golah* community in Ezra–Nehemiah. Migrants, including asylum seekers, are convenient 'outsiders' against whom a sense of 'insider' identity can be reasserted. Ethnic and religious factors remain a significant part of this process, as does the framing of the outsiders as pollutants. Those seeking asylum are, in many minds, all 'non-white' and 'non-Christian'.[31] It is not coincidental that they are often labelled 'scum' and associated with disease. Moreover, while the public discourse around asylum may not be framed in explicitly religious terms, latent fears about the de-Christianization of Britain and overt fears about its Islamization should not be underestimated. Concerns over the dilution of 'white' Britishness and Christian moral values (even if not named as such) may be more important factors than is usually allowed.

A Socio-Economic Necessity: Material Hardship and Power Struggles

The call for the exclusion of the peoples of the land and the dismissal of foreign wives was not, however, simply an ideological matter. Jerusalem was a hotbed of social and economic conflict and seethed with struggles for political power. Many were also facing multiple economic pressures. For the *golah* community, excluding the 'peoples of the land' and prohibiting mixed marriages were perceived to be social and economic necessities.

Land ownership is likely to have been a significant bone of contention between the *golah* community and the *am ha'arets*.[32] The aristocratic exiles returned to Judah to find that their property had been taken over by former peasants. The agrarian poor who had gained control of the estates of the deportees when they were in Babylon (Jer. 39:10) and now 'claimed by right of 50 years of sweat that same land' (Camp 2000: 31) clashed with the descendants of their former owners. There was not enough land to go round and a classic 'class-oriented conflict'

---

[30]   McKinlay describes what happens in Ezra–Nehemiah as a 'repeat of that discursive division of Israelite and Canaanite, that is, a feature both of the Deuteronomistic History and texts such as Lev 18:24–30, and which is now reinterpreted to refer to all intermarriage' (2004: 28).

[31]   This is not to suggest that it is only white Britons who are anti-asylum and racist. Caribbean, Asian and African immigrants who arrived in the 1950s and 1960s sometimes express antipathy towards newer arrivals.

[32]   Provan and colleagues disagree, arguing that there is no evidence for the suggestion that those returning came into conflict with those who remained and that there was plenty of land (2003: 294). Hoglund similarly argues that the Persians were reorganizing all land and the conflict could not therefore have been over land (1991).

ensued (Smith 1991: 96, Blenkinsopp 1988: 60, Yee 2003). Heavy financial burdens placed by relatively wealthy Jerusalemites on anyone trying to work the land would have exacerbated these tensions, and rural families also had to provide the temple cult with livestock, grain and wood (Neh. 10:35) and support a large tax-exempt clerical bureaucracy (Ezra 7:24) (Blenkinsopp 1988: 68–69, 258). The internal uprising mentioned in Nehemiah 5 suggests that people suffered financially because of their unpaid work on the wall and the creditors demanding payment and interest were fellow Israelites. They did so despite a drought and crop failure (Klein 1999: 779–780, Blenkinsopp 1988: 257–258). These multiple demands were made at an already difficult time. Subsistence farmers of the Judean highlands had experienced bad harvests and other calamities (for example Hag. 1:6, 10–11, Joel) and destruction and depopulation during the Babylonian period would have damaged trade, depleted the skilled artisan class and decreased productivity. The people had to pay taxes to the Persian emperor (Neh. 5:4) and Persian fiscal policy was 'harsh and unenlightened'. The people would have been forced to borrow from loan sharks at high interest rates, mortgage fields, vineyards and olive orchards, and could even have found themselves reduced to slavery (Blenkinsopp 1988: 66–67, 2009: 113–114, McNutt 1999: 196).[33] The new wall also increased the symbolic and real class separation between rich and poor by creating an urban–rural barrier (Berquist 1995: 114, Yee 2003: 143).

Struggles over the land were about more than just the money. They were also wrangles for social status and political control. In the post-exilic community, the temple was the central institution. Priests were economically and politically powerful and a man's family background, status, property and participation in the temple cult were intimately linked (Klein 1999: 747, Washington 1994: 231, Blenkinsopp 2009: 122).[34] This social system probably developed from the one adopted in exile and remained in the exiles' control when they brought it back with them to Judah (Berquist 1995). Indeed, 'jealously protective of its status and privileges', the *golah* community had two goals on their return: 'to win back the land redistributed to the peasantry … [and] to rebuild and secure control of the temple as the sociopolitical and religious center of gravity of their existence' (Blenkinsopp 1991: 53, 2009: 80). This was perhaps understandable given their lack of autonomy and control in Babylon and the probable supportive connections they had with the Persian authorities (see Blenkinsopp 1991: 50–51, Berquist 1995: 15–16). The returnees managed to manoeuvre themselves into a socially and economically privileged position and their initiative in rebuilding the temple and ongoing 'control of the "redemptive media"' meant that the *yehudim* retained higher socio-economic status than those who had never left. Their desire to maintain this status

---

[33]   For a discussion of other ways in which Persian economic policy may have increased the economic vulnerability of those in Judah and competition among them, see Hoglund (1991).

[34]   The *golah*-assembly (Ezra 2:64, Neh. 7:66) could take away your property as well as excommunicate you (Ezra 10:8) (Blenkinsopp 1991: 45).

probably explains why they refused help from the peoples of the land in rebuilding the temple and the wall (Ezra 4:3, Neh. 2:20) as it would have meant relinquishing some control (Blenkinsopp 1988: 68–69, 107, 226). It is hardly surprising that such obvious power-mongering by the returnees was met with resentment by many of those who had formerly been in control during the exile. The *am ha'arets* were understandably reluctant to give way to the *golah* newcomers.

Intermarriage as economic and political threat

The desire of the *yehudim* to hold onto their socio-economic power coupled with the fact that women were able to hold and inherit property at this time (Eskenazi 1992, Washington 1994: 235–236) meant that mixed marriages would have been regarded by them as particularly dangerous. Intermarriage was initially vital for the returnees. It provided them with the possibility of economic gain – the 'elites exchanged or parlayed their high status as imperial agents in order to gain access to the land' – while also offering socio-political advance to the *am ha'arets* – the 'natives exchanged their land to "marry up" into the ranks of the returning elite'. Yet, once they had obtained the land, the *golah* community practised endogamy – or in-group marriage – to hold onto it (Yee 2003: 144–145). They did this because intermarriage then became an economic threat: 'Exogamous marriages could threaten encroachment on the land holdings of the congregation, since "foreign" women and their children might claim land belonging to the temple collective' (Klein 1999: 747). Mixed marriage raised the potential for the transfer of one ethnic group's property to another, explaining why it was to be punished by the forfeiting of property (Ezra 10.8) (Hoglund 1991: 67). The problem was also, at another level, political in that foreign marriage

> threatened the stability of the authority structure: intermarriage for the sake of upward mobility could bring outside challenges to the power of the leadership group and, further, call into question whether this group could maintain power over the generations if inheritances passed out of the families of 'pure Israelites'. (Camp 1991: 18)

Several members of the Jerusalem community seem to have been guilty. Nehemiah, particularly in 6:18 and 13:28, gives 'the impression of treacherous power-grabbing in both temple and government through strategic marriages' and it is probable that some of the returning exiles hoped to gain advantages by '"marrying up" among those defined as "outsiders"' (Smith-Christopher 1994: 258, 260). A 'network of relationships cemented by *mariages de convenance* between the Sanballats, Tobiads, and important elements of the lay and clerical aristocracy in Jerusalem' was established (Blenkinsopp 1988: 365) and Nehemiah and his associates feared that this would undermine their power base and special authority.[35]

---

[35] As Eskenazi and Judd point out, we do not know how many members of community actually married so-called foreign women, what proportion of the population

Contemporary hostility towards asylum seekers and other migrants often takes root in fears of social, economic and political marginalization and when people feel that they have to compete with too many others for material resources. Moreover, while contemporary excluders are the powerful majority and asylum seekers the minority, exclusion may also result when those with little social or political power grip onto it tightly. The BNP is keen to play on fears to bolster their own position and indeed most people in Britain today, particularly those living in deprived communities and asylum seekers themselves, feel that they have little power and do all that they can to hold onto what they have. We all take steps to bolster our status and control our circumstances, albeit in different ways. The narrative of Ezra–Nehemiah encourages us never to underestimate the effect that very real social and economic concerns can have on the way people react to those perceived to be strangers.

A Combination of Ideological and Material Causes: A 'Multiply Stressed' Context Then and Now

A final thought on the reasons for the exclusion of the 'peoples of the land' must be added at this point. Rather than being the result of solely cultic-ethnic or solely economic-political concerns, Camp suggests that the desire to exclude foreign wives likely reflects 'a sociopsychological reality of men threatened by a *multiply stressed social situation*, including internal religio-political power struggles, economically oppressive foreign rule, and the pressures of cultural assimilation' (1991: 29. My italics). Thus it was not a matter of *either* being concerned with religious and ethnic identity *or* being concerned with power, status and economic resources. Religious and ethnic concerns co-existed with and were exacerbated by socio-economic ones (Sparks 1998: 296). Smith helpfully summarizes the situation: the returnees formed 'a self-conscious community that [was] occupied with self-preservation, both as a pure community in a religious sense, and also in a material sense' (1991: 97).

Similarly today, it is not possible to attribute hostility towards migrants to one universally applicable factor. For some people British national identity may be most important and for others fears regarding competition for jobs will be overriding. In certain churches, concerns about the theology brought by newcomers may intertwine with anxieties about breaking the law or having less attention from the minister to discourage their welcome of people seeking sanctuary. Material and ideological factors also often combine in subtle and subconscious ways.

---

they constituted or what happened to the marriages (1994: 267); see Blenkinsopp (1988: 197–200) and Clines (1984: 131) for a discussion of numbers.

Hints of Ambiguity: How Widespread and Successful was this Approach to 'Foreigners'?

Despite the evident animosity towards so-called 'foreigners' in the text, relationships and identities on the ground were, in reality, highly complex and ambiguous. The Ezra–Nehemiah group demonstrated positive attitudes towards 'outsiders' at times, depicting foreigners as God's instruments: God prompts Cyrus to send the people of Israel back to Jerusalem all three times (Ezra 1:1, 1:5, 7:6, Neh. 2:8, Throntveit 1992: 14–15). Members of the *golah* community also astutely recognize that their situation depends on certain powerful foreigners and are diplomatic when necessary. For example in a letter from the Persian governor of the province Beyond the River to King Darius, the Jewish elders are reported as having used deferential terminology familiar to Persian officials in relation to the king – 'God of heaven' – and they claim to be following his orders and Cyrus' decree (Ezra 5:11–17) (Throntveit 1992: 33). This inclusivity went beyond a cynical courting of favour from great foreigners. In Ezra 6:21, foreigners were allowed to participate in the Passover Feast.

What is more, Nehemiah worked with some of the *am ha'arets* living in Jerusalem, having been motivated to return through news from relatives (Neh. 1:2–3), and the rebuilding project he inaugurates is community-wide. Nehemiah seems happy for trading with peoples of the land to take place as long as it is not on the Sabbath or holy days and he hosts people 'from the nations around' at his table (Neh. 5:17). Craftsmen of Tyre and Sidon – Canaanite/Phoenician cities – were welcomed as workers (Ezra 3:7, Wills 2008: 63). Nehemiah's prohibition of foreigners entering the temple is really directed at Tobiah, who had a Yahwist name and was related through marriage to Judean leaders (Neh. 13:4–9, 6:18). Wills argues that Nehemiah was simply 'othering' Tobiah, a leading trader and far from an 'outsider', by pushing him 'well over an imaginary border' and giving him a foreign identity as an Ammonite. Sanballat, governor of Samaria, a northern Israelite, was similarly Yahwist and pushed over an 'imaginary border' through labelling as a 'Horonite' (2008: 72–73).[36] The sense of the 'other' was probably also constantly shifting and unclear. Whereas in Ezra 1–6, the 'Others were the external nations on the northern periphery of Judah', in the Ezra Memoir (Ezra

---

[36]   Klein points out that Sanballat's daughter married into the family of the high priest (Neh. 13:28), he had contacts in Jerusalem (Neh. 6:10–14) and two of his children mentioned in the Elephantine Papyri have Yahwistic names. Tobiah was also tied to the Jerusalem nobility and priesthood (Neh. 6:17–19, 13:4) and was probably a royal official, maybe governor of Ammon. He may have had some kind of temporary authority over Judah in co-operation/under supervision of Samaritans. His son also had a Yahwistic name (Neh. 6:18) (1999: 757). Williamson suggests that Tobiah was a junior colleague of Sanballat in Samaria, and was only associated with Ammon through his ancestry (1985: 183–184). A Tobiah is mentioned in a list of early returnees (Ezra 2:60), confusing distinctions between groups in Jerusalem further still (Camp 2000: 334).

7–10, Neh. 8–10), it seems that 'the Other on the horizon has been discovered among us, in the form of foreign women and their children' (Wills 2008: 68).[37]

It is also doubtful whether the expulsions did, in fact, happen. They may have existed only within the discourse, being far more important in terms of defining insider-outsider identity than they were in practice. No punishments are mentioned for failing to divorce so-called foreign wives and attempts to enforce such divorces probably failed. Blenkinsopp, noting the 'uncharacteristically abrupt' conclusion in Ezra 10:44 to such an apparently important episode, sees the most likely explanation for this as its lack of success (1988: 200). What is more, the 'practice of marrying outside the community was still widespread during Nehemiah's administration, and it would be impossible to explain the remarkable demographic expansion of Judaism in the following centuries if this measure had taken hold' (Blenkinsopp 1988: 200; see also 2009: 71). Camp asks, 'Was, then, the idea of compulsory divorce merely a useful political ploy designed for rhetorical appeal to the radicals but for failure in practice? Or was it even a creation of the editor of Ezra–Nehemiah, working at some later day?' (2000: 336).

The extensive opposition to Nehemiah indicates that many living in Judah at this time differed in their approach to foreigners and views on 'mixed marriage'. Ezra 10:12–14 suggests a 'reluctance to implement the proposal' and although only four men are said to have opposed the separations, the fact that they are mentioned at all indicates that they were a significant minority (Blenkinsopp 1988: 193–194, 2009: 68). Only around 110 women out of a total population of approximately 20,000 seem to have been affected (Ezra 10:18–44, Anderson 2009: 57–58, Wills 2008: 75). It is possible that the '"mixed-marriages" were considered "mixed" *only* by Ezra and his supporters, and not in the first case by the married persons themselves' (Smith-Christopher 1994: 247) and that Ezra and Nehemiah were just avid extremists. Indeed, Blenkinsopp suggests that Ezra's reaction (9:3–5) and Nehemiah's (13:25) are both 'intemperate' (1988: 177, 364).[38]

Ambiguities in relation to foreigners can be glimpsed in the Global North today. While some foreigners are regarded as a threat, others are welcomed and

---

[37] According to Smith-Christopher, Ezra and Nehemiah differ in what is meant by the term 'foreigner': 'the Ezra texts deal with an *intra-Jewish debate* while it is only the Nehemiah texts that actually discuss "foreigners" in any modern sense of the term' (1996: 123). The 'peoples of the land' are defined in Ezra 9:1 as Canaanites, Hittites, Perizzites, Jebusites, Ammonites, Moabites, Egyptians and Amorites – a stereotypical and traditional list of enemies – suggesting that the author is distinguishing pejoratively between those who had not been in exile and those who had (1996: 126); see Gen. 15:19–20, Exod. 3:8, 17, Deut. 7:1 and Judg. 3:5 for conventional lists of enemies. In Nehemiah, the issue is actually much more about 'real' foreigners (1996: 126). A word used here is '*erev* (Neh. 13:3), which probably means immigrants rather than mixture and refers most naturally to 'aliens without any Jewish ancestor' (Clines 1984: 237).

[38] See Carroll (1992), Farisani (2004c) and Fewell (2004) to hear some opposing voices. C. Hayes (2002) explores the variety of attitudes to intermarriage existing at different times.

enthused about. The points-based immigration system is testimony to this. It is also easy to split individuals or groups of foreigners artificially. People want their skills or aspects of their culture, but not other aspects of their culture nor the impact that their presence may have on health services or schooling. We may enjoy Thai food, employ Polish builders or use Cameroonian textiles, but resent the presence of Thais, Poles and Cameroonians. This confusion of attitudes exists within most people. I have heard myself speak in the same conversation about frustrations concerning African time-keeping and how much I have learned from African ways of life. It is also not uncommon to hear people speak in a derogatory way about asylum seekers but warmly about 'Joy, my friend from Zimbabwe'. Though the most hostile voices are the loudest, mixed attitudes within every segment of the established community are discernible. Finding ways to own this ambiguity and hear more positive voices is crucial.

Summary

This chapter has discussed one kind of response to strangers and strangeness found in the Bible – responses made by those inhabiting an ecology of fear. Ezra, Nehemiah and the *golah* community they led were trying to come to terms with the crisis of exile and rebuild their lives under Persian domination. Their position was precarious and this led them to react to the 'peoples of the land' who had been left behind – now strangers to them – in hostile and excluding ways. While such approaches should be denounced, it is also valuable to try to understand them. The *golah* community was looking for someone to blame for loss and the exile and the *am ha'arets* women were an easy target. It was also keen to maintain religious purity and identity and there were practical conflicts over power, land and money between the two groups. Possible connections between the post-exilic context in Judah and the contemporary ecology of fear in relation to migration raise significant challenges, which I will explore in the conclusion.

Chapter 8
Ecology of Faith: Ruth and the Syro-Phoenician Woman

> In every encounter with every stranger we are given the chance to meet the living Christ ... Through the stranger our view of self, of world, of God is deepened and expanded. Through the stranger we are given a chance to find ourselves. And through the stranger, God finds us and offers us the gift of wholeness in the midst of our estranged lives.
>
> (Palmer 1983: 67, 70)

The ecology of fear is not the only context outlined in the Bible for responding to strangers. A very different thread of material, produced by those inhabiting an ecology of faith, calls people to be open, welcoming and compassionate. This chapter explores this second thread and identifies two interrelated sub-strands – passages which exhort readers to care for 'aliens' in their midst and narratives which encourage the recognition and embrace of the stranger as a life-bringer. The stories of Ruth in the Hebrew Bible and the Syro-Phoenician Woman in the Gospel of Mark (7:24–30) provide examples. What insights do they offer into how established populations should engage with people on the move? An ecology of faith indicates a way of living and being which is trusting and compassionate towards those who are unknown. 'Faith' is used to indicate the opposite of fear rather than a system of religious doctrines and practices. It means 'complete trust or confidence in someone or something' and to be faithful means to be 'loyal, constant and steadfast' (Pearsall 1998: 660).

I privilege texts produced by ecologians of faith above those produced by ecologians of fear, seeing them as a source of potential wisdom.[1] But why take advice from the authors of Ruth and Mark and not from those of Ezra–Nehemiah? There are two reasons. One is simply that there seems to be more material which calls for the inclusion of the stranger than for her exclusion, and in later Hebrew writings and the New Testament especially, open, compassionate passages dwarf the number of hostile ones.[2] The other reason is a matter of subjective

---

[1] Olyan (2000), a Canadian immigrant to the US, also privileges Ruth over Ezra–Nehemiah.

[2] Among the numerous passages are Gen. 18, Jon., Heb. 13:2, the Parable of the Good Samaritan and Jesus' encounter with the disciples on the Emmaus Road. On Gen. 18, see Amos (2004) and West (2006). B Byrne (2000) provides relevant commentary on the Good Samaritan, the Great Banquet and the Emmaus Road encounter and Koenig (2001)

hermeneutical choice. I read the Bible as a source of life for the contemporary world and particularly for the oppressed and marginalized. I therefore always privilege stories which promote liberation above those which lead to death. Following Smith-Christopher, I believe that it is important to seek voices within the text that 'can light our path to a future coexistence by means of insights and hopeful ideals' (1996: 141–142).

A Duty of Care: 'You Shall Not Oppress the *Ger*'

The Judaeo-Christian scriptures teem with passages stating a clear duty to care for the stranger.[3] This is particularly the case in the Hebrew Bible, where general exhortations towards doing justice and caring for the poor can be found alongside more specific instructions about how to treat 'aliens'. While in Isaiah there is encouragement to 'learn to do good; seek justice, rescue the oppressed' (1:17), in Exodus and Leviticus, there are numerous exhortations such as this: 'When an alien resides with you in your land, you shall not oppress the alien. The alien who resides with you shall be to you as the citizen among you: you shall love the alien as yourself, for you were aliens in the land of Egypt' (Lev. 19:33–34).[4] Sacks notes that whereas there is only one verse in the Hebrew Bible that commands, 'You shall love your neighbour as yourself', we are instructed to 'love the stranger' in 36 places (2002: 58). Kristeva similarly points out: 'The Torah ceaselessly dwells on the duties of Jews toward foreigners, and it may be noted that no other commandment (circumcision, dietary taboos, prohibition against lying and stealing) is repeated as often' (1991: 67). It was an awareness of their own 'strangerhood' that led to this emphasis.[5] The people of Israel had first-hand knowledge of what it felt like to be outsiders and their experiences of slavery, exile and imperial domination were annually re-enacted at the Passover (Sacks 2002: 59). Having such a strong understanding of themselves as strangers and sojourners created 'a bond with [other] sojourning strangers, whom Israel must love as themselves' (McKinlay 2004: 24; see also Feldmeier 1996: 244, Kidd 1999: 83).

---

discusses an openness to strangers in the ministry of Jesus, Paul and the early Christian community; see also Spina (2005) and McKinlay (2004: 132–133) on the positive role of biblical outsiders. There are also many texts calling people not to be afraid, including Isa. 41:10 and Mt. 28:10.

   3   Duty is broadly understood along Kantian lines as a command from God which we are obligated to follow, regardless of whether it is consistent with our own happiness. The notion of duty towards the refugee is also prominent in Islam. For an introduction to values and laws connected with asylum and refugees in Islam, see 'Abd al-Rahim (2008), Abū al-Wafā (2009), Elmadmad (1991) and Hayatli (2009).

   4   Other examples include Exod. 22:21, Lev. 23:22, Deut. 10:18 and Jer. 22:3. For a discussion of biblical narratives of justice, see Groody (2007: 26–58).

   5   For examples, see Deut. 10:19b and 1 Chron. 29:15.

But who were the 'aliens' that were to be cared for and were they similar to migrants or those seeking sanctuary today? What did care entail and how were they to be treated? The word translated in English as 'stranger' or 'alien' comes from a number of Hebrew terms with slightly different meanings. The people of Israel were most frequently encouraged to love those termed *gerim* in Hebrew. According to Rendtorff, the *ger* is often mentioned in conjunction with the *toshav* and both refer to a person that 'originally came from somewhere else and lives now in a surrounding that is not his or her own'. In Leviticus 25:23, God seems to regard the Israelites and the *ger* and *toshav* living among them as on a par. It is likely that the *ger* could buy a piece of land, whereas the children of *toshavim* could be taken as slaves (*'evadim*) (Lev. 25:45), which suggests they were seen as similar to inhabitants of surrounding nations. The *sakir* was a free person working for wages. Rendtorff therefore suggests that within the Israelite community a social hierarchy existed of *ger-toshav-sakir*-slave, though the *ger* was not necessarily the wealthiest (1996: 79). The *nokrim* and *zarim* were beyond this hierarchy, being the '"true" foreigners who live[d] in their own country outside the land of Israel' (Burnside 2001: 19–21). Juxtaposing the *ger* with the *'ezrakh*, 'an original, native inhabitant of the land, a citizen', provides further clarification. The status of the *ger* in relation to the *'ezrakh* in fact changed over time. Whereas in earlier material, the focus is on simply treating the *ger* justly, in later material, the *ger* is to be almost completely included within the community (van Houten 1991: 175).

By the time the priestly laws were compiled, the *ger* had become an accepted resident in the community and was subject to many of the same laws as a native Israelite (Exod. 12:49) (Rendtorff 1996: 82). Even the stranger who had killed was to be given sanctuary on the same basis as a native. God instructed Moses to set aside 'cities of refuge' for 'the Israelites, for the resident or transient alien among them' (Num. 35:15).[6] The *ger* was also included in cultic practices, including in the Day of Atonement, the holiest day of the year (Lev. 16:29–34) (Rendtorff 1996: 83). The *gerim* remained poorer than the Israelites, however, as they were not able to own land in perpetuity and usually had to earn their living by hiring out their services as day workers.[7] According to Olyan, the *ger* was therefore always 'in a precarious position: He ha[d] no place in the lineage structure, with its advantages (such as redemption or blood vengeance); he ha[d] no claim to a part of the national patrimony'. He was also always seen 'a problem' because his

---

[6]   See also Deut. 191–13 and Josh. 201–9. For discussions of the biblical themes of sanctuary and refuge – its origins in the Pentateuch and relation to contemporary asylum-seeking – see Burnside (2010), de Vaux (1961: 160–163) and Rabben (2011). I have chosen not to explore the theme of sanctuary, as it was essentially providing protection to those who had committed crimes and thus very different from what people mean by sanctuary in relation to migrants today.

[7]   See Deut. 24:14, Epsztein (1986: 116) and de Vaux (1961: 75). Ezek. 47:22, which allows a permanent *ger* with children to inherit land, is the exception that proves this rule.

position was continually open to challenge and he was a permanent 'potential target for xenophobes' (2000: 81).[8]

Burnside translates *ger* as 'immigrant' and, unpacking the precise religious, social, legal and economic rights of the many different categories of Hebrew stranger, makes direct parallels to suggest a Christian immigration policy for the UK today (2001: 13–14; see also Spina 1983: 325–326). He argues that while all should be granted basic protection, it is 'vulnerable' and 'deserving' foreigners who should be positively welcomed. These should moreover be strongly encouraged to assimilate into British national life (2001: 67–87).[9] Transferring a model so exactly from ancient Israel to contemporary Britain is potentially dangerous. The modern nation-state is not analogous to the sixth or fifth century BCE Israelite 'nation' and the present-day immigrant cannot be understood as equivalent to a *ger*, particularly as the current word 'immigrant' refers to many different types of foreign settlers and the former category of *ger* was defined variously over time. The Hebrew Bible provides no blueprint for how people should be treated in the twenty-first century. The *ger* is therefore better translated ambiguously as 'resident alien' or 'sojourner' and understood loosely as someone who lived among the people but who remained different and was, as a result, likely to be vulnerable. Many contemporary migrants, including asylum seekers, can be understood loosely as falling within a broad, comparable category. While most hope to and some do live permanently among the established population, they are regarded as different and do not share all of the same rights. The call to protect and support *gerim* in the Israelite community can therefore also be understood as a general guiding principle for Christians wishing to relate to migrants today.

Turning briefly to the New Testament, a similar strand encouraging concern for the outsider is apparent. Jesus is often to be found mixing with those who were beyond or on the margins of mainstream Jewish society, including women, tax collectors and lepers. The challenge he poses to care for the poor, suffering and despised is made most explicit in the parables of the Good Samaritan (Lk. 10:25–37) and the Last Judgement (Mt. 25:35). Those who refuse to welcome strangers and care for those in need in this second parable find themselves consigned to eternal punishment on Judgement Day. This biblical sub-strand provides the overriding theological basis for Christian projects working alongside those seeking asylum today. Again and again, the biblical imperative to care for the 'alien' is stressed in the hope that Christians will recognize a duty to offer support. Restore, for

---

[8]　Debates surrounding the nature, identity and rights of the *ger* abound; see Epsztein (1986: 117–118), Kidd (1999) and Olyan (2000: 79–81) on the *ger* in the Holiness and Deuteronomistic texts, as well as Crüsemann (1993) and Kristeva (1991: 68).

[9]　Spencer (2004) presents similar arguments in relation to biblical teaching on 'nationhood' and 'asylum and immigration'.

example, has quoted Matthew 25:35 on fliers, and asylum-related events, seminars and retreats often contain the word 'strangers' in their titles.[10]

Encounters with Life-bringing Strangers: Introducing Ruth and the Syro-Phoenician Woman

Responses to strangers rooted in an ecology of faith go far beyond this, however. Another related sub-strand of biblical material sees the outsider not simply as one who requires help, but also as one who brings new and God-given life. The Book of Ruth tells the story of two women – Ruth, a Moabite, and Naomi, her Israelite mother-in-law – who leave the land of Moab after their husbands have died during a period of famine and journey to Israel together seeking a new life. There they encounter Boaz, a kinsman of Naomi, who offers them protection and later marries Ruth. The novella closes with the celebration of the birth of their son, Obed.[11] The dating of Ruth has been the subject of protracted debate and hinges largely on what its purpose is believed to have been.[12] The lack of a definitive date, as with Ezra–Nehemiah, need not be a matter for significant concern. What is important is that the book clearly addresses the thorny theological issue of who was to be included in the community and who excluded from it. Who was legitimately part of Israel and who was not? Whether written in the pre-exilic or post-exilic era, Ruth was intended to instruct 'the community's view of outsiders'. More specifically, it was intended 'to challenge narrow exclusivism in the life of the ancient community' (Sakenfeld 1999: 5).[13] The novella thus has the potential to offer relevant insights into how members of established populations should approach migrants today. The book was also written at a time of uncertainty and upheaval, whether that was because the people were dealing with threats to the Davidic monarchy or coming to terms with the exile, and turning to the story itself, Spina notes that Ruth 'is squarely located in an era of double jeopardy, the time when judges ruled [leaders deficient and breaking covenant with God] and a famine menaced' (2005: 119).

---

[10] For other examples, see www.beaconbradford.org, www.embraceni.org and 'What does the Bible say about Refugees?' which can be downloaded at www.sgmlifewords.com/asylum/reflect/index.html [all accessed: 25 September 2011]; see also Fraser (2007) and Chapter 6 for examples of theological reflection surrounding migration and asylum on this theme.

[11] LaCocque describes a 'novella' as 'a short story where the situations and the characters occupy a more important place than the facts' (2004: 9).

[12] See LaCocque (2004: 2–3, 18–21), Lau (2011: 44–53, 145–190), Nielsen (1997: 28–29) and Sakenfeld (1999: 1–5).

[13] Other messages co-exist within the book (Bronner 1993). Some suggest that it is a story of loyalty and faithfulness (for example Sasson 1997: 322) and others, a model of female solidarity (for example Putnam 1994, van Wijk-Bos 2001); see also Masenya (2004: 88), Trible (1978: 166–199) and van Wolde (1997: 119–126).

Thus both the authorial *and* textual contexts were precarious ones and potentially full of fear. The similarity with the context today regarding migrants is striking.

The story of the Syro-Phoenician Woman describes an occasion when Jesus goes away to Tyre to rest and is there approached by a Gentile woman. The woman asks Jesus to cast out a demon from her daughter. Jesus refuses her request, replying, 'Let the children be fed first, for it is not fair to take the children's food and throw it to the dogs'. Undaunted, the woman retorts, 'Sir, even the dogs under the table eat the children's crumbs' and Jesus then agrees to heal her daughter. The same story is told with slight differences in Matthew 15:21–28. I chose the Markan version as it was written earlier and also because, as will become clear later, the reason Jesus gives for healing the woman's daughter has particular significance.[14] It is likely that, whether penned in Rome or Syro-Palestine and whatever its date between 65 and 75 CE, the Gospel of Mark was intended to be read by a cross-racial Christian community (Kinukawa 1994: 52) living through a time of considerable social, religious, economic and political turmoil.[15] Written for a diverse community feeling fearful and vulnerable and from the perspective of a 'subjected' people (Horsley 2001: 37), stories in the Gospel of Mark may well be able to speak to contemporary established communities from the perspective of those seeking asylum.

Portraying the Stranger: The Women as Multiple Outsiders

Ruth and the Syro-Phoenician Woman are intentionally depicted as multiple outsiders in their respective contexts. Naomi fails to mention Ruth on arriving in Bethlehem and Ruth herself remains silent (1:19–20), and her existence is barely acknowledged. She is identified as a 'foreigner' seven times in the book (LaCocque 2004: 62–63) and labels herself a *nokriyah* (2:10), a word that indicated a potentially threatening foreigner and that was used in Proverbs of foreign women who could lead Israelite men astray (Bergant 2003: 51). At the time, *nokriyah* signified 'one that questions the habits and traditions' and Ruth is therefore 'not simply the foreigner, but one who is strange and different' (LaCocque 2004: 24, 70).[16] Indeed, Miller and Hayes point out that '[t]ravel and contact with other cultures, at least in pre-Hellenistic times, were rare … This general lack of outside contacts meant that society tended toward conservatism and was generally suspicious of external influences' (2006: 28). What is more, Ruth comes from Moab and is pointedly labelled Ruth the 'Moabite' (1:4, 1:22, 2:2, 2:6, 2:21, 4:5, 4:10) throughout the

---

[14] Dube (2000: 157–195), Guardiola-Sáenz (1997) and Wainwright (1995) offer readings of the Matthean text.

[15] For more on the Galilean context at this time, see Horsley (2001: 31–36) and Theissen and Merz (1998).

[16] See Begg (1992) on the categories of foreignness, otherness and not-belonging at the time.

book. It is the first marker attached to her, even before her name is stated, and thus 'her origins obliterate everything else' (LaCocque 2004: 66; see also van Wolde 1997: 1, 8). The nation of Moab was considered an arch-enemy of Israel as its people had refused to help Israelite immigrants on their way to the Promised Land (Deut. 23:4) and Moab was born as a result of an incestuous relationship between Lot and his daughters (Gen. 19:36–37). As a Moabite, Ruth would have been regarded as 'a descendent of that fruit of incest' (Kristeva 1991: 75) and being a Moabite *woman* more specifically, a 'hypersexualised threat' (Donaldson 2010: 141). Moabites were forbidden from entering the 'assembly of the Lord' (Deut. 23:3) and mixed marriages with Moabites were strictly prohibited (Ezra 9:1–2). Spina writes, 'Putting the matter bluntly, Moab [was] anathema to Israel' (2005: 121, Yee 2009: 128).[17] Moab, in this story, is also depicted as a place of famine. Donaldson notes the 'doubling of ethnic markers' in 2:6 – Ruth is described as a 'Moabite from Moab' – and argues that this is designed to emphasize the fact that Ruth is 'an alien who comes from a despised and barbaric country' (2010: 142).[18]

Ruth is a 'liminal character' (Matthews 2004: 208) for other reasons too, namely that she is a woman and a childless widow. Ruth gleans in the field (2:2–3), an activity specifically associated with being a foreigner, widow or orphan (Nielsen 1997: 54; see Lev. 19:9–10, Deut. 24:19), and Koosed notes that to 'glean one must traverse a border, step over a property line' and suggests that gleaners 'live in Borderlands', particularly 'those of class difference' (2011: 49). Barrenness would also have been considered a sign of divine disfavour. LaCocque summarizes her situation:

> Ruth the Moabite, metaphorically, excellently represents 'the other.' She was a woman in a man's world; she was a widow and without a child in a group for which infertility was a mark of shame; she was a foreigner and also an enemy – in short, she represents perfectly what psychology calls 'the repressed.' Her arrival in Bethlehem, inevitably, shakes the Judeans' sociopolitical foundations. (2004: 3)

The Syro-Phoenician Woman is similarly multiply on the outside. She has no name and is identified solely in terms of socio-cultural categories, as 'a Greek, of Syrophoenician origin'. 'Syro-Phoenician' may indicate people from a specific geographical area – the Phoenicians on the Levant in the Roman province of Syria

---

[17] Spina points to three specific episodes where Moabites are seen in negative light (Num. 22:2–6, 25:1–9, Judg. 3:12–14) (2005: 121); see also 2 Sam. 8:2 and Neh. 13:23–25. According to Darr, some rabbinical interpretation suggested that Naomi's sons had been struck down by God because they had sinned in marrying foreign women (cited in Kwok 2005: 106).

[18] Koosed warns against 'automatically read[ing] this difference as prejudice or inferiority', arguing that such negative attitudes are not explicit in the text and may be included to encourage more sympathy towards her (2011: 32–33, 47).

(France 2002: 297, Witherington 2001: 21) – or a mixed marriage (Marcus 2000: 462–463). The labelling of her as 'Greek' stresses a difference between her and Jesus in terms both of race and language (S. Miller 2004: 91) and implies that she was a Gentile rather than a Jew.[19] She is probably best understood as culturally Greek and ethnically Syrian and was therefore 'a double outsider' to those from Israelite Galilee (Horsley 2001: 212–213). Theissen describes her as a 'Hellenized Phoenician' and surmises that she was probably bilingual and integrated into Greek culture, and thus a member of the affluent upper class and a free citizen – a privileged 'Hellene' (1992: 69–72). Her strangeness is emphasized using textual and linguistic means. Ringe points out how the parenthetical introduction of details about her identity disrupts the flow of story and 'by its literary awkwardness calls attention to itself' (2001: 86). France also sees her 'double designation' as Syro-Phoenician *and* Greek as an attempt to underline her Gentile status (2002: 297). It is significant that in Matthew, Phoenician is recognized as the contemporary name for ancient Canaanites (Mt. 15:21–22), people who were grouped with Moabites in the Hebrew Bible as enemies. The Syro-Phoenician Woman and Jesus are thus depicted as 'represent[ing] separate worlds, since they differ in race, social status and gender. She is portrayed as a member of the Hellenistic world, cultured and wealthy, whereas Jesus is a Jewish man who lives as an itinerant teacher' (S. Miller 2004: 92).

The setting of the story in the region of Tyre is also significant. Tyre, an area outside and to the northwest of Galilee, was centred on a cosmopolitan coastal city and had a thriving mercantile economy. It was politically influential and ethnically mixed (Ringe 2001: 84). Tyre, along with Sidon, is usually portrayed negatively in the Hebrew Bible and its inhabitants were regarded as avaricious enemies who exploited the poorer region of Galilee for its agricultural produce. This resentment would have been exacerbated by the memory of Tyre's previous territorial expansions into Galilee (see for example Isa. 23, Ezek. 26–28, Theissen 1992: 74–75). According to Malbon, while Mark's geographical knowledge often seems confused with regards to Jesus' journeys (for example 7:31), the '"foreignness," as it were, of these cities and areas is more crucial in Mark's Gospel than their precise location or Jesus' exact itinerary in reaching them'. They were symbolically important (1991: 41, Kinukawa 1994: 53).

Like Ruth, the personal circumstances of the woman conspired to push her to the edges of respectable society. Not only was she a woman in a patriarchal society without any apparent connection with a man, but she is also associated with a daughter who is demon-possessed, a factor which is particularly significant given the discussion of purity that immediately precedes this story in the Gospel (Mk 7:1–23) (France 2002: 297, Horsley 2001: 214). Kinukawa pithily sums up

---

[19]   Witherington suggests that whereas Mark stresses her 'political and national identity', Matthew focuses on her religious affiliation (1984: 64). McKinlay notes a link with Jezebel, 'the Phoenician who crossed from Sidon to Israel but refused to acknowledge Yahweh as God' (2004: 63).

her position: in Jewish eyes, she would have been seen as '"unclean" by birth, a foreigner and a female, and "untouchable" because of her daughter who is possessed by an unclean spirit ... thus triply polluted: foreign, female, and demon-possessed' (1994: 55).

Migrants, including those seeking sanctuary, can be seen as contemporary 'Ruths' and 'Syro-Phoenician Women'. They are often regarded as outsiders by members of established populations and some reasons for their marginalization are similar.[20] They are by definition foreign and are often perceived to be ethnically 'different' by white, British people. They are also associated in many minds with threats of violence, poverty and disease (particularly sexually-transmitted diseases) and are feared as potential bringers of a dangerous 'foreign' religion (Islam) and other 'strange' cultural practices. Women seeking asylum, like Ruth and the Syro-Phoenician Woman, experience particular difficulties because of their gender.

The Women as a Source of Transformation and New Life

Given this depiction, what is so surprising is that the two women are also portrayed as sources of new life. In both of these narratives written by those inhabiting and urging an ecology of faith, the reader is called to recognize a potentially threatening outsider as a 'life-bringer' and 'God-bearer'. Ruth is revealed to be a central figure who offers a vital new lease of life to Boaz, Naomi and the whole community of Israel. Through marrying Boaz, Ruth brings him joy and also ensures that she and Naomi are no longer powerlessly stuck on the social assistance offered to widows. In addition, the birth of their son, Obed, fills Naomi's emptiness (4:13–17). Naomi had been 'bitter' (1:13), an ironic contrast to her name meaning 'pleasant' or 'sweet' (Sakenfeld 1999: 20, 28), but she is restored to fullness of life and assured of nourishment in old age through her grandson (4:15–17). The women of the town claim, after Obed's birth, that Ruth is worth more than seven sons to Naomi (4:15). Seven was the traditional number of idealized perfection (Sakenfeld 1999: 82). Obed later becomes the grandfather of the messianic King David and his name, meaning 'serving', underlines his redemptive function, rekindling and nourishing life (LaCocque 2004: 145). So it is that through the person of Ruth, the people of Israel are renewed. Ruth is mentioned in the genealogy of Jesus in Matthew 1:5 and pointing out the significance of this, Spina writes: 'Almost every single time an essential birth takes place, one observes an inexplicable combination of providence and human choices. *Even more remarkable, outsiders keep showing up to invade the narrative space and promote Israel's future and therefore God's*

---

[20]   Kwok makes interesting connections between the woman and outsiders today, including the mother of a prostitute in Jakarta and the mother of a Korean political prisoner (1994), and Kinukawa suggests parallels between the woman and Koreans living in Japan (1994: 61–65).

agenda' (2005: 136. My italics).[21] The comparisons made between Ruth and Rachel and Leah who 'built up the house of Israel' (4:11–12) emphasize that her union with Boaz is seen as strengthening the 12 tribes of Israel (Nielsen 1997: 91).

As if this were not enough, it is also Ruth who persuades the Bethlehemites to adopt a more generous and creative interpretation of the Torah. If taken literally, as it was in Ezra–Nehemiah, this would have excluded her as a *nokriyah* from being given any of the usual assistance granted to widows and aliens (LaCocque 2004: 28–32). Boaz, encouraged to adapt his understanding of the Torah law through his encounter with Ruth, represents the audience – the people of Israel – to whom the author is speaking. The 'story is told to disorient and to reorient [them] toward a new view and life' – a way of life more open to outsiders and less based on nationality and 'genetic descent' (LaCocque 2004: 32, Lau 2011: 115, 118). It is for these reasons that LaCocque claims that Ruth 'proves to be the opportune instrument of salvation history' (2004: 149) and Holbert that 'God is a Moabite widow' (cited in Fewell and Gunn 1990: 94). Or as Bergant puts it: 'The strange and potentially dangerous woman has become the agent of God's salvation ... the blessing of salvation comes from without (God) not from within (ourselves)' (2003: 52, 60). In the light of this, it is interesting that her name probably derives from the Hebrew root, *rwh*, meaning 'watering to saturation' (Donaldson 2010: 146). While a variety of interpretations of her name have been offered, LaCocque convincingly demonstrates the similarity between Ruth (רוּת) and the verb 'to satisfy' (הור) (2004: 40).[22] Ruth is the one who satisfies and quenches the thirst of a dry and struggling Israel. This series of events and changes described in Ruth grows out of and reinforces an ecology of faith, or what Sakenfeld terms a 'harmonious and joyful community'. By the end of the novella, we are able to glimpse

> a microcosm of the peaceable kingdom envisioned by the prophetic tradition. It is a human community in which the marginalized person has dared to insist upon full participation, in which the one in the center has reached out beyond societal norms to include the marginalized ... a community in which joy is the dominant note. (1999: 10)

The Syro-Phoenician Woman has a comparable role in the Markan story. While there is considerable debate about the purpose of the story, it above all shows Jesus shifting his position concerning mission to the Gentiles. It describes how his understanding of the Kingdom of God is expanded to include *all* people and how

---

[21]   A number of foreign women in the Hebrew Bible play significant roles in Israelite history, including Hagar, Rahab and Tamar (Brenner 2005: 107–108).

[22]   The Hebrew has been included here to show the visual similarity between the terms. Koehler and Baumgartner (1996: 1209) and Sasson (1997: 322) offer a similar interpretation of the name Ruth. The origin of the name Ruth is 'tantalizingly obscure' and has been variously interpreted (Campbell 1975: 56; see also Saxegaard 2010: 106).

this happens as a direct result of the actions and words of the Syro-Phoenician Woman. Susan Miller suggests that the Syro-Phoenician Woman is a 'prophetic figure' who brings Jesus 'the word of God' and describes their encounter 'as a turning point in the Gospel' (2004: 91, 111, 99). It marks the start of Jesus' mission to the Gentiles. After this episode, Jesus moves onto Decapolis and feeds the four thousand – the Gentile equivalent of the feeding of the five thousand (2004: 99–100). Before this, his concern had been exclusively with Israel. Rhoads similarly argues that 'Jesus has a genuine change of mind here' about the inclusion of Gentiles in the Kingdom of God and it is the woman who '"steals the scene"' (1994: 361). Horsley puts it this way: 'The Syrophoenician woman becomes the only person in Mark's story' who 'bests Jesus in debate' and she 'forces Jesus to expand the renewal to non-Israelites' (2001: 207). So while the woman may be an example of persistent faith against all the odds, contrasting favourably with the disciples (Williamson 1983: 16), her primary role is wider than this. She expands Jesus', and in turn the readers', understandings of who God is and what faith involves. The importance of this message is emphasized by the positioning of the story directly following a conversation about purity (7:1–23) and by its halfway 'pivotal position' in the Gospel (Kwok 1995: 75).[23]

The word the woman speaks is described as *logos* (7:29), a word usually associated with Jesus and with the proclamation of gospel (Mk 1:45, 2:2, 4:33, Jn 1). It indicates the creative power of speech (Gen. 1) and the bringing in of the abundance of the Kingdom (S. Miller 2004: 110). It becomes even more significant when it is recognized that, whereas in the Matthean version it is the woman's *faith* that brings about her daughter's healing, in the Markan version it is this *word* spoken by the woman that brings this healing about as well as a new understanding of the inclusive love of God. Perkinson's reflections on the pericope are illuminating. Whereas it is usually Jesus who gives voice to the voiceless (for example Mk 6:56), here

> a unique reversal takes place. The word of power Jesus bears crosses a border from his own interior to his social, political, religious other. Here, Jesus does not speak for the woman; the woman speaks for him. The saying of the Syro-Phoenician woman is not just an interesting rejoinder – it is *logos*, the word. (1996: 69; see also Rhoads 1994: 361)

He suggests that for a brief moment therefore, she displaces Christology: 'She briefly occupies the space (even the subject-position) of "Christ" in her speaking to and against Jesus, speaking briefly "in his place" without entirely giving up her own' (1996: 81). Ringe, for other reasons, also argues that the woman's comment is central. Noting the chiastic structure of the pericope, she points out that the woman's 'only line of dialogue – forms the hinge or focal point' in 7:28. What

---

[23]   Marcus (2000: 468) and Thiede (2004: 57) dispute that this story marks a turning point in the Gospel.

is more, the woman takes the role usually performed by Jesus, of providing the correcting question in response to a hostile question (2001: 82–83). Jesus' saying in 7:27 is a *chreia*, a common form in Greek rhetoric that conveys an example of the wit or wisdom of a philosopher or famous person. However, 'the woman's reply turns the story into a double *chreia*, with the punchline in the second half ... Hers is the defining wisdom of the story' (2001: 90).

Thus, the story portrays the woman as brimming with the divine. She brings about renewal for her daughter, herself, Jesus and the community of God and points towards the possibility of abundant life for the world. The healing of her daughter at a distance points forward to the new age when 'no disease or evil will remain', or in other words, to the new creation (S. Miller 2004: 109–111). The shared transformation occurs because the woman inhabits an ecology of faith and she, with Jesus and the author of Mark, encourages others to enter into such an ecology. The encounter with the Syro-Phoenician Woman was for Jesus '*a constructive, enlarging engagement with the Other*' (Anderson 1999: 9) or as Kinukawa puts it,

> she frees Jesus to be fully himself. Jesus, 'the boundary-breaker,' may not have needed the encounter with her to cross the racial barrier, but certainly it is the woman that has created the opportunity for him to cross it and step over to her side ... Her intuition about who Jesus should be and Jesus' sensitivity to the marginalized are drawn into one vortex and create a mutual transformation. (1994: 60–61)

Theological and Contemporary Echoes: Encounters with Strangers Can Bring New Life

The belief that the stranger can be one who brings new life is echoed by a number of theologians. Strangers can of course be dangerous: it is for good reason that children are told never to get into a car with them. It is also often unexpected people, though – those who are different from us – who turn out to be sources of insight, growth and vitality. Buber suggested that we can only come to know God and ourselves through relationship with the 'other'. He wrote, 'In the beginning is relation', and claimed that truth and freedom come through meeting and encounter rather than through believing: 'For through contact with every *Thou* we are stirred with a breath of the *Thou*, that is, of eternal life ... Where there is no sharing there is no reality' (1937: 18, 63). An encounter with another human being offers us a glimpse of God and can be disturbing and therefore potentially life-changing (Lévinas 1987, 1985). While Buber was among the first to establish the so-called dialogical principle, more recently, Brueggemann has argued that 'otherness' in terms of God, neighbour and within our self, is the very source of our being, and that we need to learn how to 'other' with courage and grace (1999: 16). Volf similarly claims that it is through encountering difference in the stranger that we can develop, gain new insights and be transformed: 'Identity is a result of the distinction from the other *and* the internalization of the relationship to the other ... The self is dialogically constructed. The other is already from the outset part of the self. I am who I am in relation to the other' (1996: 66, 91).[24] The Trinitarian model of God, indicating diversity in unity and mutual interdependence, is intrinsically dialogical. Human beings, made in the image of God, are called to mirror this divine interrelatedness in their own lives.[25]

Practitioners and theorists of Christian hospitality have also articulated the potential of strangers to expand our horizon, challenge us and bring about positive transformation. Hospitality is, as will gradually become clear, a key practice in an ecology of faith (see Wilson 2011). Ogletree recognizes,

> To offer hospitality to the stranger is to welcome something new, unfamiliar, and unknown into our life-world. On the one hand, hospitality requires a recognition of the stranger's vulnerability in an alien social world ... On the other hand, hospitality designates occasions of potential discovery which can open up our narrow, provincial worlds ... The sharing of stories may prove threatening, but not necessarily so ... The stranger does not simply challenge or subvert our assumed world of meaning; she may enrich, even transform, that world. (2003: 2–3)

Pohl likewise suggests that in 'joining physical, spiritual, and social nourishment, hospitality is a life-giving practice. It is both fruitful and fertile' (1999: 13, Nouwen 1976: 64–65).[26] For Wells, 'an ethic that lapses into responsibility for or duty to the stranger is inadequate. It misses the crucial dimension, that the stranger is a gift to the Church' (2006: 107). Reflecting directly on migration and multiculturalism, Fornet-Betancourt concludes that a 'praxis of hermeneutics of strangers implies a commitment with a horizon of understanding transformed by the strangers, in which we ourselves are transformed ... with the strangers "we are reborn"' (2008: 217–218).[27]

Given that the stranger can so often be a life-bringer, it is hardly surprising that people who work or volunteer with people seeking sanctuary speak of receiving much from those they are standing alongside. Some mention generous hospitality,

---

[24]   Connections can be made with the African concept of *Ubuntu*. There 'is a proverb: "*Motho ke motho ka batho*" which means "A person is a person through people"' (Letlhare 2001: 477).

[25]   On Trinitarian interrelationality, see Boff (2000: xvi, 48), Cunningham (1998), LaCugna (1993: 243–317, 399), Moltmann (2000) and Zizioulas (1985).

[26]   For more on hospitality, see Palmer (1983), Murray (1990), Pohl (1999) and Vanier (1997).

[27]   Wink suggests that even 'the enemy *can be* the way to God' (1999: 171). For more on the importance of strangers and otherness, see Duraisingh (2002: 193), Koyama (1993: 283) and Mursell (2005: 76).

contributions to the nation's cultural life or the joy of sharing in the birth of a baby. I have hardly ever come away from a conversation with a volunteer or project worker who has not said that they have gained more than they have given. Those who responded to a question on a survey I sent out to Enabling Christians in Serving Refugee members, 'What are some of the main joys and difficulties which you have recently faced, either as a project or personally?' frequently spoke of friendship, seeing children achieve at school and adults taking up new opportunities through training and piecing their lives back together as joys. One spoke of asylum seekers offering 'an example of resilience and courage' and another claimed, 'the people I meet bring so much more into my life. They live in the real world and most people in the UK don't!'. Ruth Davies, reflecting on her experience of visiting asylum seekers in detention as a volunteer, recognizes positive changes in herself:

> I have found visiting asylum seekers in detention heartbreakingly sad at times, often frustrating but truly beneficial and uplifting for me the visitor. I am constantly challenged to be more empathetic, and more imaginative – for example it is forbidden to hand over any gift in person so I sang and danced happy birthday for a detainee. I have witnessed the amazing strength and resilience of the human spirit in adversity which has helped me to grow as a human being. I think I now recognise trivial matters for what they are and have re-aligned my priorities. (2008)[28]

The sense of community within some support groups can give volunteers a place to belong as much as it does asylum seekers. Speaking personally, I have been astounded, challenged and touched by the trust in God and offers of friendship I have encountered. I remember one particular conversation with Fatima in which she asked me how my work was going. Her interest in my life despite all that she was struggling with challenged me in ways I could not have imagined. Standing alongside others in raw places has helped me to glimpse something 'real' and pointed towards the heart of life. Although such examples may sound trite, the ways in which we are enriched go deeper through gentle, subconscious shifts in our understanding and perspective.

Christian communities in the Global North are also being revitalized by immigrants in a range of ways, from increases in existing congregation numbers to the introduction of new worship styles and social projects, and reinvigorated theological and ecclesiological understandings (Burns 2004a, Hanciles 2007, 2008a, 2008b, Jansen and Stoffels 2008, ter Haar 1998, 2008, Levitt 2007, Orobator 2010). Stoppels has demonstrated, through a study of 23 immigrant

---

[28]   Other stories indicating how much can be gained or discovered through engaging with asylums seekers and refugees can be found in the Baptist Church Union pack (Baptist Union n.d.), Restore (2008), Smith (2008), Thompson (2003) and on the befriending page of the Restore website (2011a).

churches in The Hague, that professionals and volunteers from these churches contribute approximately 300,000 hours annually in social activities, equating to a financial input of over €10 million. Almost 39 per cent of this work, from psychosocial care and assistance to education and youth work, benefits the broader society (2008: 36). So, as Hoffmann argues, 'the strangers in our midst – be they Christians or not – do have a "mission" to the church, and particularly to "native" western Christians'. What is required, then, is a 'receiving attitude' (1989: 60). Yong even suggests, 'is it not in fact true that it is immigrants, exiles, refugees and displaced persons who are the living theologians of exile and the norm of Christian discipleship in a multireligious world?' (2008: 155) At a more practical level, immigration is vital to sustain the economy in the UK and elsewhere. Migrants make a substantial fiscal contribution (Sriskandarajah et al. 2005) and the EU requires 13 million net immigrants per year until 2050 in order to sustain a healthy working to retired population ratio (UNDP 2000).[29]

The ways in which strangers, including refugees and those seeking asylum, can be a source of potential God-given challenge, joy and wholeness of life are numerous. But how many of these are recognized and acknowledged? There are probably many gifts brought by migrants, be they practical, moral, ideological, theological or spiritual, which are currently not seen let alone received. Members of established populations are, as a result, missing potential glimpses of God and new life. Moreover, if encounters are not seen as mutually life-bringing, there may be a danger that any support offered will become an example of paternalistic one-way 'do-gooding'.

Exploring the Encounters: Characteristics and Consequences of an Ecology of Faith

Transformation, mutual liberation and new life came about in the stories of Ruth and the Syro-Phoenician Woman due to the ecology of faith inhabited by the central characters (and the authors). But what is it about an ecology of faith that enabled such change to take place? What permits Ruth and the Syro-Phoenician Woman to be God-bearers and life-bringers and why did an ecology of faith prevail given that the potential for fear and hostility on the part of the authors and the characters was so great?

One-to-One, Personal and Embodied Encounters

The first feature of both narratives to note is that they are focused around one-to-one, personal and embodied encounters between those in a position of weakness and those with power. The book of Ruth is rooted in interactions between

---

[29] On the contribution made by migrants to British national life, see MPA (2005: 48–52) and Refugee Week (2011).

individuals – between Orpah, Ruth and Naomi and between Ruth and Boaz. Whereas Ruth has no power and Naomi only a little more, Boaz is of considerable standing in the Bethlehem community. Both Ruth and Naomi need his help. Rashkow interestingly notes the use of the verb 'encounter' in 1:16–17, a verb which is found only 39 times in the Hebrew Bible and usually used negatively. Its significance here is heightened by the fact that this is the only verse where it is 'used directly *by* a woman to refer *to* a woman's actions' (1993: 31). Encounter is thus portrayed as being central. Ruth is also the only place in the Bible where the intimate, one-to-one motif of *'akhav*, meaning love, is used between women (Pardes 1992: 102). The large proportion of dialogue compared to narration in the book reveals the importance of embodied interaction. Fifty-five out of its 85 verses are spoken conversation, which is the highest ratio of dialogue to narrative in any biblical book (Sasson 1997: 320).

God's intervention is surprisingly minimal, which only emphasizes the value of human contact. God never speaks and his only direct intrusion is to bring about Ruth's pregnancy in the closing verses. To quote LaCocque again: 'God is present in the narrative in the measure that the characters become his presence for one another' (2004: 15–16. Italics omitted; Saxegaard, 2010: 195, Campbell 1975: 113). It is human beings who progress the narrative and bring about the transformations described. They thus take on the role that God performs in many stories in the Hebrew Bible. Words usually associated with God are associated with people, notably 'to cling to' (1:14, 2:8, cf. Deut. 4.4), and whereas people usually hide under God's wings, here it is Boaz in 3:9 who is invited by Ruth to spread his *kanaf* (wings) to protect her (cf. Ezek. 16:8) (Nielsen 1997: 73). God's working is 'hidden and mysterious' (Sakenfeld 1999: 15, Saxegaard 2010: 194) in Ruth and there is a 'hidden interplay between human action and God's control' (Nielsen 1997: 31). As Sakenfeld points out, the characters frequently invoke divine blessing upon one another (1:8, 2:12, 2:19–20, 3:10, 4:11) (1999: 40–41) . She suggests the key theme of the novella is therefore 'that human action is the vehicle for achieving divine blessing and the fullness of human community ... Both the loyal, faithful, and upright action of human beings and special moments of caring divine intervention are necessary along the road to a peaceable community' (1999: 59, 80). Without one-to-one human relationships, including contact between individuals and groups of Bethlehemites such as between Ruth and the young men and women who assist her in 2:15–16 and 2:22–23, the transformations and abundant life experienced by all would never have been brought about.

The story of the Syro-Phoenician Woman similarly involves a physical meeting and conversation between Jesus and the woman. Whereas in the Matthean version the disciples are present and speak out against the woman, in Mark, it is only Jesus and the woman. There is no interference from anyone else. No crowd of witnesses is present. The setting of the scene in a house in Mark, again in contrast to Matthew, intensifies the intimacy of the encounter further. They met in a personal, domestic and private space, somewhere Jesus had gone to deliberately 'escape notice' (7:24), and the woman comes close to him, bowing down at his feet (7:25). Jesus is a figure of power, being male and the person to whom the woman is turning for the healing. The woman, although wealthy, is in a position of weakness. She is a suppliant who needs Jesus' help.

This feature suggests how important basic, concrete human contact is in bringing about new attitudes and new life. Encounters between individual strangers, and also between individuals and groups, are a vital element in an ecology of faith – especially where there are differentials in power. A face-to-face encounter can lead to the building of personal relationship and it is through such relationships that assumptions and stereotypes can be broken down and support can be offered. It is no coincidence that many churches and projects engaging with asylum seekers originated with the meeting of two individuals.[30] More often than not, someone seeking asylum turns up one Sunday morning at a church and starts chatting to a regular member of the congregation and provokes a desire to offer support. Moments such as these epitomize what Ford describes as 'the intrusion of the faceless' upon us. These are moments when the lives of others who are unknown to us pierce our own being and demand a response. He suggests that Christians are called to react hospitably and prioritize those in need (1997: 10–13).

The offer of concrete, face-to-face hospitality to marginalized strangers has been a central commitment of Christianity since its early days. From the provision of food and accommodation to travelling preachers in the first century through to the call to welcome guests from every background in the seventh-century Rule of St. Benedict, the protection of Jews in Vichy France by the village of Le Chambon-sur-Lignon in the 1940s and current efforts to support those seeking asylum, Christians have affirmed the importance of engaging with people pushed towards the edges of society in real, physical ways and through offering friendship.[31] There is, in fact, a surprising link between the Greek word for love of one's kinship group, *phileo*, and the word for hospitality to the stranger, *philoxenia* (Pohl 1999: 31). What is distinctive about Christian hospitality is that it is offered to the 'least' and the weak rather than only to those who can reciprocate (Pohl 1999: 16). Hospitality can never simply be thought or talked about in the abstract. It should always be an embodied, real *practice*. Pohl, a prolific writer on this theme, puts it like this:

> Hospitality in the abstract lacks the mundane, troublesome, yet rich dimensions of a profound human practice … The twin moves of universalizing the neighbor and personalizing the stranger are at the core of hospitality. Claims of loving all humankind, of welcoming 'the other,' have to be accompanied by the hard work of actually welcoming a human being into a real place. (1999: 14, 75)

---

[30]   Included in the category of 'face-to-face' encounters are telephone calls and email, although they do not tend to facilitate the same level of human relationship as meeting in person does; see Palmer (1983: 69–70).

[31]   For a history and examples of Christian hospitality, see Hallie (1979), Kessler (2005), Malherbe (1983), Murray (1990) and Pohl (1999).

What is more, hospitality should be rooted in informal, unmediated encounters between individuals who are strangers to one another rather than in professionally structured meetings. Murray spent time at three Catholic Worker Houses in the 1980s – three of then over 60 houses belonging to the movement in the US (1990: 6) – and this helped him to realize that training can hinder 'the practice of hospitality, since it gives the trainee predefined categories into which to fit one's clients ... such a categorization process destroys the openness toward the stranger that is a requisite of hospitality in the traditional sense [providing food, shelter and companionship]'. While professional approaches do have some clear benefits, these gains can sometimes be 'outweighed by the loss of humanity, of the human touch' (1990: 4–5). Hospitality, a practice found in all ecologies of faith, is rooted in concrete, one-to-one, personal encounters. It is these encounters which facilitate the development of mutually life-giving relationships.

Courageous, Loving Boundary-Crossing

The second feature of the stories is that the stranger *and* those in power take considerable risks out of love for others. The two central women, along with the other main characters, cross multiple societal boundaries in order to help those in need. Each takes a courageous leap of faith in unknown people and risks losing social status, respectability and occasionally life itself.

According to Bronner, the main characters in the Book of Ruth 'all act in the spirit of *hesed*; some perform ordinary *hesed*, and some – especially Ruth – extraordinary *hesed*' (1993: 147–148). LaCocque also distinguishes between ordinary and extraordinary people on the basis of whether they demonstrate *hesed* (2004, Bronner 1993). What does *hesed* mean? Sakenfeld defines *hesed* as 'faithfulness in action' and notes that the Hebrew word 'encompasses both the attitude and the action' (1985: 3; see also Sakenfeld 1978). *hesed* took place within the context of a relationship and was a communal as well as an individual responsibility. It carried no penalties: 'loyalty [*hesed*] is shown in a freely undertaken carrying through of an existing commitment to another who is now in a situation of need' (1985: 104, 131). Glueck suggests that in Ruth, *hesed* is to do with familial and kinship obligations and that, in general, it 'can best be translated as religiosity, piety, kindness and love of mankind' (1967: 40–42, 69). God frequently shows *hesed* to his people (for example Exod. 20.6, Ps. 100.5) and the term is understood here as meaning goodness of heart, steadfast love and fidelity.

Ruth expresses *hesed* towards Naomi and Boaz from beginning to end, something that involves her taking considerable initiative (Lau 2011: 109). She starts by leaving everything she knows and making an overwhelming commitment to Naomi and her God (1:16–17). She had no promise from God about the future (Nielsen 1997: 49), adapting to a new culture would require 'intentional effort' (Sakenfeld 1999: 31) and her decision could have ended up with ejection from Bethlehem and even her death. Moreover, as Trible argues,

Not only has Ruth broken with family, country, and faith, but she has also reversed sexual allegiance. A young woman has committed herself to the life of an old woman rather than to the search for a husband, and she has made this commitment not 'until death do us part' but beyond death ... There is no more radical decision in all the memories of Israel. (1978: 173)[32]

It was a courageous choice of an 'enterprising woman' (van Wolde 1997: 22, 51) and according to Sakenfeld, the repeated use of the verb *shuv*, meaning 'to return' or 'go back' in different forms emphasizes the importance of the decisions she makes. The verb occurs 10 times in the departure scene and twice in the arrival scene. That Ruth 'clung' to Naomi (1:14) also suggests a powerful feeling (1999: 26, 30). Thus, as Adutwum puts it, Ruth's decision to stay with Naomi 'effects a voluntary change of identity and unforced submission to a new orientation. It calls forth commitment that defies the fear of the unknown and willingly accepts the consequences of the ultimate' (1998: 569).

On arriving in Bethlehem, Ruth continues to demonstrate risky *hesed*. References to her being molested (2:9, 2:22) in the barley field show that she is living dangerously, and working in a field among men, especially as a young foreign woman without male protector, risked her honour (Sakenfeld 1999: 43). She generously gives all of her leftover barley to Naomi (2:18). Ruth then takes Naomi's plan further, pursuing Boaz and propositioning him on the threshing floor. It is her own bold initiative to ask him to spread his cloak (3:9) over her, as Naomi had told her to wait for Boaz's instructions. While it is not clear what *kanaf* (wings) means, whether Ruth is inviting Boaz to have sex or appealing for marriage and security (excursus in notes in Fewell and Gunn 1990: 128–129), whether *margelotayw* means feet or genitals or whether Ruth uncovered herself or Boaz, all 'scholars agree, however, that Ruth's action is not an ordinary one' (Nielsen 1997: 70). Lau notes her 'determination and ability for independent thought' (2011: 105) and Koosed describes her as 'playfully mendacious, a trickster in the fields and on the threshing floor' (2011: 73). Her actions signify a total wager, 'a dangerous double or nothing', and she shows herself willing '"to die" socially on behalf of her mother-in-law' (LaCocque 2004: 83, 87, Saxegaard 2010: 139, Trible 1978: 182, Bal 1987: 83). If she had been caught by others, the consequences could have been cataclysmic. Her action is described explicitly as *hesed* (3:10) and Ruth is portrayed as acting out of charity towards Boaz (LaCocque 2004: 87).[33] Boaz, worried about having children and his virility and fertility, is very grateful to Ruth 'for she will help him out of *his* misery' (Bal 1987: 71). It is significant that this pivotal moment takes place at liminal, charged midnight and that it is the

---

[32]   Masenya similarly suggests that Ruth 'dares to challenge the patriarchal status quo by clinging not to a man but to an old woman, who is a symbol of desolation and insecurity' (2004: 89).

[33]   The word *hesed* is found three times in the book of Ruth. The other two refer to God (1:8, 2:20).

first time that Ruth's name is voiced (LaCocque 2004: 95). In naming herself – 'I am Ruth, your servant' – Boaz discovers his identity too. Nadar argues that Ruth is a 'bold initiator of change' who casts aside all oppressive roles assigned to her and subverts gender and ethnic boundaries (2001: 164, 171). Ruth is a brave and courageous woman who makes bold choices out of love for others. According to Sakenfeld, Ruth is esteemed (4:15) not just because she bore Obed, but 'because everything that she has done from the first scene until now has led to the possibility of the birth of this child of hope. It is Ruth's faithfulness, kindness, loyalty to Naomi, in a word, Ruth's *hesed*, that has led to this outcome' (1999: 82).

Ruth's actions push Boaz 'beyond himself to reply to the call of the extraordinary' (LaCocque 2004: 86). Boaz lays his status and credibility on the line when he offers Ruth protection in the fields and invites her to eat with him, and goes well beyond his social duties as a kinsman-redeemer in marrying her (2:8–14, Nielsen 1997: 86, Sakenfeld 1999: 45). Immediately after the meal, Boaz allows Ruth to take sheaves, something which gleaners had no right to (2:15), and even demands that others leave sheaves in her path (2:16). He demonstrates 'superabundant generosity' (Lau 2011: 61) and sets himself up as her protector, offering her special privileges (Nielsen 1997: 61, Sakenfeld 1999: 43, 46). After the incident on the threshing floor, Boaz gives her grain (3:15) and '[i]t would be hard to overestimate just how daring and risky a scheme' his plan to marry Ruth is (Kates 1994: 194, Saxegaard 2010: 170). He seems to combine two different laws to do so in a way that was 'strictly illegal' at the time (Bal 1987: 81).[34] What is more, Boaz daringly tricks the closest kinsman of Elimelech out of his right to his land by suggesting that he would have to take Ruth as well (4:6, Kates 1994: 195).

Both characters thus demonstrate extraordinary loyalty and love. In fact, being able to show *hesed* seems to be *dependent* on having courage and acting in extraordinary ways. As Nielsen suggests, it 'requires courage to exceed expectations that break norms, but both are rewarded in the end ... *hesed* can require a person to choose the unexpected and not just be satisfied with what the law declares' (1997: 31). While 'Orpah and the redeemer choose the safer path', Ruth and Boaz both possess '*hesed* to an unusual degree' (Nielsen 1997: 88, 86). This does not imply that Orpah and Boaz's relative are 'aberrant': they are simply ordinary (LaCocque 2004: 152). They opt for the status quo and continue to live a pattern of 'normal' reactions and expected behaviour. It is also interesting that, according to Zornberg, Boaz does *hesed* with someone who needs it rather than *to* someone (1994: 73). *Hesed*, at its purest, is a mutual act in which both parties give and receive and, as a result, the lives of the key characters and Israel are transformed. The community is encouraged to embrace and perform *hesed* in the way that Ruth and Boaz do. According to LaCocque, Ruth's *hesed* is 'contagious'

---

34   The law of the *go'el* or kinsman-redeemer allowed a man to redeem the land of a family member. The law of levirate marriage permitted a man to marry his dead brother's wife. Combining these could result in the transgression of the taboo against 'cleaving' between certain men and women (see Deut. 22:22, 23:2, Bal 1987: 80–83).

and 'liberating' and through 'her *hesed*, Ruth became a source of abundance and a fountain of hope for others'. Her '*hesed* produces *shalom*' for all (2004: 3–5, 77, 108). The rigidity of the law is transcended through their example, and loving kindness and generosity towards everyone including the 'stranger' is encouraged (2004: 27; see also Kates 1994: 198, Sakenfeld 1999: 63).

Turning to Mark, the Syro-Phoenician Woman shows analogous courage, persistence and patience for the sake of love. She too in fact performs extraordinary *hesed*. To start with, as Susan Miller notes, she goes beyond the boundaries of her own world to seek help for her daughter, ignoring social conventions and risking her personal security. 'A woman on her own was … vulnerable to attack' and the fact that her daughter was demon-possessed and a girl needing a dowry means that the woman was seeking her healing at great personal cost to herself (2004: 92–95). Next, the woman crosses a boundary of propriety by approaching Jesus and doing so inside a house. Women were not expected to leave their domestic sphere of the home or speak to a man in public, never mind enter his private dwelling. The woman is portrayed here as more daring than in Matthew, where she confronts Jesus in a public space (Kwok 1995: 74). Worse still, she kneels before Jesus. This was an act of worship (S. Miller 2004: 105), but far from bringing honour to Jesus, it was another 'serious misdeed which brings disgrace on him' (Kinukawa 1994: 54). Judaism in first century Palestine was an '"honor culture" … her solicitation is an affront to the honor status of Jesus: no woman, and especially a gentile, unknown and unrelated to this Jew, would have dared invade his privacy at home to seek a favor' (Myers 1988: 198, 203). Her actions were astounding. Wainwright describes the woman as 'a *skandalon*, a boundary-walker' and suggests that she may even have been the one who travelled out of her territory into that more familiar to Jesus. The woman, like Ruth, possibly therefore crossed a geographical boundary as well as numerous cultural and societal ones (1998: 87).

The woman's transgressions continue. Having asked Jesus for help, she receives a curt reply: 'Let the children be fed first, for it is not fair to take the children's food and throw it to the dogs' (7:27). She remains undaunted and cleverly plays on Jesus' insulting saying or 'riddle' (Rhoads 1994: 355) about dogs to turn it to her advantage. Quoting Kinukawa again: 'she has to be aggressive if she and her daughter are to live. So she uses the same word that Jesus uses but in her own way' (1994: 58). Perkinson similarly suggests that she beats Jesus as his own speech game: there is a 'power*ful* redeployment of the terms of talk … A diminutive "put-down" becomes the occasion for a savy "put-on" by a big woman holding and claiming her own' (1996: 76). She chooses to inject the word 'table' into the conversation to suggest a household dog rather than a scavenger dog (Dufton 1989: 417) and replaces the Jewish word for 'children' with a more general word, stressing to Jesus that her daughter is also a child (S. Miller 2004: 98). Her arguing of the point 'deepens her affront to Jesus' (Myers 1988: 204). The woman also calls Jesus, *Kyrie*, meaning 'Sir' – a usual polite Gentile form of address – or 'Lord'. She thus manages, according to Marcus, 'a delightful mixture of respectful address ("Lord"), seeming acceptance of an inferior position ("dogs"), and daring repartee'. It is a 'rhetorical coup' (2000: 469).

The woman, through this clever response, 'wrests a blessing from Jesus' (Marcus 2000: 470) and offers him a new vision too in the process. As noted already, it is clear that it is her *words* that have ensured this outcome. Horsley argues that the Syro-Phoenician Woman 'is vindicated because of, not in spite of, her assertive behaviour' (2001: 215; see also France 2002: 299). Her courage in cutting through so many boundaries is what brings about the characters' mutual transformation and renewed vision and hope. The story is, from beginning to end, one of 'extraordinary transgression' (Wainwright 1998: 86). Ringe describes her as an 'uppity woman' who had the sharp 'insight of the poor and outcast who can see though a situation because they have few illusions to defend' and 'the courage of those who have little more to lose and therefore can act in commitment and from faith on behalf of others, for the sake of life, wholeness, and liberation' (1990: 50, 56).[35]

Jesus also crosses some remarkable boundaries. First, he traverses a geographical border into 'alien' territory. As Perkinson puts it, the 'colonial geography of the encounter marks this moment as a kind of "point farthest out" ... He exits "the nation" proper, into a hybrid domain where three distinct cultures – Phoenician, Jewish and Hellenistic – intersect' (1996: 66). In crossing to 'Israel's outside', Jesus 'moves from speech to silence' (1996: 69). Even more surprisingly, he then violates gender and cultural taboos by entering into a conversation that would have dishonoured him and admitting that he has been beaten by her in argument (Myers 1988: 204). The significance of this scandalous concession should not be underestimated, as it effectively extended the Kingdom of God, the erstwhile preserve of the Jews, to Gentiles. His part in the encounter represented a major rupture of traditionally-received religious views as well as a shattering of everyday societal taboos. Jesus is, according to Myers, constructing a whole 'new social order'. In this episode, along with 5:21–43, Jesus 'extend[s] and deepen[s] the scope of the kingdom's social inclusivity' and the story articulates that 'the poor of the gentile world *are* included in this bias of the kingdom mission' (1988: 197–198). Kinukawa explicitly claims that Jesus 'challenges the barrier-building between the pure and the unclean and negates an artificially warranted cultic purity. He has executed another boundary-breaking feat' (1994: 52).[36] The fact that in three out of four passages recounting Jesus' action on behalf of Gentiles, he tries

---

[35]   Marcus points to other clever, wise, bright women who overcome men in argument, including the woman of Tekoa in 2 Sam. 14 who persuades King David to reverse the banishment of Absalom (2000: 464).

[36]   For more on Jesus crossing boundaries in this passage, see Williamson (1983: 137) and Witherington (2001: 231). Loader suggests that such boundary crossing was the 'exception rather than the rule for Jesus' (1996: 61, 51).

to hide what he has done (1:40–45, 7:24, 7:36–37), indicates that what occurred must have been shocking enough to warrant secrecy (Marcus 2000: 467).[37]

Transgressive boundary-crossing is thus central to the whole pericope (Rhoads 1994: 363, Loader 1996) and the Syro-Phoenician Woman and Jesus both embody this reality. It is their mutual courage and risk-taking for the love of the young woman which leads to her healing and the wider inclusion of the Gentile peoples in Jesus' mission.

The ecology of faith, as glimpsed in these two stories, involves taking risks and crossing multiple boundaries for the sake of others. The two 'strange' women courageously put their respectability, status and even lives on the line when encountering a powerful man they hope can help the people they love. These two men, in turn, engage with Ruth and the Syro-Phoenician Woman in ways that defy social norms and risk their own ruin in order to meet the women's needs. Jesus and Boaz show a willingness to change their own ingrained assumptions and ways of being.

Many migrants take significant risks to travel to a new country and find themselves continually crossing boundaries, whether of a national, geographical, societal, cultural, class, religious, educational or skills-based nature.[38] They often do this to make a better life for loved ones. People who engage with them positively also often take risks, albeit far less dramatic, to help in whatever way they can. Befrienders welcome strangers into their lives, giving generously of their time and money and engaging with different religious traditions and cultures, and those who campaign for immigrant and asylum seeker rights can provoke suspicion from neighbours and friends. In the US, such risks are becoming increasingly potent. In a series of new laws proposed in Alabama in 2011, anyone offering support to undocumented people was going to be made liable for arrest.[39] Potentially transforming and mutually life-giving relationships between migrants and members of established populations are formed because all involved dare to trust in the 'other' and put themselves in a position where their assumptions and lives may be changed. The boundary-pushing of Ruth and the overtly uppity approach of the Syro-Phoenician Woman are strategies employed by both groups at different times to achieve a better life for those seeking asylum.

There are, however, many in established populations who shy away from taking such risks, and for all sorts of reasons. Many assume that any required

---

[37]   The fourth passage is 5:19–20. Marcus suggests Old Testament precedents for the healing of Gentiles, notably Elijah's miracle for Gentile woman in Tyre and Sidon in 1 Kgs 17:8–16 (2000: 467).

[38]   On the risks taken by Mexican immigrants to the US and the ways in which these represent 'crucifixion,' see Cave (2011) and Groody (2009b).

[39]   This part of the series of laws known as HB56 was not in fact ratified, largely due to a protest made by church leaders in that state. However, many other draconian measures such as mandating that schools check the immigration status of all pupils and their parents were passed into law in September 2011.

boundary-crossing should be performed by the newcomers: asylum seekers are expected to integrate into British society by learning English (crossing the language boundary), wearing European clothes and eating European food (crossing the cultural boundary), earning enough to contribute substantially to the UK economy (often, though not always, crossing economic and/or educational boundaries) and accepting whatever housing or handouts they are given (often, crossing a class boundary from middle class to working class or 'underclass'). Established communities, from this perspective, simply need to stay where they are. Some also worry about breaking the law.[40]

Such a risk-averse and sedentary attitude is contested by biblical stories exhibiting an ecology of faith, as it is by theologians of alterity and hospitality. They concur that helping those in need requires the host, not just the stranger, to take risks and be willing to be changed. The host has to step over boundaries for the stranger, whether those are the material edges of social credibility or economic viability or the psychological–spiritual–experiential boundaries of the self. Just like Boaz and Jesus, he cannot expect to remain the same and needs to be prepared to have his understanding of the world and sense of personal being transformed. This is because, as Volf has suggested, we need to 'embrace' others and embracing someone involves welcoming, self-giving and readjusting our own identities to make space for the other to enter (1996: 29). Koyama explains why opening oneself up to create a space for the 'stranger' in this way is no easy matter: 'The way of extending hospitality to the stranger may even become the way towards martyrdom (Phil. 2:8). Christ was crucified because he extended hospitality to strangers so completely … The *theologia crucis*, or way of the cross … rejects the language of threat. It proclaims the ultimate power of self-giving love (*hesed*, *agape*)' (1993: 284–286; see also Groody 2009a: 6–9).

Concrete examples of such courageous boundary-crossing hospitality are numerous. The hiding of Jews in the village of Le Chambon-sur-Lignon (Hallie 1979), Dorothy Day and the Catholic Worker Houses for people who are homeless (Murray 1990) and L'Arche communities bringing together those with and without intellectual disabilities are only three.[41] The 'hosts' and 'guests' in all of these contexts have inhabited an ecology of faith grounded in risky attitudes and practices of loving-kindness. They, like Ruth, Boaz, the Syro-Phoenician Woman and Jesus, pose a significant challenge to anyone thinking about engaging with migrants today. Can we act in similarly extraordinary and audacious ways – ways which carry danger but may also bring about new life and hope for newcomers and ourselves?

---

[40]   People are often not sure what 'the law' is that they would be breaking, but fear collusion with someone who is in their country without legal permission.

[41]   For more on the need to open oneself up to the 'other' and on the risks inherent in hospitality, see Brueggemann (1999: 1), Ford (1997: 1–23), Murray (1990), Nouwen (1976), Vanier (1997) and Volf (1996). Hospitality goes beyond tolerance (Bretherton 2004, 2006a) and the language of justice and human rights (Sagovsky 2008: 146).

The Perspective of the Excluded in an Ecology of Faith: Who Really Benefits and On Whose Terms?

Despite apparently warm portrayals of the stranger and the transformations which they bring about, the end results are not universally life-bringing and unproblematic. An ecology of faith is no utopia. Even where authors were encouraging a more generous view towards strangers, they very easily slipped back into an exclusionary mentality. McKinlay notes in both narratives 'the double-sided potential of rupture'. Not 'only is there a rupture that opens towards a hoped-for and celebratory future, but there is also the rupture that is potentially harmful and divisive' (2004: 166). Consciously reading the texts from the standpoint of the two heroines and contemporary asylum seekers, ambiguities in the ecologies of faith they depict become apparent.

Ruth may not experience positive transformation in the way that Naomi, Boaz and Israel do. At one level, this is because she is absorbed and integrated to such a complete extent that her own identity is submerged and lost. At another level, it is because despite this, Ruth remains an 'outsider', never fully accepted in the community. Rather than being a story which encourages the kind of openness and hospitality to strangers described above, it is one in which the stranger turns out to have been *used* for the benefit of Israel. Honig discusses the ways in which Ozick and Kristeva have understood Ruth. According to Ozick, Ruth is an exemplary convert (1994). Ruth revitalizes the Israelite order by converting to Judaism while the Moabite 'other', Orpah, remains in Moab. Ruth is praised for leaving the 'childish ideas' of Moab behind (1994: 227) and according to Honig, is presented as a model émigré: 'Ozick tries to solve the problem as many multicultural Western democracies have since: by having the helpful (part of the) foreigner/stranger (Ruth) assimilate and by ensuring that the dangerous (part of the) foreigner (Orpah) leave or stay behind' (1999: 64). Honig censures Ozick for failing to question this assimilating ideology. Kristeva, by contrast, sees Ruth as a gift because she disrupts the prevailing order. But just like Ozick, Kristeva hardly mentions Orpah, indicating that once again Ruth's Moabite foreignness is not wanted. She seems to advocate cosmopolitanism without foreignness and this only 'risks becoming another form of domination, particularly when it confronts an Other that resists assimilation to it' (Honig 1999: 65–67, 69). Honig's criticism of Ozick and Kristeva is thus twofold: they judge the immigrant in terms of what she will do for *us* as a nation and they reduce Ruth's 'otherness' and 'foreignness' (1999: 54).

Ruth as an 'other', in Honig's reading, is never fully accepted in the text. The Moabite woman remains an unwelcome stranger throughout. The repetition of the word 'foreigner' indicates that Ruth '*stays* a Moabite' and Naomi's taking of Obed (4:16–17) signifies the community's continuing fear of Ruth's foreignness (1999: 60; see also Yee 2009: 130). Ruth also returns to silence at the end of the book. She lacks a meaningful relationship with Naomi and is in denial about her loss of Orpah and the Moab she represents (1999: 72). Significantly, as Honig points out, clinging and silence are, familiar moments of immigration dynamics … in contemporary multicultural democracies. One, a furious and hyperbolic assimilationism in which all connections to the motherland are disavowed. And two, a refusal of transition and a retreat into a separatist or nationalist enclave that leaves the immigrant stranded in relation to the receiving country *and* in relation to the lost homeland. (1999: 72)

Others have also seen the story of Ruth as ambivalent at best and oppressive at worst. Brenner claims that Ruth's disappearance from her own story at the end reflects her negative 'absorption' rather than her positive 'integration' (2005: 108) and Yee sees Ruth as a 'model minority' and 'perpetual foreigner' who is also exploited by Boaz as 'good foreign help' and a source of social and economic capital. She sees Ruth as an 'indictment of those of us who live in the First World who exploit the cheap labor of developing countries and poor immigrants' (2009: 128–131, 134). Lau argues that Ruth is incorporated as a 'member of the ingroup' and that 'no adjustment is required on the part of Israel as the host nation, only maintenance of the Israelite identity *status quo*' (2011: 92, 112). Dube suggests that the relationship between Ruth/Moab and Naomi/Judah is that of slave/master. Far from being a 'model of liberating interdependence between nations' therefore, Judah benefits at Moab's expense (2001: 193–194). Donaldson compares Ruth to the figure of Pocahontas in Cherokee history, whose goodness comes from loving white men and rejecting her own identity and background. She commends Orpah's decision as a courageous act of self-affirmation, choosing her indigenous mother's house over that of her alien Israelite father (2010).

McKinlay, writing from a postcolonial, feminist Pakeha New Zealand/Aotearoa perspective, regards it has having an overtly political colonial agenda (2004: 55–56): 'The story of Ruth reads almost as a hymn to boundary crossing – in the right direction; right, of course, being defined again by the storyteller' (2004: 50). Ruth denies her own language, spirituality, kinship claims and even burial on home ground and so the 'choice of returning home or going forward with Naomi posed by the storyteller turns out to have been no choice at all but a textual strategy to promote the model of Israelite faith' (2004: 53). Ruth struggles in a male-dominated and Israelite world. Another vociferous critic is Kwok, who challenges some of her own earlier positive views on Ruth and warns against reading the book as an 'idyllic tale' (2005: 101). Drawing on Schwartz, she points out that foreignness in the story is associated with scarcity and that Boaz's supposed generosity is not as great as it may seem because Naomi is his kin. Having to adopt the Israelite God as a precondition for inclusion problematically ties kinship to monotheism (Schwartz cited in Kwok 2005: 115). Thus, whether Ruth was written in the pre-exilic or post-exilic era, 'the importance of kinship and the significance of the bloodline in defining insiders and outsiders in ancient societies are underscored' (2005: 104). Even LaCocque, who sees Ruth as receiving new life, acknowledges that her son is effectively born to Naomi and that she never reaches full textual subjectivity (2004: 144–146).[42]

The Syro-Phoenician Woman, as already noted, is given no name and she soon disappears from view after the episode ends. She is permitted just one moment of semi-subjectivity. The daughter makes no appearance and has no textual voice (Donaldson 2005: 101). Is the woman therefore present in the narrative only in order to facilitate Jesus' movement from an exclusive preoccupation with Israel to an inclusion of all in the Kingdom of God? She remains on the outside despite Jesus' concession to heal her daughter. Moreover, while the woman's words to Jesus seem to be daring and challenging, the possibility that she was showing subservience to Jesus in agreeing that she and her daughter were like 'dogs' cannot be ruled out. Kwok notes that kneeling before Jesus, the woman 'humbles herself and evokes the image of a "devoted dog"' and that her speech is clearly 'framed in a christocentric and androcentric discourse' (1995: 77, 73). She looks up to him and speaks as his inferior. The woman's reply may signify her recognition of the place of Israel (Hooker 1991: 182). McKinlay's commentary (2004: 109) provokes this question: do her words reflect ironic resistance or the internalization of her place among the crumb-eating dogs?

Scholars who recognize the ambiguities in the portrayals of Ruth and the Syro-Phoenician Woman point to dangers lurking just beneath the surface of every ecology of faith. Being aware of these can help in guarding against them. It is easy for those in power to slip back into oppressive habits even if they have the best of intentions: the ecology of fear is never completely obliterated. Members of established populations, like the author of Ruth, can be so keen to absorb migrants into their society that the 'strange' aspects of their identity are devalued. They decide the terms on which those seeking sanctuary will be accepted. At an institutional level, this is seen in the governmental determination in the UK that all newcomers should learn English and pass a citizenship test. At a personal level, befrienders can also run the risk of being so welcoming that the 'other' is not allowed to be who she most authentically is. 'We' often decide what projects would be best for 'them' and, as a result, start to redefine who others are based on our own assumptions and preconceptions. Someone settling is then left with a difficult choice, as Honig hinted at: do I integrate on the terms of the established population and negate the parts of myself that are 'foreign' or do I live in an enclave, keeping my identity but risking never being accepted as one of 'them'? The personal cost, either way, to asylum seekers and other immigrants can be immense.

We should also not go so far in understanding the stranger as life-bringer that established communities regard engaging with those seeking sanctuary primarily as a wonderful opportunity for themselves. This only succeeds in turning help into exploitation. The main focus still needs to be on responding to the needs and desires of the 'stranger' without any hope of return. Sutherland makes this clear in his definition of hospitality: 'Christian hospitality is the intentional, responsible,

---

[42]   Nielsen (1997: 93) views the outcome for Ruth more positively.

and caring act of welcoming or visiting, in either public or private places, those who are strangers, enemies, or distressed, *without regard for reciprocation*' (2006: xiii; my italics). We are to help others without thinking about what may be gained by us as a result. Any benefits should be a bonus rather than a motivating factor. Similarly, Hallie points out that it is precisely the *uselessness* of strangers which makes regard of them significant. He writes, 'Helping is the nerve of intimacy, it is what intimacy is … That is why helping strangers has always had an air of mystery about it for me. How do we sometimes manage to treat outsiders, useless aliens, as if they were our intimates?' (1997: 4).

An ecology of faith grounded in positive relationships with strangers should always assume more 'give' than 'take' and it is essential to guard against viewing asylum seekers with utilitarian eyes, as abstract 'others' who exist to provide members of established populations with opportunities for growth. Offering practical, material support to asylum seekers should remain the priority. Min is adamant that we must engage with the 'other' as a concrete human being, embedded in a network of socio-historical relations. Political praxis and liberation must be introduced into abstract or interpersonal theologies of the 'other'. As he somewhat ironically suggests, one 'would think that the compelling priority of the starving other is to find food as such, not a face-to-face relationship with millions of people whose taxes pay for the food' (2004: 21). Koyama similarly proposes the need for 'uncushioned neighborology' (1999: 67) which is not about abstract relationality, but about embodied relationships. For Ogletree, the opposition between egoism and altruism is in fact false as selfhood is effected precisely in the radical capacity for self-giving to the other without limit (2003: 92).[43] It is only when we give without hope of return that we ourselves can receive and grow. Suggesting that working with migrants is enriching is both self-indulgent and self-defeating unless engagement is primarily about offering something of the self, materially and personally. This poses some challenging questions: what motivates our engagement with those seeking asylum? Is it simply a desire to help those in need without hope for return (which, as has already been suggested, risks being paternalistic)? Or is it because we get something out of it (which risks being exploitative)? Finding a way of treading the fine line between these two motivations so that we avoid the twin pitfalls of paternalism and exploitation is essential.

Complex Character Portrayals: Allowing the Stranger to be Real

The oppression and exploitation of Ruth and the Syro-Phoenician Woman can, however, be exaggerated. Ruth does find a home, new life and security in Bethlehem and the Syro-Phoenician Woman does have her wish granted. As Sakenfeld

---

[43]   Ogletree offers a fuller discussion, exploring and charting a middle course between the views of Tillich and Lévinas; see also Ford (1999), who mediates between Lévinas and Jungel.

suggests of Ruth, while it is not an unproblematic idyll, 'one must be careful not to throw the proverbial baby out with the bath water' (1999: 10).[44] What the noted ambiguities actually point to is that Ruth and the Syro-Phoenician Woman are both complex. They are allowed by their authors to be real, multidimensional characters.

Ruth, as she has so far been presented, is one of two types. Either she is a virtuous and courageous woman, demonstrating *hesed* towards Naomi and Boaz and taking extraordinary risks in order to transform all of their lives for the better; or she is a vulnerable, exploited and oppressed dependent who never really comes out of the shadows. The truth probably lies in a synthesis of these two poles. Brenner argues that Ruth, Naomi and Boaz have different and changing roles (1993: 76), and Fewell and Gunn encourage readers to see the characters in Ruth as 'complex people, not merely built around a single primary trait, like loyalty, altruism or generosity' (1990: 15).[45] To start with, Ruth is likely to have had multiple and conflicting motivations for travelling to Judah and taking the actions she did. The famine in Moab, family and marriage networks and love for Naomi are simply three which are mentioned. Brenner, writing in the first person, suggests that she may in reality have 'clung' to Naomi for selfish reasons. She refers to the 'complexity of my motives ... I am shrewd, practical, and self-serving first, as well as kind and loyal. And what's wrong with that, instead of an idealized portrait of a selfless hanger-on?' (2005: 105). Fewell and Gunn argue that for Ruth, destitution in Moab would undoubtedly have been a significant push factor and suggest that Boaz probably acted so warmly to Ruth out of a sense of paternalistic care and sexual attraction (1990: 30, 41, 55, 85; see also Yee 2009: 133). Naomi's changing levels of concern and attention to Ruth in the novella suggests an attitude towards her which varied according to Naomi's needs (Fewell and Gunn 1990: 76–77, 82).

Moreover, it is entirely possible that Ruth is both dependent and submissive *and* takes substantial self-motivated risks in order to transform her and Naomi's present into a better future. Resisting easy definition, she is a bundle of blurred identities and traits. Those who see her as a submissive and obedient daughter and wife and those who suggest she was a daring, devious and subversive initiator of change can both be right. The fact that she is consistently labelled a Moabite,

---

[44]   Sakenfeld argues that Ruth made a choice to be kind, caring and loyal and that Naomi 'taking' the child at the end simply highlights the reversal of Naomi's opening lament. It is a survival story and 'every aspect of its ending' cannot therefore be regarded 'as the desire of God for all times and places' (1999: 13, 83, 87). Koosed argues that postcolonial readings of Ruth risk 'historical anachronism' as they read contemporary imperialism back into the text and are therefore too harsh in their criticisms (2011: 26–29, 40, 49). She suggests, for example, that Ruth may refuse to raise her son in order to avoid becoming a model Israelite wife and mother, and if so, this indicates her resistance to assimilation (2011: 118).

[45]   Sasson designates characters in Ruth as certain folk-tale 'types' (1989).

for example, may imply that she retained aspects of her own cultural identity while also becoming a member of Israelite society (Sakenfeld 1999: 32). Koosed describes Ruth's character as 'unsettled and unsettling' – 'a border crosser who embodies plurality' (2011: 2, 63, 48) – and Saxegaard claims that Ruth's identity is 'mysterious'. 'She is simultaneously a foreign Moabite and a faithful daughter-in-law, a seductive handmaid, and a worthy woman' (2010: 105, 128). This kind of hybridity is, significantly, often a resistance strategy practised by the oppressed to disrupt categories upon them imposed by the powerful (Yee 2010: 200). Sakenfeld points to the complexity of who is at the margin and who at the centre in the book. While Ruth is marginalized textually, the Bethlehemite/Judahite community was in reality a small and struggling community in the Persian Empire at the time. Ruth thus represents the '"center," the dominant non-Israelite and non-Yahwistic culture' and the margin simultaneously (1999: 87–88). Maluleke presents a similar argument, warning against over-romanticizing Ruth and seeing her only as a positive role model, a viewpoint which incidentally eases middle-class consciences by enabling us to believe that 'Ruths' can subvert our current systems. Noting Ruth's limitations, fear, selfishness and deviousness, he writes:

> Stop the cult that wishes to see positive and successful role models everywhere … Many African Ruths are not 'successful'. Patriarchy, culture and globalization will not let them succeed … We must appreciate those who try and fail in their resistance … The Ruths of Africa are not roaring successes. But *the Ruths of Africa are human, they are humanizing, and they are real*. (2001: 244–245, 248–249. My italics)

Ruth comes across as 'real' precisely because she is not easily pigeonholed. She cannot be described simply as either a vulnerable angel or a wily go-getter. Probably out for her own advantage, she did much for others at the same time.

In the story of the Syro-Phoenician Woman, the woman is simultaneously privileged and oppressed. Though an educated, upper-class Greek, she would have been marginalized due to her daughter's condition and beyond Jesus' concern being a Gentile. She displays behaviour which is subservient at one moment, bowing before Jesus, and spirited at another, challenging his replies. Kwok names this complexity and hybridity. The woman, '[a]s an outsider … stands simultaneously at the boundaries of the privileged and the marginalized'. She is neither fully Other nor not Other. We therefore need to 'guard against a simple and reductionist understanding of the Other … The Other is never a homogeneous group; there is always the Other within the Other' (1995: 75, 82). There is interestingly no evidence to suggest that the woman became a Christian – she simply goes on her way – and it may well be that she managed to claim 'inclusion without losing her identity' (Rebera 2001: 110). As far as the contemporary reader can tell, she received healing for her daughter without being required to surrender her identity.

The stories of Ruth and the Syro-Phoenician Woman reveal that an ecology of faith does not deal in *types* of person but with *real* individuals. They indicate the falsity of the blanket and monochrome stereotypes so often attached to asylum seekers, refugees and immigrants. Employing dichotomized labels such as successful immigrant/oppressed outsider and vulnerable victim/cunning initiator are neither accurate nor helpful. Migrants are complex individuals, with inevitably mixed motivations for coming to the Global North and hybrid identities. Many asylum seekers also experience multiple statuses concurrently as the Syro-Phoenician Woman did: while often wealthy and privileged in their countries of origin, they find themselves at the bottom of the societal ladder in the receiving country. We are *all* – members of established populations too – 'real' people with multifaceted motivations and personalities and reductionist, simplistic categorizations, whether positive or negative, benefit no one. Consciously recognizing and speaking of asylum seekers and refugees in more realistic, human and humanizing ways is important.

A corollary of this is that, in an ecology of faith, the stranger is allowed to remain 'strange'. Their hybridity is respected rather than squashed in order to force the 'other' to become like 'us'. Conversely, members of established populations are also encouraged to retain their unique particularity. Honouring human particularity requires the maintenance of flexible boundaries on both the part of migrants and established populations. In the language of hospitality, the 'host' is required to allow the 'guest' to remain 'other'. Their strangeness is not to be diminished. As Murray puts it, the 'host must also allow the guest to remain in some sense a stranger, must accept that she or he will not fully understand the mystery of this other person' (1990: 18). Volf makes it clear that the host's very ability to receive from the other is dependent on allowing them to be different. In what he describes as act three of embracing another – closing the arms – maintaining one's boundaries and allowing the 'other' to be irreducibly 'other' is critical. Not only is this 'embrace proper ... unthinkable without *reciprocity*', but

> a *soft touch* is necessary. I may not close my arms around the other too tightly, so as to crush her and assimilate her, otherwise I will be engaged in a concealed power-act of exclusion ... Similarly, I must keep the boundaries of my own self firm, offer resistance, otherwise I will be engaged in a self-destructive act of abnegation. At no point in the process may the self deny either the other or itself. (1996: 143)[46]

In order for this to happen, the host needs to create a 'friendly emptiness where strangers can enter and discover themselves as created free ... Hospitality is not a subtle invitation to adopt the life style of the host, but the gift of a chance for the guest to find his [*sic*] own' (Nouwen 1976: 69). The stranger is invited into this warm, open space on her own terms but at the same time, the host also shows

---

[46]   See also Anderson (1999: 12–14) and Palmer (1983: 68) on allowing the stranger to remain 'strange'. The Trinity holds together the notion of diversity in unity or strangeness in togetherness (Cunningham 1998: 271).

herself clearly. The host needs to wait on the stranger, wasting time (Newman 2007: 180), in order to discover her irreducible particularity and she also needs to allow the stranger to speak the truth, however painful it may be to hear. Simultaneously, the host needs to retain her integrity by speaking and living her truth. Boundaries should be 'semi-permeable', at once firm and flexible: 'Without boundaries, there will be no system into which anyone could be invited; without hospitality, the system will dry up, will turn in on itself and die' (Westerhoff 2004: xii, 83).

Living in an ecology of faith is not to adopt a wishy-washy uncritical capitulation to whatever the stranger demands. It is rather about inhabiting a posture of respect towards the 'strangeness' of the stranger and an openness to being changed by this, while gently holding onto a sense of self. Boaz and Jesus did not relinquish their essence, but simply shifted their self-understanding and entered into the truth of their own identities more fully. Members of established populations need to discover ways of treading this delicate line between allowing the stranger to be who they are, on their own terms, while not feeling that their own integrity is being compromised. Being transformed by strangers can actually affirm our deepest integrity rather than undermine it.

Summary

This chapter has explored the second broad strand of responses to strangers in the Bible – responses made by those inhabiting an ecology of faith. One sub-strand of this material encourages Christians to do their duty towards the *gerim* of today, including asylum seekers. Another sub-strand, exemplified in the stories of Ruth and the Syro-Phoenician Woman, goes further and encourages us to see the stranger as a potential life-bringer. Living in the ecology of faith depicted in both narratives involves one-to-one, embodied encounters and courageous risk-takng by the stranger and host, and allows the stranger to remain strange, complex and ambiguous. It requires wariness on the part of the established population against slipping back into an ecology of fear and unintentional oppression and exploitation of the outsider and a maintenance of gentle boundaries. Creating such an environment is clearly no easy task and it is to this that the concluding chapter now turns.

PART IV
Conclusion

Chapter 9
Moving Our Encounters On

> The point is, we are all human. We must help and support each other. The Church likes everyone to live a normal life in society and not be isolated. They think we must live equally together under this roof, we must help the needy ... Christians understand asylum seekers and refugees and act. They are open to the asylum seeker's story and try to help.
>
> (Hassan in Group Interview 2007)

> Diverse currents swirl about Europe: currents of panic, cruelty and hatred; a strong current of obtuse selfishness, oblivious to its likely consequences; and a current of sanity and humanity. Only if this last predominates will there be hope of averting disaster for the world outside Europe and within it.
>
> (Dummet 2001: 152–153)

Engaging with the ecology of fear surrounding migration today and creating ecologies of faith are far from easy tasks. How are Christian FBOs doing on this front and where might we go from here? Churches are already making a substantial and valuable contribution to the support of migrants, including asylum seekers and refugees, in the UK and across the globe. In this chapter, I hope to weave together the threads of the book and suggest some concrete ways in which churches could continue, deepen and expand some of their current practices. How might we move our encounters on?

Encounters of Grassroots Service

Encounters of grassroots service form the core of church work with asylum seekers – and indeed, other migrants – at present and such a focus remains essential. Those seeking sanctuary often speak, above all else, of the informal friendship they have been offered through church-related groups. The provision of advice, activities and outings, the sharing of celebrations, English language classes, money for bus tickets, clothes for children, case support (churches are often seen as a last hope when an appeal has been refused) and the opportunities for volunteering that churches present can help to counter the isolation, fear, disempowerment, enforced passivity and poverty often experienced by people seeking sanctuary. Churches and other FBOs also provide a space in which asylum seekers can meet others in a similar situation, and in removal centres, meetings with visitors are often the only friendly contact that internees experience. Churches thus offer various 'social resources' – personal relationships providing emotional, informational and tangible support (Ryan et al. 2008: 7) – vital to newcomers' ability to transcend the ecology of fear. They contribute to the adaptive capabilities and psychological well-being of migrants, regardless of faith affiliation or background. In an ecology in which asylum seekers both mistrust and are mistrusted (Daniel and Knudsen 1995: 1), churches can be a lifeline. They can provide an interim haven for those who have lost one home and do not as yet have a new one. The range of networks and resources they proffer can also provide a basis upon which people can build if leave to remain is granted. While Christian organizations are by no means alone in offering an open door, they are among the most significant bodies making such a contribution and are physically present in every local community. Such encounters, as we have seen in the stories of Ruth and the Syro-Phoenician Woman, generate and sustain an ecology of faith. One-to-one, face-to-face, embodied relationships, which have a desire to help the 'other' in need at their heart, are its life-blood. Through engaging in such relationships, churches are helping to make what Hallie calls an 'eye [in] the hurricane' of 'the indifferent, destructive forces in the world' (1997: 53).

The Importance of Migrant Agency, Mutuality, Motivation, Training and Integrity

The ways in which Christian FBOs seek to help others can sometimes however amplify rather than reduce their difficulties. Good intentions are not enough to ensure that an ecology of faith prevails over one of fear. As Hallie puts it, 'People can be treated by other people in ways that look benign but are really destructive … There is a way of helping people that fills their hands but breaks their hearts. What is kindness to the helper can be cruelty to the helped' (1997: 207). Mutuality needs to lie at the heart of all encounters between migrants and supporters, and Christians must go beyond an approach that is only about duty towards one that is also about reciprocally enriching relationship and flourishing (Snyder 2007).[1] This helps to guard against the paternalism that is an inherent risk of offering care. Given that it is often strangers who act as bearers of new, God-given life, people standing in solidarity with migrants should more consciously tune into the possibility that those whom they encounter may be offering them surprising insights and glimpses of the divine. Opening ourselves up to the possibility that we might be changed is risky and even when intentions are well-meant, Thompson recognizes that 'our instinct to control is so strong that we manage people rather than empower them, supervise rather than liberate them, oversee rather than support them' (2003: 33).

Practising mutuality involves engaging with newcomers as dynamic, contributing 'survivors' and subjects rather than as vulnerable, 'passive innocents' (Mares 2003: 347) and guarding against imposing assumptions about what best assists adaptation. We need to ask ourselves: how do we foster dignity and

---

1   Wilson has suggested relating to asylum seekers as 'neighbours' rather than as 'guest/host' for similar reasons (2005: 81).

agency? How do we struggle *with* rather than struggle *for*? (Koopman 2008). This is particularly important given that refugees are constructed as 'bare life', as exceptions to the norm and without agency. As Bretherton argues, 'churches must overcome the exclusion of refugees by abiding with them as persons able to express themselves within and act upon a common world' – an approach he characterizes as 'the hallowing of bare life' (2010: 159). Essentially, it is vital to glean from migrants what *they* would like and to what extent and in which ways they actually wish to get involved with a church or organization. Some people seeking asylum become de facto members of the historic mainstream churches they attend – rather than simply being recipients of their services – and act *with* established community Christians as volunteers in projects or to challenge policy. Offering full participation in programmes, in terms of practical day-to-day arrangements, planning and management, wherever possible is crucial. While this may sometimes be difficult due to the transitory, stressful nature of many migrants' lives, it should still be held as an ideal. Relationships with established community Christians may not, however, be able to fulfill many people's needs for new social resources and migrants often help to settle one another through friendship, informal networks and alternative churches or faith traditions. Given this, could churches also more actively seek to provide spaces in which migrants who wish to could organize themselves?

Listening is crucial to the respecting of agency and should be undertaken with an awareness of the power a befriender inherently has over someone in the asylum system, resulting from having legal resident status and familiarity with the society. Migrants need to be allowed to be themselves – to be 'real' – with an array of mixed motivations for leaving their countries of origin and turning up at churches, approaches to survival and future plans. Emotional webs of uncertainty, fear, joy and hope need to be honoured and friends should guard against suffocating or absorbing the 'otherness' of strangers with kind suggestions. Morisy's notion of 'warm encounter' is helpful as it indicates an encounter which involves neither cold calling nor being too hot (1997: 30), as is the concept of 'hanging out' suggested by Rodgers (2004). Church-based groups need to offer an interested and compassionate engagement – a warm hanging out – without being stifling or imposing. Sharing some of one's own personal story and needs can help to foster mutuality. The moment when Fatima asked me how my work was going was the moment that we began to be friends rather than 'helper' and 'helped'. self-exposure involves taking risks, as the boundaries of the inner self are often the hardest to cross and allowing others to help us can be difficult. Courageous boundary-crossing is though, as I argued in Chapter 8, a defining feature of an ecology of faith.

Interrogation of our motivations and training would also be beneficial. Do we get involved because of a need to be needed or because of the longings and hopes of those we seek to support? While everyone inevitably has mixed motivations, the opposite danger of paternalism is exploitation – using migrants for our own ends – and solidarity with those who are struggling must remain our primary motivation. Engaging in encounters with migrants in order to be enriched is self-indulgent unless accompanied by a genuine effort to ameliorate their situation. The line between paternalism and exploitation is a fine tightrope to walk. Training and education concerning some of the issues affecting those seeking sanctuary is already offered in many church contexts. Although one of the benefits of church-based encounters is the personal or amateur touch (Sutherland 2006: 79), it may be helpful for supporters to have a greater understanding of the range of issues affecting those seeking asylum. For example, how well do volunteers grapple with the differing practical and psychological needs of asylum-seeking men and women? As Reilly has claimed, a 'standard package' approach does not always meet people's needs (1996: 16). Churches finally need to be wary of exploitation by governments that have, in line with the developments described in Chapter 1, made cut-backs in asylum support and then expected FBOs to plug the gaps (Bloch and Schuster 2002: 398, Logan 2000, Cohen 2003: 157–159). Faith-based groups need to maintain their integrity and engage in encounters of grassroots service for the benefit of migrants rather than to help balance national budgets and maintain state reputations with regards to welfare provision.

Expanding the Focus: Creating Crucibles for an Ecology of Faith and Engaging with Deprivation

Given the importance of contact between members of established communities and those seeking sanctuary in transrupting the ecology of fear, as discussed in Chapters 5 and 8, churches should also consider expanding their horizon to include those who are anti-asylum and anti-immigration. Engaging with the ecology of fear, rather than dismissing it out of hand – which usually only succeeds in entrenching people further in their views – is vital. Faith communities have the potential to act as a space in which bridges can be built between those who are different (CULF 2006: 25, Furbey et al. 2006). Through their buildings and the diversity of their membership, churches could offer a crucible for an ecology of faith, enacting and bringing into being the kind of diverse, cosmopolitan communities which the stories of Ruth and the Syro-Phoenician Woman point towards. Spaces that draw members of established communities and migrants together in conversation and shared activities – especially those that have mutual benefit – have a crucial role to play in fostering relationships that can expose stereotypes, create collective memories and identities and thereby counter scapegoating (D'Onofrio and Munk 2004: 43–46, Lewis 2005: 55, Ward 2008: 48–49). Law suggests that churches are called to be 'fear-miners' and provide contexts within which people can speak honestly 'without being judged or belittled' (2007: 43) and as Sacks puts it, the 'greatest single antidote to violence is *conversation*, speaking our fears, listening to the fears of others, and in that sharing of vulnerabilities discovering a genesis of hope' (2002: 2, Forrester 2005b: 105–107). CULF named such spaces as 'proximity spaces' (2006: 83) and hosting 'dialogues between groups in the community who are, or may be, in conflict' is, according to Palmer, a central public vocation of the Church (1983: 131). Their permanent commitment to a particular place means that they are ideally situated to do so (CULF 2006: 80). Facilitating friendly encounters between those who fear one another – creating intentional proximity ecologies of faith – could therefore be an important additional way in which churches could support migrants. Interfaith dialogue is one necessary facet of many of these encounters (Yong 2008). We need to be performing ecologies in which people can learn to take risks and cross boundaries. The ecology of faith can only become a reality through, to coin a phrase of Castillo Guerra, humanizing 'the societies of destination, so that they are hospitable societies' (2008: 262).

Engagement with people living in urban areas of deprivation for their own sake is however also vital. It is all too easy for predominantly middle-class churches to call on society at large to embrace the stranger. There is a tendency to split society into those who are 'good', in favour of asylum seekers, and those who are 'bad', against them. FBOs supportive of migrants criticize all hostility and concentrate solely on encounters with those seeking sanctuary. A more complex compassion is necessary. We need to recognize that sometimes, reluctance to share already inadequate public spaces and overstretched public services is natural. We need to be wary of demanding an openness and generosity which we ourselves can seem unable or unwilling to offer. At present, churches rarely succeed in offering those living in contexts of urban deprivation the front-line, daily support that they are being asked to show asylum seekers. Iveson is thus right to warn:

> Any demand that all urban inhabitants adopt a cosmopolitan openness to others will have a fundamentally different meaning for weak groups than it will for those who have voluntarily fortified themselves in enclaves of privilege. In some instances, the construction of fragile boundaries which limit engagements with others is all that protects the weak from annihilation. (2006: 81)

Churches wishing to stand alongside migrants should consider generating and sustaining more encounters of grassroots service with others who are marginalized.

Encounters with the Powers

Encounters of grassroots service make little long-term sense unless accompanied by advocacy and lobbying. Encounters with the powers are crucial. A band-aid approach that patches up some of the wounds of those who have experienced fear in their countries of origin and a flawed, deterrent-based asylum system will do little to decisively transrupt the ecology of fear. Graham has challenged the 'broadly curative model of "crisis-management"' and asks, 'Is the aim of care the amelioration of existential and personal distress and trouble, or the pursuit of proactive projects to establish social justice?' (1996: 52–53, Pattison 1997: 208–220). Churches have an inescapably political role (Bonhoeffer 1995: 344–346, Davey 2001: 107) and political engagement takes a variety of forms, from publishing responses to government White Papers to awareness-raising and lobbying (Bartley 2006: 64–67).[2] Encountering the powers helps to insure against the danger of being co-opted into government agendas. As Bartley suggests, adopting 'an identity as a provider of welfare, more professional, better motivated and better able than others to deliver what the government has undertaken to provide' is 'unlikely to be distinct enough' (2006: 158, Leech 2005: 141). This said, a thin tightrope between prophecy and pastoral care sometimes needs to be trodden: chaplains in removal centres can understandably be reluctant to speak about their work or centre conditions for fear that their posts may be cut.

How might church-related groups redouble their efforts to influence asylum and immigration policy and to tackle other aspects of the ecology of fear? In some ways, it is a matter of continuing what is already being done. Christians need to carry on representing the voices of those seeking sanctuary to the 'powers', be these politicians, journalists, lawyers, judges or civil servants, in contexts where their own voices are rarely if ever heard (Forrester 2001: 72). In the UK, the top-down influence of Church of England bishops in the House of Lords on immigration and asylum bills and bottom-up campaigns calling for asylum seekers' right to work and an end to policy-induced destitution have brought about changes. Witnessing in court on behalf of those seeking sanctuary is also important. While MRAs may not be able to speak out, other church members with insights into circumstances in removal centres need to make irreducibly present those who have been relegated to invisibility behind walls and wire. Challenging media misrepresentations of migrants and providing all of the actors in the asylum system, from the general public to those working in government positions, with accurate information should remain a focus of FBOs at local and national levels. Providing people with facts can make a significant dent in the ecology of fear (D'Onofrio and Munk 2004: 45). Rabbi Julia Neuberger argues that the Church in the UK has been 'at its most impressive' in the area of refugees and asylum seekers, precisely because it has taken on a leading 'prophetic role' and been unpartisan concerning the faith-backgrounds of those seeking sanctuary (2006: 29–30). She notes that 'the Church has used and uses its voice to raise the awkward points' and 'contributes to public debate by posing searching questions' (2006: 34). The same is true of churches in the US concerning undocumented immigration. In the ecologies of faith portrayed in Ruth and Mark, the strangers were not simply cared for: their presence led to the questioning and disruption of established legal norms and categorizations of who was 'in' and who was 'out'. Or to use more contemporary language, the strangers were a spur to systemic change.

---

2   The nature and extent of church engagement varies according to the size and nature of particular denominations. The Church of England, as the Established Church, continues to have a privileged political position in the UK.

Widening the Horizon: Global and Transnational Engagement

The injection of more energy in some areas may be beneficial. To start with, we could do more to link our efforts to support those seeking asylum with efforts to tackle the root causes of their flight. Any engagement with societal issues today must have an eye to the global dimensions involved (Green 2001: 30, Davey 2001, Reader 2008) and churches need to be more aware of global dynamics of forced migration outlined in Chapter 4. Given that much forced migration and the ecology of fear are transnational, paths out of an ecology of fear into an ecology of faith are also likely to be transnational. Churches have an inbuilt tendency towards parochialism – they focus on their local patch – and the deliberate cultivation of a more outward-looking stance is therefore necessary. What is more, the 'development of more comprehensive and cohesive strategies to address forced migration in its complexity' is vital (Martin et al. 2005: 3). Could churches begin to link locally-oriented support with the efforts of international humanitarian organizations to assist development, peacekeeping and the infrastructure building in nations which seek this? A number of Christian FBOs, from Christian Aid to mission agencies, are working with communities to reduce poverty, improve healthcare and education, address gender inequalities and reduce the flow of arms. While those migrating to the Global North are the presenting face of these problems, the connection is rarely made and church-based organizations tend to focus *either* on the domestic context *or* on development. Churches should moreover point out the causal link between foreign policy (such as the invasion of Iraq in 2001) and the numbers of asylum seekers arriving in Europe and North America. Finally, as De La Torre has suggested reflecting on immigration to the US, there is a need to 'move beyond the virtue of hospitality' and address the culpability of the Global North in perpetuating the global inequality (and resulting exploitation and poverty) and violence that force people to move (2010).[3]

How might churches participate in other ways in the global forced migration regime? Refugee resettlement is undertaken successfully by FBOs in the US and ECSR supported resettlement in the UK through the statutory Gateway Protection Programme until ECSR folded in 2011. JRS is one example of a Christian organization engaging with all durable solutions and with the institution of UNHCR, and at local, regional and international levels. This said, FBOs need to remain alert to the danger of being into being co-opted into any programmes or 'solutions' which essentially serve the restrictive migration agendas of states.[4] Citizens for Sanctuary has, for example, received criticism from some other NGOs for cooperating with the UKBA in the voluntary returns scheme. Churches could, in addition, challenge current definitions of migrants, refugees and asylum seekers and inject more accurate and less restrictive definitions into debates (Harvey

---

3 On the need to address root causes of refugee movements, see also Forecast (2002: 42), Logan (2000: 146), MPA (2005: 56) and Pontifical Council (2004: 13).

4 For a similar argument in relation to FBOs in Australia, see Wilson (2011).

et al. 2006: 6). Policies drawn up using categories that bear little resemblance to the complex realities of people's motivations and circumstances need to be challenged.[5] One of the strengths of churches, as Ferris pointed out, is that they 'are not bound by the internationally accepted UN definition of refugees' (1993: 20). The recent discussion stimulated by the suggestion of the IAC to rename 'asylum seekers' as those 'seeking sanctuary' has been one helpful step along this path. Churches could also help to ensure that the voices of asylum seekers have greater representation in institutions such as UNHCR and the EU.

Collaborating

Effective responses require increased collaboration. Christian FBOs sometimes have little awareness of the ways in which others are working, and countering the 'fragmentation of effort' (Smillie cited in Weiss 2001: 226) is a constant battle. While there are a number of coalitions and networks, coordination is sporadic. A church leader, for example, may arrange to speak with the UK immigration minister without being aware of grassroots campaigns underway on the same issue. Networks can focus on one particular constituency – evangelical, Roman Catholic or those who simply happen to have heard of them – and neglect to engage with others. Putting more energy into building on existing and creating collaborative partnerships with other Christian groups, faith communities and 'secular' organizations could be beneficial (Furbey et al. 2006: 51, D'Onofrio and Munk 2004: 47, Wilson 2005: 73–78). The IPPR report concluded that establishing links between different faith groups and making joint statements about the rights of asylum seekers was key (Lewis 2005: 58). Achieving a cohesive, shared approach is notoriously elusive as networking and joint approaches are rarely funded and thus, understandably, do not take priority in workloads. Could national church bodies perhaps consider funding a visionary post that has a specific but wide-ranging task to coordinate activities on advocacy and lobbying?

Despite the risks discussed, partnership with the state and corporate interests should not be dismissed (Baker 2007: 109), and churches could also investigate the possibility of working with fellow churches in countries of origin and countries to which refused asylum seekers are returned. As Gill has pointed out, church-based groups do often have access to political structures and figures and can be effective in working with the state to bring about changes in the asylum system (2010). Sometimes, it is hard to decide whether co-operation or resistance is going to bring the most benefit to those seeking sanctuary. Churches are among the few global bodies with organic roots in communities all over the world and could therefore be instrumental in formulating a detailed picture of the pre-flight, flight, post-flight and, where it happens, return experiences of forced migrants. As suggested

---

5   For one reworking of the distinction between refugees and economic migrants, drawing on Catholic Social Thought, and creation of a 'moral definition' of a refugee rooted in human dignity, see Llanos (2010).

above, a transnational issue requires transnational responses and transnational, global networks such as churches could therefore be key international players. While the Roman Catholic Church has noted the need for such home-host country collaboration (Pontifical Council 2004: 50) and JRS is rooted in many contexts, it is unclear how well such coordination works in practice. The transnational workings of other denominations on asylum and refugee matters seem virtually non-existent. FBOs rooted in mainstream, historic denominations also need to recognize that some immigrant churches in Europe are contributing to debates and calling for more open policies (see for example Van der Meulen 2008). In what ways might collaboration between these groups be fostered? Indeed, partnering with refugees, asylum seekers and other migrants is crucial. Church-based groups need to recognize and point to the ways in which asylum seekers are themselves practising resistance, in political, social and media arenas, through 'disruptive acts', and they need to offer 'solidaristic engagements' in response (Squire 2009: 165–166, O'Neill 2010).

Putting Our Own House in Order

Gritty realism is also necessary, as bringing about an ecology of faith will only be successful if we put our own house in order. As Williams recognizes, the role of the Church as prophet and judge must be accompanied by self-criticism and self-awareness (2002: 46). Churches need to acknowledge that Christians are not all in favour of helping the stranger, and there are often deep-seated reasons for this including the evidence in the scriptures to support such a view. What is needed, as Forrester argues, is a 'serious dialogue among [their] diverse membership around themes that really matter' (2001: 73) and all Christians need to be encouraged not to fuel a wider ecology of fear. As CULF put it, churches 'with fearful congregations can become the ecclesiastical equivalents of gated communities' (2006: 84). More Christians could be encouraged to offer support. Even in contexts where personal encounters with asylum seekers are unlikely, offering prayer, making financial donations or simply challenging misconceptions that arise in conversation would all be valuable. Church leaders need to preach on issues of migration and asylum (see Lewis 2005: 58) and while they sometimes shy away from doing so because of the risk of compassion fatigue or because energy is focused on building up the congregation, this is a false dichotomy.[6] As I argued in Chapter 8, our own identity, understanding and relationship to God grow *through* our engagement with strangers. Creative preaching that explores this dynamic rather than demands support of yet another social justice 'good cause' is likely to reinvigorate congregations and individuals in their journeys of faith as well as supporting those seeking asylum. Migration also needs to be given more consideration in theological training institutions. Given its salience in the

---

6   Scott notes the particular effect of church leaders on congregational attitudes and projects relating to asylum-seeking (2003: 43–44).

contemporary world, the failure of many institutions (more so in the UK than in the US) to encourage embryo ministers to think around the implications of migration for church life in the twenty-first century is a significant omission.

The culpability of Christians in asylum seekers' current difficulties has deep-seated roots. Anglican Christianity is embedded in conceptions of British nationality and Christian missionaries accompanied European imperialists who carved territories into artificially constructed nation-states, cutting across tribal and established allegiances and exploiting their human and material resources. Christians must own the part their forebears and tradition have played in creating a number of the underlying push factors that cause refugees to flee today and the fiercely defended state borders that they encounter. Territorially-bounded ecclesiologies are also unhelpful. Orobator, writing of Roman Catholic Church, notes that it 'lays a heavy emphasis on territoriality' (2005: 172) and the same could be said of other denominations. While a local focus can be helpful, it can also mean that issues relating to those 'on the move' all too easily fall between the gaps of diocesan, circuit, parish or congregational concern. Mendieta helpfully summarizes the challenge: 'On the one hand, the new church must find a place beyond the nation-states of political modernity; but on the other hand, it must do so with a post-colonialist and post-imperialist attitude' (2001: 22). Developing new structures to plug the gaps is crucial.

Realism needs to extend beyond ourselves to include migrants and what is being asked for from policy-makers. Asylum seekers are complex people, as all human beings are, and well-meant but naive, monochrome portrayals of them as vulnerable and helpless must be eschewed. These do nothing to enhance the credibility of Christian advocacy or the agency and self-esteem of those seeking sanctuary. We also need to recognize that there is a need for an asylum system and for the rights and needs of established communities to be heard. Policy-makers and implementers are treading a narrow tightrope themselves and while challenging hostility and injustice outright is central, turning certain powerful people into scapegoats will only serve to fuel rather than transrupt the ecology of fear. Thus yet another tightrope – between mounting clear, forthright and courageous challenges to injustice and offering a nuanced understanding and presentation of the issues involved – must be walked. The former attracts attention, while the latter honours the complexity of those seeking sanctuary and helps to build credibility among policy-makers and implementers.

A Promising Model: The City of Sanctuary Movement

The City of Sanctuary (COS) Movement is a growing attempt to create ecologies of faith, rooted in grassroots relationships, service and local advocacy and operating in collaborative and embodied ways. It aims 'to build a culture of hospitality' and 'to create a network of towns and cities throughout the country which are proud to be places of safety, and which include people seeking sanctuary fully in the life of their communities' (COS 2011). It began in 2005, with Sheffield becoming the first City of Sanctuary in 2007, and draws together a range of community groups, RCOs, asylum seekers and members of established communities. The movement 'seeks to influence the political debate on sanctuary indirectly through cultural change' (COS 2011) and promotes an 'alternative discourse' rooted in 'rethinking the city along relational lines' (Darling 2010: 131). In Sheffield, welcome signs and postcards have visually marked the city, local organizations and businesses have been approached and 'active engagements between asylum seekers and local residents' have been facilitated and encouraged through events including meals and concerts. This has provided a base from which 'political calls for rights could arise' organically. In 2009, Sheffield City Council voted to adopt the City of Sanctuary manifesto as a series of policy priorities (Darling 2010: 132, 136).[7] Churches have been involved with the movement from its inception: its founder and president is a former President of the Methodist Conference, Inderjit Bhogal. This model is one which merits attention, involvement and expansion. If a majority of cities in the UK – and also other towns and rural areas – committed themselves to being places of sanctuary, an ecology of faith could spread organically. Such a model also has the potential to be shared with other nation-states.

Encounters in Worship

Given the spiritual significance of faith for many migrants, encounters with those seeking sanctuary in worship are essential. Worship is a context within which care can be experienced (Willimon 1979) and a liberative ecology of faith can be nurtured. Lathrop suggests that worship should turn us 'inside out' (1999: 202) or as Hovda puts it, 'Good liturgical celebration, like a parable, takes us by the hairs of our heads, lifts us momentarily out of the cesspool of injustice we call home, puts us in the promised and challenging reign of God, where we are treated like we have never been treated anywhere else' (1994: 220; see also Saliers 1994, Forrester 2005a: 103–111). Special asylum-seeking focused services and the welcoming of those seeking sanctuary into ordinary Sunday worship can be sustaining and transformative for all who participate in them. The nurturing of those wishing to be baptized is also important. Considering a number of factors in two broad areas could re-energize and deepen such encounters.[8]

---

7   For more on the COS movement, see Darling et al. (2010).

8   Bevans similarly recognizes a twofold challenge: 'The mission of the world's migrants, is on the one hand, to call the church to its full catholic reality as the pilgrim people of God, a people who follow the lead of the "God of the Tent"; on the other hand, the local church's mission is to incorporate its newest arrivals into its full mission of preaching, serving, and witnessing to the reign of God' (2008: 99).

Transrupting and Renewing Our Worship

The recognition that strangers can bring new life suggests that migrants may be nudging churches to renew their liturgical practices and self-understanding. Do the experiences of asylum seekers, for instance, call Christians to rediscover the practice of lament? Mursell stresses the importance of this practice for those in exile: 'the exile must first come to terms with the present, and one way to do that is through lament. In the language of spirituality, lament might be described as the way you respond when faith and experience collide painfully with one another' (2005: 40). While many churches are poor at creating spaces where traumatic stories can be voiced publicly, it is vital to bring raw pain, rage and profound unanswered questions before God and one another. As Brueggemann suggests, bringing to public expression fears and terrors and speaking of the 'real deathliness that hovers over us and gnaws within us' is a form of prophecy in the contemporary numbed world (2001: 45. Italics omitted). In creating a space for those seeking sanctuary to voice their lament within worship, others may feel permission to do the same.[9]

Migrants also challenge and reinvigorate Christian understandings and experiences of the Eucharist. Balasuriya argued in the 1970s that the Eucharist had been 'domesticated within the dominant social establishments of the day. Its radical demands have been largely neutralized. Its cutting edge has been blunted … Why is it that persons and people who proclaim Eucharistic love and sharing deprive the poor people of the world of food, capital, employment, and even land?' (1979: xi–xii). His claim that the Eucharist has to result in liberative action for the oppressed remains pertinent in relation to migration today. Celebrating a meal intended to embody love and transrupt destructive forces is heresy if it fails to nurture justice and mutuality within and beyond the participating congregation. Groody suggests that in a world full of walls and barriers, the Eucharist should witness 'to the primacy of God's universal, undivided, and unrestricted love' (2007: 213).[10] Or to put it differently, the Eucharist should foster an ecology of faith. The presence of asylum seekers at Eucharistic tables reminds us that the Church is not supposed to be a club of socially, economically, culturally or ethnically similar people engaged in an exclusive religious practice that has little meaning beyond church walls. The Eucharist is a radically socially inclusive and political act in which 'the other [should be] encountered and social difference transcended' and where all should be able to experience the hospitality of God (see Sheldrake 2001: 114). It is an act that should encourage and equip Christians to go out and strive for

---

9   For more on lament, see Galloway (2006) and O'Connor (2002). Celebration is, of course, also important (Fornet-Betancourt 2008: 210).

10   For more on the Eucharist as an embodiment of and resource for liberation and justice, see Boff (1993: 69–70), Cavanaugh (1998, 2002: 4–5), Forrester (1997: 245, 2000: 103), Hilton (1998) and Sagovsky (2002).

justice and equality in our world.[11] Groody has described how he participated in a mass in El Paso, Texas on the US–Mexico border. Half of the congregation was on one side of the fence and half on the other side. The liturgy was an expression of 'common solidarity as a people of God beyond political constructions' (2008: 299) and made a powerful public statement.[12] What might other acts of liturgical-political defiance in relation to migration and asylum-seeking look like?

Understanding scripture in its fullness also requires the presence of asylum seekers. Christians cannot hope to enter into a multi-vocal Bible which narrates the lives and speaks from the perspective of many 'on the move' without the interpretations and insights of contemporary migrants. As Wells points out, 'a diverse Bible requires – almost creates – a diverse people to be able to read it' (2006: 157). Could those seeking sanctuary also call Christians to rediscover their identity as a people who inhabit the tension between being 'on the move' and being rooted? Asylum seekers remind us that Christians are both strangers *and* those who have a longing for and promise of home. They equally remind us that we discover who we are through our communion with others in and beyond the body of Christ. Knowing who we are and having confidence in this ambivalent, other-oriented and transitory-rooted identity can in turn help us to welcome strangers (Newman 2007: 33). Migrants could help Christians to recognize the properly incarnational nature of liturgy (Barnard 2008, Klomp 2008) and Burns suggests that fellowship with asylum seekers 'might help to vivify an understanding of the communion of saints, an underdeveloped doctrinal theme' (2004b). In summary, it may be that the presence of those seeking sanctuary could help to encourage a transformative ecology of faith in Christian worship. Allowing migrants to challenge in these ways would incidentally help to avoid the danger of only preaching to the already converted in specially tailored services. It is also important to recognize that, in many places, congregations have in fact become dependent upon migrants for their numeric viability and cultural, ethnic and spiritual vitality (for example, Cacciottolo 2010).[13]

Prioritizing Humanity and Involvement

Encounters in worship need to offer a space in which those seeking asylum can be 'real' and in which co-creation and co-involvement are encouraged. Services focusing specifically on the issue of asylum can provide a space for solidarity and

---

11   See also the vision of Schmitmeyer, cited in Andrews (2002: 71–73).

12   See also the film *One Border, One Body* (2008).

13   Catto (2008), Hanciles (2007, 2008a, 2008b), Hirschman (2007: 411–412), ter Haar (2008, 1998) and Marquardt (2005) explore some of the ways in which immigrants are transforming existing congregations and establishing new ones. Speaking of immigrant churches, Jansen and Stoffels suggest that they bring to the Global North 'Responsibility for the society at large, Regeneration of the missionary vocation, and Representation of a Christianity that is not resigned to secularization' (2008: 7–8).

focused reflection, but ironically risk reinforcing the negative labelling of people as 'asylum seekers'. 'Ordinary' worship contexts in which people are known primarily as mothers or doctors or teenagers or Iraqis rather than as 'asylum seekers' may therefore be more humanizing and empowering. In all liturgies, in order to counter the danger of engaging in liturgy *about* asylum seekers rather than *with* them, the participation of migrants needs to be prioritized where migrants welcome this opportunity. Guest has explored the social functions of worship within a community and argues that the way in which we worship has a significant effect on our relationships with one another: 'Worship events are often key contexts in which relations of power are negotiated ... At such events, norms of authority and hierarchy are often implicit in the very structure of devotional practice' (Guest in Cameron et al. 2005: 100). Churches therefore need to ask themselves some important questions. Who is allowed to speak, pray, read and administer the sacrament in services? Are asylum seekers and refugees consulted about important decisions? Are the experiences of migrants given space to be heard? If English is not someone's first language, are they trying to find ways in which service booklets and conversation may be available in other mother tongues? How might congregations offer warm welcome without stepping over the line into interrogation or absorption? Essentially, churches need to provide a space where migrants are offered more respect and access to power than they are in the widespread ecology of fear.[14] Finally, churches should be cautious with regards to requests for conversion and allow people to grow in Christian faith at their own pace. While honouring people's wishes, those who have mixed motivations for making such a request could regret it later. Baptism should never be seen as an easy opportunity for church growth. Wingate's suggestion to be 'appropriately cautious' is apt (2005: 139).

Encounters in Theology

Encounters in theology are the least tangible of the four. Theological reflection on issues surrounding migration often takes place in the process of the other three types of encounter outlined above: we do our 'God-talk' implicitly as we endeavour to do our 'God-walk'. Understandings of God emerge and grow through encounters with migrants and within the active nurturing of an ecology of faith. More explicit encounters in theology, including this book and some of the literature I have drawn upon, are usually addressed primarily to those working within the Church and academy. They hope to provide sustenance and motivation for Christians supporting migrants, inspire and encourage others to become involved and hint at directions for ongoing work. How might these theological encounters be developed further?

---

14   See Wells (2006: 132–224) for more on inclusion and welcome in church services.

Theology needs to be offered to wider society as well as to the Church: it is ideally always public theology. Forrester defines public theology as 'talk about God, which claims to point to publicly accessible truth, to contribute to public discussion by witnessing to a truth which is relevant to what is going on in the world and to the pressing issues facing people and societies today' (2000: 127).[15] Theologies surrounding asylum and migration remain, at present, largely church-oriented. This is partly because many in the academy are suspicious of theological discourse and policy-makers are wary of associating too closely with any one faith community and thereby alienating those of another or no faith. Conversely, theologians struggle to find a way of making their discourse intelligible and ideas relevant to those outside the Christian community. As a result, as Pattison has suggested, theology tends to find itself serving 'the interests and needs of the churches, their hierarchy and clerisy' and speaking to a 'small, hypothetical audience of other scholars and theologians' (2007: 213, 217). He states: 'One of the most depressing things about contemporary Western Christian thought and practice is that it has largely failed to impact creatively and positively upon those who are not church members. It has become a tolerated, if somewhat dull and dusty, private indulgence for those who "like that kind of thing"' (2007: 194).

One way through this impasse is to transcend it. Christian theologians may be able to develop a voice in the secular academy, among policy-makers, within other faith communities and, indeed, with migrants, by imagining and contributing an alternative ecology – a radical and re-enchanted vision of society – which is so attractive that others are drawn to engage with it. This is likely to be more energizing than presenting a set of dry moral requirements. To quote Pattison again, 'Interesting performance and positive lure are much more likely to be of interest to non-theologians than defensive posturing ... theology needs to become imaginatively irritating and adhesive' (2007: 221). Without a dream of a more harmonious and mutually enriching future in relation to migration, it will be hard to step out of the present quagmire of fear. As Forrester suggests, 'a re-igniting of utopian hopes' can act 'as the engine of social transformation' (2001: 5). Tightropes must again be walked. Theologians need to balance speaking in a language which others can understand with the call to be distinctive, daring and to speak of fundamental meaning and the divine. We need to avoid, according to Forrester, 'simply adding the voice of theology to what everyone else is saying already' (2010: 441) or as Williams puts it, the 'contribution of the Church must always be something on another level from that of the various bodies struggling for dominance and access. It must simply offer a radically different imaginative landscape, in which people can discover possibilities of change' (2005: 17).[16] Theological visions need to be confident, positive, proactive and hopeful while at

---

15   For more on public theology, see Forrester (1997: 31–37, 2000, 2004a), Graham and Lowe (2009), Pattison (2007: 197–228) and Thiemann (1991).

16   For more on the importance of imagination, see Brueggemann (2001, 1997), Cavanaugh (2002: 4), Metz (1980: 89–91) and Wells (2006: 36).

the same time open to challenge from others in dialogue and willing to shift and change. They should lead to a sustained and sharp critique of current situations and the posing of transruptive, awkward questions.

This book stepped into the borderlands of such a vision and critique surrounding asylum-seeking and immigration. Bringing into being a better ecology surrounding migration requires input from a range of scholars, practitioners and, above all, immigrants, refugees and asylum seekers.[17] While I have touched on migrants' experiences of churches, more probing studies based on primary research are necessary. How do people seeking sanctuary experience interactions with various FBOs? How do these experiences compare with their interactions with secular organizations? How do people who are not Christian experience church-based initiatives, and if they have not engaged with such programmes, what are the reasons underpinning this disengagement? Furthermore, in what ways does the agency of asylum seekers overlap or come into conflict with that of Christian groups? Theological and biblical reflection from the perspectives of those seeking sanctuary is also vital, and this needs to be heard in their own words. Which biblical narratives resonate with asylum seekers' experiences and what light might people seeking sanctuary cast on textual interpretation? How has the experience of being strangers affected people's understandings of God, the Church or the Eucharist? Theological methodology and biblical hermeneutics also need to be explored in the light of asylum-seeking. Phan, an immigrant to the US from Vietnam, has suggested that in an era of extensive migration, a 'Betwixt and Between' theological method is essential and that theology can no longer be undertaken from only one perspective (2003). The pervasive reality of migration points towards a recognition that local, liberation, postcolonial and subaltern theologies can no longer be seen as theologies of the majority world – as optional extra add-ons – but rather as intrinsic to *any* theology wishing to be considered meaningful. While some reflections are available from the perspective of relatively privileged migrants (a number of which have been woven into this study), the experience of being a *forced* migrant may present new and challenging insights.

Important work considering appropriate ethical foundations for borders and immigration, citizenship and integration policies is now emerging (for example, Bretherton 2006b, Reed 2010, Gerschutz and Lorentzen 2009). Roman Catholic scholars, in particular, have been developing arguments surrounding human rights, sovereignty, solidarity and migrants – including the protection of refugees – sometimes drawing on Roman Catholic Social Teaching (Baggio and Brazal 2008, O'Neill 2007, Battistella 2008, Hollenbach 2008, 2010, Orobator 2010, Tomasi 2010, Kerwin 2008, 2009, Tulud Cruz 2011, Rowlands 2011). While biblical material and theological constructs can never provide a policy blueprint, Christian theology may be able to offer broad, relevant and engaging principles (in conjunction with the insights of others) upon which more just and equitable

---

17   People can, of course, inhabit more two or more of these categories at the same time. Some migrants are themselves scholars and practitioners.

policies for everyone in society could be based. Groody has begun to develop a systematic theology arising from migration, seeing migration as 'a way of thinking about God and what it means to be human in the world': he explores the notion of crossing borders in relation to the concepts of *imago dei*, incarnation, mission and kingdom (2009a). More remains to be done on both fronts. Exploring why certain congregations respond to the needs of migrants, including those seeking sanctuary, while others do not would also be valuable. Is it predominantly theological, geographical or socio-economic factors which lead to the presence of an ecology of fear in one place and an ecology of faith in another? What support is being offered to those seeking sanctuary among African-initiated or other immigrant congregations and by those from other faith communities? There may be shared theological visions or possibilities of practical collaboration. Finally, it would be interesting to consider what encounters churches are involved in and what influence they wield at an international or transnational level in relation to forced migration, whether through the UNHCR or WCC or other avenues. Empirical studies, as well as broader social scientific analysis and theological reflection, would be helpful in all of these areas.

A Not-So-Final Word …

Churches can be proud of the extensive, varied and valuable contribution they make in supporting some of the most marginalized people in local, regional, national and international communities. While there will undoubtedly be many more challenges ahead for asylum seekers and any who come alongside them, there is also plenty to celebrate. Fatima and Annette are both building new, hope-filled lives and Christians have made many dents in the ecology of fear. In this book, I have hoped to offer a few new insights into the encounters between migrants and churches and suggest some practical steps which could be taken along the path out of an ecology of fear and towards the establishment of a more widespread, life-bringing and vibrant ecology of faith. It has not said all that needs to be said on asylum-seeking, migration, theology and churches. Many more voices must be heard and avenues of research travelled. As Georgi advises, the 'real miracle of the kingdom of God is to become like children again. Never feel too good to be beginners again. Stay perennial students, true scholars, that is. Never take possession of anything, not even of the insight of your own answers' (2005: 369). A final word – if there can be one – belongs to Annette, with whose story this book began. She responded to a question about her experience of churches thus:

> Governments are the same in my country and here – they make me feel a stranger, like I don't belong – but the Church and some Christian people help me to feel at home. I got to know friends who gave me comfort and support … If there was not church in this country, many people would die. (2008)

Appendix
Church-based Migrant, Refugee and Asylum Seeker Support Organizations

The following list of organizations supporting migrants, refugees and asylum seekers is simply designed to indicate a few organizations it is possible to become involved with (mainly in the UK and US), as well as some resources for exploration. It is far from exhaustive.

UK

Boaz Trust

A Christian organization serving destitute asylum seekers in Greater Manchester through providing accommodation, weekly food parcels, legal services, English and craft classes and undertaking campaigning and advocacy. http://boaztrust.org. uk.

CHASTE

Churches Against Sex Trafficking in Europe. www.chaste.org.uk.

Citizens for Sanctuary

A Citizen Organising Foundation campaign to secure justice for people fleeing persecution and rebuild public support for sanctuary. www.citizensforsanctuary. org.uk.

City of Sanctuary Movement

A movement to build a culture of hospitality for people seeking sanctuary in the UK, involving a growing number of cities. www.cityofsanctuary.org.

Jesuit Refugee Service UK

Based at the Hurtado Jesuit Centre in Wapping, London. JRS has a Day Centre and a Detention Outreach Programme. www.jrsuk.net.

Restore

A project of Birmingham Churches Together which includes befriending, a summer holiday programme for children, women's and men's activities groups and awareness-raising. www.restore-uk.org.

US

Episcopal Migration Ministries and Church World Service

National refugee resettlement agencies, working with regional organizations such as Refugee Immigration Ministry (www.r-i-m.net) and Refugee Resettlement and Immigration Services of Atlanta (www.rrisa.org) to place newly arriving refugees in communities across the US. www.episcopalchurch.org/emm. www.churchworldservice.org/site/PageServer?pagename=action_what_assist_main. RIM also runs a Spiritual Care Givers Program, involving volunteers visiting those held in detention facilities.

Jubilee Partners

An intentional Christian community based in Comer, Georgia, offering hospitality to newly arrived refugees and seeking to help them begin to feel safe and confident in the US before they move to their own apartment. www.jubileepartners.org.

National Council of Churches USA: Ecumenical Resources for Immigration Ministries

Information concerning Church World Service programmes and the Interfaith Immigrant Coalition, and statements, policies and best practices adopted by faith communities. www.ncccusa.org/immigration/immigmain.html.

New Sanctuary Movement

A movement seeking to respond to the needs of immigrant workers and their families, and to support coalitions working on comprehensive immigration reform. Local branches are comprised of a range of faith communities who work in partnership with other local and regional support and advocacy organizations. www.newsanctuarymovement.org.

United Methodist Church National Plan for Hispanic/Latino Ministries

Website including plans for congregational and leadership development, information on immigration issues and campaigning, and resources. http://new. gbgm-umc.org/plan/hispanic.

US Conference of Catholic Bishops

Catholic Social Teaching on Immigration and the Movement of Peoples, including discussion questions and activities for parishes. http://usccb.org/issues-and-action/ human-life-and-dignity/immigration/catholic-teaching-on-immigration-and-the-movement-of-peoples.cfm.

Australia

Hotham Mission Asylum Seeker Project

Based in Melbourne, Hotham Mission ASP offers casework, housing, subsistence support, one-to-one support link-ups, men's and women's groups to asylum seekers living in the community, as well as advocacy and research. http://hothammission. org.au.

Regional and Global

Churches Commission for Migrants in Europe

CCME, an ecumenical body, works on behalf of churches in Europe on national and European policies concerning labour trafficking, refugee protection, anti-trafficking, development and inclusivity and diversity. www.ccme.be.

Jesuit Refugee Service

JRS works in a range of ways in situations of conflict and displacement across the globe, as well as in countries of resettlement and asylum. www.jrs.net.

References

'Abd al-Rahim, M. 2008. 'Asylum: A Moral and Legal Right in Islam'. *Refugee Survey Quarterly*, 27(2), 15–23.

Abū al-Wafā, A. 2009. *The Right to Asylum between Islamic Shari'ah and International Refugee Law: A Comparative Study*. Riyadh: UNHCR.

Ackroyd, P. R. 1968. *Exile and Restoration: A Study of Hebrew Thought of the Sixth Century BC*. London: SCM Press.

Adutwum, O. 1998. 'Ruth', in *The International Bible Commentary: A Catholic and Ecumenical Commentary for the Twenty-First Century*, edited by W. R. Farmer et al. Collegeville: Liturgical Press, 566–571.

Agamben, G. 1998. *Homo Sacer: Sovereign Power and Bare Life*. Trans. D. Heller-Roazen. Stanford: Stanford University Press.

Agamben, G. 2005. *State of Exception*. Trans. K. Attell. Chicago: University of Chicago Press.

Ager, A. and Ager, J. 2011. 'Faith and the Discourse of Secular Humanitarianism'. *Journal of Refugee Studies*, 24(3), 456–472.

Ager, A. and Strang, A. 2008. 'Understanding Integration. A Conceptual Framework'. *Journal of Refugee Studies*, 21(2), 166–191.

Agier, M. 2008. *On the Margins of the World: The Refugee Experience Today*. Trans. D. Fernbach. Cambridge and Malden: Polity Press.

Agier, M. 2011. *Managing the Undesirables: Refugee Camps and Humanitarian Government*. Trans. D. Fernbach. Cambridge and Malden, MA: Polity Press.

Ahearn, F., Loughry, M. and Ager, A. 1999. 'The Experience of Refugee Children', in *Refugees: Perspectives on the Experience of Forced Migration*, edited by A. Ager. London and New York: Continuum, 215–236.

Ahn, J. J. 2011. *Exile as Forced Migrations: A Sociological, Literary, and Theological Approach on the Displacement and Resettlement of the Southern Kingdom of Judah*. Berlin and New York: Walter De Gruyter.

Akenson, D. H. 1992. *God's Peoples: Covenant and Land in South Africa, Israel and Ulster*. Ithaca and London: Cornell University Press.

Aldred, J. O. 2005. *Respect: Understanding Caribbean British Christianity*. Peterborough: Epworth.

Alexander, C. 2000. '(Dis)Entangling the "Asian Gang": Ethnicity, Identity, Masculinity', in *Un/settled Multiculturalisms: Diasporas, Entanglements, Transruptions*, edited by B. Hesse. London and New York: Zed Books, 123–147.

Amin, A. 2002. *Ethnicity and the Multicultural City: Living with Diversity*. London: Economic and Social Research Council.

Amnesty International. 2006. *Down and Out in London: The Road to Destitution for Rejected Asylum Seekers*. London: Amnesty International UK.

Amos, C. 2004. *The Book of Genesis*. Peterborough: Epworth.

Andersen, T. 2011. 'Illegal Immigrant Charged with 6th DUI in Boxborough'. *Boston Globe* [Online, 26 September]. Available at: http://articles.boston.com/2011-09-26/news/30205129_1_illegal-immigrant-immigration-status-face-deportation [accessed: 12 October 2011].

Anderson, B. 1991. *Imagined Communities: Reflections on the Origin and Spread of Nationalism*. Rev. edn. London and New York: Verso.

Anderson, C. B. 2009. 'Reflections in an Interethnic/Racial Era on Interethnic/Racial Marriage in Ezra', in *They Were All Together in One Place? Toward Minority Biblical Criticism*, edited by R. C. Bailey, T. B. Liew and F. F. Segovia. Atlanta: Society of Biblical Literature, 47–64.

Anderson, H. 1999. 'Seeing the Other Whole: A Habitus for Globalisation', in *Globalisation and Difference: Practical Theology in a World Context*, edited by P. Ballard and P. Couture. Cardiff: Cardiff Academic Press, 3–17.

Anderson, H. 2005. 'The Bible and Pastoral Care', in *The Bible in Pastoral Practice: Readings in the Place and Function of Scripture of the Church*, edited by P. Ballard and S. R. Holmes. London: Darton, Longman and Todd, 195–211.

Andrews, D. 2002. 'The Lord's Table, the World's Hunger: Liturgy, Justice, and Rural Life', in *Liturgy and Justice: To Worship God in Spirit and Truth*, edited by A. Y. Koester. Collegeville: Liturgical Press, 63–73.

Annette. 2008. Interview (Meeting) with Annette. Birmingham, 19 December.

Appadurai, A. 1996. *Modernity at Large: Cultural Dimensions of Globalization*. Minneapolis: University of Minnesota Press.

Arango, J. 2004. 'Theories of International Migration', in *International Migration in the New Millennium: Global Movement and Settlement*, edited by D. Joly. Aldershot and Burlington: Ashgate, 15–35.

Armstrong, K. 2001. *The Battle for God: Fundamentalism in Judaism, Christianity and Islam*. London: HarperCollins.

Asylum Welcome. 2008. Asylum Welcome [Online]. Available at: www.asylum-welcome.org [accessed: 18 December 2008].

Ateek, N. S. 2006. 'A Palestinian Perspective: Biblical Perspectives on the Land', in *Voices from the Margin: Interpreting the Bible in the Third World*, edited by R. S. Sugirtharajah. 3rd edn. Maryknoll: Orbis, 227–234.

Atherton, J. 2000. *Public Theology for Changing Times*. London: SPCK.

Augustine. 1972. *Concerning the City of God against the Pagans*, edited by D. Knowles. Trans. H. Bettenson. Harmondsworth: Penguin.

Baggio, F. and Brazal, A. M. (eds). 2008. *Faith on the Move: Toward a Theology of Migration in Asia*. Manila: Ateneo de Manila University Press.

Baker, C. R. 2007. *The Hybrid Church in the City: Third Space Thinking*. Aldershot: Ashgate.

Baker, C. R. 2009. 'Blurred Encounters? Religious Literacy, Spiritual Capital and Language', in *Faith in the Public Realm: Controversies, Policies and Practices*, edited by A. Dinham, R. Furbey and V. Lowndes. Bristol: Polity Press, 105–122.

Baker, C. R. and Skinner, H. 2006. *Faith in Action: The Dynamic Connection between Spiritual and Religious Capital*. Manchester: William Temple Foundation. Available at: www.wtf.org.uk/activities/documents/FaithinAction_000.pdf [accessed: 9 May 2011].

Bal, M. 1987. *Lethal Love: Feminist Literary Readings of Biblical Love Stories*. Bloomington and Indianapolis: Indiana University Press.

Balasuriya, T. 1979. *The Eucharist and Human Liberation*. London: SCM Press.

Balci, B. 2007. 'Central Asian Refugees in Saudi Arabia: Religious Evolution and Contributing to the Reislamization of their Motherland'. *Refugee Survey Quarterly*, 26(2), 12–21.

Balibar, E. and Wallerstein, I. 1991. *Race, Nation, Class: Ambiguous Identities*. London and New York: Verso.

Ballard, P. 2011. 'The Bible in Theological Reflection: Indications from the History of Scripture'. *Practical Theology*, 4(1), 35–47.

Ballard, P. and Holmes, S. R. 2005. 'General Introduction: The Underlying Issues, Challenges and Possibilities', in *The Bible in Pastoral Practice: Readings in the Place and Function of Scripture in the Church*, edited by P. Ballard and S. R. Holmes. London: Darton, Longman and Todd, xiii–xxiii.

Ballard, P. and Pritchard, J. 1996. *Practical Theology in Action: Christian Thinking in the Service of Church and Society*. London: SPCK.

Baptist Union [of Great Britain and BMS World Mission]. n.d. 'Welcoming the Stranger: Working with Refugees and Asylum Seekers. Resource Pack'. Didcot: Baptist Union of Great Britain and BMS World Mission.

Barnard, M. 2008. 'African Worship in an Amsterdam Business District: Liturgy in Immigrant Churches', in *A Moving God: Immigrant Churches in the Netherlands*, edited by M. Jansen and H. Stoffels. Zurich: Lit Verlag GmbH & Co. KG Wien, 115–137.

Barnett, M. 2011. 'Humanitarianism, Paternalism, and the UNHCR', in *Refugees in International Relations*, edited by A. Betts and G. Loescher. Oxford: Oxford University Press, 105–132.

Barth, F. 1969. *Ethnic Groups and Boundaries: The Social Organization of Culture Difference*. Bergen and London: Universitetsforlaget and Allen & Unwin.

Bartholomew, C. and Hughes, F. (eds). 2004. *Explorations in a Christian Theology of Pilgrimage*. Aldershot: Ashgate.

Bartley, J. 2006. *Faith and Politics After Christendom: The Church as a Movement for Anarchy*. Milton Keynes: Paternoster.

Barton, M. 2005. *Rejection, Resistance and Resurrection: Speaking out on Racism in the Church*. London: Darton, Longman and Todd.

Battistella, G. 2008. 'Migration and Human Dignity: From Policies of Exclusion to Policies Based on Human Rights', in *A Promised Land, A Perilous Journey:*

Theological Perspectives on Migration, edited by D. G. Groody and G. Campese. Notre Dame, IN: University of Notre Dame Press, 177–191.

Bauman, Z. 1992. 'Soil, Blood and Identity'. *The Sociological Review*, 40(4), 675–701.

Bauman, Z. 1998. *Globalization: The Human Consequences*. Cambridge: Polity.

Bauman, Z. 2001. *Community: Seeking Safety in an Insecure World*. Cambridge: Polity.

Bauman, Z. 2004. 'Living (Occasionally Dying) Together in an Urban World', in *Cities, War and Terrorism: Towards an Urban Geopolitics*, edited by S. Graham. Oxford: Blackwell, 110–119.

Bauman, Z. 2005. *Liquid Life*. Cambridge and Malden: Polity.

BBC. 2001. 'Councils "Overspend on Asylum Seekers"'. *BBC News* [Online, 5 April]. Available at: http://news.bbc.co.uk/1/hi/uk_politics/1261116.stm [accessed: 1 November 2008].

BBC. 2004. 'Asylum Seeker's Church Rescue Bid'. *BBC News* [Online, 29 November]. Available at: http://news.bbc.co.uk/1/hi/england/bristol/4052953.stm [accessed: 30 December 2010].

BBC. 2011. 'Net Migration Total up by a Fifth'. *BBC News* [Online, 25 August]. Available at: www.bbc.co.uk/news/uk-14663354 [accessed: 12 October 2011].

BEACON [Bradford Ecumenical Asylum Concern]. 2008. BEACON [Online]. Available at: www.beaconbradford.org [accessed: 18 December 2008].

Beaumont, J. 2008. 'Faith Action on Urban Issues'. *Urban Studies*, 45(10), 2019–2034.

Beck, U. 1992. *Risk Society: Towards a New Modernity*. Trans. M. Ritter. London, Thousand Oaks, CA and New Delhi: Sage.

Beck, U. 1999. *World Risk Society*. Cambridge: Polity.

Beck, U. 2006. *Cosmopolitan Vision*. Cambridge and Malden: Polity.

Beckford, R. 2000. *Dread and Pentecostal: A Political Theology for the Black Church in Britain*. London: SPCK.

Bedford, N. E. 2005. 'To Speak of God from More Than One Place: Theological Reflections from the Experience of Migration', in *Latin American Liberation Theology: The Next Generation*, edited by I. Petrella. Maryknoll: Orbis, 95–118.

Begg, C. T. 1992. 'Foreigner', in *The Anchor Bible Dictionary, D-G*, Vol. 2, edited by D. N. Freedman. New York: Doubleday, 829–830.

Behloul, S. M. 2007. 'From "Problematic" Foreigners to "Unproblematic" Muslims: Bosnians in the Swiss Islam-Discourse'. *Refugee Survey Quarterly*, 26(2), 22–35.

Benhabib, S. 2004. *The Rights of Others: Aliens, Residents and Citizens*. Cambridge: Cambridge University Press.

Bennett, F. and Roberts, M. 2004. *From Input to Influence: Participatory Approaches to Research and Inquiry into Poverty*. York: Joseph Rowntree Foundation.

Berg, L. and Millbank, J. 2009. 'Constructing the Personal Narratives of Lesbian, Gay and Bisexual Asylum Claimants'. *Journal of Refugee Studies*, 22(2), 195–223.

Bergant, D. 2003. 'Ruth: The Migrant Who Saved the People', in *Migration, Religious Experience, and Globalization*, edited by G. Campese and P. Ciallella. New York: Center for Migration Studies, 49–61.

Berquist, J. 1995. *Judaism in Persia's Shadow: A Social and Historical Approach*. Minneapolis: Augsburg Fortress.

Berry, J. W. 1992. 'Acculturation and Adaptation in a New Society'. *International Migration*, 30, 69–85.

Betts, A. 2009. *Forced Migration and Global Politics*. Malden, MA and Oxford: Wiley-Blackwell.

Betts, A. 2011a. 'International Cooperation in the Refugee Regime', in *Refugees in International Relations*, edited by A. Betts and G. Loescher. Oxford: Oxford University Press, 53–84.

Betts, A. 2011b. 'Introduction: Global Migration Governance', in *Global Migration Governance*, edited by A. Betts. Oxford and New York: Oxford University Press, 1–33.

Bevans, S. 2002. *Models of Contextual Theology*. Rev. edn. Maryknoll: Orbis.

Bevans, S. 2008. 'Mission *among* Migrants, Mission *of* Migrants: Mission of the Church', in *A Promised Land, A Perilous Journey: Theological Perspectives on Migration*, edited by D. G. Groody and G. Campese. Notre Dame: Notre Dame University Press, 89–106.

Bhabha, H. K. 1994. *The Location of Culture*. London and New York: Routledge.

Bhabha, H. K. 1996. 'Culture's In-Between', in *Questions of Cultural Identity*, edited by S. Hall and P. du Gay. London, Thousand Oaks and New Delhi: Sage, 53–60.

BID [Bail for Immigration Detainees] and Asylum Aid. 2005. *Justice Denied: Asylum and Immigration Legal Aid – a System in Crisis*. London: BID and Asylum Aid.

Black, R. 1998. *Refugees, Environment and Development*. Harlow: Longman.

Black, R. 2001. 'Fifty Years of Refugee Studies: From Theory to Policy'. *International Migration Review*, 35(1), 57–78.

Blair, T. 2008. *Faith and Globalisation*, The Cardinal's Lectures, Westminster Cathedral, London, 3 April.

Blenkinsopp, J. 1988. *Ezra–Nehemiah*. Old Testament Library. London: SCM Press.

Blenkinsopp, J. 1991. 'Temple and Society in Achaemenid Judah', in *Second Temple Studies 1. Persian Period*, JSOT Supplement Series 117, edited by P. R. Davies. Sheffield: JSOT Press/Sheffield Academic Press, 22–53.

Blenkinsopp, J. 2009. *Judaism, The First Phase: The Place of Ezra and Nehemiah in the Origins of Judaism*. Grand Rapids: William B. Eerdmans.

Blits, J. 1989. Hobbesian Fear. *Political Theory*, 17(3), 417–431.

Bloch, A. 2002. *The Migration and Settlement of Refugees in Britain*. Basingstoke: Palgrave Macmillan.

Bloch, A. and Levy, C. 1999. *Refugees, Citizenship and Social Policy in Europe*. Basingstoke: Macmillan.

Bloch, A. and Schuster, L. 2002. 'Asylum and Welfare: Contemporary Debates'. *Critical Social Policy*, 22(3), 393–414.

Bloch, A. and Schuster, L. 2005. 'At the Extremes of Exclusion: Deportation, Detention and Dispersal'. *Ethnic and Racial Studies*, 28(3), 491–512.

Bloqueau, J.-M. 2005. Talk by Fr Jean-Marie Bloqueau, Priest at Notre Dame de France Church, London Churches Refugee Network meeting, 23 October.

BMA [British Medical Association]. 2008. 'Asylum Seekers and their Health'. *BMA* [Online]. Available at: www.bma.org.uk/ap.nsf/Content/asylumseekershealth. jsp [accessed: 2 November 2008].

BNP [British National Party]. 2006. *Council Election Manifesto* [Online]. Available at: www.bnp.org.uk/election2006/manifesto2006.pdf [accessed: 10 January 2007].

BNP. 2008. BNP [Online]. Available at: www.ccob.co.uk [accessed: 28 November 2008].

Board, D. 2008. *Jerusalem, and New Jerusalem*. Speech, Fifth Annual Conference, Churches Refugee Network, Carr's Lane United Reformed Church, Birmingham, 17 May.

Boaz Trust. 2008. Boaz Trust Projects [Online]. Available at: www.boaztrust.org. uk/projects [accessed: 18 December 2008].

Boaz Trust. 2011. Boaz Trust [Online]. Available at: www.boaztrust.org.uk [accessed: 3 October 2011].

Boff, C. 1987. *Theology and Praxis: Epistemological Foundations*. Trans. R. R. Barr. Maryknoll: Orbis.

Boff, L. 1993. *The Path to Hope: Fragments from a Theologian's Journey*. Trans. P. Berryman. Maryknoll: Orbis.

Boff, L. 2000. *Holy Trinity, Perfect Community*. Trans. P. Berryman. Maryknoll: Orbis.

Boff, L. and Boff, C. 1987. *Introducing Liberation Theology*. Trans. P. Burns. Maryknoll: Orbis.

Bohmer, C. and Shuman, A. 2008. *Rejecting Refugees: Political Asylum in the 21st Century*. London and New York: Routledge.

Bonhoeffer, D. 1995. *Ethics*. Edited by E. Bethge, trans. N. Horton Smith. Rev. edn. New York: Touchstone/Simon & Schuster.

Bonifacio, G. T. and Angeles, V. S. M. (eds). 2010. *Gender, Religion, and Migration: Pathways of Integration*. Lanham: Lexington Books.

Bookman, M. Z. 2006. *Tourists, Migrants and Refugees: Population Movements in Third World Development*. Boulder and London: Lynne Rienner.

Boswell, C. and Geddes, A.. 2011. *Migration and Mobility in the European Union*. Basingstoke: Palgrave Macmillan.

Boyarin, D. 1994. *A Radical Jew: Paul and the Politics of Identity*. Berkeley, Los Angeles and London: University of California Press.

Bradstock, A. and Trotman, A. 2003. *Asylum Voices: Experiences of People Seeking Asylum in the United Kingdom*. London: CTBI.

Braidotti, R. 1994. *Nomadic Subjects: Embodiment and Sexual Difference in Contemporary Feminist Theory*. New York: Columbia University Press.

Bralo, Z. and Morrison, J. 2005. 'Immigrants, Refugees and Racism: Europeans and Their Denial', in *International Migration and Security: Opportunities and Challenges*, edited by E. Guild and J. van Selm. London and New York: Routledge, 113–128.

Brenner, A. 1993. 'Naomi and Ruth', in *A Feminist Companion to Ruth*, edited by A. Brenner. Sheffield: Sheffield Academic Press, 70–84.

Brenner, A. 2005. *I am ...: Biblical Women Tell Their Own Stories*. Minneapolis: Augsburg Fortress.

Bretherton, L. 2004. 'Tolerance, Education and Hospitality: A Theological Proposal'. *Studies in Christian Ethics*, 17(1), 80–103.

Bretherton, L. 2006a. *Hospitality as Holiness: Christian Witness Amid Moral Diversity*. Aldershot: Ashgate.

Bretherton, L. 2006b. 'The Duty of Care to Refugees, Christian Cosmopolitanism, and the Hallowing of Bare Life'. *Studies in Christian Ethics*, 19(1), 39–61.

Bretherton, L. 2010. *Christianity and Contemporary Politics: The Conditions and Possibilities of Faithful Witness*. Oxford and Malden: Wiley-Blackwell.

Brett, M. G. 1996. 'Interpreting Ethnicity; Method, Hermeneutics, Ethics', in *Ethnicity and the Bible*, edited by M. G. Brett. Boston and Leiden: Brill, 3–22.

Brettell, C. B. and Hollifield, J. F. (eds). 2002. *Migration Theory: Talking Across Disciplines*. New York and London: Routledge.

Brewer, J. and Hunter, A. 2006. *Foundations of Multimethod Research: Synthesizing Styles*. Thousand Oaks, London and New Delhi: Sage.

Bronner, L. L. 1993. 'A Thematic Approach to Ruth in Rabbinic Literature', in *A Feminist Companion to Ruth*, edited by A. Brenner. Sheffield: Sheffield Academic Press: 146–169.

Brower, D. 2008. Interview (Meeting) with the Revd Deirdre Brower, Minister, Nazarene Church, Longsight, Manchester, Bristol, 17 July.

Brown, R. 2000. *Group Processes*. 2nd edn. Oxford: Blackwell.

Brown Douglas, K. 2005. *What's Faith Got To Do With It? Black Bodies/Christian Souls*. Maryknoll: Orbis.

Browning, D. S. 1991. *A Fundamental Practical Theology: Descriptive and Strategic Proposals*. Minneapolis: Augsburg Fortress.

Brubaker, R. 1992. *Citizenship and Nationhood in France and Germany*. Cambridge and London: Harvard University Press.

Brubaker, R. 2005. 'The "Diaspora" Diaspora'. *Ethnic and Racial Studies*, 28(1), 1–19.

Brueggemann, W. 1993. 'Trajectories in Old Testament Literature and the Sociology of Ancient Israel', in *The Bible and Liberation: Political and*

Social Hermeneutics, edited by N. K. Gottwald and R. A. Horsley. Rev. edn. Maryknoll and London: Orbis and SPCK, 201–226.

Brueggemann, W. 1997. *Cadences of Home: Preaching among Exiles*. Louisville: Westminster John Knox.

Brueggemann, W. 1999. *The Covenanted Self: Explorations in Law and Covenant*. Minneapolis: Fortress.

Brueggemann, W. 2001. *The Prophetic Imagination*. 2nd edn. Minneapolis: Augsburg Fortress.

Brueggemann, W. 2002. *The Land: Place as Gift, Promise, and Challenge in Biblical Faith*. 2nd edn. Minneapolis: Augsburg Fortress.

Brueggemann, W. 2008. *A Pathway of Interpretation: The Old Testament for Pastors and Students*. Eugene: Cascade Books.

BSA [British Sociological Association]. 2002. *Statement of Ethical Practice* [Online]. Available at: www.sociology.org.uk/as4bsoce.pdf [accessed: 4 August 2008].

Buber, M. 1937. *I and Thou*. Trans. R. G. Smith. Edinburgh: T & T Clark.

Burman, E. 2010. 'Explicating the Tactics of Banal Exclusion: A British Example', in *Gender and Migration: Feminist Interventions*, edited by I. Palmary, E. Burman, K. Chantler and P. Kiguwa. London and New York: Zed Books, 119–138.

Burns, S. 2004a. *Welcoming Asylum Seekers: Struggles and Joys in the Local Church*. Cambridge: Grove Books.

Burns, S. 2004b. 'A Blessing from Overseas'. *Church Times*, 28 May, 9.

Burnside, J. 2001. *The Status and Welfare of Immigrants: The Place of the Foreigner in Biblical Law and its Relevance to Contemporary Society*. Cambridge: Jubilee Centre.

Burnside, J. 2010. 'Exodus and Asylum: Uncovering the Relationship between Biblical Law and Narrative'. *Journal for the Study of the Old Testament*, 34(3), 243–266.

Busher, D. 2010. 'Refugee Women: Twenty Years On'. *Refugee Survey Quarterly*, 29(2), 4–20.

Byrne SJ, B. 2000. *The Hospitality of God: A Reading of Luke's Gospel*. Collegeville: Liturgical Press.

Byrne, L. 2000. *The Journey is My Home*. London: Hodder & Stoughton.

Byron, G. L. 2002. *Symbolic Blackness and Ethnic Difference in Early Christian Literature*. London and New York: Routledge.

Cacciottolo, M. 2010. 'Papal Visit: Have Immigrants Saved the Catholic Church?'. *BBC News* [Online, 12 September]. Available at: www.bbc.co.uk/news/uk-11067661 [accessed: 6 December 2010].

CAFOD [Catholic Agency for Overseas Development]. 2008. *Refugees: Prayers and Liturgy* [Online]. Available at: www.cafod.org.uk/worship/refugees [accessed: 18 December 2008].

Cahalan, K. A. 2010. 'Pastoral Theology or Practical Theology? Limits and Possibilities', in *Keeping Faith in Practice: Aspects of Catholic Pastoral*

Theology, edited by J. Sweeney, G. Simmonds and D. Lonsdale. London: SCM Press, 99–116.

Callamard, A. 1999. 'Refugee Women: A Gendered and Political Analysis of the Refugee Experience', in *Refugees: Perspectives on the Experience of Forced Migration*, edited by A. Ager. London and New York: Continuum, 196–214.

Cameron, H., Bhatti, D., Duce, C., Sweeney, J., and Watkins, C. 2010. *Talking about God in Practice: Theological Action Research and Practical Theology*. London: SCM Press.

Cameron, H., Richter, P., Davies, D. and Ward, F. (eds). 2005. *Studying Local Churches: A Handbook*. London: SCM Press.

Camp, C. V. 1991. 'What's So Strange About the Strange Woman?', in *The Bible and the Politics of Exegesis*, edited by D. Jobling, P. L. Day and G. T. Sheppard. Cleveland: Pilgrim Press, 17–31.

Camp, C. V. 2000. *Wise, Strange and Holy: The Strange Woman and the Making of the Bible*. JSOT Supplement Series 320. Sheffield: JSOT Press/Sheffield Academic Press.

Campbell, A. 2000. 'The Nature of Practical Theology', in *The Blackwell Reader in Pastoral and Practical Theology*, edited by J. Woodward and S. Pattison. Oxford: Blackwell, 77–88.

Campbell Jr, E. F. 1975. *Ruth: A New Translation with Introduction and Commentary*. Anchor Bible. New York: Doubleday.

CAP [Church Action on Poverty]. 2006. *Poverty Action Sunday Pack* [Online]. Available at: www.church-poverty.org.uk/resources/phawresources/PAS/povery-action 2006/PovertyActionSundaypack2006.pdf/view [accessed: 18 December 2008].

CAP [Church Action on Poverty]. 2008. *Living Ghosts Campaign* [Online]. Available at: www.church-poverty.org.uk/campaigns/livingghosts [accessed: 20 November 2008].

Carey, G. 2008. 'It isn't Racist to Want a Cap on Immigration'. *The Times*, 10 September.

Carroll, J. 2001 *Constantine's Sword: The Church and the Jews: A History*. Boston and New York: Houghton Mifflin.

Carroll, R. P. 1991. 'Textual Strategies and Ideology in the Second Temple Period', in *Second Temple Studies 1. Persian Period*, edited by P. R. Davies. JSOT Supplement Series 117. Sheffield: JSOT Press/Sheffield Academic Press, 108–124.

Carroll, R. P. 1992. 'Coopting the Prophets: Nehemiah and Nodiah', in *Priests, Prophets and Scribes: Essays on the Formation and Heritage of Second Temple Judaism in Honour of Joseph Blenkinsopp*, edited by E. Ulrich, J. Wright, R. P Carroll and P. R. Davies. JSOT Supplement Series 149. Sheffield: JSOT Press/Sheffield Academic Press, 87–99.

Carroll, R. P. 1997. 'Deportation and Diasporic Discourses in the Prophetic Literature', in *Exile: Old Testament, Jewish and Christian Conceptions*, edited by J. M. Scott. Leiden, New York and Köln: Brill, 63–85.

Carroll, R. P. 1998. 'Exile! What Exile? Deportation and the Discourses of Diaspora', in *Leading Captivity Captive: 'The Exile' as History and Ideology*, edited by L. Grabbe. JSOT Supplement Series 278. Sheffield: JSOT Press/ Sheffield Academic Press, 62–79.

Carroll R., M. D. 2008. *Christians at the Border: Immigration, the Church, and the Bible*. Grand Rapids: Baker Academic.

Carulla, S. B. 2007. 'Resocialization of "Desplazados" in Small Pentecostal Congregations in Bogotá, Colombia'. *Refugee Survey Quarterly*, 26(2), 36–46.

Castelli, E. 1991. *Imitating Paul: A Discourse of Power*. Louisville: Westminster John Knox.

Castells, M. 2000a. *The Rise of the Network Society*. The Information Age: Economy, Society and Culture. Vol. I. 2nd edn. Oxford and Malden: Blackwell.

Castells, M. 2000b. *End of Millennium*. The Information Age: Economy, Society and Culture. Vol. III. 2nd edn. Oxford and Malden: Blackwell.

Castells, M. 2004. *The Power of Identity*. The Information Age: Economy, Society and Culture. Vol. II. 2nd edn. Oxford and Malden: Blackwell.

Castillo Guerra, J. E. 2008. 'A Theology of Migration: Toward an Intercultural Methodology', in *A Promised Land, A Perilous Journey: Theological Perspectives on Migration*, edited by D. G. Groody and G. Campese. Notre Dame, IN: Notre Dame University Press, 243–270.

Castles, S. 2000. *Ethnicity and Globalization*. London, Thousand Oaks and New Delhi: Sage.

Castles, S. 2002. 'Migration and Community Formation under Conditions of Globalization'. *International Migration Review*, 36(4), 1143–1168.

Castles, S. 2003. 'Towards a Sociology of Forced Migration and Social Transformation'. *Sociology*, 37(1), 13–34.

Castles, S. 2004. *Migration Fundamentals: Confronting the Realities of Forced Migration* [Online]. Available at: www.migrationinformation.org/Feature/ display.cfm?id=222 [accessed: 16 January 2009].

Castles, S. 2007. 'The Factors that Make and Unmake Migration Policies', in *Rethinking Migration: New Theoretical and Empirical Perspectives*, edited by A. Portes and J. DeWind. New York: Berghahn, 29–61.

Castles, S. and Davidson, A. 2000. *Citizenship and Migration: Globalization and the Politics of Belonging*. Basingstoke: Macmillan.

Castles, S. and Loughna, S. 2005. 'Trends in Asylum Migration to Industrialized Countries, 1990–2001', in *Poverty, International Migration and Asylum*, edited by G. J. Borjas and J. Crisp. Basingstoke: Palgrave Macmillan, 39–69.

Castles, S. and Miller, M. J. 2009. *The Age of Migration: International Population Movements in the Modern World*. 4th edn. New York and London: Guilford Press.

Castles, S. and Van Hear, N. 2011. 'Root Causes', in *Global Migration Governance*, edited by A. Betts. Oxford and New York: Oxford University Press, 287–306.

Catto, R. 2008. 'Non-Western Christian Missionaries in England: Has Mission been Reversed?', in *Mission and Migration*, edited by S. Spencer. Calver: Cliff College, 109–118.

Cavanaugh, W. T. 1998. *Torture and Eucharist: Theology, Politics, and the Body of Christ*. Oxford and Malden: Blackwell.

Cavanaugh, W. T. 2002. *Theopolitical Imagination: Discovering the Liturgy as a Political Act in an Age of Global Consumerism*. London and New York: T & T Clark.

Cave, Damien. 2011. 'Crossing Over, and Over'. *New York Times*, 2 October.

Cave, Dave. 2003. *Discovering Ezra and Nehemiah*. Crossway Bible Guides. 2nd edn. Leicester: Crossway Books.

CCME [Churches' Commission for Migrants in Europe]. 2011. CCME [Online]. Available at: www.ccme.be [accessed: 26 October 2011].

Cenada, S. 2003. 'Women Asylum Seekers in the UK', in *Exile and Asylum: Women Seeking Refuge in 'Fortress Europe'*, edited by A. Treacher, A. Coombes, C. Alexander, L. Bland and P. Alldred. Feminist Review 73. Basingstoke: Palgrave Macmillan, 126–128.

Centre for Social Justice. 2008. *Asylum Matters: Restoring Trust in the UK Asylum System*. London: Centre for Social Justice.

Chaillot, C. 2007. 'Some Aspects of the Situation of Refugees from the Oriental Orthodox Christian Churches'. *Refugee Survey Quarterly*, 26(2), 47–56.

Chantler, K. 2010. 'Women Seeking Asylum in the UK: Contesting Conventions', in *Gender and Migration: Feminist Interventions*, edited by I. Palmary, E. Burman, K. Chantler, L. Bland and P. Alldred. London and New York: Zed Books, 104–118.

Cheng, P. C. 2011. *Radical Love: An Introduction to Queer Theology*. New York: Seabury Books.

Childs, B. S. 1974. *Exodus: A Commentary*. London: SCM Press.

Chimni, B. S. 1998. 'The Geopolitics of Refugee Studies: A View from the South'. *Journal of Refugee Studies*, 11(4), 350–374.

Chimni, B. S. 2001. 'Reforming the International Refugee Regime: A Dialogic Model'. *Journal of Refugee Studies*, 14(2), 151–168.

Chimni, B. S. 2009. 'The Birth of a "Discipline": From Refugee to Forced Migration Studies'. *Journal of Refugee Studies*, 22(1), 11–29.

Church in Wales. 2008. *Press Release: Refugees and Asylum Seekers Receive Support* [Online]. Available at: www.churchinwales.org.uk/press/display_press_release.php?prid=4512 [accessed: 3 October 2011].

Citizens for Sanctuary. 2011. Citizens for Sanctuary [Online]. Available at: www.citizensforsanctuary.org.uk [accessed: 8 October 2011].

Clarke, G. 2008. 'Faith-based Organizations and International Development: An Overview', in *Development, Civil Society and Faith-based Organizations. Bridging the Sacred and the Secular*, edited by G. Clarke and M. Jennings. Basingstoke: Palgrave Macmillan, 17–45.

Clarke, N. and Nandy, L. 2008. *Living on the Edge of Despair: Destitution amongst Asylum Seeking and Refugee Children*. London: Children's Society. Available at: www.childrenssociety.org.uk/resources/documents/Research/ Living_on_the_edge_of_despair_destitution_amongst_asylum_seeking_and_ refugee_children_6115_full.pdf [accessed: 27 November 2008].

Clark-King, E. 2004. *Theology By Heart: Women, the Church and God*. Peterborough: Epworth.

CLEAR [City Life Education and Action for Refugees]. 2008. CLEAR [Online]. Available at: www.clearproject.org.uk [accessed: 18 December 2008].

CLG [Communities and Local Government]. 2010. *2008–2009 Citizenship Survey: Community Cohesion Topic Report*. London: CLG. Available at: www.communities. gov.uk/publications/corporate/statistics/citizenshipsurvey200809cohesion [accessed: 12 January 2012].

Clifford, J. 1999. 'Diasporas', in *Migration, Diasporas and Transnationalism*, edited by S. Vervotec and Robin Cohen. Cheltenham and Northampton, MA: Edward Elgar, 215–251.

Clines, D. J. A. 1978. *The Theme of the Pentateuch*. JSOT Supplement Series 10. Sheffield: JSOT Press/Sheffield Academic Press.

Clines, D. J. A. 1984. *Ezra, Nehemiah, Esther*. New Century Bible Commentary. Grand Rapids: William B Eerdmans.

Cloke, P. 2010. 'Theo-Ethics and Radical Faith-based Praxis in the Postsecular City', in *Exploring the Postsecular: The Religious, the Political and the Urban*, edited by A. Molendijk, J. Beaumont and C. Jedan. Leiden and Boston: Brill, 223–241.

Cohen, Robin. 1994. *Frontiers of Identity: The British and the Others*. London and New York: Longman.

Cohen, Robin (ed.). 1996. *Theories of Migration*. International Library of Studies on Migration 1. Cheltenham and Brookfield: Edward Elgar.

Cohen, Robin. 2006. *Migration and its Enemies: Global Capital, Migrant Labour and the Nation-state*. Aldershot and Burlington: Ashgate.

Cohen, Robin. 2008. *Global Diasporas: An Introduction*. 2nd edn. Abingdon and New York: Routledge.

Cohen, S. 2003. *No One is Illegal: Asylum and Immigration Control Past and Present*. Stoke on Trent and Sterling: Trentham Books.

Coleman, S. and Eade, J. 2004. 'Introduction: Reframing Pilgrimage', in *Reframing Pilgrimage: Cultures in Motion*, edited by S. Coleman and J. Eade. London and New York: Routledge, 1–25.

Collinson, S. 2011. 'Forced Migration in the International Political Economy', in *Refugees in International Relations*, edited by A. Betts and G. Loescher. Oxford: Oxford University Press, 305–323.

Colville, R. 2006a. 'The Perfect Scapegoat'. *Refugees*, 142(1), 7–13. Geneva: UNHCR.

Colville, R. 2006b. 'Words and Images'. *Refugees*, 142(1), 14–19. Geneva: UNHCR.

Colwell, J. 2005. 'The Church as Ethical Community', in *The Bible in Pastoral Practice: Readings in the Place and Function of Scripture in the Church*, edited by P. Ballard and S. R. Holmes. London: Darton, Longman and Todd, 212–224.

Community Links. 2005. *Small Places, Close to Home: Projects led by Refugee and Asylum-seeking Communities*. London: Community Links.

Cone, J. H. 1990. *A Black Theology of Liberation*. Twentieth anniversary edn. Maryknoll: Orbis.

Copeland, M. S. 2004. 'Living Stones in the Household of God', in *Living Stones in the Household of God: The Legacy and Future of Black Theology*, edited by L. E. Thomas. Minneapolis: Augsburg Fortress, 183–188.

Corbey, R. and Leerssen, J. T. (eds). 1991. *Alterity, Identity, Image: Selves and Others in Society and Scholarship*. Amsterdam and Atlanta: Rodopi.

COS [City of Sanctuary]. 2011. COS [Online]. Available at: www.cityofsanctuary. com [accessed: 20 August 2011].

Coton, J. 2007. *Alltogether for Asylum Justice: Asylum Seekers' Conversion to Christianity*. London: Evangelical Alliance. Available at: www.eauk. org/public-affairs/socialjustice/upload/alltogether-for-asylum-justice.pdf [accessed: 26 November 2008].

Coulton, N. 2007. 'Asylum Injustice'. *The Times* [Online, 30 April]. Available at: www.timesonline.co.uk/tol/comment/letters/article1722947.ece [accessed: 27 November 2008].

Coulton, N. 2008. Interview (Meeting) with the Very Revd Nicholas Coulton, Oxford, 29 July.

Coventry Peace House. 2006. *I Came Here for Safety: The Reality of Detention and Destitution for Asylum Seekers*. Coventry: Coventry Peace House. Available at: http://covpeacehouse.org.uk/files/I%20came%20here%20for%20safety. pdf [accessed: 4 August 2008].

Cox, J. 2011. Interview (Telephone) with Jonathan Cox, Lead Organizer, Citizens for Sanctuary, 13 April.

Crawley, H. 1999. 'Women and Refugee Status: Beyond the Public/Private Dichotomy in UK Asylum Policy', in *Engendering Forced Migration: Theory and Practice*, edited by D. Indra. New York and Oxford: Berghahn, 308–333.

Crawley, H. 2001. *Refugees and Gender: Law and Process*. Bristol: Jordan.

Crawley, H. 2005. *Evidence on Attitudes to Asylum and Immigration: What We Know, Don't Know and Need to Know*. Working Paper No. 23. Oxford: Centre on Migration, Policy and Society [COMPAS]. Available at: www.compas. ox.ac.uk/publications/working_papers.shtml [accessed: 20 January 2009].

Crisp, J. 2003. *A New Asylum Paradigm? Globalization, Migration and the Uncertain Future of the International Refugee Regime*. New Issues in Refugee Research. Working Paper No. 100. Geneva: UNHCR. Available at: www. unhcr.org/3fe16d835.pdf [accessed: 22 August 2011].

Crisp, J. 2004. *The Local Integration and Local Settlement of Refugees: A Conceptual and Historical Analysis*. New Issues in Refugee Research.

Working Paper No. 102. Geneva: UNHCR. Available at: www.unhcr.org/ doclist/research/3bbc18ed5/skip-60.html [accessed: 20 January 2009].

Crisp, J. 2008. *Beyond the Nexus: UNHCR's Evolving Perspective on Refugee Protection and International Migration*. New Issues in Refugee Research. Paper No. 155. Available at: http://reliefweb.int/sites/reliefweb.int/files/ reliefweb_pdf/node-23904.pdf [accessed: 16 August 2011].

Crosby, M. H. 1988. *House of Disciples: Church, Economics, and Justice in Matthew*. Maryknoll: Orbis Books.

Cross, L. 2005. Interview (Meeting) with Lindsay Cross, Co-ordinator of WERS, Newcastle, 20 January.

Crossan, J. D. 1991. *The Historical Jesus: The Life of a Mediterranean Jewish Peasant*. Edinburgh: T & T Clark.

Crüsemann, F. 1993. '"You Know the Heart of a Stranger" (Exodus 23.9). A Recollection of the Torah in the Face of New Nationalism and Xenophobia', in *Migrants and Refugees*, edited by D. Mieth and L. S. Cahill. London and Maryknoll: SCM Press and Orbis, 95–109.

CULF [Commission on Urban Life and Faith]. 2006. *Faithful Cities: A Call for Celebration, Vision and Justice. The Report from the Commission on Urban Life and Faith*. Peterborough and London: Methodist Publishing House and Church House Publishing.

Cunningham, D. S. 1998. *These Three are One: The Practice of Trinitarian Theology*. Oxford: Blackwell.

da Lomba, S. 2010. 'Legal Status and Refugee Integration: A UK Perspective'. *Journal of Refugee Studies*, 23(4), 415–436.

Daily Star. 2003. 'Asylum Seekers Eat Our Donkeys'. *Daily Star*, 31 August, 1.

Dalferth, I. 2010. 'Post-secular Society: Christianity and the Dialectics of the Secular'. *Journal of the American Academy of Religion*, 78(2), 317–345.

Daniel, B. 2010. *Neighbor: Christian Encounters with 'Illegal' Immigration*. Louisville: Westminster John Knox.

Daniel, E. V. and Knudsen, J. C. 1995. 'Introduction', in *Mistrusting Refugees*, edited by E. V. Daniel and J. C. Knudsen. Berkeley and Los Angeles: University of California Press, 1–12.

Darling, J. 2010. 'A City of Sanctuary: The Relational Re-imagining of Sheffield's Asylum Politics'. *Transactions of the Institute of British Geographers*, 35(1), 125–140.

Darling, J., Barnett, C. and Eldridge, S. 2010. 'City of Sanctuary: A UK Initiative for Hospitality'. *Forced Migration Review*, 34, 46–47.

Davey, A. 1995. 'Being Church as Political Praxis', in *Liberation Theology UK*, edited by C. Rowland and J. Vincent. Sheffield: Urban Theology Unit, 55–74.

Davey, A. 1999. 'Globalization as Challenge and Opportunity in Urban Mission: An Outlook from London'. *International Review of Mission*, 88(351), 381–389.

Davey, A. 2001. *Urban Christianity and Global Order: Theological Resources for an Urban Future*. London: SPCK.

Davies, R. 2008. 'Visiting Asylum Seekers in Detention: A Personal View'. *JRS–UK News*, Spring, 2. London: Jesuit Refugee Service.

Davis, F., Paulhus, E. and Bradstock, A. 2008. *Moral, But No Compass – Government, Church and the Future of Welfare. A Report for the Church of England and to the Nation*. Chelmsford: Matthew James.

Dawson, A. 1999. 'The Origins and Character of the Base Ecclesial Community: A Brazilian Perspective', in *The Cambridge Companion to Liberation Theology*, edited by C. Rowland. Cambridge: Cambridge University Press, 109–128.

Deaux, K. 2006. *To Be An Immigrant*. New York: Russell Sage Foundation.

Decker, M. R., Oram, S., Gupta, J. and Silverman, J. G. 2009. 'Forced Prostitution and Trafficking for Sexual Exploitation Among Women and Girls in Situations of Migration and Conflict: Review and Recommendations for Reproductive Health Care Personnel', in *Women, Migration, and Conflict: Breaking a Deadly Cycle*, edited by S. F. Martin and J. Tirman. Dordrecht and New York: Springer, 63–86.

Deeks, D. (ed.). 2006. *Asylum Principles: Statement for Churches Working on Asylum Issues*. London: CTBI/CCRJ.

Denscombe, M. 2007. *The Good Research Guide for Small-Scale Social Research Projects*. 3rd edn. Maidenhead: Open University Press and McGraw-Hill Education.

De Genova, N. and Peutz, N. (eds). 2010. *The Deportation Regime: Sovereignty, Space and the Freedom of Movement*. Durham, NC and London: Duke University Press.

De La Torre, M. 2010. 'Moving Beyond Hospitality'. *Journal of Lutheran Ethics*, 10(4). Available at: www.elca.org/What-We-Believe/Social-Issues/Journal-of-Lutheran-Ethics/Issues/April-2010/Moving-Beyond-Hospitality.aspx [accessed: 12 January 2012].

de Raadt, P. 2006. Interview (Telephone) with Puck de Raadt, Co-ordinator, Bail Circle, 2 May.

de Vaux, R. 1961. *Ancient Israel: Its Life and Institutions*. Trans. J. McHugh. London: Darton, Longman and Todd.

de Wet, C. (ed.). 2006. *Development-Induced Displacement: Problems, Policies and People*. Studies in Forced Migration. Vol. 18. New York and Oxford: Berghahn.

DFID [Department for International Development]. 2007. *Moving Out of Poverty – Making Migration Work Better for Poor People*. London: DFID. Available at: www.migrationdrc.org/publications/other_publications/Moving_Out_of_Poverty.pdf [accessed: 22 August 2011].

Dolnik, S. 2011. 'Asylum Ploys Feed on News To Open Door'. *The New York Times*, 13 July, 1.

Doná, G. and Berry, J. W. 1999. 'Refugee Acculturation and Re-acculturation', in *Refugees: Perspectives on the Experience of Forced Migration*, edited by A. Ager. London and New York: Continuum, 169–195.

Donaldson, L. E. 2005. 'Gospel Hauntings: The Postcolonial Demons of New Testament Criticism', in *Postcolonial Biblical Criticism: Interdisciplinary Intersections*, edited by S. D. Moore and F. F. Segovia. London and New York: T & T Clark, 97–113.

Donaldson, L. E. 2010. 'The Sign of Orpah: Reading Ruth Through Native Eyes', in *Hope Abundant: Third World and Indigenous Women's Theology*, edited by P.-L. Kwok. Maryknoll: Orbis, 138–151.

D'Onofrio, L. and Munk, K. 2004. *Understanding the Stranger: Final Report*. London: ICAR.

Dorais, L. J. 2007. 'Faith, Hope and Identity: Religion and the Vietnamese Refugees'. *Refugee Survey Quarterly*, 26(2), 57–68.

Douglas, M. 1984. *Purity and Danger: An Analysis of Concepts of Pollution and Taboo*. Paperback edn. London: Ark Paperbacks.

Douglas, M. 2001. *In the Wilderness: The Doctrine of Defilement in the Book of Numbers*. Rev. edn. Oxford and New York: Oxford University Press.

Douglas, M. 2004. *Jacob's Tears: The Priestly Work of Reconciliation*. Oxford and New York: Oxford University Press.

Dube, M. W. 2000. *Postcolonial Feminist Interpretation of the Bible*. St Louis: Chalice Press.

Dube, M. W. 2001. 'Divining Ruth for International Relations', in *Other Ways of Reading: African Women and the Bible*, edited by M. W. Dube. Atlanta and Geneva: Society of Biblical Literature and WCC Publications, 179–195.

Duffield, M. 2001. *Global Governance and the New Wars: The Merging of Development and Security*. London and New York: Zed Books.

Dufton, F. 1989. 'The Syrophoenician Woman and Her Dogs'. *Expository Times*, 100, 417.

Dulles, A. 1983. *Models of Revelation*. Dublin: Gill and Macmillan.

Dulles, A. 1987. *Models of the Church*. Expanded edn. New York: Doubleday.

Dummet, M. 2001. *On Immigration and Refugees*. London and New York: Routledge.

Duncan, G. (ed.). 2002. *Seeing Christ in Others: An Anthology for Worship, Meditation and Mission*. New edn. Norwich: Canterbury.

Duncan, G. (ed.). 2005. *Entertaining Angels: A Worship Anthology on Sharing Christ's Hospitality*. Norwich: Canterbury.

Duraisingh, C. 2002. 'Encountering Difference in a Plural World: A Pentecost Paradigm for Mission', in *Waging Reconciliation: God's Mission in a Time of Globalization and Crisis*, edited by I. T. Douglas. New York: Church Publishing Incorporated, 171–212.

Dustman, C. and Preston, I. 2003. *Racial and Economic Factors in Attitudes to Immigration*. London: University College, London and Institute for Fiscal Studies. Available at: http://doku.iab.de/grauepap/2003/coll_dustmann.pdf [accessed: 26 October 2008].

Eade, J. and Sallnow, M. (eds). 2000. *Contesting the Sacred: The Anthropology of Christian Pilgrimage*. Rev. edn. Urbana and Chicago: University of Illinois Press.

Eby, J., Iverson, E., Smyers, J. and Kekic, E. 2011. 'The Faith Community's Role in Refugee Resettlement in the US'. *Journal of Refugee Studies*, 24(3), 586–605.

ECSR [Enabling Christians in Serving Refugees]. 2008. *ECSR/SGM Lifewords Toolkit* [Online]. Available at: www.sgmlifewords.com/asylum/index.html [accessed: 18 December 2008].

Edwards, J. R. 2007. 'A Biblical Perspective on Immigration Policy', in *Debating Immigration*, edited by C. Swain. Cambridge and New York: Cambridge University Press, 46–62.

Eggers, D. 2006. *What is the What: The Autobiography of Achak Deng. A Novel*. New York: Vintage Books.

Ehrenreich, B. and Hochschild, A. R. (eds). 2002. *Global Woman: Nannies, Maids and Sex Workers in the New Economy*. London: Granta Books.

Ekklesia. 2005. 'Stop using Asylum Seekers as Political Footballs, say Churches'. *Ekklesia* [Online, 12 April]. Available at: www.ekklesia.co.uk/content/news_syndication/article_050412wyec.shtml [accessed: 20 April 2005].

Eliot, T. S. 1959. *The Four Quartets: Burnt Norton, East Coker, The Dry Salvages and Little Gidding*. London and Boston: Faber & Faber.

Eliot, T. S. 1990. 'Journey of the Magi', in *The Waste Land and Other Poems*. London: Faber & Faber, 65–66.

Ellin, N. (ed.). 1997. *Architecture of Fear*. New York: Pinceton Architectural Press.

Elliott, J. H. 2005. *A Home for the Homeless: A Social-Scientific Criticism of 1 Peter, Its Situation and Strategy*. New edn. Eugene: Wipf and Stock.

Elmadmad, K. 1991. 'An Arab Convention on Forced Migration: Desirability and Possibilities'. *International Journal of Refugee Law*, 3(3), 461–481.

EmbraceNI. 2008. EMBRACE [Online]. Available at: www.embraceni.org [accessed: 18 December 2008].

Epsztein, L. 1986. *Social Justice in the Ancient Near East and the People of the Bible*. Trans. J. Bowden. London: SCM Press.

Eskenazi, T. C. 1992. 'Out from the Shadows: Biblical Women in the Postexilic Era'. *Journal for the Study of the Old Testament*, 54, 25–43.

Eskenazi, T. C. and Judd, E. P. 1994. 'Marriage to a Stranger in Ezra 9–10', in *Second Temple Studies 2. Temple and Community in the Persian Period*, edited by T. C. Eskenazi and K. H. Richards. JSOT Supplement Series 175. Sheffield: JSOT Press/Sheffield Academic Press, 266–285.

ESRC [Economic and Social Research Council] Seminar. 2006. 'Appendix: Guidelines Funded through the Economic and Research Council Seminar Series: "Eliciting the Views of Refugee People Seeking Asylum"', in *Doing Research with Refugees: Issues and Guidelines*, edited by B. Temple and R. Moran. Bristol: Policy Press, 203–206.

Essed, P., Frerks, G. and Schrijvers, J. 2004. 'Introduction: Refugees, Agency and Social Transformation', in *Refugees and the Transformation of Societies: Agency, Policies, Ethics and Politics*, edited by P. Essed, G. Frerks and J. Schrijvers. New York and Oxford: Berghahn, 1–16.

Etherington, K. 2004. *Becoming a Reflexive Researcher: Using Our Selves in Research*. London and Philadelphia: Jessica Kingsley.

Evans, C. A. 1997. 'Aspects of Exile and Restoration in the Proclamation of Jesus and the Gospels', in *Exile: Old Testament, Jewish and Christian Conceptions*, edited by J. M. Scott. Leiden, New York and Köln: Brill, 299–328.

Faist, T. 1997. 'The Crucial Meso-Level', in *International Migration, Immobility and Development: Multidisiplinary Perspectives*, edited by T. Hammar, G. Brochmann, K. Tamas and T. Faist. Oxford and New York: Berg, 187–217.

Faist, T. 2000. *The Volume and Dynamics of International Migration and Transnational Social Spaces*. Oxford and New York: Oxford University Press.

Faist, T. 2010. 'Transnationalisation: Its Conceptual and Empirical Relevance', in *Migration in a Globalised World: New Research Issues and Prospects*, edited by C. Audebert and M. K. Doraï. Amsterdam: Amsterdam University Press, 79–105.

Farisani, E. 2004a. 'The Composition and Date of Ezra–Nehemiah'. *Old Testament Essays*, 17(2), 208–230.

Farisani, E. 2004b. 'A Sociological Analysis of Israelites in Babylonian Exile'. *Old Testament Essays*, 17(3), 380–388.

Farisani, E. 2004c. 'Ethnicity in Ezra–Nehemiah'. *Theologia Viatorum*, 28(1), 24–55.

Farnell, R. 2009. 'Faiths, Government and Regeneration: A Contested Discourse', in *Faith in the Public Realm: Controversies, Policies and Practices*, edited by A. Dinham, R. Furbey and V. Lowndes. Bristol: Policy Press, 183–202.

Favell, A. 2001. *Philosophies of Integration: Immigration and the Idea of Citizenship in France and Britain*. 2nd edn. Basingstoke: Palgrave.

Fekete, L. 2005. *The Deportation Machine: Europe, Asylum and Human Rights*. London: Institute of Race Relations.

Felder, C. H. 1991. 'Race, Racism and the Biblical Narratives', in *Stony the Road we Trod: African American Biblical Interpretation*, edited by C. H. Felder. Minneapolis: Augsburg Fortress, 127–145.

Feldmeier, R. 1996. 'The "Nation" of Strangers: Social Contempt and its Theological Interpretation in Ancient Judaism and Early Christianity', in *Ethnicity and the Bible*, edited by M. G. Brett. Boston and Leiden: Brill, 241–270.

Fennelly, K. 2008. 'Prejudice Towards Immigrants in the Midwest', in *New Faces in New Places: The Changing Geography of American Immigration*, edited by D. Massey. New York: Russell Sage Foundation, 151–178.

Fernandez, E. S. 2006. 'Exodus-toward-Egypt: Filipino-Americans' Struggle to Realise the Promised Land in America', in *Voices from the Margin: Interpreting the Bible in the Third World*, edited by R. S. Sugirtharajah. 3rd edn. Maryknoll: Orbis, 242–257.

Ferris, E. G. 1990. 'The Churches, Refugees, and Politics', in *Refugees and International Relations*, edited by G. Loescher and L. Monahan. Oxford: Clarendon, 159–177.

Ferris, E. G. 1993. *Beyond Borders: Refugees, Migrants and Human Rights in the Post-Cold War Era*. Geneva: WCC Publications.

Ferris, E. G. 2011. 'Faith and Humanitarianism: It's Complicated'. *Journal of Refugee Studies*, 24(3), 606–625.

Fewell, D. N. 2004. 'Ezra and Nehemiah', in *Global Bible Commentary*, edited by D. Patte. Nashville: Abingdon, 127–134.

Fewell, D. N. and Gunn, D. M. 1990. *Compromising Redemption: Relating Characters in the Book of Ruth*. Louisville: Westminster John Knox.

Feyissa, A. and Horn, R. 2008. 'There is More Than One Way of Dying: An Ethiopian Perspective on the Effects of Long-term Stays in Refugee Camps', in *Refugee Rights: Ethics, Advocacy, and Africa*, edited by D. Hollenbach. Washington, DC: Georgetown University Press, 13–26.

Fiddian-Qasmiyeh, E. 2010. '"Ideal" Refugee Women and Gender Equality Mainstreaming in the Sahrawi Refugee Camps: "Good Practice" for Whom?'. *Refugee Survey Quarterly*, 29(2), 64–84.

Fiddian-Qasmiyeh, E. 2011. 'The Pragmatics of Performance: Putting "Faith" in Aid in the Sahrawi Refugee Camps'. *Journal of Refugee Studies*, 24(3), 533–547.

Fiddian-Qasmiyeh, E. and Qasmiyeh, Y. 2010. 'Muslim Asylum-Seekers and Refugees: Negotiating Identity, Politics and Religion in the UK'. *Journal of Refugee Studies*, 23(3), 294–314.

Finkelstein, I. and Na'aman, N. 1994. *From Nomadism to Monarchy: Archaeological and Historical Aspects of Early Israel*. Jerusalem and Washington, DC: Yad Izhak Ben-Zvi, Israel Exploration Society and Biblical Archaeology Society.

Finlay, A. 2001. 'Reflexivity and the Dilemmas of Identification: An Ethnographic Encounter in Northern Ireland', in *Researching Violently Divided Societies: Ethical and Methodological Issues*, edited by M. Smyth and G. Robinson. New York: United Nations University Press, 55–76.

Fishbane, M. 1985. *Biblical Interpretation in Ancient Israel*. Oxford: Oxford University Press.

Floyd-Thomas, S. M. and Pinn, A. B. (eds). 2010. *Liberation Theologies in the US: An Introduction*. New York and London: New York University Press.

Flynn, D. 2005. 'New Border, New Management: The Dilemmas of Modern Immigration Policies'. *Ethnic and Racial Studies*, 28(3), 463–490.

Flynn, D., Ford, R. and Somerville, W. 2010. 'Immigration and the Election'. *Renewal*, 18(3/4), 102–114. Available at: http://renewal.org.uk/files/Renewal_autumn_2010_Flyn_et_al_immigration.pdf [accessed: 7 February 2012].

Fontaine, C. R. 2010. '"Here Comes This Dreamer": Reading Joseph the Slave in Multicultural and Interfaith Contexts', in *Genesis*, edited by A. Brenner, A. C. Lee and G. A. Yee. Minneapolis: Fortress, 131–145.

Forbes Martin, S. 2004. *Refugee Women*. 2nd edn. Lanham: Lexington Books.

Ford, D. F. 1997. *The Shape of Living*. London: Fount.

Ford, D. F. 1999. *Self and Salvation: Being Transformed*. Cambridge: Cambridge University Press.

Forecast, H. 2002. '"Am I My Brother's Keeper?" Ethical and Human Issues behind the Search for and Provision of Asylum in the UK'. *Epworth Review*, 29(4), 36–43.

Fornet-Betancourt, R. 2008. 'Hermeneutics and Politics of Strangers: A Philosophical Contribution on the Challenge of *Convivencia* in Multicultural Societies', in *A Promised Land, A Perilous Journey: Theological Perspectives on Migration*, edited by D. G. Groody and G. Campese. Notre Dame, IN: University of Notre Dame Press, 210–224.

Forrester, D. B. 1997. *Christian Justice and Public Policy*. Cambridge: Cambridge University Press.

Forrester, D. B. 1999. 'Theology in Fragments: Practical Theology and the Challenge of Post-modernity', in *Globalisation and Difference: Practical Theology in a World Context*, edited by P. Ballard and P. Couture. Cardiff: Cardiff Academic Press, 129–133.

Forrester, D. B. 2000. *Truthful Action: Explorations in Practical Theology*. Edinburgh: T & T Clark.

Forrester, D. B. 2001. *On Human Worth: A Christian Vindication of Equality*. London: SCM Press.

Forrester, D. B. 2004a. 'The Scope of Public Theology', in *The Future of Christian Social Ethics: A Special Edition of Studies in Christian Ethics 17 (2). Essays on the Work of Ronald H Preston, 1913–2001*, edited by E. Graham and E. D. Reed. London and New York: Continuum, 5–19.

Forrester, D. B. 2004b. 'Working in the Quarry: A Response to the Colloquium', in *Public Theology for the 21st Century*, edited by W. F. Storrar and A. R. Morton. London and New York: T & T Clark, 431–438.

Forrester, D. B. 2005a. *Theological Fragments: Explorations in Unsystematic Theology*. London and New York: T & T Clark International.

Forrester, D. B. 2005b. *Apocalypse Now? Reflections on Faith in a Time of Terror*. Aldershot and Burlington: Ashgate.

Forrester, D. B. 2010. *Forrester on Christian Ethics and Practical Theology: Collected Writings on Christianity, India, and the Social Order*. Farnham: Ashgate.

France, R. T. 2002. *The Gospel of Mark: A Commentary on the Greek Text*. Grand Rapids and Carlisle: William B Eerdmans and Paternoster.

Fraser, G. 2007. 'Christians are Called to Welcome Strangers'. *Church Times*, 29 June, 11.

Freedman, J. 2007. *Gendering the International Asylum and Refugee Debate.* Basingstoke: Palgrave Macmillan.

Freeman, G. 2007. 'Immigrant Incorporation in Western Democracies', in *Rethinking Migration: New Theoretical and Empirical Perspectives*, edited by A. Portes and J. De Wind. New York and Oxford: Berghahn, 122–146.

Freyne, S. 1985. 'Villifying the Other and Defining the Self: Matthew's and John's Anti-Jewish Polemic in Focus', in *'To See Ourselves As Others See Us': Christians, Jews, 'Others' in Late Antiquity*, edited by J. Neusner and E. S. Frerichs. Chico: Scholars Press, 117–143.

Friedman, J. 2004a. 'Introduction', in *Worlds on the Move: Globalization, Migration and Cultural Security*, edited by J. Friedman and S. Randeria. London and New York: I. B. Tauris and Co, xiii–xix.

Friedman, J. 2004b. 'Globalization, Transnationalization, and Migration: Ideologies and Realities of Global Transformation', in *Worlds on the Move: Globalization, Migration and Cultural Security*, edited by J. Friedman and S. Randeria. London and New York: I. B. Tauris and Co, 63–88.

Furbey, R. 2010. Presentation at Migration, Racism and Religion: A Conference on Faith Organizations, Sanctuary and Civil Society. University of East London, 4 February.

Furbey, R., Dinham, A., Farnell, R., Finneron, D., and Wilkinson, G. 2006. *Faith as Social Capital: Connecting or Dividing?* Bristol: Policy Press.

Furedi, F. 2005. *Culture of Fear: Risk-taking and the Morality of Low Expectation.* Rev. edn. London and New York: Continuum.

Galloway, K. 2006. 'Singing the Lord's Song', in *Worship: Window of the Urban Church*, edited by T. Stratford. London: SPCK, 11–24.

Geddes, A. 2000. *Immigration and European Integration: Towards Fortress Europe?* Manchester and New York: Manchester University Press.

Geddes, A. 2003. *The Politics of Migration and Immigration in Europe.* London, Thousand Oaks and New Delhi: Sage.

Geddes, A. 2005. 'Immigration and the Welfare State', in *International Migration and Security: Opportunities and Challenges*, edited by E. Guild and J. van Selm. London and New York: Routledge, 159–173.

Geddes, A. 2008. *Immigration and European Integration: Beyond fortress Europe?* 2nd edn. Manchester and New York: Manchester University Press.

Gellner, E. 1997. *Nationalism.* London: Weidenfeld & Nicolson.

Gentleman, A. 2011. 'Child Detention: Has the Government Broken its Promise to End it?'. *Guardian* [Online, 17 October]. Available at: www.guardian.co.uk/uk/2011/oct/17/child-detention-government-broken-promise/print [accessed: 20 October 2011].

Georgi, D. 2005. *The City in the Valley: Biblical Intepretation and Urban Theology.* Atlanta: Society of Biblical Literature.

Gerschutz, J. M. and Lorentzen, L. A. 2009. 'Integration Yesterday and Today: New Challenges for the US and the Church', in *And You Welcomed Me:*

Migration and Catholic Social Teaching, edited by D. Kerwin and J. M. Gerschutz. Lanham: Lexington Books, 123–148.

Ghanea, N. 2007. 'Europeanization of Citizenship and Asylum Policy: A Case Study of the U.K.', in *New Regionalism and Asylum Seekers: Challenges Ahead*, edited by S. Kneebone and F. Rawlings-Sanaei. New York and Oxford: Berghahn, 111–135.

Ghosh, B. (ed.). 2000. *Managing Migration: Time for a New International Regime?* Oxford and New York: Oxford University Press.

Gibney, Mark. 2002. 'Certain Violence, Uncertain Protection', in *Global Changes in Asylum Regimes: Closing Doors*, edited by D. Joly. Basingstoke: Palgrave Macmillan, 15–37.

Gibney, Matthew J. 2002. 'Security and the Ethics of Asylum after 11 September'. *Forced Migration Review*, 13(June), 40–42.

Gibney, Matthew J. 2003. 'The State of Asylum: Democratisation, Judicialisation and Evolution of Refugee Policy', in *The Refugee Convention 50 Years On: Globalisation and International Law*, edited by S. Kneebone. Aldershot: Ashgate, 19–45.

Gibney, Matthew J. 2004. *The Ethics and Politics of Asylum: Liberal Democracy and the Response to Refugees*. Cambridge: Cambridge University Press.

Gibney, Matthew J. 2006. '"A Thousand Little Guantanamos": Western States and Measures to Prevent the Arrival of Refugees', in *Displacement, Asylum, Migration: The Oxford Amnesty Lectures 2004*, edited by K. E. Tunstall. Oxford: Oxford University Press, 139–169.

Gibney, Matthew J. 2008. 'Asylum and the Expansion of Deportation in the United Kingdom'. *Government and Opposition*, 43(2), 146–167.

Gibney, Matthew J. and Hansen, R. 2005. 'Asylum Policy in the West: Past Trends, Future Possibilities', in *Poverty, International Migration and Asylum*, edited by G. J. Borjas and J. Crisp. Basingstoke: Palgrave Macmillan, 70–96.

Gill, N. 2010. 'Tracing Imaginations of the State: The Spatial Consequences of Different State Concepts among Asylum Activist Organizations'. *Antipode*, 42(5), 1048–1070.

Gilroy, P. 2004. *After Empire: Melancholia or Convivial Culture?* Abingdon: Routledge.

Girard, R. 1986. *The Scapegoat*. Trans. Y. Freccero. London: Athlone Press.

Girard, R. 1996. *The Girard Reader*, edited by J. G. Williams. New York: Crossroad.

Girard, R. 2001. *I See Satan Fall Like Lightning*. Trans. J. G. Williams. Maryknoll: Orbis.

Glueck, N. 1967. *Ḥesed in the Bible*, edited by E. L. Epstein. Trans. A. Gottschalk. Cincinnati: Hebrew Union College Press.

Gold, J. 2008. 'Bishop tells Christians to Oppose BNP'. *Christian Today* [Online, 20 September]. Available at:
www.christiantoday.com/article/bishop.tells.christians.to.oppose.bnp/21461.htm [accessed: 27 November 2008].

Gooder, P. 2000. *The Pentateuch: A Story of Beginnings*. London and New York: Continuum.

Gordon-Carter, G. 2003. *An Amazing Journey: The Church of England's Repsonse to Institutional Racism*. London: Church House Publishing.

Grabbe, L. 1998. *Ezra–Nehemiah*. London and New York: Routledge.

Goździak, E. M. 2002. 'Spiritual Emergency Room: The Role of Spirituality and Religion in the Resettlement of Kosovar Albanians'. *Journal of Refugee Studies*, 15(2), 136–152.

Goździak, E. M. 2008. 'Pray God and Keep Walking: Religion, Gender, Identity, and Refugee Women', in *Not Born a Refugee Woman: Contesting Identities, Rethinking Practices*, edited by M. Hajdukowski-Ahmed, N. Khanlou and H. Moussa. New York and Oxford: Berghahn, 180–195.

Goździak, E. M. and Shandy, D. J. 2002. 'Editorial Introduction: Religion and Spirituality in Forced Migration'. *Journal of Refugee Studies*, 15(2), 129–135.

Graham, E. L. 1995. Making the Difference: Gender, Personhood and Theology. London and New York: Mowbray.

Graham, E. L. 1996. *Transforming Practice: Pastoral Theology in an Age of Uncertainty*. London and New York: Mowbray.

Graham, E. L. 1999. 'Towards a Practical Theology of Embodiment', in *Globalisation and Difference: Practical Theology in a World Context*, edited by P. Ballard and P. Couture. Cardiff: Cardiff Academic Press, 79–84.

Graham, E. L. 2000. 'Practical Theology as Transforming Practice', in *The Blackwell Reader in Pastoral and Practical Theology*, edited by J. Woodward and S. Pattison. Oxford: Blackwell, 104–117.

Graham, E. L. 2008. 'Why Practical Theology Must Go Public'. *Practical Theology*, 1(1), 11–17.

Graham, E. L. and Lowe, S. 2009. *What Makes a Good City? Public Theology and the Urban Church*. London: Darton, Longman and Todd.

Graham, E. L., Walton, H. and Ward, F. 2005. *Theological Reflection: Methods*. London: SCM Press.

Graham, S. (ed.). 2004a. *Cities, War, and Terrorism: Towards an Urban Geopolitics*. Oxford, Malden and Carlton: Blackwell.

Graham, S. 2004b. 'Introduction: Cities, Warfare, and States of Emergency', in *Cities, War and Terrorism: Towards an Urban Geopolitics*, edited by S. Graham. Oxford, Malden and Carlton: Blackwell, 1–25.

Green, L. 2001. *The Impact of the Global: An Urban Theology*. New City Special, 13. 2nd edn. Sheffield: Urban Theology Unit and Benfoy Press.

Griffiths, D., Sigona, N. and Zetter, R. 2005. *Refugee Community Organisations and Dispersal: Networks, Resources and Social Capital*. Bristol: Policy Press.

Groody, D. G. 2007. *Globalization, Spirituality and Justice: Navigating the Path to Peace*. Maryknoll: Orbis.

Groody, D. G. 2008. 'Fruit of the Vine and Work of Human Hands: Immigration and the Eucharist', in *A Promised Land, A Perilous Journey: Theological*

Perspectives on Migration, edited by D. G. Groody and G. Campese. Notre Dame: University of Notre Dame Press, 299–315.

Groody, D. G. 2009a. 'Crossing the Divide: Foundations of a Theology of Migration and Refugees', in *And You Welcomed Me: Migration and Catholic Social Teaching*, edited by D. Kerwin and J. M. Gerschutz. Lanham: Lexington Books, 1–30.

Groody, D. G. 2009b. 'Jesus and the Undocumented: A Spiritual Geography of a Crucified People'. *Theological Studies*, 70(2), 298–316.

Groody, D. G. and Campese, G. (eds). 2008. *A Promised Land, A Perilous Journey: Theological Perspectives on Migration*. Notre Dame: University of Notre Dame Press.

Group Interview. 2007. Interview (Meeting) with Ali, Jean-Paul, Hassan, Ahmad and Jeremy Thompson, Birmingham, 18 May. The first four names are pseudonyms.

Guardiola-Sáenz, L. A. 1997. 'Borderless Women and Borderless Texts: A Cultural Reading of Matthew 15.21–28'. *Semeia*, 78, 69–81.

Guild, E. 2006. 'Protection, Threat and Movement of Persons: Examining the Relationships of Terrorism and Migration in EU Law after 11 September 2001', in *Forced Migration and Global Processes: A View from Forced Migration Studies*, edited by F. Crépeau, D. Nakache, M. Collyer, N. Goetz and A. Hansen. Lanham: Lexington Books, 295–317.

Guild, E. and van Selm, J. (eds). 2005. International Migration and Security: Opportunities and Challenges. Abingdon and New York: Routledge.

Gundry, R. H. 1993. *Mark: A Commentary on His Apology for the Cross*. Grand Rapids: William B Eerdmans.

Gutiérrez, G. 1974. *A Theology of Liberation: History, Politics and Salvation*. Trans. C. Inda and J. Eagleson. London: SCM Press.

Gutiérrez, G. 1983. *The Power of the Poor in History: Selected Writings*. London: SCM Press.

Gutiérrez, G. 2003. 'The Situation and Tasks of Liberation Theology Today', in *Opting for the Margins: Postmodernity and Liberation in Christian Theology*, edited by J. Rieger. Trans. J. B. Nickoloff. Oxford: Oxford University Press, 89–104.

Gutiérrez, G. 2008. 'Poverty, Migration, and the Option for the Poor', in *A Promised Land, A Perilous Journey: Theological Perspectives on Migration*, edited by D. G. Groody and G. Campese. Notre Dame: Notre Dame University Press, 76–86.

Gutmann, A. (ed.). 1994. *Multiculturalism: Examining the Politics of Recognition*. Princeton: Princeton University Press.

Gwynn, R. 2001. *Huguenot Heritage: The History and Contributions of the Huguenots in Britain*. 2nd edn. Brighton and Portland: Sussex Academic Press.

Habel, N. C. 1995. *The Land is Mine: Six Biblical Land Ideologies*. Minneapolis: Augsburg Fortress.

Habermas, J. 2008. 'Notes on a Post-Secular Society' [Online]. Available at: www.signandsight.com/features/1714.html [accessed: 9 May 2011].

Haddad, E. 2008a. 'The External Dimension of EU Refugee Policy: A New Approach to Asylum?'. *Government and Opposition*, 43(2), 190–205.

Haddad, E. 2008b. *The Refugee in International Society: Between Sovereigns*. Cambridge: Cambridge University Press.

Hagan, J. 2008. 'Faith for the Journey: Religion as a Resource for Migrants', in *A Promised Land, A Perilous Journey: Theological Perspectives on Migration*, edited by D. G. Groody and G. Campese. Notre Dame: Notre Dame University Press, 3–19.

Hagan, J. and Ebaugh, H. R. 2003. 'Calling Upon the Sacred: Migrants' Use of Religion in the Migration Process'. *International Migration Review*, 37(4), 1145–1162.

Haigh, G. 2008. Interview (Telephone) with Gillian Haigh, Actions and Outreach Coordinator, Mothers' Union, Bradford Diocese, 27 November.

Hajdukowski-Ahmed, M., Khanlou, N. and Moussa, H. 2008. 'Introduction', in *Not Born a Refugee Woman: Contesting Identities, Rethinking Practices*, edited by M. Hajdukowski-Ahmed, N. Khanlou and H. Moussa. New York and Oxford: Berghahn, 1–23.

Hall, J., Brooke, T. and Brennan, B. 2005. Interview (Meeting) with Rev. John Hall, Coventry Diocesan Officer for Social Responsibility, Tim Brooke and Sister Brenda Brennan, Churches Together for Refugees in Coventry, Coventry, 10 February.

Hall, S. 1996. 'Introduction: Who Needs "Identity"?', in *Questions of Cultural Identity*, edited by S. Hall and P. du Gay. London, Thousand Oaks and New Delhi: Sage, 1–17.

Hall, S. 1997. 'The Spectacle of the "Other"', in *Representation: Cultural Representations and Signifying Practices*, edited by S. Hall. Milton Keynes and London: Open University and Sage, 223–279.

Hall, S. 2000. 'Conclusion: The Multi-cultural Question', in *Un/settled Multiculturalisms: Diasporas, Entanglements, Transruptions*, edited by B. Hesse. London and New York: Zed Books, 209–241.

Hallie, P. 1979. *Lest Innocent Blood be Shed*. London: Michael Joseph.

Hallie, P. 1997. *Tales of Good and Evil, Help and Harm*. New York: HarperCollins.

Hammar, T. 1985. 'Introduction', in *European Immigration Policy: A Comparative Study*, edited by T. Hammar. Cambridge: Cambridge University Press, 1–13.

Hammar, T., Brochmann, G., Tamas, K. and Faist, T. (eds). 1997. *International Migration, Immobility and Development: Multidisciplinary Perspectives*. Oxford and New York: Berg.

Hampshire, J. 2009. 'Disembedding Liberalism? Immigration Politics and Security in Britain since 9/11', in *Immigration Policy and Security: U.S., European, and Commonwealth Perspectives*, edited by T. E. Givens, G. P. Freeman and D. L. Leal. New York: Routledge, 109–129.

Hampshire, J. and Saggar, S. 2006. *Migration, Integration and Security in the UK Since July 7* [Online]. Available at: www.migrationinformation.org/Feature/display.cfm?ID=383 [accessed: 30 May 2008].

Hanciles, J. J. 2007. 'Migration', in *Dictionary of Mission Theology: Evangelical Foundations*, edited by J. Corrie. Nottingham and Downers Grove: Inter-Varsity Press, 225–227.

Hanciles, J. J. 2008a. 'Migration and Mission: The Religious Significance of the North–South Divide', in *Mission in the 21st Century: Exploring the Five Marks of Global Mission*, edited by A. Walls and C. Ross. London: Darton, Longman and Todd, 118–129.

Hanciles, J. J. 2008b. *Beyond Christendom: Globalization, African Migration, and the Transformation of the West*. Maryknoll: Orbis.

Hansard. 2007. *Text for 13 June 2007* [Online]. Available at: www.publications.parliament.uk/pa/ld200607/ldhansrd/text/70613–0006.htm#07061372000393, www.publications.parliament.uk/pa/ld200607/ldhansrd/text/70613–0004.htm#07061372000388 [accessed: 18 December 2008].

Hansen, R. 2000. *Citizenship and Immigration in Post-War Britain: The Institutional Origins of a Multicultural Nation*. Oxford: Oxford University Press.

Hansen, R. 2003. 'Migration to Europe since 1945: Its History and its Lessons', in *The Politics of Migration: Managing Opportunity, Conflict and Change*, edited by S. Spencer. Oxford: Blackwell, 25–38.

Hansen, R. and Weil, P. (eds). 2001. *Towards a European Nationality: Citizenship, Immigration and Nationality Law in the EU*. Basingstoke: Palgrave.

Hardin, R. 2004. 'Terrorism and Group-Generalized Distrust', in *Distrust*, edited by R. Hardin. New York: Russell Sage Foundation, 278–297.

Harding, S. (ed.). 2006. *The Stranger Within: Towards a More Progressive Asylum Policy*. Special Edition of *The Common Good: Christianity, Progressive Politics and Social Justice*, 194 (Summer). London: Christian Socialist Movement.

Harff, B. and Gurr, T. R. 2004. *Ethnic Conflict in World Politics*. 2nd edn. Boulder and Oxford: Westview Press.

Hargreaves, A. G. 2001. 'Media Effects and Ethnic Relations in Britain and France', in *Media and Migration: Constructions of Mobility and Difference*, edited by R. King and N. Wood. London and New York: Routledge, 23–37.

Harpur, J. 2002. *Sacred Tracks: 2000 Years of Christian Pilgrimage*. London: Frances Lincoln.

Harrell-Bond, B. 1986. *Imposing Aid: Emergency Assistance to Refugees*. Oxford: Oxford University Press.

Harrell-Bond, B. 1999. 'The Experience of Refugees as Recipients of Aid', in *Refugees: Perspectives on the Experience of Forced Migration*, edited by A. Ager. London and New York: Continuum, 136–168.

Harris, A. 2010. '"A Place to Grow Spiritually and Socially": The Experiences of Young Pilgrims to Lourdes', in *Religion and Youth*, edited by S. Collins-Mayo and B. P. Dandelion. Farnham: Ashgate, 149–158.

Harvey, A., Pemberton, C. and Armour, R. 2006. *Asylum Reflections: A Theological Companion to Asylum Principles*. London: CCRJ/CTBI. Available at: www.ctbi.org.uk/pdf_view.php?id=22 [accessed: 7 January 2009].

Haslam, D. 1996. *Race for the Millennium: A Challenge to Church and Society*. London: Church House.

Hastrup, K. and Olwig, K. F. 1997. 'Introduction', in *Siting Culture: The Shifting Anthropological Object*, edited by K. Hastrup and K. F. Olwig. London and New York: Routledge, 1–14.

Hauerwas, S. 1981. *A Community of Character: Toward a Constructive Christian Social Ethic*. Notre Dame, IN: University of Notre Dame Press.

Hauerwas, S. and Willimon, W. H. 1989. *Resident Aliens: A Provocative Christian Assessment of Culture and Ministry for People Who Know that Something is Wrong*. Nashville: Abingdon Press.

Hayatli, M. 2009. 'Islam, International Law and the Protection of Refugees and IDPs', in *Islam, Human Rights and Displacement. Forced Migration Review* Supplement, 2–3. Available at: www.fmreview.org/FMRpdfs/Human-Rights/islam-human-rights.pdf [accessed: 12 January 2012].

Hayes, C. E. 2002. *Gentile Impurities and Jewish Identities: Intermarriage and Conversion from the Bible to the Talmud*. Oxford: Oxford University Press

Hayes, D. 2002. 'From Aliens to Asylum Seekers: A History of Immigration Controls and Welfare in Britain', in *From Immigration Controls to Welfare Controls*, edited by S. Cohen, B. Humphries and E. Mynott. London and New York: Routledge, 30–46.

Hayter, T. 2003. 'No Borders: The Case Against Immigration Controls', in *Exile and Asylum: Women Seeking Refuge in 'Fortress Europe'*, edited by A. Treacher, A. Coombes, C. Alexander, L. Bland and P. Alldred. Feminist Review 73. Basingstoke: Palgrave Macmillan, 6–18.

Hayter, T. 2004. *Open Borders: The Case Against Immigration Controls*. 2nd edn. London and Ann Arbor: Pluto.

Hayward, L., Hajdukowski-Ahmed, M., Ploeg, J. and Trollope, K. 2008. '"We Want to Talk, They Give Us Pills": Identity and Mental Health of Refugee Women from Sudan', in *Not Born a Refugee Woman: Contesting Identities, Rethinking Practices*, edited by M. Hajdukowski-Ahmed, N. Khanlou and H. Moussa. New York and Oxford: Berghahn, 196–214.

HCIDC [House of Commons International Development Committee]. 2004. *Migration and Development: How to Make Migration Work for Poverty Reduction*. Sixth Report of Session 2003–2004. Vol. 1. HC 79–1. London: HCIDC. Available at: www.publications.parliament.uk/pa/cm200304/cmselect/cmintdev/79/79.pdf [accessed: 20 January 2009].

Heidegger, M. 1971. *Poetry, Language, Thought*. Trans. A. Hofstadter. New York: Harper Colophon.

Held, D., McGrew, A., Goldblatt, D. and Perraton, J. 1999. *Global Transformations: Politics, Economics and Culture*. Cambridge: Polity.

Hendrickson, B. and Seegmiller, B. 2007. *Religious Studies Engaged in Refugee Studies: Potential Contributions*. Refuge and Rejection: The Humanities in the Study of Forced Migration, 3. Arizona: Department of History, Arizona State University. Available at: www.asu.edu/clas/history/proj/refugee/article/h_s_intro.htm [accessed: 10 September 2007].

Hennig, R. 2011. 'Concern over Burundians in Tanzania'. *Afrol News* [Online, 19 June]. Available at: www.afrol.com/articles/12820 [accessed: 14 October 2011].

Hermkens, A.-K., Jansen, W. and Notermans, C. (eds). 2009. *Moved by Mary: The Power of Pilgrimage in the Modern World*. Farnham: Ashgate.

Hesse, B. 2000a. 'Introduction: Un/Settled Multiculturalisms', in *Un/settled Multiculturalisms: Diasporas, Entanglements, Transruptions*, edited by B. Hesse. London and New York: Zed Books, 1–30.

Hesse, B. (ed.) 2000b. *Un/settled Multiculturalisms: Diasporas, Entanglements, Transruptions*. London and New York: Zed Books.

Heyward, C. 1998. 'Jesus of Nazareth/Christ of Faith: Foundations of a Reactive Christology', in *Lift Every Voice: Constructing Christian Theologies from the Underside*, edited by S. B. Thistlethwaite and M. P. Engel. Maryknoll: Orbis, 197–206.

Heywood, D. 2004. *Divine Revelation and Human Learning: A Christian Theory of Knowledge*. Explorations in Practical, Pastoral and Empirical Theology. Aldershot: Ashgate.

Hilton, D. 1998. *Table Talk: Looking at the Communion Table from the Outside and the Inside*. London: URC.

Hirschman, C. 2007. 'The Role of Religion in the Origins and Adaptation of Immigrant Groups in the US', in *Rethinking Migration: New Theoretical and Empirical Perspectives*, edited by A. Portes and J. DeWind. New York and Oxford: Berghahn, 391–418.

HO [Home Office]. 2002a. *Nationality, Immigration and Asylum Bill*. London: HMSO.

HO [Home Office]. 2002b. *Secure Borders, Safe Haven: Integration with Diversity in Modern Britain*. White Paper. London: HMSO.

HO [Home Office]. 2004. *Asylum and Immigration (Treatment of Claimants, etc) Act*. London: HMSO.

HO [Home Office]. 2005. *Controlling our Borders: Making Migration Work for Britain: Five Year Strategy for Asylum and Immigration*. London: HO.

HO [Home Office]. 2006a. *Fair, Effective, Transparent and Trusted: Rebuilding Confidence in Our Immigration System*. London: HMSO.

HO [Home Office]. 2006b. *A Points-based System: Making Migration Work for Britain*. London: HMSO.

HO [Home Office]. 2008. *Asylum Statistics United Kingdom 2007*. Home Office Statistical Bulletin 11/08. London: HO. Available at: www.homeoffice.gov.uk/rds/immigration-asylum-stats.html [accessed: 20 January 2009].

HO [Home Office]. 2011. *Control of Immigration: Quarterly Statistical Summary, United Kingdom. Quarter 4 (2010) October–December*. London: HO. Available at: www.homeoffice.gov.uk/publications/science-research-statistics/research-statistics/immigration-asylum-research/control-immigration-q4-2010/control-immigration-q4-2010?view=Binary [accessed: 16 August 2011].

HO [Home Office]. 2012. *Children Entering Detention Held Solely under Immigration Act Powers. December 2011*. [Online]. Available at: www.homeoffice.gov.uk/publications/science-research-statistics/research-statistics/immigration-asylum-research/child-detention-dec2011?view=Standard&pub ID=976700 [accessed: 9 February 2012].

Hobbs, T. R. 2002. 'The Political Jesus: Discipleship and Disengagement', in *The Social Setting of Jesus and the Gospels*, edited by W. Stegemann, B. J. Malina and G. Theissen. Minneapolis: Augsburg Fortress, 251–281.

Hoffmann, G. 1989. 'Solidarity with Strangers as Part of the Mission of the Church'. *International Review of Mission*, 78, 53–61.

Hoglund, K. 1991. 'The Achaemenid Context', in *Second Temple Studies 1. Persian Period*, edited by P. R. Davies. JSOT Supplement 117. Sheffield: JSOT Press/Sheffield Academic Press, 54–72.

Holland, J. 2005. 'Introduction: Roots of the Pastoral Circle in Personal Experiences and Catholic Social Tradition', in *The Pastoral Circle Revisited: A Critical Quest for Truth and Transformation*, edited by F. Wijsen, P. Henriot and R. Mejía. Maryknoll: Orbis, 1–12.

Holland, J. and Henriot, P. 1983. *Social Analysis: Linking Faith and Justice*. Rev. edn. Maryknoll: Orbis.

Hollands, M. 2001. 'Upon Closer Acquaintance: The Impact of Direct Contact with Refugees on Dutch Hosts'. *Journal of Refugee Studies*, 14(3), 295–314.

Hollenbach, D. (ed.). 2008. *Refugee Rights: Ethics, Advocacy, and Africa*. Washington, DC: Georgetown University Press.

Hollenbach, D. (ed.). 2010. *Driven From Home: Protecting the Rights of Forced Migrants*. Washington, DC: Georgetown University Press.

Hollifield, J. 2007. 'The Emerging Migration State', in *Rethinking Migration: New Theoretical and Empirical Perspectives*, edited by A. Portes and J. DeWind. New York and Oxford: Berghahn, 62–89.

Holmes, C. 1988. *John Bull's Island: Immigration and British Society, 1871–1971*. Basingstoke: Macmillan Press.

Holmes, C. 1991. *A Tolerant Country? Immigrants, Refugees and Minorities in Britain*. London: Faber & Faber.

Holmgren, F. C. 1987. *Ezra and Nehemiah: Israel Alive Again*. International Theological Commentary. Grand Rapids and Edinburgh: William B. Eerdmans and Handsel Press.

Home Affairs Committee. 2011. *Ninth Report: The Work of the UK Border Agency (November 2010–March 2011)* [Online]. Available at: www.publications.parliament.uk/pa/cm201012/cmselect/cmhaff/929/92902.htm [accessed: 9 February 2012].

Hondagneu-Sotelo, P. 2008. *God's Heart Has No Borders: How Religious Activists are Working for Immigrant Rights*. Berkeley and Los Angeles: University of California Press.

Honig, B. 1999. 'Ruth, The Model Emigrée: Mourning and the Symbolic Politics of Immigration', in *Ruth and Esther: A Feminist Companion to the Bible (Second Series)*, edited by A. Brenner. Sheffield: Sheffield Academic Press, 50–74.

Hooker, M. D. 1991. *The Gospel According to St Mark*. London: A & C Black.

hooks, b. 1991. *Yearning: Race, Gender, and Cultural Politics*. London: Turnaround.

Hope Projects. 2011. Hope Projects [Online]. Available at: www.hope-projects.org.uk [accessed: 2 October 2011].

Horsley, R. A. 2001. *Hearing the Whole Story: The Politics of Plot in Mark's Gospel*. Louisville: Westminster John Knox.

Hovda, R. 1994. 'The Vesting of Liturgical Ministers', in *Robert Hovda: The Amen Corner*, edited by J. F. Baldovin. Collegeville: Liturgical Press, 213–233.

Hug, J. 2005. 'Redeeming Social Analysis: Recovering the Hidden Religious Dimensions of Social Change', in *The Pastoral Circle Revisited: A Critical Quest for Truth and Transformation*, edited by F. Wijsen, P. Henriot and R. Mejía. Maryknoll: Orbis, 196–210.

Hughes, G. 1986. *In Search of a Way: Two Journeys of Spiritual Discovery*. 2nd edn. London: Darton, Longman and Todd.

Hume, B. 1984. *To Be A Pilgrim*. London: SPCK.

Huntington, S. P. 1996. *The Clash of Civilizations and the Remaking of World Order*. New York: Simon & Schuster.

Huysmans, J. 1995. 'Migrants as a Security Problem: Dangers of "Securitizing" Societal Issues', in *Migration and European Integration: The Dynamics of Inclusion and Exclusion*, edited by R. Miles and D. Thränhardt. London: Pinter, 53–72.

Huysmans, J. 2006. *The Politics of Insecurity: Fear, Migration and Asylum in the EU*. Abingdon and New York: Routledge.

Hynes, P. 2011. *The Dispersal and Social Exclusion of Asylum Seekers: Between Liminality and Belonging*. Bristol: Policy Press.

Hynes, P. and Sales, R. 2010. 'New Communities: Asylum Seekers and Dispersal', in *Race and Ethnicity in the 21st Century*, edited by A. Bloch and J. Solomos. Basingstoke: Palgrave Macmillan, 39–61.

IAC [Independent Asylum Commission]. 2007–2008. Hearings [Online]. Available at: www.humanrightstv.com/channel/7 [accessed: 6 August 2008].

IAC [Independent Asylum Commission]. 2008a. *Fit For Purpose Yet? The Independent Asylum Commission's Interim Findings*. London: IAC.

IAC [Independent Asylum Commission]. 2008b. *Saving Sanctuary*. London: IAC.

IAC [Independent Asylum Commission]. 2008c. *Safe Return*. London: IAC.

IAC [Independent Asylum Commission]. 2008d. *Deserving Dignity*. London: IAC.

Ibrahim, M. 2005. 'The Securitization of Migration. A Racial Discourse'. *International Migration*, 34(5), 163–187.

ICAR [Information Centre about Asylum Seekers and Refugees in the UK]. 2004. *Media Image, Community Impact: Assessing the Impact of Media and Political Images of Refugees and Asylum Seekers on Community Relations in London*. London: ICAR/King's College, London.

ICAR [Information Centre about Asylum Seekers and Refugees in the UK]. 2007. *Reporting Asylum: The UK Press and the Effectiveness of PCC Guidelines, January–March 2005*. London: ICAR.

Iftikhar, A. 2008. 'Presumption of Guilt: September 11 and the American Muslim Community', in *Keeping Out the Other: A Critical Introduction to Immigration Enforcement Today*, edited by D. Brotherton and P. Kretsedemas. New York: Columbia University Press, 108–137.

Ignatieff, M. 2001. *The Needs of Strangers*. 1st Picador USA edn. New York: Picador USA.

Inge, J. 2003. *A Christian Theology of Place*. Explorations in Practical, Pastoral and Empirical Theology. Aldershot: Ashgate.

IOM [International Organization for Migration]. 2010. *World Migration Report. The Future of Migration: Building Capacities for Change*. Geneva: IOM. Available at: http://publications.iom.int/bookstore/free/WMR_2010_ENGLISH.pdf [accessed: 15 October 2011].

IOM [International Organization for Migration]. 2011. *Fact and Figures: Global Estimates and Trends* [Online]. Available at: www.iom.int/jahia/Jahia/about-migration/facts-and-figures/lang/en [accessed: 14 October 2011].

IOM [International Organization for Migration]. 2011b. *Identifying International Migrants* [Online]. Available at: www.iom.int/jahia/Jahia/about-migration/developing-migration-policy/identify-intl-migrants [accessed: 15 October 2011].

Isasi-Díaz, A. M. 1998a. 'Solidarity: Love of Neighbor in the 21st Century', in *Lift Every Voice: Constructing Christian Theologies from the Underside*, edited by S. B. Thistlethwaite and M. P. Engel. Rev. edn. Maryknoll: Orbis, 30–39.

Isasi-Díaz, A. M. 1998b. 'The Bible and *Mujerista* Theology', in *Lift Every Voice: Constructing Christian Theologies from the Underside*, edited by S. B. Thistlethwaite and M. P. Engel. Rev. edn. Maryknoll: Orbis, 267–275.

Isin, E. F. and Wood, P. K. 1999. *Citizenship and Identity*. London, Thousand Oaks and New Delhi: Sage.

Isiorho, D. 2002. 'Black Theology in Urban Shadow: Combating Racism in the Church of England'. *Black Theology: An International Journal*, 1(1), 29–48.

Ivereigh, A. 2010. *Faithful Citizens: A Practical Guide to Catholic Social Teaching and Community Organising*. London: Darton, Longman and Todd.

Iveson, K. 2006. 'Strangers in the Cosmopolis', in *Cosmopolitan Urbanism*, edited by J. Binnie, J. Holloway, S. Millington and C. Young. London and New York: Routledge, 70–86.

Jackson, G. and Dube, D. 2006. *'What am I Living for?' Living on the Streets of Leicester. A Report on Destitute Asylum Seekers and Refugees*. Leicester: Leicester Refugee and Asylum Seekers' Voluntary Sector Forum and Diocese of Leicester. Available at: www.refugee-action.org.uk/campaigns/documents/LVSFDestitutionReport2006.pdf [accessed: 3 December 2008].

Jacobs, M. (ed.) 1987. *Faith or Fear? A Reader in Pastoral Care and Counselling*. London: Darton, Longman and Todd.

Jacobsen, K. and Landau, L. B. 2003. 'The Dual Imperative in Refugee Research: Some Methodological and Ethical Considerations in Social Science Research on Forced Migration'. *Disasters*, 27(3), 185–206.

Jacobson, D. 1996. *Rights Across Borders: Immigration and the Decline of Citizenship*. Baltimore and London: Johns Hopkins University Press.

Jagessar, M. N. 2008. *A Service of Word and Table* [Online]. Available at: www.lifewords.info/asylum/reflect/services.html [accessed: 18 December 2008].

Jansen, M. 2008. 'The Wind Beneath My Wings: Migration and Religion in the Life Stories of Filipina Domestic Workers in Amsterdam', in *A Moving God: Immigrant Churches in the Netherlands*, edited by M. Jansen and H. Stoffels. Zurich: Lit Verlag GmbH & Co. KG Wien, 61–78.

Jansen, M. and Stoffels, H. 2008. 'Introduction', in *A Moving God: Immigrant Churches in the Netherlands*, edited by M. Jansen and H. Stoffels. Zurich: Lit Verlag GmbH & Co. KG Wien, 3–12.

Japhet, S. 1983. 'People and Land in the Restoration Period', in *Das Land Israel in biblischer Zeit*, edited by G. Strecker. Göttingen: Vandenhoeck and Ruprecht, 103–125.

Japhet, S. 1994. 'Composition and Chronology in the Book of Ezra–Nehemiah', in *Second Temple Studies 2. Temple and Community in the Persian Period*, edited by T. C. Eskenazi and K. H. Richards. JSOT Supplement Series 175. Sheffield: JSOT Press/Sheffield Academic Press, 189–216.

Jayaweera, H. and Choudhury, T. 2008. *Immigration, Faith and Cohesion: Evidence from Local Areas with Significant Muslim Populations*. York: Joseph Rowntree Foundation.

JCHR [Joint Committee on Human Rights]. 2007. *The Treatment of Asylum Seekers*. Tenth Report of Session 2006–07. Vol. 1. Report and Formal Minutes. HL 81–1. HC 60–1. London: Stationery Office.

Joly, D. 1996. *Haven or Hell? Asylum Policies and Refugees in Europe*. Basingstoke: Macmillan.

Joly, D. 2002. 'Introduction', in *Global Changes in Asylum Regimes: Closing Doors*, edited by D. Joly. Basingstoke: Palgrave Macmillan, 1–14.

Joly, D. 2004. 'Between Exile and Ethnicity', in *International Migration in the New Millennium: Global Movement and Settlement*, edited by D. Joly. Aldershot: Ashgate, 143–179.

Jones, J. 2000. 'This is a Good Time to Remember that Jesus was an Asylum-seeker too'. *The Independent on Sunday* [Online, 22 December]. Available at: www. independent.co.uk/opinion/commentators/james-jones-this-is-a-good-time-to-remember-that-jesus-was-an-asylumseeker-too-629150.html [accessed: 7 December 2008].

Joppke, C. 1998a. 'Immigration Challenges the Nation-state', in *Challenge to the Nation-state: Immigration in Western Europe and the US*, edited by C. Joppke. Oxford: Oxford University Press, 5–46.

Joppke, C. 1998b. 'Asylum and State Sovereignty: A Comparison of the US, Germany, and Britain', in *Challenge to the Nation-state: Immigration in Western Europe and the US*, edited by C. Joppke. Oxford: Oxford University Press, 109–152.

Joppke, C. and Morawska, E. 2003. 'Integrating Immigrants in Liberal Nation-states: Policies and Practices', in *Towards Assimilation and Citizenship: Immigrants in Liberal Nation-states*, edited by C. Joppke and E. Morawska. Basingstoke: Palgrave Macmillan, 1–36.

JRS [Jesuit Refugee Service]. 2004. *Detention in Europe: Administrative Detention of Asylum-seekers and Irregular Migrants*. Observation and Position Document. Brussels: JRS – Europe.

JRS [Jesuit Refugee Service]. (ed.). 2005. *God in Exile: Towards a Shared Spirituality with Refugees*. Rome: JRS.

JRS [Jesuit Refugee Service]. 2007. *Annual Report 2007*. Rome: JRS.

JRS [Jesuit Refugee Service]. 2008. Liturgy Resources [Online]. Available at: www.jrsuk.net [accessed: 18 December 2008].

Kaldor, M. 2001. *New and Old Wars: Organized Violence in a Global Era*. Cambridge: Polity.

Kanstroom, D. 2007. *Deportation Nation: Outsiders in American History*. Cambridge: Harvard University Press.

Käsemann, E. 1984. *The Wandering People of God: An Investigation of the Letter to the Hebrews*. Trans. R. A. Harrisville and I. L. Sandberg. Minneapolis: Augsburg.

Kates, J. A. 1994. 'Women at the Center: *Ruth and Shavuot*', in *Reading Ruth: Contemporary Women Reclaim a Sacred Story*, edited by J. A. Kates and G. T. Reimer. New York: Ballantine Books, 187–198.

Kaye, R. 1997. 'Redefining the Refugee: The UK Media Portrayal of Asylum Seekers', in *The New Migration in Europe: Social Constructions and Social Realities*, edited by K. Koser and H. Lutz. Basingstoke: Macmillan, 163–182.

Keen, D. 2008. *Complex Emergencies*. Cambridge: Polity Press.

Keifert, P. R. 1992. *Welcoming the Stranger: A Public Theology of Worship and Evangelism*. Minneapolis: Augsburg Fortress.

Kelley, N. and Stevenson, J. 2006. *First do no Harm: Denying Healthcare to People whose Asylum Claims have Failed*. London: Refugee Council. Available at: www.refugeecouncil.org.uk/policy/position/2006/healthcare.htm [accessed: 20 January 2009].

Kelly, L. 2005. 'Researching Refugees and Asylum Seekers – some Methdological Issues'. Presentation at the Postgraduate Methodology Seminar Day: Refugee Research Issues. York, 11 March.

Kennedy, P. and Murphy-Lawless, J. 2003. 'The Maternity Care Needs of Refugee and Asylum Seeking Women in Ireland', in *Exile and Asylum: Women Seeking Refuge in 'Fortress Europe'*, edited by A. Treacher, A. Coombes, C. Alexander, L. Bland and P. Alldred. 2003. Feminist Review 73. Basingstoke: Palgrave Macmillan, 39–53.

Kerr, R. 2008. Interview (Telephone) with Richard Kerr, Race Relations Panel, Presbyterian Church in Ireland and Member of EmbraceNI, 28 November.

Kerwin, D. 2008. 'The Natural Rights of Migrants and Newcomers: A Challenge to U.S. Law and Policy', in *A Promised Land, A Perilous Journey: Theological Perspectives on Migration*, edited by D. G. Groody and G. Campese. Notre Dame, IN: University of Notre Dame Press, 192–209.

Kerwin, D. 2009. 'Rights, the Common Good, and Sovereignty in Service of the Human Person', in *And You Welcomed Me: Migration and Catholic Social Teaching*, edited by D. Kerwin and J. M. Gerschutz. Lanham: Lexington Books, 93–121.

Kessler, D. (ed.) 2005. *Receive One Another: Hospitality in Ecumenical Perspective*. Geneva: WCC Publications.

Kibreab, G. 1999. 'Revisiting the Debate on People, Place, Identity and Displacement'. *Journal of Refugee Studies*, 12(4), 384–410.

Kibreab, G. 2004. 'Refugeehood, Loss and Social Change: Eritrean Refugees and Returnees', in *Refugees and the Transformation of Societies: Agency, Policies, Ethics and Politics*, edited by P. Essed, G. Frerks and J. Schrijvers. New York and Oxford: Berghahn, 19–30.

Kidd, J. R. 1999. *Alterity and Identity in Israel. The in the Old Testament*. Berlin and New York: Walter de Gruyter.

Kinukawa, H. 1994. *Women and Jesus in Mark: A Japanese Feminist Perspective*. Maryknoll: Orbis.

Kjaerum, M. 2002. 'Human Rights Organisations and the Formation of Refugee Regimes', in *Global Changes in Asylum Regimes*, edited by D. Joly. Basingstoke: Palgrave Macmillan, 204–214.

Klein, R. W. 1999. 'The Books of Ezra & Nehemiah: Introduction, Commentary, and Reflections', in *The New Interpreter's Bible*, Vol. III, edited by L. E. Keck, T. G. Long, B. C. Birch et al. Nashville: Abingdon, 661–851.

Klomp, M. 2008. 'Make a Joyful Noise unto the Lord! The Sound of Liturgy in the Wesley Methodist Church', in *A Moving God: Immigrant Churches in the Netherlands*, edited by M. Jansen and H. Stoffels. Zurich: Lit Verlag GmbH & Co. KG Wien, 139–157.

Kneebone, S. (ed.) 2003. *The Refugees Convention 50 Years On: Globalisation and International Law*. Aldershot: Ashgate.

Kneebone, S. (ed.) 2009. *Refugees, Asylum Seekers and the Rule of Law: Comparative Perspectives*. Cambridge and New York: Cambridge University Press.

Knoppers, G. N. 2007. 'Nehemiah and Sanballat: The Enemy Without or Within?', in *Judah and Judeans in the Fourth Century B.C.E.*, edited by O. Lipschits, G. N. Knoppers and R. Albertz. Winona Lake: Eisenbrauns, 305–331.

Koehler, L. and Baumgartner, W. 1996. *The Hebrew and Aramaic Lexicon of the Old Testament*. Vol. 3. Trans. M. E. J. Richardson. Leiden: Brill.

Koenig, J. 2001. *New Testament Hospitality: Partnership with Strangers as Promise and Mission*. Eugene: Wipf and Stock.

Kofman, E., Phizacklea, A., Raghuram, P. and Sales, R. 2000. *Gender and International Migration in Europe: Employment, Welfare and Politics*. London and New York: Routledge.

Kohli, R. K. and Mitchell, F. (eds). 2007. *Working with Unaccompanied Asylum Seeking Children: Issues for Policy and Practice*. Basingstoke: Palgrave Macmillan.

Koopman, S. 2008. 'Imperialism Within: Can the Master's Tools Bring Down Empire?'. *ACME: An International E-Journal for Critical Geographies*, 7(2), 283–307.

Koopmans, R. and Statham, P. 2000a. 'Migration and Ethnic Relations as a Field of Political Contention: An Opportunity Structure Approach', in *Challenging Immigration and Ethnic Relations Politics: Comparative European Perspectives*, edited by R. Koopmans and P. Statham. Oxford: Oxford University Press, 13–56.

Koopmans, R. and Statham, P. 2000b. 'Challenging the Liberal Nation-state? Postnationalism, Multiculturalism, and the Collective Claims-making of Migrants and Ethnic Minorities in Britain and Germany', in *Challenging Immigration and Ethnic Relations Politics: Comparative European Perspectives*, edited by R. Koopmans and P. Statham. Oxford: Oxford University Press, 189–232.

Koosed, J. L. 2011. *Gleaning Ruth: A Biblical Heroine and Her Afterlives*. Columbia: University of South Carolina Press.

Koser, K. 1998. 'Out of the Frying Pan and into the Fire: A Case Study of Illegality amongst Asylum Seekers', in *The New Migration in Europe: Social Constructions and Social Realities*, edited by K. Koser and H. Lutz. Basingstoke: Macmillan, 185–198.

Koser, K. 2011a. 'Internally Displaced Persons', in *Global Migration Governance*, edited by A. Betts. Oxford and New York: Oxford University Press, 210–223.

Koser, K. 2011b. 'The Impacts of the Global Economic and Financial Crisis', in *Security, Insecurity and Migration in Europe*, edited by G. Lazaridis. Farnham: Ashgate, 67–80.

Koser, K. and Lutz, H. 1998. 'The New Migration in Europe: Contexts, Constructions and Realities', in *The New Migration in Europe: Social Constructions and*

Social Realities, edited by K. Koser and H. Lutz. Basingstoke: Macmillan, 1–17.

Koyama, K. 1993. '"Extend Hospitality to Strangers" – A Missiology of the Theologia Crucis'. *International Review of Mission*, LXXXII(327), 283–295.

Koyama, K. 1999. *Water Buffalo Theology*. Rev. edn. Maryknoll: Orbis.

Kramer, R. M. 2004. 'Collective Paranoia: Distrust Between Social Groups', in *Distrust*, edited by R. Hardin. New York: Russell Sage Foundation, 136–166.

Kristeva, J. 1982. *Powers of Horror: An Essay on Abjection*. Trans. L. S. Roudiez. New York: Columbia University Press.

Kristeva, J. 1991. *Strangers to Ourselves*. Trans. L. S. Roudiez. New York: Columbia University Press.

Kundnani, A. 2001. 'In a Foreign Land: The New Popular Racism'. *Race and Class*, 43(2), 41–60.

Kundnani, A. 2007. *The End of Tolerance: Racism in 21st Century Britain*. London and Ann Arbor: Pluto.

Kunz, E. F. 1973. 'The Refugee in Flight: Kinetic Models and Forms of Displacement'. *International Migration Review*, 7(2), 125–146.

Kunz, E. F. 1981. 'Exile and Resettlement: Refugee Theory'. *International Migration Review*, 15(1), 42–51.

Kunz, R., Lavenex, S. and Panizzon, M. (eds). 2011. *Multilayered Migration Governance: The Promise of Partnership*. London and New York: Routledge.

Kwok, P.-L. 1994. 'Worshipping with Asian Women: A Homily on Jesus Healing the Daughter of a Canaanite Woman', in *Feminist Theology from the Third World: A Reader*, edited by U. King. London: SPCK, 236–242.

Kwok, P.-L. 1995. *Discovering the Bible in the Non-Biblical World*. Maryknoll: Orbis.

Kwok, P.-L. 1998. 'Discovering the Bible in the Non-Biblical World', in *Lift Every Voice: Constructing Christian Theologies from the Underside*, edited by S. B. Thistlethwaite and M. P. Engel. Rev. edn. Maryknoll: Orbis, 276–288.

Kwok, P.-L. 2005. *Postcolonial Imagination and Feminist Theology*. London: SCM Press.

Kwok, P.-L. 2007. 'A Theology of Border Passage', in *Border Crossings: Cross-cultural Hermeneutics*, edited by D. N. Premnath. Maryknoll: Orbis, 103–117.

Kwok, P.-L. (ed.). 2010. *Hope Abundant: Third World and Indigenous Women's Theology*. Maryknoll: Orbis.

Kymlicka, W. 1995. *Multicultural Citizenship: A Liberal Theory of Minority Rights*. Oxford: Clarendon.

Kymlicka, W. 2001. *Politics in the Vernacular: Nationalism, Multiculturalism, and Citizenship*. Oxford: Oxford University Press

LaCocque, A. 2004. *Ruth: A Continental Commentary*. Trans. K. C. Hanson. Minneapolis: Augsburg Fortress.

LaCugna, C. M. 1993. *God For Us: The Trinity and Christian Life*. Paperback edn. San Francisco: HarperSanFrancisco.

Lambert, J. 2002. *Refugees and the Environment: The Forgotten Element of Sustainability*. London and Brussels: Greens and European Free Alliance in the European Parliament.

Lammers, E. 2007. 'Researching Refugees: Preoccupations with Power and Questions of Giving'. *Refugee Survey Quarterly*, 26(3), 72–81.

Langer, J. 1997. *The Bend in the Road: Refugees Writing*. Nottingham: Five Leaves.

Larson, D. W. 2004. 'Distrust: Prudent, If Not Always Wise', in *Distrust*, edited by R. Hardin. New York: Russell Sage Foundation, 34–59.

Lartey, E. Y. 2000. 'Practical Theology as a Theological Form', in *The Blackwell Reader in Pastoral and Practical Theology*, edited by J. Woodward and S. Pattison. Oxford: Blackwell, 128–134.

Lartey, E. Y. 2006. *Pastoral Theology in an Intercultural World*. Peterborough: Epworth.

Lathrop, G. W. 1999. 'Liturgy and Mission in a North American Context', in *Inside Out: Worship in an Age of Mission*, edited by T. Schattauer. Minneapolis: Fortress Press, 201–212.

Latvus, K. 2007. 'The Bible in British Urban Theology: An Analysis by a Finnish Companion', in *Reading Other-Wise: Socially Engaged Biblical Scholars Reading with Their Local Communities*, edited by G. O. West. Atlanta: Society of Biblical Literature, 133–140.

Lau, P. H. W. 2011. *Identity and Ethics in the Books of Ruth: A Social Identity Approach*. Berlin and New York: Walter De Gruyter.

Lavenex, S. 2001. *The Europeanisation of Refugee Policies: Between Human Rights and Internal Security*. Aldershot and Burlington: Ashgate.

Law, E. 2007. *Finding Intimacy in a World of Fear*. St Louis: Chalice Press.

Layton-Henry, Z. 2004. 'Britain: From Immigration Control to Migration Management', in *Controlling Immigration: A Global Perspective*, edited by W. A. Cornelius, T. Tsuda, P. L. Martin and J. Hollifield. 2nd edn. Stanford: Stanford University Press, 297–333.

Lazaridis, G. (ed.). 2011. *Security, Insecurity and Migration in Europe*. Farnham: Ashgate.

Leaning, J. 2001. 'Ethics of Research in Refugee Populations'. *The Lancet*, 357, 5 May, 1432–1433.

Leaning, J., Bartels, S. and Mowafi, H. 2009. 'Sexual Violence during War and Forced Migration', in *Women, Migration and Conflict: Breaking a Deadly Cycle*, edited by S. F. Martin and J. Tirman. Dordrecht and New York: Springer, 173–199.

Leech, K. 2005. *Race: Changing Society and the Churches*. London: SPCK.

Legal Action for Women. 2006. *A 'Bleak House' in Our Times: An Investigation into Women's Rights Violations at Yarl's Wood Removal Centre*. London: Crossroad Books.

Letlhare, B. 2001. 'Corporate Personality in Botswana and Ancient Israel: A Religio-cultural Comparison', in *The Bible in Africa: Transactions,*

Trajectories and Trends, edited by G. O. West and M. W. Dube. Boston and Leiden: Brill, 474–480.

Levenson, J. D. 1996. 'The Universal Horizon of Biblical Particularism', in *Ethnicity and the Bible*, edited by M. G. Brett. Boston and Leiden: Brill, 143–169.

Lévinas, E. 1985. *Ethics and Infinity: Conversations with Philippe Nemo*. Trans. R. A. Cohen. Pittsburgh: Duquesne University Press.

Lévinas, E. 1987. *Time and the Other [and Additional Essays]*. Pittsburgh: Duquesne University Press.

Lévinas, E. 1993. *Outside the Subject*. Trans. M. B. Smith. London: Athlone Press.

Levitt, P. 2003. '"You Know, Abraham Was Really the First Immigrant": Religion and Transnational Migration'. *International Migration Review*, 37(3), 847–873.

Levitt, P. 2007. *God Needs No Passport: Immigrants and the Changing Religious Landscape*. New York: New Press.

Levitt, P. 2008. 'Religion as a Path to Civic Engagement'. *Ethnic and Racial Studies*, 31(4), 766–791.

Lewis, M. 2005. *Asylum: Understanding Public Attitudes*. London: IPPR.

Lewis Taylor, M. 2003. 'Subalternity and Advocacy as *Kairos* for Theology', in *Opting for the Margins: Postmodernity and Liberation in Christian Theology*, edited by J. Rieger. Oxford: Oxford University Press, 23–44.

Ley, D. 2008. 'The Immigrant Church as an Urban Service Hub'. *Urban Studies*, 45(10), 2057–2074.

Lincoln, A. T. 2004. 'Pilgrimage and the New Testament', in *Explorations in a Christian Theology of Pilgrimage*, edited by C. Bartholomew and F. Hughes. Aldershot: Ashgate, 29–49.

Lindley, A. 2011. 'Remittances', in *Global Migration Governance*, edited by A. Betts. Oxford and New York: Oxford University Press, 242–265.

Linke, U. and Taana Smith, D. 2009. 'Fear: A Conceptual Framework', in *Cultures of Fear: A Critical Reader*, edited by U. Linke and D. Taana Smith. London and New York: Pluto Press, 1–17.

Lister, R. 2004. *Poverty*. Cambridge: Polity.

Llanos, C. 2010. 'Refugees or Economic Migrants: Catholic Thought on the Moral Roots of the Distinction', in *Driven from Home: Protecting the Rights of Forced Migrants*, edited by D. Hollenbach. Washington, DC: Georgetown University Press, 249–269.

Loader, W. 1996. 'Challenged at the Boundaries: A Conservative Jesus in Mark's Tradition'. *Journal for the Study of the New Testament*, 63, 45–61.

Loescher, G. 1993. *Beyond Charity: International Cooperation and the Global Refugee Crisis*. New York: Oxford University Press.

Loescher, G. 2000. 'Forced Migration in the Post-Cold War Era: The Need for a Comprehensive Approach', in *Managing Migration: Time for a New International Regime?*, edited by B. Ghosh. Oxford and New York: Oxford University Press, 190–219.

Loescher, G. and Milner, J. 2011. 'UNHCR and the Global Governance of Refugees', in *Global Migration Governance*, edited by A. Betts. Oxford and New York: Oxford University Press, 189–209.

Loescher, G. and Scanlan, J. A. 1986. *Calculated Kindness: Refugees and America's Half-Open Door: 1945 to the Present*. New York: Free Press.

Loescher, G., Betts, A. and Milner, J. 2008. *The United Nations High Commissioner for Refugees (UNHCR): The Politics and Practice of Refugee Protection into the Twenty-first Century*. London and New York: Routledge.

Lofland, L. H. 1973. *A World of Strangers: Order and Action in Urban Public Space*. New York: Basic Books.

Logan, P. 2000. 'Open and Shut Case: The Asylum Crisis', in *Street Credo: Churches in the Community*, edited by M. Simmons. London: Lemos and Crane, 137–147.

Loughry, M. 2008. 'The Representation of Refugee Women in Our Research and Practice', in *Not Born a Refugee Woman: Contesting Identities, Rethinking Practices*, edited by M. Hajdukowski-Ahmed, N. Khanlou and H. Moussa. New York and Oxford: Berghahn, 166–172.

Lovell, N. (ed.). 1998. *Locality and Belonging*. London and New York: Routledge.

Lykes, M. B. 2010. 'No Easy Road to Freedom: Engendering and Enculturating Forced Migration', in *Driven from Home: Protecting the Rights of Forced Migrants*, edited by D. Hollenbach. Washington, DC: Georgetown University Press, 71–93.

Malbon, E. S. 1991. *Narrative Space and Mythic Meaning in Mark: The Biblical Seminar 13*. Sheffield: JSOT Press/Sheffield Academic Press.

Malfait, R. and Scott-Flynn, N. 2005. *Destitution of Asylum-Seekers and Refugees in Birmingham*. Birmingham: Restore and Church Urban Fund.

Malherbe, A. J. 1983. *Social Aspects of Early Christianity*. 2nd edn. Philadelphia: Fortress.

Malkki, L. H. 1995. *Purity and Exile: Violence, Memory and National Cosmology among Hutu Refugees in Tanzania*. Chicago and London: University of Chicago Press.

Malkki, L. H. 1997. 'Speechless Emissaries: Refugees, Humanitarianism, and Dehistoricization', in *Siting Culture: The Shifting Anthropological Object*, edited by K. F. Olwig and K. Hastrup. London and New York: Routledge, 223–254.

Malloch, M. S. and Stanley, E. 2006. 'The Detention of Asylum Seekers in the UK: Representing Risk, Managing the Dangerous'. *Punishment and Society*, 7(1), 53–71.

Maluleke, T. S. 2001. 'African "Ruths," Ruthless Africas: Reflections of an African Mordecai', in *Other Ways of Reading: African Women and the Bible*, edited by M. W. Dube. Atlanta and Geneva: Society of Biblical Literature and WCC Publications, 237–251.

Marcus, J. 2000. *Mark 1–8: A New Translation with Introduction and Commentary*. Anchor Bible. New York: Doubleday.

Mares, P. 2003. 'Distance Makes the Heart Grow Fonder: Media Images of Refugees and Asylum Seekers', in *Refugees and Forced Displacement: International Security, Human Vulnerability and the State*, edited by E. Newman and J. van Selm. Tokyo and New York: UN University Press, 330–349.

Marfleet, P. 2006. *Refugees in a Global Era*. Basingstoke: Palgrave Macmillan.

Marfleet, P. 2011. 'Understanding "Sanctuary": Faith and Traditions of Asylum'. *Journal of Refugee Studies*, 24(3), 440–455.

Marquardt, M. F. 2005. 'Structural and Cultural Hybrids: Religious Congregational Life and Public Participation of Mexicans in the New South', in *Immigrant Faiths: Transforming Religious Life in America*, edited by K. Leonard, A. Stepick, M. Vasquez and J. Holdaway. Walnut Creek: AltaMira, 189–218.

Marrujo, O. R. 2003. 'Immigrants at Risk, Immigrants as Risk: Two Paradigms of Globalization', in *Migration, Religious Experience and Globalization*, edited by G. Campese and P. Ciallella. New York: Center for Migration Studies, 17–28.

Marrus, M. R. 2002. *The Unwanted: European Refugees from the First World War Through the Cold War*. Philadelphia: Temple University Press.

Martin, P. L., Martin, S. F. and Weil, P. 2006. *Managing Migration: The Promise of Cooperation*. Lanham and Oxford: Lexington Books.

Martin, S. F. 2001. 'Forced Migration and Professionalism'. *International Migration Review*, 35(1), 226–243.

Martin, S. F. and Tirman, J. (eds). 2009. *Women, Migration, and Conflict: Breaking a Deadly Cycle*. Dordrecht and New York: Springer.

Martin, S. F., Fagen, P. W., Jorgensen, K., Mann-Bondat, L., and Schoenholtz, A. 2005. *The Uprooted: Improving Humanitarian Responses to Forced Migration*. Lanham: Lexington Books.

Masenya, M. 2004. 'Ruth', in *Global Bible Commentary*, edited by D. Patte. Nashville: Abingdon, 86–91.

Massey, Doreen S. 2007. *World City*. Cambridge: Polity.

Massey, Douglas, Arango, J., Hugo, G., Kouaouci, A., Pellegrino, A. and Taylor, J. E. 1998. *Worlds in Motion. Understanding International Migration at the End of the Millennium*. Oxford: Clarendon.

Mason, E. 2007. 'Keeping Up with Refugee Research'. *Refugee Survey Quarterly*, 26(3), 149–161.

Matthews, V. H. 2004. *Judges and Ruth: The New Cambridge Bible Commentary*. Cambridge: Cambridge University Press.

Mauser, U. 1963. *Christ in the Wilderness: The Wilderness Theme in the Second Gospel and its Basis in the Biblical Tradition*. London: SCM Press.

Mayer, J.-F. 2007. 'Introduction: "In God Have I Put My Trust": Refugees and Religion'. *Refugee Survey Quarterly*, 26(2), 6–10.

McAdam, J. 2011. 'Environmental Migration', in *Global Migration Governance*, edited by A. Betts. Oxford and New York: Oxford University Press, 153–188.

McFague, S. 1987. *Models of God: Theology for an Ecological, Nuclear Age*. Philadelphia: Fortress.

McGhee, D. 2001a. 'Persecution and Social Group Status: Homosexual Refugees in the 1990s'. *Journal of Refugee Studies*, 14(1), 20–42.

McGhee, D. 2001b. 'Homosexuality and Refugee Status in the United Kingdom'. *Sociological Research Online*, 6(1). Available at: www.socresonline.org. uk/6/1/mcghee.html [accessed: 20 November 2008].

McGhee, D. 2005. 'Cohesion Strategies in Contemporary Britain'. *Sociological Research Online*, 10(3). Available at: www.socresonline.org.uk/10/3/mcghee. html [accessed: 20 December 2011].

McKinlay, J. E. 2004. *Reframing Her: Biblical Women in Postcolonial Focus*. Sheffield: Sheffield Phoenix Press.

McLoughlin, D. 2005. *Fear, Hate and the Stranger*. Talk to the West Midlands Region Churches Forum, 1 February.

McLoughlin, D. 2006. *Strange God, Strange Jesus and Strange Neighbours: A Reflection on the Limits of the Kingdom of God*. Unpublished Lecture, National Catholic Refugee Forum Conference, 13 May.

McMichael, C. 2002. '"Everywhere is Allah's Place": Islam and the Everyday Life of Somali Women in Melbourne, Australia'. *Journal of Refugee Studies*, 15(2), 171–188.

McNutt, P. 1999. *Reconstructing the Society of Ancient Israel*. London and Louisville, KY: SPCK and Westminster John Knox.

McSpadden, L. A. 1998. '"I Must Have My Rights!" The Presence of State Power in the Resettlement of Ethiopian and Eritrean Refugees', in *Power, Ethics and Human Rights: Anthropological Studies of Refugee Research and Action*, edited by R. M. Krulfeld and J. L. MacDonald. Lanham: Rowman & Littlefield, 147–172.

McTernan, O. 2003. *Violence in God's Name: Religion in an Age of Conflict*. London: Darton, Longman and Todd.

Meeks, W. A. 2003. *The First Urban Christians: The Social World of the Apostle Paul*. 2nd edn. New Haven and London: Yale University Press.

Meertens, D. 2004. 'A Life Project out of Turmoil: Displacement and Gender in Colombia', in *Refugees and the Transformation of Societies: Agency, Policies, Ethics and Politics*, edited by P. Essed, G. Frerks and J. Schrijvers. New York and Oxford: Berghahn, 69–80.

Mehta, L. (ed.). 2009. *Displaced by Development: Confronting Marginalisation and Gender in Justice*. New Delhi: Sage Publications India.

Mein, A. 2006. *Ezekiel and the Ethics of Exile*. Paperback edn. Oxford: Oxford University Press.

Mendieta, E. 2001. 'Invisible Cities: A Phenomenology of Globalization *from Below*'. *City*, 5(1), 7–26.

Merton, T. 1958. *Thoughts in Solitude*. London: Burns & Oates.

Mertus, J. 2003. 'Sovereignty, Gender, and Displacement', in *Refugees and Forced Displacement: International Security, Human Vulnerability, and the State*, edited by E. Newman and J. van Selm. Tokyo and New York: UN University Press, 250–273.

Methodist Church. 2008. *Worship and Bible Study* [Online]. Available at: www.
methodist.org.uk/index.cfm?fuseaction=opentoworld.content&cmid=833
[accessed: 27 November 2008].

Methodist Church. 2011a. *Methodist Church Responses to Consultations on
Immigration and Asylum* [Online]. Available at: www.methodist.org.uk/index.
cfm?fuseaction=opentoworld.content&cmid=830 [accessed: 8 October 2011].

Methodist Church. 2011b. *Conference Resolutions and Policies* [Online].
Available   at: www.methodist.org.uk/index.cfm?fuseaction=opentoworld.
content&cmid=829 [accessed: 8 October 2011].

Methodist Church. 2011c. *Asylum and Immigration* [Online]. Available at: www.
methodist.org.uk/index.cfm?fuseaction=opentoworld.content&cmid=827
[accessed: 8 October 2011].

Metz, J. B. 1980. *Faith in History and Society: Toward a Practical Fundamental
Theology*. Trans. D. Smith. London: Burns & Oates.

Meyer, B. and Geschiere, P. 1999. 'Globalization and Identity: Dialectics of
Flow and Closure. Introduction', in *Globalization and Identity: Dialectics of
Flow and Closure*, edited by B. Meyer and P. Geschiere. Oxford and Malden:
Blackwell, 2–15.

Meyers, C. 2005. *Exodus*. The New Cambridge Bible Commentary. New York:
Cambridge University Press.

Migration Watch. 2011. *Advisory Council: Biographical Notes* [Online]. Available
at: www.migrationwatch.co.uk/profile_council.php [accessed: 26 October
2011].

Mijoga, H. B. 1991. 'Refugees Unfold the Stories of the Bible'. *Religion in
Malawi*, 3, 16–24.

Miller, G. 2004. *A Newcastle/Iranian Experience*. Unpublished Reflection,
Newcastle Cathedral.

Miller, G. 2005. Interview (Meeting) with Revd Geoff Miller, Newcastle, 20
January.

Miller, J. M. and Hayes, J. H. 2006. *A History of Ancient Israel and Judah*. 2nd
edn. Louisville and London: Westminster John Knox.

Miller, S. 2004. *Women in Mark's Gospel*. London and New York: T & T Clark.

Milner, J. 2011. 'Refugees, Peacebuilding, and the Regional Dynamics of
Conflict', in *Refugees in International Relations*, edited by A. Betts and G.
Loescher. Oxford: Oxford University Press, 261–284.

Milwood, R. A. 1997. *Liberation and Mission: A Black Experience*. London:
African Caribbean Education Resource Centre.

Min, A. K. 2004. *The Solidarity of Others in a Divided World: A Postmodern
Theology After Postmodernism*. New York and London: T&T Clark
International.

Mintz, A. 1996. *Hurban: Responses to Catastrophe in Hebrew Literature*.
Syracuse: Syracuse University Press.

Molendijk, A., Beaumont, J. and Jedan, C. (eds). 2010. *Exploring the Postsecular:
The Religious, the Political and the Urban*. Leiden and Boston: Brill.

Moltmann, J. 2000. 'Perichoresis: An Old Magic Word for a New Trinitarian Theology', in *Trinity, Community and Power: Mapping Trajectories in Wesleyan Theology*, edited by M. D. Meeks. Nashville: Kingswood/Abingdon, 111–125.

Moltmann, J. 2002. *Theology of Hope: On the Ground and the Implications for a Christian Eschatology*. New edn. London: SCM Press.

Moorhead, C. 2005. *Human Cargo: A Journey Among Refugees*. London: Chatto & Windus.

Morgan, T. 2004. 'Packing 5 Years into 20 Minutes'. *CMS Mission Xtra*, 31. London: Church Mission Society.

Morgan, T. 2006. Email, 27 April.

Morisy, A. 1997. *Beyond the Good Samaritan: Community Ministry and Mission*. London and Herndon: Mowbray.

Morris, C. 2006. *Things Shaken – Things Unshaken: Reflections on Faith and Terror*. Peterborough: Epworth.

Morton, A. R. 2004. 'Duncan Forrester: A Public Theologian', in *Public Theology for the 21st Century*, edited by W. F. Storrar and A. R. Morton. London and New York: T & T Clark, 25–36.

Mote, A. 2003. *OverCrowded Britain: Our Immigration Crisis Exposed*. Petersfield: Tanner.

Mountz, A. 2011. 'The Enforcement Archipelago: Detention, Haunting, and Asylum on Islands'. *Political Geography*: doi:10.1016/j.polgeo.2011.01.005

Moxnes, H. 2003. *Putting Jesus in His Place: A Radical Vision of Household and Kingdom*. Louisville: Westminster John Knox.

Moxon, S. 2004. *The Great Immigration Scandal*. Exeter: Imprint Academic.

MPA [Mission and Public Affairs Council]. 2005. *A Place of Refuge: A Positive Approach to Asylum Seekers and Refugees in the UK*. London: Church House Publishing.

Mulvey, G. 2010. 'When Policy Creates Politics: The Problematizing of Immigration and the Consequences for Refugee Integration in the UK'. *Journal of Refugee Studies*, 23(4), 437–462.

Murray, H. 1990. *Do Not Neglect Hospitality: The Catholic Worker and the Homeless*. Philadelphia: Temple University Press.

Mursell, G. 2005. *Praying in Exile*. London: Darton, Longman and Todd.

Myers, C. 1988. *Binding the Strong Man: A Political Reading of Mark's Story of Jesus*. Maryknoll: Orbis.

Mynott, E. 2002. 'From a Shambles to a New Apartheid: Local Authorities, Dispersal and the Struggle to Defend Asylum Seekers', in *From Immigration Controls to Welfare Controls*, edited by S. Cohen, B. Humphries and E. Mynott. London and New York: Routledge, 106–125.

Nadar, S. 2001. 'A South African Indian Womanist Reading of the Character of Ruth', in *Other Ways of Reading: African Women and the Bible*, edited by M. W. Dube. Atlanta and Geneva: Society of Biblical Literature and WCC Publications, 159–175.

Naish, T. J. 2005. *'The Possibility of Displacement': Imagery of Displacement and the Theology of Christian Mission*. Unpublished PhD Dissertation. Bristol: Trinity College.

Nazir-Ali, M. 1998. *Citizens and Exiles: Christian Faith in a Plural World*. London: SPCK.

Nelson-Pallmeyer, J. 2005. *Is Religion Killing Us? Violence in the Bible and the Quran*. Paperback edn. New York and London: Continuum.

Neuberger, J. 2006. 'Richard Harries and the Issues of Our Time', in *Public Life and the Place of the Church: Reflections to Honour the Bishop of Oxford*, edited by M. Brierley. Aldershot: Ashgate, 23–35.

Neuman, W. L. 2006. *Social Research Methods: Qualitative and Quantitative Approaches*. 5th edn. Boston: Allyn and Bacon.

Neusner, J. 1997. 'Exile and Return as the History of Judaism', in *Exile: Old Testament, Jewish, and Christian Conceptions*, edited by J. M. Scott. Leiden, New York and Köln: Brill, 221–337.

Newman, Edward. 2003. 'Refugees, International Security, and Human Vulnerability: Introduction and Survey', in *Refugees and Forced Displacement: International Security, Human Vulnerability and the State*, edited by E. Newman and J. van Selm. Tokyo and New York: UN University Press, 3–30.

Newman, Elizabeth. 2007. *Untamed Hospitality: Wecloming God and Other Strangers*. Grand Rapids: Brazos Press.

Nickoloff, J. B. (ed.). 1996. *Gustavo Gutiérrez: Essential Writings*. Maryknoll: Orbis.

Niebuhr, H. R. 1951. *Christ and Culture*. New York: Harper & Brothers.

Niederwimmer, K. 1998. *The Didache: A Commentary on the Didache*, edited by H. W. Attridge. Trans. L. M. Maloney. Minneapolis: Augsburg Fortress.

Nielsen, K. 1997. *Ruth: A Commentary*. Old Testament Library. London: SCM Press.

Noth, M. 1972. *A History of the Pentateuchal Traditons*. Trans. B. W. Anderson. Englewood Cliffs: Prentice Hall.

Notre Dame. 2008. Notre Dame Church [Online]. Available at: www.notredamechurch.co.uk/eng/outreach.html [accessed: 18 December 2008].

Nouwen, H. J. 1976. *Reaching Out*. Glasgow: Collins.

Nyers, P. 2006. *Rethinking Refugees: Beyond States of Emergency*. New York and Abingdon: Routledge.

O'Connell Killen, P. and de Beer, J. 1994. *The Art of Theological Reflection*. New York: Crossroad.

O'Connor, K. M. 2002. *Lamentations & the Tears of the World*. Maryknoll: Orbis.

O'Donoghue, P. 2001. *Any Room at the Inn? Reflections on Asylum Seekers*. London: Office for Refugee Policy of the Catholic Bishops' Conference of England and Wales.

O'Neill, M. 2010. *Asylum, Migration and Community*. Bristol: Policy Press.

O'Neill, W. 2007. 'Rights of Passage: The Ethics of Forced Displacement'. *Journal of the Society of Christian Ethics*, 27(1), 113–135.

Office for Refugee Policy [of the Catholic Bishops' Conference of England and Wales]. 2004. *The Dispossessed: A Brief Guide to the Catholic Church's Concern for Refugees and Migrants*. London: Office for Refugee Policy of the Catholic Bishops' Conference of England and Wales.

Ogletree, T. W. 2003. *Hospitality to the Stranger: Dimensions of Moral Understanding*. Louisville: Westminster John Knox.

Oliver, K. 2001. *Witnessing: Beyond Recognition*. Minneapolis: University of Minnesota Press.

Olyan, S. M. 2000. *Rites and Ranks: Hierarchy in Biblical Representations of Cult*. Princeton: Princeton University Press.

Orji, N. 2011. 'Faith-based Aid to People Affected by Conflict in Jos, Nigeria: An Analysis of the Role of Christian and Muslim Organizations'. *Journal of Refugee Studies*, 24(3), 473–492.

Orobator, A. E. 2005. *From Crisis to Kairos: The Mission of the Church in the Time of HIV/AIDS, Refugees and Poverty*. Nairobi: Paulines Publications Africa.

Orobator, A. E. 2008. 'Key Ethical Issues in the Practices and Policies of Refugee-Serving NGOs and Churches', in *Refugee Rights: Ethics, Advocacy, and Africa*, edited by D. Hollenbach. Washington, DC: Georgetown University Press, 225–244.

Orobator, A. E. 2010. 'Justice for the Displaced: The Challenge of a Christian Understanding', in *Driven from Home: Protecting the Rights of Forced Migrants*, edited by D. Hollenbach. Washington, DC: Georgetown University Press, 37–53.

Osmer, R. R. 2008. *Practical Theology: An Introduction*. Grand Rapids: William B. Eerdmans.

O'Sullivan, M. 2009. 'The Intersection between the International, the Regional and the Domestic: Seeking Asylum in the UK', in *Refugees, Asylum Seekers and the Rule of Law: Comparative Perspectives*, edited by S. Kneebone. Cambridge and New York: Cambridge University Press, 228–280.

Owens, P. 2011. 'Beyond "Bare Life": Refugees and the "Right" to Have Rights', in *Refugees in International Relations*, edited by A. Betts and G. Loescher. Oxford: Oxford University Press, 133–150.

Ozick, C. 1994. 'Ruth', in *Reading Ruth: Contemporary Women Reclaim a Sacred Story*, edited by J. A. Kates and G. T. Reimer. New York: Ballantine Books, 211–232.

Padovani, F. 2006. 'Involuntary Resettlement in the Three Gorges Dam Area in the Perspectice of Forced Migration Due to Hydraulic Planning in China', in *Forced Migration and Global Processes: A View from Forced Migration Studies*, edited by F. Crépeau, D. Nakache, M. Collyer, N. Goetz and A. Hansen. Lanham and Oxford: Lexington Books, 91–123.

Pain, R. and Smith, S. J. 2008. 'Fear: Critical Geopolitics and Everyday Life', in *Fear: Critical Geopolitics and Everyday Life*, edited by R. Pain and S. J. Smith. Aldershot: Ashgate, 1–19.

Palmer, P. J. 1983. *The Company of Strangers: Christians and the Renewal of America's Public Life*. New York: Crossroad.

Panayi, P. 1994. *Immigration, Ethnicity and Racism in Britain, 1815–1945*. Manchester and New York: Manchester University Press.

Pannell, I. 2011. 'Libya Conflict: Black African Migrants Caught in Backlash'. *BBC News* [Online, 18 September]. Available at: www.bbc.co.uk/news/world-africa-14965062 [accessed: 25 October 2011].

Pantazis, C., Gordon, D. and Levitas, R. (eds). 2006. *Poverty and Social Exclusion in Britain: The Millennium Survey*. Bristol: Policy Press.

Papademetriou, D. G. 2003. 'Managing Rapid and Deep Change in the Newest Age of Migration', in *The Politics of Migration: Managing Opportunity, Conflict and Change*, edited by S. Spencer. Oxford: Blackwell, 39–58.

Papadopoulos, T. 2011. 'Immigration and the Variety of Migrant Integration Regimes in the European Union', in *Migration and Welfare in the New Europe: Social Protection and the Challenge of Integration*, edited by E. Carmel, A. Cerami and T. Papadopoulos. Bristol: Policy Press, 23–47.

Papastergiadis, N. 2000. *The Turbulence of Migration: Globalization, Deterritorialization and Hybridity*. Cambridge: Polity.

Pardes, I. 1992. *Countertraditions in the Bible: A Feminist Approach*. Cambridge: Harvard University Press.

Parekh, B. 2000. *Rethinking Multiculturalism: Cultural Diversity and Political Theory*. Basingstoke: Macmillan.

Parekh, B. 2008. *A New Politics of Identity: Political Principles for an Interdependent World*. Basingstoke and New York: Palgrave Macmillan.

Parsitau, D. S. 2011. 'The Role of Faith and Faith-based Organizations among Internally Displaced Persons in Kenya'. *Journal of Refugee Studies*, 24(3), 493–512.

Patel, P. 2010. *Faith Organizations and Migrants Today: The Gender Question?* Presentation at Migration, Racism and Religion: A Conference on Faith Organizations, Sanctuary and Civil Society. University of East London, 4 February. Available at: www.uel.ac.uk/cmrb/conferencepapers.htm [accessed: 9 May 2011].

Pattison, S. 1997. *Pastoral Care and Liberation Theology*. Paperback edn. London: SPCK.

Pattison, S. 2000a. *Shame: Theory, Therapy, Theology*. Cambridge: Cambridge University Press.

Pattison, S. 2000b. 'Some Straw for the Bricks: A Basic Introduction to Theological Reflection', in *The Blackwell Reader in Pastoral and Practical Theology*, edited by J. Woodward and S. Pattison. Oxford: Blackwell, 135–145.

Pattison, S. 2007. *The Challenge of Practical Theology: Selected Essays*. London and Philadelphia: Jessica Kingsley.

Pattison, S. and Woodward, J. 2000. 'An Introduction to Pastoral and Practical Theology', in *The Blackwell Reader in Pastoral and Practical Theology*, edited by J. Woodward and S. Pattison. Oxford: Blackwell, 1–19.

Pearsall, J. (ed.). 1998. *The New Oxford Dictionary of English*. Oxford: Oxford University Press.

Pecan [Peckham Evangelical Churches Action Network]. 2008. PECAN [Online]. Available at: www.pecan.org.uk [accessed: 20 December 2008].

Penninx, R., Kraal, K., Martiniello, M. and Vervotec, S. 2004. 'Introduction: European Cities and Their New Residents', in *Citizenship in European Cities: Immigrants, Local Politics and Integration Policies*, edited by R. Penninx, K. Kraal, M. Martiniello and S. Vervotec. Aldershot: Ashgate, 1–16.

Perkinson, J. 1996. 'A Canaanite Word in the Logos of Christ; or the Difference the Syro-Phoenician Woman Makes to Jesus'. *Semeia*, 75, 61–85.

Petrella, I. 2006. *The Future of Liberation Theology: An Argument and Manifesto*. London: SCM Press.

Phan, P. C. 2003. 'The Experience of Migration in the US as a Source of Intercultural Theology', in *Migration, Religious Experience, and Globalization*, edited by G. Campese and P. Ciallella. New York: Center for Migration Studies, 143–169.

Phan, P. C. 2008. 'Migration in the Patristic Era: History and Theology', in *A Promised Land, A Perilous Journey: Theological Perspectives on Migration*, edited by D. G. Groody and G. Campese. Notre Dame, IN: University of Notre Dame Press, 35–61.

Phillimore, J. 2009. 'Restrictionism versus Liberalism? The Rupture between Asylum and Integration in the EU', in *Europe's Established and Emerging Immigrant Communities: Assimilation, Multiculturalism or Integration*, edited by C. Howson and M. Sallah. Stoke on Trent: Trentham Books, 47–64.

Pickering, M. 2001. *Stereotyping: The Politics of Representation*. Basingstoke: Palgrave.

Pickering, S. 2011. *Women, Borders, and Violence: Current Issues in Asylum, Forced Migration, and Trafficking*. New York: Springer.

Pirouet, M. L. 2006. 'Why Religion Matters', in *Doing Research with Refugees: Issues and Guidelines*, edited by B. Temple and R. Moran. Bristol: Policy Press, 167–182.

Platten, S. 1996. *Pilgrims*. London: HarperCollins.

Pohl, C. D. 1999. *Making Room: Recovering Hospitality as a Christian Tradition*. Grand Rapids and Cambridge: William B. Eerdmans.

Pontifical Council [for the Pastoral Care of Migrants and Itinerant People]. 2004. *The Love of Christ Towards Migrants – Erga migrantes caritas Christi*. London: Catholic Truth Society.

Poore, P. 2005. 'Migration: A Threat or an Asset to Health?', in *International Migration and Security: Opportunities and Challenges*, edited by E. Guild and J. van Selm. London and New York: Routledge, 174–190.

Portes, A. 1999. 'Conclusion: Towards a New World – The Origins and Effects of Transnational Activities'. *Ethnic and Racial Studies*, 22(2), 463–477.

Portes, A., Guarnizo, L. E. and Landolt, P. 1999. 'The Study of Transnationalism: Pitfalls and Promise of an Emergent Research Field'. *Ethnic and Racial Studies*, 22(2), 217–237.

Potts, K. and Brown, L. 2005. 'Becoming an Anti-Oppressive Researcher', in *Research As Resistance: Critical, Indigenous and Anti-Oppressive Approaches*, edited by L. Brown and S. Strega. Toronto: Canadian Scholars' Press, 255–286.

Powell, W. and Leather, S. 2002. *Asylum Seeker & Refugee Befriending Pack: 'When I was a Stranger You Welcomed Me'*. Teddington: Tearfund.

Praxis. 2008. Praxis. [Online]. Available at: www.praxis.org.uk [accessed: 20 December 2008].

Premnath, D. N. 2007a. 'Introduction', in *Border Crossings: Cross-cultural Hermeneutics*, edited by D. N. Premnath. Maryknoll: Orbis, 1–12.

Premnath, D. N. 2007b. 'Margins and Mainstream: An Interview with R S Sugirtharajah', in *Border Crossings: Cross-cultural Hermeneutics*, edited by D. N. Premnath. Maryknoll: Orbis, 153–165.

Price, M. 2009. *Rethinking Asylum: History, Purpose and Limits*. Cambridge and New York: Cambridge University Press.

Pries, L. (ed.) 1999. *Migration and Transnational Social Spaces*. Aldershot: Ashgate.

Prior, J. 2006. *Destitute and Desperate: A Report on the Numbers of 'Failed' Asylum Seekers in Newcastle upon Tyne and the Services Available to Them*. Newcastle: Open Door (North East).

Prochaska, F. 2006. *Christianity and Social Service in Modern Britain: The Disinherited Spirit*. Oxford: Oxford University Press.

Provan, I., Long, V. P. and Longman III, T. 2003. *A Biblical History of Israel*. Louisville and London: Westminster John Knox.

Putnam, R. A. 1994. 'Friendship', in *Reading Ruth: Contemporary Women Reclaim a Sacred Story*, edited by J. A. Kates and G. T. Reimer. New York: Ballantine Books, 44–54.

Rabben, L. 2011. *Give Refuge to the Stranger: The Past, Present, and Future of Sanctuary*. Walnut Creek: Left Coast Press.

Rajkumar, P. 2010. *Dalit Theology and Dalit Liberation: Problems, Paradigms and Possibilities*. Farnham: Ashgate.

Rashkow, I. 1993. 'Ruth: The Discourse of Power and the Power of Discourse', in *A Feminist Companion to Ruth*, edited by A. Brenner. Sheffield: Sheffield Academic Press, 26–41.

Reader, J. 2008. *Reconstructing Practical Theology: The Impact of Globalization*. Aldershot: Ashgate.

Rebera, R. W. 2001. 'The Syrophoenician Woman: A South Asian Feminist Perspective', in *A Feminist Companion to Mark*, edited by A-J. Levine. Sheffield: Sheffield Academic Press, 101–110.

Reddie, A. G. 2003. *Nobodies to Somebodies: A Practical Theology for Education and Liberation*. Peterborough: Epworth.

Reddie, A. G. 2006a. *Black Theology in Transatlantic Dialogue*. Basingstoke: Palgrave Macmillan.

Reddie, A. G. 2006b. *Dramatizing Theologies: A Participative Approach to Black God-Talk*. London and Oakville: Equinox.

Reddie, A. G. 2008. 'People Matter Too! The Politics and Method of doing Black Liberation Theology (the Ferguson Lecture – the University of Manchester, 18th October 2007)'. *Practical Theology*, 1(1), 43–64.

Reed, E. 2010. 'Refugee Rights and State Sovereignty: Theological Perspectives on the Ethics of Territorial Borders'. *Journal of the Society of Christian Ethics*, 30(2), 59–78.

Reed, K. 2003. 'Gendering Asylum: The Importance of Diversity and Context', in *Exile and Asylum: Women Seeking Refuge in 'Fortress Europe'*, edited by A. Treacher, A. Coombes, C. Alexander, L. Bland and P. Alldred. Feminist Review 73. Basingstoke: Palgrave Macmillan, 114–118.

Refugee Action. 2006. *The Destitution Trap: Research into Destitution among Refused Asylum Seekers in the UK*. London: Refugee Action. Available at: www.refugee-action.org.uk/campaigns/documents/RA_DestReport_Final_ LR.pdf [accessed: 7 June 2008].

Refugee Council. 2004a. *Agenda for Integration*. London: Refugee Council. Available at: www.refugeecouncil.org.uk/policy/responses/2004/Integration. htm [accessed: 21 January 2009].

Refugee Council. 2004b. *Hungry and Homeless: The Impact of the Withdrawal of State Support on Asylum Seekers, Refugee Communities and the Voluntary Sector*. London: Refugee Council.

Refugee Council. 2007. *The New Asylum Model*. Briefing Paper. London: Refugee Council. Available at: www.refugeecouncil.org.uk/policy/briefings/2007/nam. htm [accessed: 21 January 2009].

RSC [Refugee Studies Centre]. 2007. 'Ethical Guidelines for Good Research Practice'. *Refugee Survey Quarterly*, 26(3), 163–172.

Refugee Week. 2011. *Famous Refugees* [Online]. Available at: www.refugeeweek. org.uk/InfoCentre/famous-refugees.htm [accessed: 27 September 2011].

Reilly, R. 1996. *Towards a Co-ordinated Strategy: The Voluntary Sector Response to the Withdrawal of Social Security Benefits from Asylum Seekers*. Unpublished Policy Report. London: Social and Pastoral Action, Catholic Diocese of Westminster.

Rendtorff, R. 1996. 'The *Gēr* in the Priestly Laws of the Pentateuch', in *Ethnicity and the Bible*, edited by M. G. Brett. Boston and Leiden: Brill, 77–87.

Restore. 2008. *Annual Report 2007*. Birmingham: Restore. Available at: www. restore-uk.org [accessed: 21 November 2008].

Restore. 2011a. Restore [Online]. Available at: www.restore-uk.org [accessed: 2 October 2011].

Restore. 2011b. *Annual Report 2010*. Birmingham: Restore. Available at: www. restore-uk.org [accessed: 3 October 2011].

Rhoads, D. M. 1994. 'Jesus and the Syropheonician Woman in Mark: A Narrative-Critical Study'. *Journal of the American Academy of Religion*, 62(2), 343–375.

Richardson, J. 2003. 'Reading the Bible in the City: Urban Culture, Local Context and the Right to Interpret'. *Anvil*, 20(2), 105–116.

Rieger, J. 2001. *God and the Excluded: Visions and Blind Spots in Contemporary Theology*. Minneapolis: Augsburg Fortress.

Rieger, J. 2003a. 'Introduction: Opting for the Margins in a Postmodern World', in *Opting for the Margins: Postmoderntiy and Liberation in Christian Theology*, edited by J. Rieger. Oxford: Oxford University Press, 3–22.

Rieger, J. 2003b. 'Theology and the Power of the Margins in a Postmodern World', in *Opting for the Margins: Postmodernity and Liberation in Christian Theology*, edited by J. Rieger. Oxford: Oxford University Press, 179–199.

Ringe, S. 1990. 'A Gentile Woman's Story', in *Feminist Theology: A Reader*, edited by A. Loades. London: SPCK, 49–57.

Ringe, S. 2001. 'A Gentile Woman's Story, Revisited: Rereading Mark 7.24–31', in *A Feminist Companion to Mark*, edited by A-J. Levine. Sheffield: Sheffield Academic Press, 79–100.

Robertson, R. 1995. 'Glocalization: Time-Space and Homogeneity-Heterogeneity', in *Global Modernities*, edited by M. Featherstone, S. Lash and R. Robertson. London, Thousand Oaks and New Delhi: Sage, 25–44.

Robin, C. 2004. *Fear: The History of a Political Idea*. Oxford and New York: Oxford University Press.

Robinson, V. 1998. 'The Importance of Information in the Resettlement of Refugees in the UK'. *Journal of Refugee Studies*, 11(2), 146–160.

Robinson, V., Andersson, R. and Musterd, S. 2003. *Spreading the 'Burden'? A Review of Policies to Disperse Asylum Seekers and Refugees*. Bristol: Policy Press.

Rodgers, G. 2004. '"Hanging Out" with Forced Migrants: Methodological and Ethical Challenges'. *Forced Migration Review*, 21(September), 48–49.

Rogers, R. 1997. *Cities for a Small Planet*. London: Faber.

Rosenau, J. N. 2004. 'Emergent Spaces, New Places, and Old Faces: Proliferating Identities in a Globalizing World', in *Worlds on the Move: Globalization, Migration and Cultural Security*, edited by J. Friedman and S. Randeria. London and New York: I. B. Tauris and Co., 23–62.

Rosenberg, D. 2006. *Immigration* [Online]. Available at: www.channel4.com/culture/microsites/O/origination/immigration_t.html [accessed: 6 January 2009].

Rowlands, A. 2011. 'On the Temptations of Sovereignty: The Task of Catholic Social Teaching and the Challenge of UK Asylum Seeking'. *Political Theology*, 12(6), 843–869.

Rudiger, A. 2006. 'Integration of New Migrants', in *Refugees and Other New Migrants: A Review of the Evidence on Successful Approaches to Integration*, edited by S. Spencer. Oxford: Centre on Migration, Policy and Society

[COMPAS], 4–21. Available at: www.compas.ox.ac.uk/publications/papers/ Refugees_new%20migrants-Dec06.pdf [accessed: 20 January 2009].

Rudiger, A. 2007. *Prisoners of Terrorism? The Impact of Anti-Terrorism Measures on Refugees and Asylum Seekers in Britain*. London: Refugee Council and Oxfam.

Rudolph, C. 2006. *National Security and Immigration: Policy Development in the US and Western Europe Since 1945*. Stanford: Stanford University Press.

Ruiz, J.-P. 2007. 'Abram and Sarai Cross the Border: Reading Genesis 12.10–20 with People on the Move', in *Border Crossings: Cross-cultural Hermeneutics*, edited by D. N. Premnath. Maryknoll: Orbis, 15–34.

Ruiz, J.-P. 2009. '"They Could Not Speak the Language of Judah": Rereading Nehemiah 13 between Brooklyn and Jerusalem', in *They Were All Together in One Place? Toward Minority Biblical Criticism*, edited by R. C. Bailey, T. B. Liew and F. F. Segovia. Atlanta: Society of Biblical Literature, 79–95.

Runesson, A. 2011. *Exegesis in the Making: Postcolonialism and New Testament Studies*. Biblical Interpretation Series 103. Leiden and Boston: Brill.

Rutherford, J. 2005. 'Fallen Among Thieves', in *Mediactive: Issue 4*, edited by J. Rutherford. London: Barefoot, 71–89.

Rutter, J. 2006. *Refugee Children in the UK*. Maidenhead: Open University Press.

Ryan, D., Dooley, B. and Benson, C. 2008. 'Theoretical Perspectives on Post-Migration Adaptation and Psychological Well-being among Refugees: Towards a Resource-based Model'. *Journal of Refugee Studies*, 21(1), 1–18.

Sacks, J. 2002. *The Dignity of Difference: How to Avoid the Clash of Civilizations*. London and New York: Continuum.

Sadler Jr, R. S. 2005. *Can a Cushite Change His Skin? An Examination of Race, Ethnicity and Othering in the Hebrew Bible*. New York and London: T & T Clark.

Sadoway, G. 2008. 'The Gender Factor in Refugee Determination and the Effect of "Gender Guidelines"', in *Not Born a Refugee Woman: Contesting Identities, Rethinking Practices*, edited by M. Hajdukowski-Ahmed, N. Khanlou and H. Moussa. New York and Oxford: Berghahn, 244–253.

Sager, R. 2010. *Faith, Politics, and Power: The Politics of Faith-based Initiatives*. New York: Oxford University Press.

Saggar, S. 2003. 'Immigration and the Politics of Public Opinion', in *The Politics of Migration: Managing Opportunity, Conflict and Change*, edited by S. Spencer. Oxford and Malden: Blackwell, 178–194.

Sagovsky, N. 2002. 'The Eucharist and the Practice of Justice'. *Studies in Christian Ethics*, 15(1), 75–96.

Sagovsky, N. 2005. 'Faith in Asylum', *Gore Lecture*, Westminster Abbey, London, 15 February.

Sagovsky, N. 2007. 'Destitute by Government Design'. *Church Action on Poverty News*, (Winter 2007), 5.

Sagovsky, N. 2008. 'Exile, Seeking Asylum in the UK and the *Missio Dei*', in *Mission and Migration*, edited by S. Spencer. Calver: Cliff College, 141–157.

Said, E. W. 1988. 'Michael Walzer's *Exodus and Revolution*: A Canaanite Reading', in *Blaming the Victims: Spurious Scholarship and the Palestinian Question*, edited by E. Said and C. Hitchens. London and New York: Verso, 161–178.

Said, E. W. 1991. *Orientalism: Western Conceptions of the Orient*. London: Penguin.

Sakenfeld, K. D. 1978. *The Meaning of Ḥesed in the Hebrew Bible: A New Inquiry*. Missoula: Scholars Press.

Sakenfeld, K. D. 1985. *Faithfulness in Action: Loyalty in Biblical Perspective*. Philadelphia: Fortress.

Sakenfeld, K. D. 1999. *Ruth*. Interpretation: A Bible Commentary for Teaching and Preaching. Louisville: John Knox.

Sales, R. 2002. 'The Deserving and the Undeserving? Refugees, Asylum Seekers and Welfare in Britain'. *Critical Social Policy*, 22(3), 456–478.

Sales, R. 2007. *Understanding Immigration and Refugee Policy: Contradictions and Continuities*. Bristol: Policy Press.

Saliers, D. E. 1994. *Worship as Theology: Foretaste of Glory Divine*. Nashville: Abingdon.

Sampson, E. E. 1999. *Dealing with Differences: An Introduction to the Social Psychology of Prejudice*. Orlando: Harcourt Brace College.

Sandercock, L. 2003. *Cosmopolis II: Mongrel Cities of the 21st Century*. London and New York: Continuum.

Sassen, S. 1998a. 'The *de facto* Transnationalizing of Immigration Policy', in *Challenge to the Nation-state: Immigration in Western Europe and the US*, edited by C. Joppke. Oxford: Oxford University Press, 49–85.

Sassen, S. 1988b. *The Mobility of Labor and Capital: A Study in International Investment and Labor Flow*. Cambridge: Cambridge University Press.

Sassen, S. 1999. *Guests and Aliens*. New York: New Press.

Sassen, S. 2006a. *Cities in a World Economy*. 3rd edn. Thousand Oaks, London and New Delhi: Pine Forge Press/Sage.

Sassen, S. 2006b. 'The Repositioning of Citizenship and Alienage: Emergent Subjects and Spaces for Politics', in *Displacement, Asylum, Migration: The Oxford Amnesty Lectures 2004*, edited by K. E. Tunstall. Oxford: Oxford University Press, 176–203.

Sasson, J. M. 1989. *Ruth: A New Translation with a Philological Commentary and a Formalist-Folklorist Interpretation*. 2nd edn. Sheffield: Sheffield Academic Press.

Sasson, J. M. 1997. 'Ruth', in *The Literary Guide to the Bible*, edited by R. Alter and F. Kermode. London: Fontana, 320–328.

Savage, S.-J. 2005. 'The Efficacy and Justifiability of Policies to Disperse Asylum Seekers: A Case Study of Disperal under the UK's Immigration and Asylum Act of 1999', in *Refugee Crises and International Response: Towards Permanent Solutions?*, edited by A. Bolesta. Warsaw: Leon Koźmiński Academy of Entrepreneurship and Management, 217–246.

Saxegaard, K. M. 2010. *Character Complexity in the Book of Ruth*. Tübingen, Germany: Mohr Siebeck.

Sayyid, S. 2000. 'Beyond Westphalia: Nations and Diasporas – the Case of the Muslim Umma', in *Un/settled Multiculturalisms: Diasporas, Entanglements, Transruptions*, edited by B. Hesse. London and New York: Zed Books, 33–50.

Schaeffer, J. 1990. *Sanctuary and Asylum: A Handbook for Commitment*. Geneva: World Alliance of Reformed Churches.

Schmeidl, S. 2001. 'Conflict and Forced Migration: A Quantitative Review, 1964–1995', in *Global Migrants, Global Refugees: Problems and Solutions*, edited by A. R. Zolberg and P. M. Benda. New York: Berghahn, 62–94.

Schmidt, A. 2007. '"I Know What You're Doing", Reflexivity and Methods in Refugee Studies'. *Refugee Survey Quarterly*, 26(3), 82–99.

Schotsmans, P. 1993. 'Ethnocentricity and Racism: Does Christianity have a Share in the Responsibility', in *Migrants and Refugees*, edited by D. Mieth and L. S. Cahill. London and Maryknoll: SCM Press and Orbis, 87–94.

Schreiter, R. J. 1997. *The New Catholicity: Theology between the Global and the Local*. Maryknoll: Orbis.

Schuster, L. 2000. 'A Comparative Analysis of the Asylum Policy of Seven European Governments'. *Journal of Refugee Studies*, 13(1), 118–132.

Schuster, L. 2003. *The Use and Abuse of Political Asylum in Britain and Germany*. London and Portland: Frank Cass.

Schuster, L. and Solomos, J. 2004. 'Race, Immigration and Asylum: New Labour's Agenda and its Consequences'. *Ethnicities*, 4(2), 267–287.

Schwager, R. 2000. *Must there be Scapegoats? Violence and Redemption in the Bible*. New edn. Trans. M. L. Assad. New York and Leominster: Crossroad and Gracewing.

Schwartz, R. M. 1997. *The Curse of Cain: The Violent Legacy of Monotheism*. Chicago and London: University of Chicago Press.

Scott, S. F. 2003. *Welcoming Refugees? A Study of Host Community Attitudes as seen in Church Related Projects in Leicester*. Unpublished MA Dissertation. London: University of East London.

Sedmak, C. 2002. *Doing Local Theology: A Guide for Artisans of a New Humanity*. Maryknoll: Orbis.

Segovia, F. F. 1995a. '"And They Began to Speak in Other Tongues": Competing Modes of Discourse in Contemporary Biblical Criticism', in *Reading from this Place: Volume 1: Social Location and Biblical Interpretation in the US*, edited by F. F. Segovia and M. A. Tolbert. Minneapolis: Fortress, 1–32.

Segovia, F. F. 1995b. 'Toward a Hermeneutics of the Diaspora: A Hermeneutics of Otherness and Engagement', in *Reading from this Place: Volume 1: Social Location and Biblical Interpretation in the US*, edited by F. F. Segovia and M. A. Tolbert. Minneapolis: Fortress, 57–73.

Segovia, F. F. 1998. 'Biblical Criticism and Postcolonial Studies: Toward a Postcolonial Optic', in *Postcolonial Bible*, edited by R. S. Sugirtharajah. The Bible and Postcolonialism, 1. Sheffield: Sheffield Academic Press, 49–65.

Segovia, F. F. 2000. *Decolonizing Biblical Studies: A View from the Margins.* Maryknoll: Orbis.

Segundo, J. L. 1976. *The Liberation of Theology.* Trans. J. Drury. Maryknoll: Orbis.

Sellner, E. C. 2004. *Pilgrimage: Exploring a Great Spiritual Practice.* Notre Dame: Sorin Books.

Senior, D. 2008. '"Beloved Aliens and Exiles": New Testament Perspectives on Migration', in *A Promised Land, A Perilous Journey: Theological Perspectives on Migration*, edited by D. G. Groody and G. Campese. Notre Dame: University of Notre Dame Press, 20–34.

Sennett, R. 1993. *The Conscience of the Eye: The Design and Social Life of Cities.* New edn. London and Boston: Faber & Faber.

Sennett, R. 2002. *The Fall of Public Man.* London: Penguin.

Sentamu, J. 2008. *The Road to Recovery: Neighbourliness and Mercy, Community and Service.* The Archbishop of York's Temple Address to the Evangelical Alliance. London: Royal Society, 28 November. Available at: www.archbishopofyork.org/2042 [accessed: 29 November 2008].

Shandy, D. J. 2002. 'Nuer Christians in America'. *Journal of Refugee Studies*, 15(2), 213–221.

Sheldrake, P. 2001. *Spaces for the Sacred: Place, Memory and Identity.* London: SCM Press.

Short, J. R. 2004. *Global Metropolitan: Globalizing Cities in a Capitalist World.* London and New York: Routledge.

Silove, D. 2004. 'The Global Challenge of Asylum', in *Broken Spirits: The Treatment of Traumatized Asylum Seekers, Refugees, War and Torture Victims*, edited by J. P. Wilson and B. Droždek. New York and Hove: Brunner-Routledge, 13–31.

Simmel, G. 1950. 'The Stranger', in *The Sociology of Georg Simmel*, edited by K. H. Wolff. Glencoe: Free Press, 402–408.

Sivanandan, A. 2001. 'Poverty is the New Black'. *Race and Class*, 43(2), 1–5.

Skeldon, R. 2010. 'Migration and Development over Twenty Years of Research: Progress and Prospects', in *Migration in a Globalised World: New Research Issues and Prospects*, edited by C. Audebert and M. K. Doraï. Amsterdam: Amsterdam University Press, 145–159.

Slack, J. 2008. 'Migrants Arriving from Overseas will be Brought "Under Control" Hints New Immigration Minister'. *Daily Mail*, 6 October.

Slee, N. 2004. *Women's Faith Development: Patterns and Processes.* Explorations in Practical, Pastoral and Empirical Theology. Aldershot: Ashgate.

Slessarev-Jamir, H. 2011. *Prophetic Activism: Progressive Religious Justice Movements in Contemporary America.* New York and London: New York University Press.

Smart, K. and Fullegar, S. 2008. *The Destitution Tally: An Indication of the Extent of Destitution among Asylum Seekers and Refugees. Refugee Agencies Policy*

Response. London: Refugee Council, Refugee Action, Migrant Helpline, Scottish Refugee Council and Welsh Refugee Council.

Smillie, I. and Minear, L. 2004. *The Charity of Nations: Humanitarian Action in a Calculating World*. Bloomfield: Kumarian Press.

Smith, C. 1996. 'Introduction: Correcting a Curious Neglect, or Bringing Religion Back in', in *Disruptive Religion: The Force of Faith in Social Movement Activism*, edited by C. Smith. New York and London: Routledge, 1–25.

Smith, D. L. 1989. *The Religion of the Landless: The Social Context of the Babylonian Exile*. Bloomington: Meyer-Stone Books.

Smith, D. L. 1991. 'The Politics of Ezra: Sociological Indicators of Postexilic Judean Society', in *Second Temple Studies 1. Persian Period*, edited by P. R. Davies. JSOT Supplement Series 117. Sheffield: JSOT Press/Sheffield Academic Press, 73–97.

Smith, G. 2008. *They Come Back Singing: Finding God with the Refugees*. Chicago: Loyola Press.

Smith, J. Z. 1985. 'What A Difference A Difference Makes', in *'To See Ourselves as Others See Us': Christians, Jews, 'Others' in Late Antiquity*, edited by J. Neusner and E. S. Frerichs. Chico: Scholars Press, 3–48.

Smith, N. 2002. 'New Globalism, New Urbanism: Gentrification as Global Urban Strategy'. *Antipode*, 34(3), 427–450.

Smith-Christopher, D. L. 1994. 'The Mixed Marriage Crisis in Ezra 9–10 and Nehemiah 13: A Study of the Sociology of the Post-Exilic Judean Community', in *Second Temple Studies 2. Temple and Community in the Persian Period*, edited by T. C. Eskenazi and K. H. Richards. JSOT Supplement Series 175. Sheffield: JSOT Press/Sheffield Academic Press, 243–265.

Smith-Christopher, D. L. 1996. 'Between Ezra and Isaiah: Exclusion, Transformation, and Inclusion of the "Foreigner" in Post-Exilic Biblical Theology', in *Ethnicity and the Bible*, edited by M. G. Brett. Leiden: Brill, 117–142.

Smith-Christopher, D. L. 1997. 'Reassessing the Historical and Sociological Impact of the Babylonian Exile (597/587–539 BCE)', in *Exile: Old Testament, Jewish and Christian Conceptions*, edited by J. M. Scott. Boston and Leiden: Brill, 7–36.

Smith-Christopher, D. L. 2002. *Biblical Theology in Exile*. Minneapolis: Augsburg Fortress Press.

Snyder, S. 2007. 'The Dangers of "Doing Our Duty": Reflections on Churches Engaging with People Seeking Asylum in the UK'. *Theology*, 110(857), 351–360.

Snyder, S. 2011. 'Un/settling Angels: Faith-based Organizations and Asylum-seeking in the UK'. *Journal of Refugee Studies*, 24(3), 565–585.

Soggin, J. A. 1999. *An Introduction to the History of Israel and Judah*. 3rd edn. Trans. J. Bowden. London: SCM Press.

Solimano, A. 2010. *International Migration in the Age of Crisis and Globalization: Historical and Recent Experiences*. Cambridge: Cambridge University Press.

Solomos, J. 2003. *Race and Racism in Britain*. 3rd edn. Basingstoke: Palgrave Macmillan.

Somerville, W. 2007. *Immigration under New Labour*. Bristol: Policy Press.

Soysal, Y. N. 1994. *Limits of Citizenship: Migrants and Postnational Membership in Europe*. Chicago and London: University of Chicago Press.

Sparks, K. L. 1998. *Ethnicity and Identity in Ancient Israel: Prolegomena to the Study of Ethnic Sentiments and Their Expression in the Hebrew Bible*. Winona Lake: Eisenbrauns.

Spencer, N. 2004. *Asylum and Immigration: A Christian Perspective on a Polarised Debate*. Milton Keynes: Paternoster.

Spencer, Sarah. 2003. 'Introduction', in *The Politics of Migration: Managing Opportunity, Conflict and Change*, edited by S. Spencer. Oxford: Blackwell, 1–24.

Spencer, Sarah. 2011. *The Migration Debate*. Bristol: Policy Press.

Spina, F. A. 1983. 'Israelites as *gerîm*, "Sojourners," in Social and Historical Context', in *The Word of the Lord Shall Go Forth*, edited by C. Meyers and M. O'Connor. Winona Lake: Eisenbrauns, 321–335.

Spina, F. A. 2005. *The Faith of the Outsider: Exclusion and Inclusion in the Biblical Story*. Grand Rapids and Cambridge: William B. Eerdmans.

Squire, V. 2009. *The Exclusionary Politics of Asylum*. Basingstoke: Palgrave Macmillan.

Sriskandarajah, D. 2006. 'Migration Madness: Five Policy Dilemmas'. *Studies in Christian Ethics*, 19(1), 21–37.

Sriskandarajah, D., Cooley, L. and Reed, H. 2005. *Paying Their Way: The Fiscal Contribution of Immigrants in the UK*. London: IPPR.

Statham, P. 2003. 'Understanding Anti-Asylum Rhetoric: Restrictive Politics or Racist Publics?', in *The Politics of Migration: Managing Opportunity, Conflict and Change*, edited by S. Spencer. Oxford and Malden: Blackwell, 163–177.

Stegemann, W. 1996. 'Anti-Semitic and Racist Prejudices in Titus 1:10–16', in *Ethnicity and the Bible*, edited by M. G. Brett. Boston and Leiden: Brill, 271–294.

Stepick, A., Rey, T. and Mahler, S. J. (eds). 2009. *Churches and Charity in the Immigrant City: Religion, Immigration and Civic Engagement in Miami*. New Brunswick: Rutgers University Press.

Stoppels, S. 2008. 'Count their Blessings: Social Return on Investment of Immigrant Churches in The Hague', in *A Moving God: Immigrant Churches in the Netherlands*, edited by M. Jansen and H. Stoffels. Zurich: Lit Verlag GmbH & Co. KG Wien, 31–47.

Strang, A. and Ager, A. 2010. 'Refugee Integration: Emerging Trends and Remaining Agendas'. *Journal of Refugee Studies*, 23(4), 589–607.

Sugirtharajah, R. S. 1996. 'Orientalism, Ethnonationalism and Transnationalism: Shifting Identities and Biblical Interpretation', in *Ethnicity and the Bible*, edited by M. G. Brett. Boston and Leiden: Brill, 421–429.

Sugirtharajah, R. S. 1998a. 'Biblical Studies after the Empire: From a Colonial to a Postcolonial Mode of Interpretation', in *The Postcolonial Bible*, edited by R. S. Sugirtharajah. The Bible and Postcolonialism, 1. Sheffield: Sheffield Academic Press, 12–22.

Sugirtharajah, R. S. 1998b. 'A Postcolonial Exploration of Collusion and Construction in Biblical Interpretation', in *The Postcolonial Bible*, edited by R. S. Sugirtharajah. The Bible and Postcolonialism, 1. Sheffield: Sheffield Academic Press, 91–116.

Sugirtharajah, R. S. 1999. 'Thinking about Vernacular Hermeneutics Sitting in a Metropolitan Study', in *Vernacular Hermeneutics*, edited by R. S. Sugirtharajah. The Bible and Postcolonialism, 2. Sheffield: Sheffield Academic Press, 92–115.

Sugirtharajah, R. S. 2001. *The Bible and the Third World: Precolonial, Colonial and Postcolonial Encounters*. Cambridge: Cambridge University Press.

Sugirtharajah, R. S. 2002. *Postcolonial Criticism and Biblical Interpretation*. Oxford: Oxford University Press.

Sugirtharajah, R. S. 2003. *Postcolonial Reconfigurations: An Alternative Way of Reading the Bible and Doing Theology*. London: SCM Press.

Sugirtharajah, R. S. 2006a. 'Charting the Aftermath: A Review of Postcolonial Criticism', in *The Postcolonial Biblical Reader*, edited by R. S. Sugirtharajah. Malden, Oxford and Carlton: Blackwell, 7–32.

Sugirtharajah, R. S. 2006b. 'Postcolonial Biblical Interpretation', in *Voices from the Margin: Interpreting the Bible in the Third World*, edited by R. S. Sugirtharajah. 3rd edn. Maryknoll: Orbis, 64–84.

Sullivan, M. 2003. 'Swan Bake: Asylum Seekers Steal the Queen's Birds for Barbecues. *The Sun*, 4 July.

Summerfield, D. 2005. '"My Whole Body is Sick … My Life is Not Good": A Rwandan Asylum Seeker Attends a Psychiatric Clinic in London', in *Forced Migration and Mental Health: Rethinking the Care of Refugees and Displaced Persons*, edited by D. Ingleby. New York: Springer, 97–114.

Sung, J. M. 2005. 'The Human Being as Subject: Defending the Victims', in *Latin American Liberation Theology: The Next Generation*, edited by I. Petrella. Maryknoll: Orbis, 1–19.

Sutherland, A. 2006. *I Was A Stranger: A Christian Theology of Hospitality*. Nashville: Abingdon.

Suvin, D. 2005. 'Displaced Persons'. *New Left Review*, 31(Jan/Feb), 107–123.

Swanstrom, T. 2002. 'Are Fear and Urbanism at War?'. *Urban Affairs Review*, 38(1), 135–140.

Swinton, J. and Mowat, H. 2006. *Practical Theology and Qualitative Research*. London: SCM Press.

Tajfel, H. 1981. *Human Groups and Social Categories: Studies in Social Psychology*. Cambridge: Cambridge University Press.

Temple, B. and Moran, R. (eds). 2006. *Doing Research with Refugees: Issues and Guidelines*. Bristol: Policy Press.

Temple, B. and Moran, R., with Fayas, N., Haboninana, S., McCabe, F., Mohamed, Z., Noori, A. and Rahman, N. 2005. *Learning to Live Together: Developing Communities with Dispersed Refugee People Seeking Asylum*. York: Joseph Rowntree Foundation. Available at: www.jrf.org.uk/bookshop/details.asp?pubID=665 [accessed: 15 January 2009].

ter Haar, G. 1998. *Halfway to Paradise: African Christians in Europe*. Cardiff: Cardiff Academic Press.

ter Haar, G. 2008. 'African Christians in Europe', in *Mission and Migration*, edited by S. Spencer. Calver: Cliff College, 31–52.

Terry, F. 2002. *Condemned to Repeat? The Paradox of Humanitarian Action*. Ithaca and London: Cornell University Press.

Theissen, G. 1992. *The Gospels in Context: Social and Political History in the Synoptic Tradition*. Trans. L. M. Maloney. Edinburgh: T & T Clark.

Theissen, G. and Merz, A. 1998. *The Historical Jesus: A Comprehensive Guide*. Trans. J. Bowden. London: SCM Press.

Theunissen, M. 1984. *The Other: Studies in the Social Ontology of Husserl, Heidegger, Sartre, and Buber*. Trans. C. Macann. Cambridge and London: Massachusetts Institute of Technology Press.

Thiede, C. P. 2004. *The Cosmopolitan World of Jesus: New Light from Archaeology*. London: SPCK.

Thiemann, R. F. 1991. *Constructing a Public Theology: The Church in a Pluralistic Culture*. Louisville: Westminster John Knox.

Thistlethwaite, S. B. and Cairns, G. F. (eds). 1994. *Beyond Theological Tourism: Mentoring as a Grassroots Approach to Theological Education*. Maryknoll: Orbis.

Thomas, H. 1997. *The Slave Trade: The History of the Atlantic Slave Trade, 1440–1870*. London: Picador.

Thomas, P. 2009. 'Community Cohesion, the "Death of Multiculturalism" and Work with Young People', in *Europe's Established and Emerging Immigrant Communities: Assimilation, Multiculturalism or Integration*, edited by C. Howson and M. Sallah. Stoke on Trent: Trentham Books, 149–161.

Thomas, R. S. 2000. *Collected Poems: 1945–1990*. London: Phoenix.

Thompson, B. D. 2003. *Shelter from the Storm: Caring for the Victims of Kosovo*. Peterborough: Epworth.

Thompson, J., Pattison, S. and Thompson, R. 2008. *SCM Studyguide to Theological Reflection*. London: SCM Press.

Throntveit, M. A. 1992. *Ezra–Nehemiah*. Interpretation: A Bible Commentary for Teaching and Preaching. Louisville: John Knox.

Tidball, D. 2004. 'The Pilgrim and the Tourist: Zygmunt Bauman and Postmodern Identity', in *Explorations in a Christian Theology of Pilgrimage*, edited by C. Bartholomew and F. Hughes. Aldershot: Ashgate, 184–200.

Tirman, J. (ed.). 2004. *The Maze of Fear: Security and Migration after 9/11*. New York: New Press.

Toğral, B. 2011. 'Convergence of Securitization of Migration and "New Racism" in Europe: Rise of Culturalism and Disappearance of Politics', in *Security, Insecurity and Migration in Europe*, edited by G. Lazaridis. Farnham: Ashgate, 219–237.

Tomasi, S. 2010. 'Human Rights as a Framework for Advocacy on Behalf of the Displaced: The Approach of the Catholic Church', in *Driven from Home: Protecting the Rights of Forced Migrants*, edited by D. Hollenbach. Washington, DC: Georgetown University Press, 55–69.

Tracy, D. 1981. *The Analogical Imagination: Christian Theology and the Culture of Pluralism*. London: SCM Press.

Tracy, D. 1988. *Plurality and Ambiguity: Hermeneutics, Religion, Hope*. London: SCM Press.

TTI [*Transatlantic Trends: Immigration*]. 2010. Key Findings. A Survey by the German Marshall Fund of the US, Bradley Foundation, Compagnia di San Paolo, Barrow Cadbury Trust and Fundación BBVA. Available at: http://trends.gmfus.org/immigration/doc/TTI2010_English_Key.pdf [accessed: 9 February 2012].

Treacher, A., Coombes, A., Alexander, C., Bland, L. and Alldred, P. 2003. 'Editorial', in *Exile and Asylum: Women Seeking Refuge in 'Fortress Europe'*, edited by A. Treacher, A. Coombes, C. Alexander et al. Feminist Review 73. Basingstoke: Palgrave Macmillan, 1–4.

Trible, P. 1978. *God and the Rhetoric of Sexuality*. London: SCM Press.

Trible, P. 1984. *Texts of Terror: Literary-Feminist Readings of Biblical Narratives*. Philadelphia: Fortress.

Tulud Cruz, G. 2010. *An Intercultural Theology of Migration: Pilgrims in the Wilderness*. Leiden and Boston: Brill.

Tulud Cruz, G. 2011. 'Towards an Ethic of Risk: Catholic Social Teaching and Immigration Reform'. *Studies in Christian Ethics*, 24(3), 294–310.

Turner, S. 2004. 'New Opportunities: Angry Young Men in a Tanzanian Refugee Camp', in *Refugees and the Transformation of Societies: Agency, Policies, Ethics and Politics*, edited by P. Essed, G. Frerks and J. Schrijvers. New York and Oxford: Berghahn, 94–105.

Turton, D. 1996. 'Migrants and Refugees: A Mursi Case Study', in *In Search of Cool Ground: War, Flight and Homecoming in North-east Africa*, edited by T. Allen. Geneva: United Nations Research Institute for Social Development, 96–110.

Turton, D. 2003. *Refugees, Forced Resettlers and 'Other Forced Migrants': Towards a Unitary Study of Forced Migration*. New Issues in Refugee Research. Working Paper No. 94. Geneva: UNHCR. Available at: www.unhcr.org/doclist/research/3bbc18ed5/skip-60.html [accessed: 20 January 2009].

UKBA [United Kingdom Border Agency]. 2012. *Asylum* [Online]. Available at: www.ukba.homeoffice.gov.uk/asylum [accessed: 18 June 2012].

UNDP [United Nations Development Programme]. 2000. *Replacement Migration: Is it a Solution to Declining and Ageing Populations?* New York: UN.

Available at: www.un.org/esa/population/publications/migration/migration. htm [accessed: 5 November 2008].

UNHCR [United Nations High Commissioner for Refugees]. 1991. *Guidelines on the Protection of Refugee Women*. Geneva: UNHCR. Available at: www.unhcr. org/3d4f915e4.html [accessed: 26 October 2011].

UNHCR [United Nations High Commissioner for Refugees]. 2006. *The State of the World's Refugees: Human Displacement in the New Millennium*. Oxford and New York: Oxford University Press.

UNHCR [United Nations High Commissioner for Refugees]. 2008a. *2007 Global Trends: Refugees, Asylum-Seekers, Returnees, Internally Displaced and Stateless Persons*. Geneva: UNHCR. Available at: www.unhcr.org/statistics/ STATISTICS/4852366f2.pdf [accessed: 12 January 2012].

UNHCR [United Nations High Commissioner for Refugees]. 2008b. *UNHCR Handbook for the Protection of Women and Girls*. Geneva: UNHCR. Available at: www.unhcr.org/refworld/docid/47cfc2962.html [accessed: 26 October 2011].

UNHCR [United Nations High Commissioner for Refugees]. 2010. *Convention and Protocol Relating to the Status of Refugees*. Geneva: UNHCR. Available at: www.unhcr.org/protect/PROTECTION/3b66c2aa10.pdf [accessed: 15 October 2011].

UNHCR [United Nations High Commissioner for Refugees]. 2011a. *2010 Global Trends: 60 Years and Still Counting*. Geneva: UNHCR. Available at: www. unhcr.org/4dfa11499.html [accessed: 15 August 2011].

UNHCR [United Nations High Commissioner for Refugees] 2011b. *Asylum Levels and Trends in Industrialized Countries 2010: Statistical Overview of Asylum Applications Lodged in Europe and Selected Non-European Countries*. Geneva: UNHCR. Available at: www.unhcr.de/fileadmin/user_upload/ dokumente/06_service/zahlen_und_statistik/2010AsylumTrendsIndus.pdf [accessed: 5 January 2012].

UNHCR/Asylum Aid. 2011. *Mapping Statelessness in the United Kingdom*. London: UNHCR/Asylum Aid. Available at: www.asylumaid.org.uk/data/files/ publications/174/Mapping_Statelessness.pdf [accessed: 9 February 2012].

UN Initiative to Fight Human Trafficking. 2011. Human Trafficking: The Facts [Online]. Available at: www.unglobalcompact.org/docs/issues_doc/labour/ Forced_labour/HUMAN_TRAFFICKING_-_THE_FACTS_-_final.pdf [accessed: 5 June 2011].

Unruh, H. R. and Sider, R. J. 2005. *Saving Souls, Serving Society: Understanding the Faith Factor in Church-based Social Ministry*. Oxford: Oxford University Press.

URC [United Reformed Church]. n.d. *Responding to Refugees & Asylum Seekers*. Unpublished Leaflet. London: Racial Justice Committee, United Reformed Church.

Urry, J. 2003. *Global Complexity*. Cambridge: Polity.

Valtonen, K. 1998. 'Resettlement of Middle Eastern Refugees in Finland: The Elusiveness of Integration'. *Journal of Refugee Studies*, 11(1), 38–60.

Van der Meulen, M. 2008. 'Being Illegal is like Fishing without a Permit: African Churches, Illegal Immigration, and the Public Sphere', in *A Moving God: Immigrant Churches in the Netherlands*, edited by M. Jansen and H. Stoffels. Zurich: Lit Verlag GmbH & Co. KG Wien, 49–59.

Van Hear, N. 1998. *New Diasporas: The Mass Exodus, Dispersal and Regrouping of Migrant Communities*. London: University College London Press.

Van Hear, N. 2006a. 'Conclusion: Re-casting Societies in Conflict', in *Catching Fire: Containing Forced Migration in a Volatile World*, edited by N. Van Hear and C. McDowell. Lanham: Lexington Books, 213–221.

Van Hear, N. 2006b. '"I Went as Far as My Money Would Take Me": Conflict, Forced Migration and Class', in *Forced Migration and Global Processes: A View from Forced Migration Studies*, edited by F. Crépeau, D. Nakache, M. Collyer, N. Goetz and A. Hansen. Lanham: Lexington Books, 125–127.

Van Hear, N., Brubaker, R. and Bessa, T. 2009. *Managing Migration for Human Development: The Growing Salience of Mixed Migration*. UN Development Programme Human Development Reports Research Paper 2009/20. New York: UNDP.

van Houten, C. 1991. *The Alien in Israelite Law*. JSOT Supplement Series 107. Sheffield: JSOT Press/Sheffield Academic Press.

van Houtum, H. and Pijpers, R. 2008. 'On Strawberry Fields and Cherry Picking: Fear and Desire in the Bordering and Immigration Policies of the European Union', in *Fear: Critical Geopolitics and Everyday Life*, edited by R. Pain and S. J. Smith. Aldershot: Ashgate, 157–173.

Vanier, J. 1997. *Our Journey Home: Rediscovering a Common Humanity Beyond Our Differences*. Trans. M. Parham. London: Hodder & Stoughton.

Van Liempt, I. and Bilger, V. (eds). 2009. *The Ethics of Migration Research Methodology: Dealing with Vulnerable Immigrants*. Eastbourne: Sussex Academic Press.

van Munster, R. 2009. *Securitizing Immigration: The Politics of Risk in the EU*. Basingstoke: Palgrave Macmillan.

van Selm, J. 2005. 'Introduction: Immigration: Opportunities and Challenges for the Developed World', in *International Migration and Security: Opportunities and Challenges*, edited by E. Guild and J. van Selm. London and New York: Routledge, 1–7.

van Selm, J. 2007. 'The Europeanization of Refugee Policy', in *New Regionalism and Asylum Seekers: Challenges Ahead*, edited by S. Kneebone and F. Rawlings-Sanaei. New York and Oxford: Berghahn, 79–109.

Van Seters, J. 1975. *Abraham in History and Tradition*. New Haven and London: Yale University Press.

van Wijk-Bos, J. W. H. 2001. *Ruth and Esther: Women in Alien Lands*. Nashville: Abingdon.

van Wolde, E. 1997. *Ruth and Naomi*. Trans. J. Bowden. London: SCM Press.

Vaux, T. 2001. *The Selfish Altruist*. London: Earthscan Publications.

Väyrynen, R. 2005. 'Illegal Immigration, Human Trafficking and Organized Crime', in *Poverty, International Migration and Asylum*, edited by G. J. Borjas and J. Crisp. Basingstoke: Palgrave Macmillan, 143–170.

Verdirame, G. and Harrell-Bond, B. 2005. *Rights in Exile: Janus-Faced Humanitarianism*. Studies in Forced Migration, 17. New York and Oxford: Berghahn.

Vervotec, S. 1999. 'Conceiving and Researching Transnationalism'. *Ethnic and Racial Studies*, 22(2), 447–462.

Vervotec, S. 2006. *The Emergence of Super-Diversity in Britain*. Working Paper No. 25. Oxford: Centre on Migration, Policy and Society [COMPAS]. Available at: www.compas.ox.ac.uk/publications/working_papers.shtml [accessed: 20 January 2009].

Vervotec, S. 2007. 'Migrant Transnationalism and Modes of Transformation', in *Rethinking Migration: New Theoretical and Empirical Perspectives*, edited by A. Portes and J. DeWind. New York: Berghahn, 149–180.

Vijayajumar, L. and Jotheeswaran, A. T. 2010. 'Suicide in Refugees and Asylum Seekers', in *Mental Health of Refugees and Asylum Seekers*, edited by D. Bhugra, T. Craig and K. Bhui. Oxford: Oxford University Press, 195–210.

Vincent, J. (ed.). 2006. *Mark: Gospel of Action. Personal and Community Responses*. London: SPCK.

Virilio, P. 2005. *City of Panic*. Trans. J. Rose. Oxford and New York: Berg.

Volf, M. 1996. *Exclusion and Embrace: A Theological Exploration of Identity, Otherness and Reconciliation*. Nashville: Abingdon.

Wainwright, E. M. 1995. 'A Voice from the Margin: Reading Matthew 15.21–28 in an Australian Feminist Key', in *Reading from this Place: Volume II: Social Location and Biblical Intepretation in Global Perspective*, edited by F. F. Segovia and M. A. Tolbert. Philadelphia: Fortress, 132–153.

Wainwright, E. M. 1998. *Shall We Look for Another? A Feminist Rereading of the Matthean Jesus*. Maryknoll: Orbis.

Wali, S. 1994. 'I Realized I was the Enemy', in *Women in Exile*, edited by M. Afkhami. Charlottesville and London: University Press of Virginia, 124–139.

Walton, H. and Hass, A. W. (eds). 2000. *Self/Same/Other: Re-envisioning the Subject in Literature and Theology*. Sheffield: Sheffield Academic Press.

Ward, K. 2008. *Local Experiences of Migration: Consulting Coventry*. London: ICAR. Available at: www.icar.org.uk/?lid=10088 [accessed: 26 October 2011].

Ward, K., Amas, N. and Lagnado, J. 2008. *Supporting Disabled Refugees and Asylum Seekers: Opportunities for New Approaches*. London: Metropolitan Support Trust/ICAR. Available at: www.refugeesupport.org.uk/documents/MST_RCU_DisabilityFullReport_1108.pdf [accessed: 26 October 2011].

Warner, D. 1999. 'Deterritorialization and the Meaning of Space: A Reply to Gaim Kibreab'. *Journal of Refugee Studies*, 12(4), 411–416.

Warrior, R. A. 2006. 'A Native American Perspective: Canaanites, Cowboys and Indians', in *Voices from the Margin: Interpreting the Bible in the Third World*, edited by R. S. Sugirtharajah. 3rd edn. Maryknoll: Orbis, 235–241.

Washington, H. C. 1994. 'The Strange Woman of Proverbs 1–9 and Post-Exilic Judaean Society', in *Second Temple Studies 2. Temple and Community in the Persian Period*, edited by T. C. Eskenazi and K. H. Richards. JSOT Supplement Series 175. Sheffield: JSOT Press/Sheffield Academic Press, 217–242.

Watson, S. D. 2009. *The Securitization of Humanitarian Migration: Digging Moats and Sinking Boats*. Abingdon and New York: Routledge.

Watters, C. 2008. *Refugee Children: Towards the Next Horizon*. New York: Routledge.

WCC [World Council of Churches]. 2008. *Global Platform for Reflection and Analysis. Finding Sanctuary: Migration, Community and the Churches* [Online]. Available at: www.oikumene.org/?id=4244 [accessed: 31 July 2008].

Weems, R. J. 1991. 'Reading *Her Way* through the Struggle: African American Women and the Bible', in *Stony the Road We Trod: African American Biblical Interpretation*, edited by C. H. Felder. Minneapolis: Augsburg Fortress, 55–77.

Weil, S. 1987. *The Need for Roots: Prelude to a Declaration of Duties Towards Mankind*. London and New York: Ark Paperbacks.

Weiner, M. 1995. *The Global Migration Crisis: Challenge to States and to Human Rights*. New York: HarperCollins College.

Weiss, T. G. 2001. 'Reforming the International Humanitarian Delivery System for Wars', in *Global Migrants, Global Refugees: Problems and Solutions*, edited by A. R. Zolberg and P. M. Benda. New York and Oxford: Berghahn, 206–242.

Weiss, T. G. and Korn, D. A. 2006. *Internal Displacement: Conceptualization and its Consequences*. Abingdon: Routledge.

Welch, M. and Schuster, L. 2008. 'American and British Constructions of Asylum Seekers: Moral Panic, Detention, and Human Rights', in *Keeping Out the Other: A Critical Introduction to Immigration Enforcement Today*, edited by D. Brotherton and P. Kretsedemas. New York: Columbia University Press, 138–158.

Weller, P. 1987. *Sanctuary – the Beginning of a Movement?* Runnymede Commentary No. 1. London: Runnymede Trust.

Weller, P. 1989. *The Multi-Faith Dimensions of Sanctuary in the United Kingdom*. Centre for the Study of Religion and Society Pamphlet Library No. 21. Canterbury: University of Kent.

Weller, P. (ed.). 2007. *Migration Principles: Statement for Churches Working on Migration Issues*. London: CTBI/CCRJ.

Weller, P. 2009. 'How Participation Changes Things: "Inter-faith", "Multi-faith" and a New Public Imagination', in *Faith in the Public Realm: Controversies, Policies and Practices*, edited by A. Dinham, R. Furbey and V. Lowndes. Bristol: Polity Press, 63–81.

Wells, S. 2006. *God's Companions: Reimagining Christian Ethics*. Oxford, Malden and Carlton: Blackwell.

WERS [West End Refugee Service]. 2008. *Annual Report 2007–2008*. Available at: www.wers.org.uk/docs/report/WERS_annual_report_07–08.pdf [accessed: 29 December 2008].

WERS [West End Refugee Service]. 2011. WERS. [Online]. Available at: www.wers.org.uk [accessed: 3 October 2011].

West, G. O. 1999a. *The Academy of the Poor: Towards a Dialogical Reading of the Bible*. Interventions, 2. Sheffield: Sheffield Academic Press.

West, G. O. 1999b. 'The Bible and the Poor: A New Way of Doing Theology', in *The Cambridge Companion to Liberation Theology*, edited by C. Rowland. Cambridge: Cambridge University Press, 129–152.

West, G. O. 2006. *Genesis: The People's Bible Commentary*. Oxford: Bible Reading Fellowship.

Westerhoff, C. A. 2004. *Good Fences: The Boundaries of Hospitality*. Harrisburg: Morehouse.

Westermann, C. 1986. *Genesis 12–36: A Commentary*. Trans. J. J. Scullion. London: SPCK.

Westin, C. 1999. 'Regional Analysis of Refugee Movements: Origins and Response', in *Refugees: Perspectives on the Experience of Forced Migration*, edited by A. Ager. London and New York: Continuum, 24–45.

Whitehead, T. 2011. 'Fears of a New Asylum Crisis – Think Tank'. *Telegraph* [Online, 29 April]. Available at: www.telegraph.co.uk/news/uknews/immigration/8480414/Fears-of-new-asylum-crisis-think-tank.html [accessed: 29 April 2011].

Whitelam, K. W. 1996. *The Invention of Ancient Israel: The Silencing of Palestinian History*. London and New York: Routledge.

Wigley, B. 2006. 'Relief and Development as Flawed Models for the Provision of Assistance to Refugees in Camps', in *Forced Migration and Global Processes: A View from Forced Migration Studies*, edited by F. Crépeau, D. Nakache, M. Collyer, N. Goetz and A. Hansen. Lanham: Lexington Books, 159–185.

Wijsen, F. 2005. 'The Practical–Theological Spiral: Bridging Theology in the West and the Rest of the World', in *The Pastoral Circle Revisited: A Critical Quest for Truth and Transformation*, edited by F. Wijsen, P. Henriot and R. Mejía. Maryknoll: Orbis, 108–126.

Williams, D. S. 1993. *Sisters in the Wilderness: The Challenge of Womanist God-Talk*. Maryknoll: Orbis.

Williams, R. 2002. *Resurrection: Interpreting the Easter Gospel*. 2nd edn. London: Darton, Longman and Todd.

Williams, R. 2005. 'Urbanization, the Christian Church and the Human Project', in *Spirituality in the City*, edited by A. Walker. London: SPCK, 15–26.

Williams, R. 2008. *Archbishop Supports Calls for End to Detention of Children Seeking Asylum* [Online, 9 July]. Available at: www.archbishopofcanterbury.org/articles.php/1231/archbishop-supports-calls-for-end-to-detention-of-children-seeking-asylum [accessed: 8 October 2011].

Williams, R. 2010a. *Archbishop Expresses Concern over Refugee Protection* [Online, 7 October]. Available at: www.archbishopofcanterbury.org/articles. php/932/archbishop-expresses-concern-over-refugee-protection [accessed: 8 October 2011].

Williams, R. 2010b. *Enriching the Arguments: The Refugee Contribution to British Life*. Council for Assisting Refugee Academics, University College London, 12 May. Available at: www.archbishopofcanterbury.org/articles. php/576/archbishops-cara-lecture [accessed: 8 October 2011].

Williamson, H. G. M. 1985. *Ezra, Nehemiah*. Word Biblical Commentary, 16. Waco: Word Books.

Williamson, H. G. M. 1987. *Ezra and Nehemiah*. Old Testament Guides. Sheffield: Sheffield Academic Press.

Williamson, L. 1983. *Mark*. Louisville: John Knox.

Willimon, W. H. 1979. *Worship as Pastoral Care*. Nashville: Abingdon.

Wills, L. 2008. *Not God's People: Insiders and Outsiders in the Biblical World*. Lanham: Rowman & Littlefield.

Wilson, Erin. 2011. 'Much to be Proud of, Much to be Done: Faith-based Organizations and the Politics of Asylum in Australia'. *Journal of Refugee Studies*, 24(3), 1–17.

Wilson, E.-J. 2005. *The Church and Refugees in the UK: An Opportunity for Mutual Enrichment*. Unpublished MTh Dissertation. Belfast: Institute of Theology, Queen's University.

Wilson, J. P. 2004. 'The Broken Spirit: Posttraumatic Damage to the Self', in *Broken Spirits: The Treatment of Traumatized Asylum Seekers, Refugees, War and Torture Victims*, edited by J. P. Wilson and B. Droždek. New York and Hove: Brunner-Routledge, 109–157.

Winder, R. 2005. *Bloody Foreigners: The Story of Immigration to Britain*. Paperback edn. London: Abacus.

Wingate, A. 2005. *Celebrating Difference, Staying Faithful: How to Live in a Multi-Faith World*. London: Darton, Longman and Todd.

Wink, W. 1999. *The Powers That Be: Theology for a New Millennium*. New York: Galilee/Doubleday.

Wistrich, R. S. (ed.). 1999. *Demonizing the Other: Antisemitism, Racism and Xenophobia*. Amsterdam: Harwood Academic.

Witherington III, B. 1984. *Women in the Ministry of Jesus: A Study of Jesus' Attitudes to Women and their Roles as Reflected in His Earthly Life*. Cambridge: Cambridge University Press.

Witherington III, B. 2001. *The Gospel of Mark: A Socio-Rhetorical Commentary*. Grand Rapids: William B. Eerdmans.

Wogaman, J. P. and Strong, D. M. (eds). 1996. *Readings in Christian Ethics: A Historical Sourcebook*. Louisville: Westminster John Knox.

Wong, W. C. 2010. '"Same Bed, Different Dreams": An Engendered Reading of Families in Migration in Genesis and Hong Kong', in *Genesis*, edited by A. Brenner, A. C. C. Lee and G. A. Yee. Minneapolis: Fortress, 191–210.

Wood, W. B. 2001. 'Ecomigration: Linkages between Environmental Change and Migration', in *Global Migrants, Global Refugees: Problems and Solutions*, edited by A. R. Zolberg and P. M. Benda. New York and Oxford: Berghahn, 42–61.

Woodcock, A and Tapsfield, J. 2011. 'David Cameron Plea in Illegal Immigrants Push'. *Independent* [Online, 10 October]. Available at: www.independent.co.uk/news/uk/politics/david-cameron-plea-in-illegal-immigrants-push-2368451.html [accessed:12 October 2011].

World Bank. 2006. *Global Economic Prospects 2006: Economic Implications of Remittances and Migration*. Washington, DC: World Bank. Available at: http://econ.worldbank.org/WBSITE/EXTERNAL/EXTDEC/EXTDECPROSPECTS/GEPEXT/EXTGEP2006/0,,menuPK:1026834~pagePK:64167702~piPK:64167676~theSitePK:1026804,00.html [accessed: 22 August 2011].

Wright, J. L. 2007. 'A New Model for the Composition of Ezra–Nehemiah', in *Judah and Judeans in the Fourth Century B.C.E.*, edited by O. Lipschits, G. N. Knoppers and R. Albertz. Winona Lake: Eisenbrauns, 333–348.

Wright, N. T. 1996. *Jesus and the Victory of God*. London: SPCK.

Yee, G. A. 2003. *Poor Banished Children of Eve: Women as Evil in the Hebrew Bible*. Minneapolis: Augsburg Fortress.

Yee, G. A. 2009. '"She Stood in Tears Amid the Alien Corn": Ruth, the Perpetual Foreigner and Model Minority', in *They Were All Together in One Place? Toward Minority Biblical Criticism*, edited by R. C. Bailey, T. B. Liew and F. F. Segovia. Atlanta: Society of Biblical Literature, 119–140.

Yee, G. A. 2010. 'Postcolonial Biblical Criticism', in *Methods for Exodus*, edited by T. B. Dozeman. Cambridge: Cambridge University Press, 193–233.

Yin Yap, S., Byrne, A. and Davidson, S. 2011. 'From Refugee to Good Citizen: A Discourse Analysis of Volunteering'. *Journal of Refugee Studies*, 24(1), 157–170.

Yong, A. 2008. *Hospitality and the Other: Pentecost, Christian Practices, and the Neighbor*. Maryknoll: Orbis.

YouGov/*Mail on Sunday*. 2005. *YouGov/Mail on Sunday Survey Results* [Online]. Available at: www.yougov.com/archives/pdf/DBD050101001_1.pdf [accessed: 30 May 2008].

Young, I. M. 2000. *Inclusion and Democracy*. Oxford: Oxford University Press.

Zabaleta, M. R. 2003. 'Exile', in *Exile and Asylum: Women Seeking Refuge in 'Fortress Europe'*, edited by A. Treacher, A. Coombes and C. Alexander, L. Bland and P. Alldred. Feminist Review 73. Basingstoke: Palgrave Macmillan, 19–38.

Zanchettin, M. 2005. 'Asylum and Refugee Protection after September 11: Towards Increasing Restrictionism?', in *Refugee Crises and International Response: Towards Permanent Solutions?*, edited by A. Bolesta. Warsaw: Leon Koźmiński Academy of Entrepreneurship and Management, 141–180.

Zanre, L. 2005. Interview (Meeting) with Louise Zanre, Director of JRS–UK, London, 6 October.

Zetter, R. 1991. 'Labeling Refugees: Forming and Transforming of a Bureaucratic Identity'. *Journal of Refugee Studies*, 4(1), 39–62.

Zetter, R. 1999. 'International Perspectives on Refugee Assistance', in *Refugees: Perspectives on the Experience of Forced Migration*, edited by A. Ager. London and New York: Continuum, 46–82.

Zetter, R. 2007. 'More Labels, Fewer Refugees: Remaking the Refugee Label in an Era of Globalization'. *Journal of Refugee Studies*, 20(2), 172–192.

Zetter, R., Griffiths, D. and Sigona, N. 2005. 'Social Capital or Social Exclusion? The Impact of Asylum-Seeker Dispersal on UK Refugee Community Organizations'. *Community Development Journal*, 40(2), 169–181.

Zetter, R., Griffiths, D., Sigona, N., Flynn, D., Pasha, T. and Beynon, R. 2006. *Immigration, Social Cohesion and Social Capital: What are the Links?* York: Joseph Rowntree Foundation.

Zizioulas, J. D. 1985. *Being as Communion: Studies in Personhood and the Church*. Crestwood: St Vladimir's Seminary Press.

Zolberg, A. R. 2001. 'Introduction: Beyond the Crisis', in *Global Migrants, Global Refugees: Problems and Solutions*, edited by A. R. Zolberg and P. M. Benda. New York and Oxford: Berghahn, 1–16.

Zolberg, A. R., Suhrke, A. and Aguayo, S. 1989. *Escape from Violence: Conflict and the Refugee Crisis in the Developing World*. New York and Oxford: Oxford University Press.

Zornberg, A. 1994. 'The Concealed Alternative', in *Reading Ruth: Contemporary Women Reclaim a Sacred Story*, edited by J. A. Kates and G. T. Reimer. New York: Ballantine Books, 65–81.

Films and TV Programmes

The Asylum Seeker. 2004. TV, BBC2. 4 December.

Dispatches: Keep Them Out. 2004. TV, Channel Four. 6 May.

God Grew Tired of Us. 2006. Film. Prod. C. Quinn and T. Walker. Newmarket Films.

In This World. 2003. Film. Dir. M. Winterbottom. 87 minutes.

One Border, One Body: Immigration & the Eucharist. 2008. Film. Dir. J. C. Frey. Exec. Prod. D. G. Groody CSC and Jack Lorenz. 30 minutes.

Rain in a Dry Land. 2007. Film. Anne Makepeace Productions and Independent Television Service.

Index